ADVENTURES WITH HARDY BULBS

BOOKS BY LOUISE BEEBE WILDER

ADVENTURES IN A SUBURBAN GARDEN

WHAT HAPPENS IN MY GARDEN

THE FRAGRANT PATH

ADVENTURES WITH HARDY BULBS

ADVENTURES WITH HARDY BULBS

by

LOUISE BEEBE WILDER

Illustrated by

WALTER BEEBE WILDER

COLLIER BOOKS

MACMILLAN PUBLISHING COMPANY

NEW YORK

COLLIER MACMILLAN PUBLISHERS

LONDON

Collier Books
Macmillan Publishing Company
866 Third Avenue, New York, NY 10022
Collier Macmillan Canada, Inc.

Library of Congress Cataloging-in-Publication Data
Wilder, Louise Beebe, 1878–1938.
  Adventures with hardy bulbs / by Louise Beebe Wilder.
  p. cm.
  Reprint. Originally published: New York:
  Macmillan, 1936.
  Includes bibliographical references.
  ISBN 0–02–040840–4
  1. Bulbs.   I. Title.
SB425.W57   1990   89–71161   CIP
635.9′44–dc20

Macmillan books are available at special discounts for bulk
purchases for sales promotions, premiums, fund-raising, or
educational use. For details, contact:
Special Sales Director
Macmillan Publishing Company
866 Third Avenue
New York, NY 10022

First Collier Books Edition 1990

10 9 8 7 6 5 4 3 2 1

PRINTED IN THE UNITED STATES OF AMERICA

To

WALTER BEEBE WILDER

In grateful recognition of his able assistance in grow-
ing the bulbs, keeping the records, and for his work of
illustrating this book with pen and camera

CONTENTS

Contents

PART II—*Continued*

FOREWORD

It is a singular piece of good news that Louise Beebe Wilder's *Adventures with Hardy Bulbs* is available once again, in a new edition from its original publisher, some fifty-four years after its first appearance in 1936. Surely more of her books will follow, coming back into print to gain Mrs. Wilder a new following to match the many admirers her books and magazine articles earned her in the years between the end of World War I and her death in 1938.

The 1920s and 1930s were a golden age in America for writing about gardening. Earlier periods produced their isolated classics, such as Charles Dudley Warner's droll and often hilarious account, *My Summer in a Garden* (1870), and Celia Thaxter's lyrical and affecting book, just recently reprinted, *An Island Garden* (1894). These books teach again the ancient lesson that really good horticultural writing transcends its time, offering pleasure, instruction, and inspiration to readers decades and even centuries after the writers have ceased to breathe and walk the earth. But the period between the two world wars was special in the United States as regards horticultural writing for several reasons. For one thing, the word *gardener* was beginning to change meaning, to shed its denotation of the professional gardener and hired help who together took care of a garden that someone else owned. The days of the great estates had not yet ended but were on the wane, and the owner of the garden and the person who planned and tended it were gradually becoming one and the same. Another point of considerable importance was the emergence of a community of like-minded horticultural writers, editors, and landscape architects who together began to educate the public about the pleasures of gardening and about the great wealth of plants at their disposal. Professor Liberty Hyde Bailey of Cornell University, one of the true giants of horticulture, was still writing prolifically on matters both practical and aesthetic. Richardson Wright, himself the author of many delightful books that have stood the test

ix

of time, exerted great influence on the development of a truly American style of horticulture in his position as editor of *House & Garden,* a magazine that under his direction was the single most important source of ideas and information about gardens and gardening of its time. There are other names that could be mentioned, but I will stop at Herbert Durand and Beatrix Farrand, for my topic is Louise Beebe Wilder, and among distinguished company she was clearly a luminary.

Mrs. Wilder did much more than her share to teach a nation to garden, and she did it by writing with uncommon grace combined with botanical precision. Although her books show a broad command of literature, including the literature of the garden, there is precious little trace of the secondhand in her writings and none of the second-rate. Horticultural writers unfortunately are well practiced in the arts of plagiarism, and have been so since ancient times. The temptation to wear authority on their sleeves leads them to borrow from other writers, especially when the topic is a plant they do not know. Plagiarism in turn leads to the perpetuation of nonsense, as in the solemn report of the great seventeenth-century herbalist John Gerard that there be trees that bear as fruits barnacles that soon turn to geese.

There are no barnacle-geese in anything Louise Beebe Wilder wrote, because she addressed her topics with genuine authority, not its pretense. She observed—no, she *experienced*—the plants she described (the broader word is necessary, given her keen concern for fragrance) directly and firsthand in the two gardens she made just north of New York City. The breadth of her horticultural interests was vast, and her influence during her lifetime and after her death was pervasive. She introduced Americans to the ideas of rock gardening and of raising alpine plants. She wrote repeatedly about the intelligent use of color, about designing pleasant combinations of color for herbaceous borders, and about avoiding clashes. (But she knew her own mind and stood her own ground when hers was a minority opinion: in the received wisdom, magenta is despised and mocked and recommended for exile from any decent garden. Mrs. Wilder liked it and said so, often—and occasionally at considerable length.) And no one in America has written more completely and informatively than she on the hardy bulbs that are the topic of this volume, the objects of her affectionate adventures.

A word of warning is perhaps due here about some of the bulbs in this book. The world of gardening changes much more slowly than, say, the world of fashion. It changes at a more glacial pace, but change it does. Some of the cultivars of common bulbs like tulips and narcissus that *Adventures with Hardy Bulbs* discusses are no longer available commercially. There are also new cultivars—such as the many superb daffodils bred in Oregon since World War II by Grant Mitsch—that have come along since Wilder's book. Certain of the rarer genera are very difficult to come by at all. There is some temptation to revise the book, to bring it up to date by deleting some bulbs and adding others and also, in a few instances, changing the scientific names of plants to accord with the most recent thinking of botanists, or more precisely taxonomists. This temptation has been resisted, and wisely so, I think, for some good reasons. First, *Adventures with Hardy Bulbs* is a classic, and classics are best left untampered with, except in cases in which the first edition did violence to the writer's text by bowdlerizing it or otherwise cleaning it up for public consumption. Second, the slowly changing world of horticulture will continue to change. Cultivars thought to have gone out of existence may be discovered again and returned to commerce. New cultivars thought to be superior will in their turn be superseded. Making the text conform to the standards of 1990 is no guarantee that it will be accurate in every detail in 2000. What we have here is a treasure— the best thinking and best writing of one of our very best garden writers in 1936. I was in diapers then, but I still read Mrs. Wilder on this and every other subject with relish, finding in her much nourishment and encouragement. So will others.

Finally, it must be noted that some "adventures with hardy bulbs" were difficult to pursue, even for Louise Beebe Wilder, in the 1930s. A plant quarantine, lasting roughly from the end of World War I to the end of World War II, cut off absolutely the supply of bulbs from overseas during these years. A few American growers, such as The Daffodil Mart in tidewater Virginia, filled the gap as best they could, but finding true rarities was difficult, often impossible. Today's gardeners have a much easier time of it, and if in the case of bulbs discussed in this book they find some frustration in the search, they may all the better understand Mrs. Wilder's achievement.

While I agree with the decision not to tamper with the text, I must add my word in this introduction about an issue of some importance. Some species of hardy bulbs are being collected in the wild in their native habitats in the Mediterranean Basin, to the point of their being threatened with extinction. Hardy cyclamens are a major example, but the problem also arises with some narcissus and tulips. Heightened environmental awareness of the ecosystem and its fragility makes it a moral imperative—one unknown in the 1930s—that gardeners not contribute to the loss of native species in such a way that their gardens are zoos of what was once a living world and free. Montrose Nursery in Hillsborough, North Carolina, specializes in raising from seed hardy cyclamens that gardeners can grow and love without guilt or uneasy consciences. Just recently, two much larger mail-order concerns, Burpee and Smith & Hawken, have announced their policy not to sell any bulb or other plant that may have been collected to its endangerment. Here, I think, we find the counsel of wisdom, if not perfection.

Introductions to books reprinted are supposed to be solemn, thus overlooking a few gritty and personal truths. The truth is, I'm glad *Adventures with Hardy Bulbs* can be bought once again without resorting to fine antiquarian bookdealers who may not have it in stock or to pawing through book bins in secondhand stores. I'm glad, because "my" copy was borrowed from a friend a year ago. Lately, she has left increasingly more urgent messages on my answering machine. Original editions of Louise Beebe Wilder are in short supply. This new edition of one of her finest books may preserve friendships between those who lend it out and those who borrow it.

ALLEN LACY

PROPAGANDA

IT has been said by an eminent explorer that adventures are an indication of incompetency, of failure to foresee and provide against all possible contingencies; but he fails to point out that it is precisely this failure to anticipate every eventuality that makes adventure irresistible to certain minds, that provides the age-old impulse to leave the beaten path for new and untracked regions, geographical or mental. Were this not so, we should all be following cut and dried, or exact occupations like accountancy or compiling dictionaries.

Where there is no uncertainty, there can be no thrilling interest; never that delicious round-the-corner feeling, tingling and anticipatory, that is the portion of those who advance, not knowing just what they are going to meet, or how they will meet it.

"Tomorrow is, ah, whose?"

That is the query that puts the eternal punch into the common round. It may be yours, it may be mine; it is ours to seek.

Nor need one fare to the far corners of the earth to find adventure. Adventure is of the mind—a mental attitude toward everyday events wherever experienced. One does not have to sit through the long night of an antarctic winter with an Admiral Byrd to know this, or to explore uncharted airways. Adventure may be met with any day, any hour, on one's doorstep, just around the corner; it may lurk in the subway, on a bus top, in the garden. Particularly in the garden, for gardening, whether of window-ledge dimensions or a matter of acres, is fraught with adventure. It is not the peaceful pottering, "idly busy" occupation that some of its exponents would have us believe; it is a pursuit that requires patience for careful industry and research, courage for experiment and hazard; it requires of us curiosity, perseverance, hardihood.

Perhaps it will be thought that I am seeking to provide myself with an alibi when I insist that it is what I do not know rather than what I do know, that makes gardening eternally interesting to me, that keeps me turning horticultural corners after thirty years or more, and still with that alert exhilaration that I should not feel, if I knew what awaited me. If I knew more, I should enjoy less. Of this I am certain. That is not to say that one should not be ever trying to know, seeking the truth, but that one should never reach a state of serene content with one's knowledge, for that is the point where adventure ends and stagnation begins.

Thus, this account of my adventures over a period of many years with bulbous plants is offered, not as a last word on their culture, but rather as a stimulant, as, in fact, propaganda. There are not enough bulbous plants grown in this country; there is not enough proemial curiosity concerning them. There are plenty of big Tulips grown, many Daffodils, a good many Crocuses, some Snowdrops, and a few others, but there is a vast reservoir of beauty and interest that is seldom tapped by any save the gardener with an explorative or adventurous turn of mind. The result of this state of affairs is a genuine loss of beauty to the world, a sad missing of delight by the individual.

For those who like to specialize in their gardening, or who possess the collector's instinct, it would be difficult to fix upon a more rewarding solution than bulbous plants in general, or one or more genera of bulbous plants: Narcissus, Crocuses, Sisyrinchiums, whatever. It is when we begin to specialize that we seem to get under the very skin of our craft, so to speak, when we know the purest and most absorbing preoccupation.

The study of bulbous plants takes one far into the "well-lit past of horticulture," and some of what is to be found there is set down in the following pages in the belief that readers will like to know not only that a plant blooms at a certain season, is such a color, is such a height, but a little also of its life history—whence it came, by whom found, that it grew in the gardens of Crispin van de Pass, or Parkinson, that Gerard had it from his worthy friend Robinus of Paris, or whoever; in short, that centuries ago it thrust out of the earth and flowered, making a light for the eyes of humankind, just as it does in our gardens today.

Unless otherwise stated, I have grown, or attempted to grow, all the bulbs hereafter enumerated, in my two gardens, the one in Rockland County, New York, the other in Westchester County; the first a cold garden, snow-blanketed as a rule in winter, brilliantly sunny in summer, the soil well on the sandy side with a good deal of lime in it; the second subjected to muggish summers, freeze-and-thaw winters, having a clay subsoil, and a good deal of shade. These gardens, while only a few miles apart in point of distance, are widely separated in the physical characteristics they offer.

What I have set down is simply my own experience with a number of hardy bulbous plants and a very few tender ones. There are numerous notable omissions. There is nothing said of Lilies; they should not be treated lightly or briefly; nothing of the Orchidaceous plants, for they require a book to themselves.

I have regretfully left out Trilliums because of the increasing stoutness of the book, Eremurus because I know nothing about them, Oriental Hyacinths because any reliable catalogue will tell you all you need to know of their culture; the tuberous rooted Delphiniums, Corydalis, Dicentras, Ranunculus, and others because of that impending threat of stoutness; but my modest hope is that there is enough in the book to make it a pleasant and stimulating companion along a path that I have found increasingly interesting and rewarding.

LOUISE BEEBE WILDER

BRONXVILLE, NEW YORK
   March, 1936

ADVENTURES WITH HARDY BULBS

PART I

THE ADVENTURE BEGINS

Perhaps in growing bulbs there is less of adventure, less of uncertainty and hazard, than in growing most other kinds of plants; that is to say, at the outset. Bury a clean, sound, mature bulb in the ground, and the reward is far more certain than when we buy what we believe to be a sound bond or security. The old triplet comes to mind:

> Clean and round,
> Heavy and sound,
> In every bulb a flower.

That, at any rate, is the thumbnail history of the first year, assuming, of course, that we have not planted shrinking South Africans in frosty New England, or sunk drought lovers in a marsh. Sufficient food is stored in the bulb or corm to bring forth a perfect flower or flowers the first year. After that, other factors enter in. Continuance, increase, that comfortable settling down and spreading about that proclaims the happily situated plant, depends upon a knowledge of, and attention to, its needs and preferences.

Bulbous plants are, however, pretty generally reasonable in their demands. Not many have obscure yearnings that tax our ingenuity to grasp and solve. The majority are content with a nourishing, gritty soil, porous and free from fresh manure, and many like a bit of lime in some form. Nearly all must be protected from stagnant moisture, particularly during the resting period, though they will put up with any reasonable amount of rainfall during the growing season. Certain of them like more sunshine than others, certain of them for the best results should be planted early, others late.

A few, like Calochortus and Fritillarias, are more incalculable; their wants are not to be summed up in a few words, or satisfied by the impatient hit-or-miss gardener. I have at times thought that like some persons, they do not, themselves, know what they want. Just plain cussed, as our farmer friends would say. But

3

this is, of course, being unfair to them, for somewhere they thrive, somewhere they are amiable and exuberant. The fault lies in ourselves, that we too often try to fit them to conditions that are easily within our compass but physically antagonistic to them.

But one day, probably when we least expect it, we, like love, or perhaps because of love, find a way. The reward in satisfaction is great, what some one has called a triumph of hope over experience, when we see some hitherto bit of perversity making flirtatious eyes at us and plainly wanting to be friends. At such a felicitous moment, we may recall Browning's diver—that there were two points in his adventure:

> One—when a beggar, he prepares to plunge.
> One—when a prince, he rises with his pearl.

When we have succeeded in making a Fritillaria really happy, we have arisen with our pearl.

And now, at the risk of being tedious, a word should be said as to the use of the term "bulb." In catalogues, in books, by gardeners generally, the term is loosely employed to designate not only true bulbs, but other forms of underground storehouses more properly known as corms, tubers, and rhizomes.

In as few words as possible, a true bulb is "a subterranean bud consisting of fleshy leaves closely packed round a woody core, whence roots proceed downward and stems upward." If you cut through a bulb you will find firmly compressed within it the infant flower and leaves.

Examples of true bulbs are Tulips, Lilies, Narcissus, Alliums, and Hyacinths. The outstanding difference between a true bulb and a corm is that a corm is a quite hard and solid body, and if cut through, shows no trace of leaves or scales. Crocuses, Brodiaeas, and Colchicums grow from corms.

A bulb will survive year after year and increase its kind by means of offsets. A corm dies annually, but before doing so, produces a new corm or corms upon its top or sides, nourished at the expense of the old corm, which gradually withers away, and by the action of the leaves out in the sunlight. In a bulb, the flower stem arises from the base; in a corm, from the summit.

A tuber is a short thickened portion of underground stem, a storehouse of food, furnished with "eyes" or buds from which the plant arises, feeding upon its stored food until its roots develop. Cyclamens, Winter Aconites, and certain Anemones and Oxalises grow from tubers. The swollen horizontal roots of the Bearded Iris and the Solomon's Seal are examples of rhizomes.

Certain bulbs are referred to as tunicated. This means literally "covered by coats," as in the Onion. Others are said to be imbricated. In these the thickened leaves or scales overlap one another as in the bulb of the Lily and of some Fritillarias. Apparently it takes more than one coat to justify the expression "tunicated." The fibrous husks which inclose such corms as Crocuses and Brodiaeas and the Gladiolus, and which are often called tunics, do not, from the botanist's standpoint, make these corms tunicated, but sheathed.

These wrappings, whatever they may be, are most interesting when examined, and vary greatly. Those of the Tulip are thin and satiny, and occasionally lined with "wool"; those of *Iris reticulata* are neatly and intricately woven; the husk that incloses Brodiaeas is rough and coarse; Crocus tunics vary a great deal.

All, whether bulb, corm tuber, or rhizome, are alike in being herbaceous, that is, having no permanent woody stem above ground (dying down in winter), and perennial—living by some means from year to year.

At the outset, this book was designed to cover only hardy bulbs and corms; but immediately there were Anemones, Cyclamens, Winter Aconites, and other tubers importuning for admission, and when the bars were down, a few rhizomes crept in. Most of those here treated of belong to the class of plants known as monocotyledons, the chief difference between these and the dicotoledons being that the former have only one seed leaf, while the latter have two. (For more complete definition see any botany or garden dictionary.) Important in the latter class mentioned in this book are Cyclamen, Anemone, Lycoris, and Oxalis.

Bulbous plants are the saving and very gracious grace of many gardens. They are, as I have said, a friendly lot on the whole, versatile and various, and one or other of them, often many of them, may be had in bloom over the whole period of the growing year; sometimes, indeed, individuals make their audacious appearance at seasons that the hardiest of us would hesitate to characterize as "growing," anticipating and extending the gardener's pleasure in a way that is in the highest degree heartening.

Of course locality and climate will have something to do with this extension and anticipation. I am writing from the neighborhood of New York City—lower Westchester County—where sub-zero temperatures are not unusual, where frosts often fall before the end of September, where a spiteful freeze often interrupts April's friendly advances. More than once I have seen the Japanese Quince bushes angrily lurid beneath a pall of snow, Daffodils fluttering above a white blanket, Snowdrops piercing sheer ice; but over a few years, bulbs have flowered in this garden during every month. During ten months is practically the rule.

And this class of plants offers to the gardener not only this cheering omnipresence, but a vast and dazzling array of colors, forms, and types for every sort of garden usage; for beds, for borders, for naturalizing in grass, on rough banks, in meadows, in woods, by stream or pondside, for the rock garden, there are suitable kinds. And there is always room for a few more, usually for many more.

When you think your garden is crowded, look about carefully, and you will discover nooks and corners into which a few bulbs may be tucked away; beneath the shrubs and lightly shadowing trees, in grassy places, on the lee side of hedges, between the herbaceous plants in the borders, wedged among paving stones—in all sorts of places, these cheerful, willing flowers will grow and blossom.

Not all kinds are equally docile under cultivation. A few are notably upstage, and meet our advances with a conspicuous lack of coöperation; not all are equally showy. Some, indeed, are inconsiderable trinkets worth growing merely because they are quaint or amusing; but some of these small things, bestowed in out-of-the-way corners, nourish and sustain the spirit even in greater degree than do the splendors that force themselves insistently upon our attention.

If rare and expensive species and varieties are wanted, a few will do to begin with. If the increase is looked after and cherished, there will soon be a nice stock. I would urge all gardeners to label carefully and clearly their colonies of bulbs; it adds much to the interest and friendliness with which we regard them if we can call them by their names, and it is a positive duty to be able to identify them accurately for visitors whose attention they have attracted.

One bit of consideration is the due and the necessity of all bulbous plants (i.e., corms, tubers and rhizomes). After flowering, the foliage should be allowed to ripen naturally, that is, to turn yellow and die down, before it is cut off. No housemaidish idea of keeping things looking tidy should cause us to ignore this fundamental requirement of this class of plants.

And for the best of reasons. The storage of food in the bulb for future use in the making of flowers, depends upon the activity of the leaves out in the light as well as of the roots in the dark earth. Cut off the leaves while they are still green and active, and you have cut off a main food supply without which health, even life, cannot be sustained.

When the leaves turn yellow, the plant is telling us in plain terms that its work of laying in supplies for the coming year is completed, and that we may now clean up. Not to regard this information offered by the plant itself, is in the highest degree foolhardy and leads only to loss and final desolation.

A few years of being shorn of its leaves, and the bulb gives up the struggle and dies. Many so-called by-the-day men employed in suburban neighborhoods make a practice of this brutal cleaning up because their employers, ignorant of the function of the yellowing leaves, like to see things looking nice and neat, and the "gardeners" know no better. This practice probably explains the fact, in part at least, that so few luxuriant spreads of bulbs are to be found in suburban neighborhoods, and often answers the complaint of individuals that something always eats their bulbs, or that nothing will grow in their soil.

Plenty of water and sunlight during the ripening period is important, and enables the bulb to restore its tone after the effort of flowering. When the leaves are finally cut away, a light mulch of sand and leafmold is an appreciated attention.

Of course yellowing foliage is not ornamental, and in order to prevent its being too conspicuous, some little thought and trouble should be taken to plant the bulbs where it will be more or less hidden. It is seldom a good plan to plant in the forefront of borders bulbs that are to be left in the ground; better to set them in clumps and colonies among the springing perennials toward the middle or at the back where the new green of the hardy plants will screen them. Shrubbery borders are commonly less on view than the main herbaceous borders, and here, as in woodland, they may be left to finish their work in peace and comfort, and with offense to none.

Bulb-planting time, according to species and climate, extends from the first of August through November. The depth to plant varies with the size of the bulb, and sometimes with the species or variety. A simple guide, and one that will serve for almost all bulbs, is to bury them to three times their own depth.

The question of how close to plant is often asked. It is almost always a question of individual taste. How closely do you like to see them massed? Do you prefer to see each flower, or spike of flowers, outlined against a background of its own foliage, or other greenery? To the bulbs, it is generally a matter of indifference; they are a gregarious lot and do not at all mind being crowded, provided that there is sufficient nourishment in the soil to support them.

Personally, I like Crocuses massed almost to the clotted stage, Snowdrops in close fountains, Daffodils far enough apart for each flower to show all its beauty.

Where the soil is poor, it should be deeply dug and enrichment added, but not of a kind that would harm the bulbs. Bonemeal is the best fertilizer for bulbs. It gives up its properties slowly and as needed. It may be spread over the ground, and gently scratched, in the spring or fall. Horse manure should never be used in soil where bulbs are to be planted—it is too hot and hasty in its action; but very old cow manure dug in the year before planting, or used as a mulch spread in the autumn, and scratched in the spring, is beneficial. But it must be old and well rotted. This also prevents the bulbs from being thrown out of the ground by the action of the frost in winter.

If bulbs are to be lifted and stored over the summer, as is sometimes done with Tulips and some others, they should be allowed to remain in the ground until the foliage is ripe, or if necessary, they may be carefully lifted and heeled into the earth in some by-place where they will not be in the way. When the foliage is quite ripe, the bulbs may be lifted and stored in a cool airy place in paper boxes or bags, after they are dry enough for a gentle rubbing to remove adhering soil and the old skins. To dry them in sun is apt to cause the skins to split and the bulb to dry and shrivel.

Bulbs which have been taken out of the ground and stored over the summer, should be sharply watched for signs of activity, and if they are beginning to grow, should be put into the earth at once.

Crocuses are especially eager to get to work, and should usually be replanted in July and August, at the latest. If for any pressing reason a bulb must be moved from one situation to another before its leaves are ripe, the operation should be carried out with the minimum of interference with the functioning of the leaves and roots. It is best to dig it up with a clump of earth and at once transfer it to its new home, where it should be kept watered until the foliage is ripe. On no account should the roots be exposed to drying air.

Certain bulbs lose all their roots during the resting period in summer, and these may be moved with impunity at any time after the foliage has yellowed. Among these are Tulips and Spanish Irises. They come from climates where the summers are hot and comparatively rainless, so we must endeavor in their case to provide a period of complete rest for them. This is true also of Calochortus. (See sections on these species.)

The majority of bulbs may be left in the ground year after year to look after themselves until they make it plain by a falling off in flowering that they need to be taken up and given fresh soil and more space in which to grow. This is especially true of Narcissus, Muscaris, Snowdrops, Chionodoxas, Scillas, Camassias, Leucojums, Fritillarias, and Puschkinias; also Erythroniums. Mr. W. R. Dykes, however, is inclined to believe that *Fritillaria Imperialis,* the Crown Imperial, flowers best when it is lifted annually and replanted after about a month.

In formal beds of Tulips or Hyacinths, it is best to plant new bulbs every year in order to avoid irregularities in the flowering and height of the stems that would spoil the patterned effect aimed at. Such bulbs as are taken up from these formal beds may be distributed in less conspicuous places.

The word "hardy," as used in the following pages, is to be understood as meaning that the bulb under consideration will survive out of doors over the winter with only such covering as is given the garden in the ordinary course of its care in the neighborhood of New York, and usually as far north as Boston.

In some instances I have been able to ascertain the fact that certain kinds are hardy much farther north, but I should not, and do not, take anyone's word as to the hardiness of a plant.[1] All sorts of

[1] See "Hardiness," *The Garden Dictionary,* edited by Norman Taylor (Houghton Mifflin Company, 1936).

factors enter in. If you want to grow a bulb, do so, and try it in more than one situation, in more than one kind of soil, with and without covering. You will have some happy surprises, some disappointments, but you will have learned something definite about your bulb; that is, about its behavior under the conditions that you are able to give it.

The care of new bulbs before they are planted, is an important matter often neglected. The boxes and bags should be opened at once so that air may freely circulate among the bulbs, and they should be placed in a dry and airy place. If planting must be delayed, the bulbs are best emptied out of their containers and spread on trays or papers (carefully labeled); otherwise they may begin to grow in the bags, sending up shoots and forming roots which may be injured in the later handling, using up their stored strength to no purpose.

Bulbs that have flowered for us in pots should, when their beauty is past, be placed in some shaded, outdoor place, and the pots kept moist until the foliage has ripened thoroughly. The bulbs may then be turned out of the pots, dried in the shade and cleaned, and in the autumn planted out in the shrubbery borders. But be sure not to neglect watering, so that the bulb will be able to garner strength after the unnatural process of forcing that it has been subjected to.

THE USE OF LITTLE BULBS IN THE
ROCK GARDEN

THE debt owed by rock gardeners to little bulbs is not to be overestimated. It is they, and not the slothful herbaceous plants, that bring the first relief to winter-jaded senses, and answer the need for assurance that spring is really just around the corner.

Long before the ordinary rock plants have thought of stretching their little green limbs preparatory to awakening, the small bulbs and corms and tubers are not only awake, but up and doing. All over the brown and rocky hills, wherever the shallow terraces and gentle slopes afford a foothold, tiny spears, sheaths, and noses are thrusting through the wet and sullen earth.

Turn back the snow almost any winter day in the neighborhood of New York, and you will find some of these apostles of a new order edging upward. At an audaciously early date, while snows still fly and frosts are a nightly occurrence, the naked earth bursts into an incredible flowering—not a poor-spirited, niggardly flowering, but whole-hearted, generous, even sumptuous.

Innumerable little bells swing merrily in the breeze, "Buttercups" glow, chalices open wide to the touch of the sun, bubbles and vases of many hues materialize miraculously; there are spreads of blue that put the pale spring sky to shame, fountains of frost that gleam more whitely than real frosts, Anemones as frail as shells, blue-white, rose, cochineal, tiny Daffodils like yellow lanterns, wedges of seed pearls—such an array! and all disporting themselves like children loosed, if not from durance vile, at least from a constraint they are obviously glad to escape.

Nor is this spring manifestation all the performance of which small bulbous things are capable in the rock garden. Scarcely a week of the growing year but owes something to one or other of them, and they are among the flowers that say a smiling and reassuring farewell to us upon the very threshold of winter.

This is no glamorous tale of Arabian Nights' entertainment. It is in many gardens, and might be in all, the gayest of realities.

The amazing fact is that such an opportunity is not embraced by all rock gardeners. That it is not, can only be for the reason that it is not generally known how easily pleased are the majority of little bulbs, how easily acquired, how inexpensive. I say the majority because there are, of course, exceptions to every rule. A few, like the Fritillarias, are stand-offish, and a few, because they are rare or scarce, are expensive; but it takes a very few gathered into a little close colony to make a bright spot, and most of them increase their numbers, as time goes on, in a gratifying manner.

There are little bulbs for every situation that the rock garden provides, for sun, for shade, for damp, for dry. Most of them thrive in a nourishing soil composed of good loam and humus, free from manure but made easily pervious to moisture by the addition of sharp sand. The majority will stand any amount of moisture in the spring, but do not object to drought in summer; some, indeed, demand droughty conditions after they have bloomed, else they are unable to ripen their bulbs. Among these are the native Calochortus and Brodiaeas and Irises of the *reticulata* and *persica* types.

The majority, again, may be planted any time in September or October that is convenient. But here, also, there are exceptions. The small Tulip species should be put aside until November. Early-planted bulbs are subject to the disease known as "fire." The Calochortus should also be planted in November, late rather than early.

On the other hand, certain bulbs should not be kept out of the ground a day longer than necessary, for in the dry air virtue goes out of them, they lose vitality and substance, and consequently the buds are born "blind," and frequently there is no flowering even in later years.

Among those that should be planted not later than August, are Snowdrops, Winter Aconites, Erythroniums, Fritillarias, Autumn Crocuses, and Colchicums. The small Daffodils should be planted in September for the best results, as should Grape Hyacinths (they make a fall growth), *Brodiaea uniflora* (Triteleia), and *Iris reticulata*. Spring Crocuses are best planted early also, as they are always eager to make a start. For the rest, September and October will do very well.

The depth to plant is roughly three times the depth of the

bulb, and a point which must be insisted upon as strongly in the rock garden as in any other part of the garden or grounds is that the foliage must be allowed to ripen thoroughly before it is cut off, and never prematurely removed in the interest of tidiness. This, of course, necessitates some ingenuity on the part of the gardener in placing the bulbs where their yellowing foliage will not mar the picture as a whole. They may be planted in close groups behind or among small herbaceous plants whose developing greenery will hide the sorry ending of the bulbs. Or certain creepers may be planted above their heads. This has the double advantage of furnishing a setting for them and of keeping the flowers free from spattering mud thrown up by heavy rains.

A few such associations may be suggested here: various Crocus species planted under *Androsace sarmentosa* or beneath the silver patchwork of *Antennaria dioica rosea;* any of the more hearty bulbous things, such as the Muscaris, beneath *Arabis procurrens.* This close-matting plant is good also as a covering for *Scilla hispanica* and thrives, as does the Scilla, in shade.

Ceratostigma plumbaginoides (Plumbago) makes a good companion planting for the late-flowering Alliums, such as *A. odorum* or *A. stellatum. Tulipa silvestris* may be grown effectively behind a white cascade of Foam Flower, *Tiarella cordifolia. Oxalis rosea* may be sown over the heads of the shade-loving Scillas, such as *S. sibirica,* and provides bloom in that region for the rest of the season.

Iris reticulata and the variety *Krelagei* thrive here on a warm slope, and come up well under a carpet of white-flowered Thyme. *Arenaria montana* and Brodiaeas associate well. Muscari Heavenly Blue is effective piercing mats of *Phlox subulata.* They flower at the same time. *Leucojum aestivum* comes cheerfully through Moneywort (*Lysimachia Nummularia*). Snowdrops of the *nivalis* group and Winter Aconites thrive under English Ivy. *Tulipa Clusiana* looks well behind a wave of the pale-colored *Alyssum saxatile citrinum.* This makes a charming and showy picture for a high place on the rock garden in full sun.

Do not make the mistake of using the ordinary *Alyssum saxatile,* with its heads of sharp yellow flowers. The creamy form is much better. Small Daffodils do well beneath the flat blanket of *Veronica repens,* or the looser weave of *V. Nummularia.* Colchicums are not put out by a ground cover of *Veronica filiformis*, or the stronger growing Moneywort.

Verbena chamaedryfolia (grown as an annual) with flaming scarlet flowers, may be planted to spread over areas where spring bulbs have died away, and the tender Zephyranthes will come up through it and flower through the summer. *Verbena venosa* (*V. rigida*), that flowers the first year from seed, may tumble over a rock to cover the spot where below it some bulb is taking itself off in an untidy manner. Its heads of purple flowers continue throughout the season.

In this garden *V. venosa* self-sows. *Cyclamen neapolitanum* thrives happily enmeshed with the wire-thin branches of *Muehlenbeckia nana*, Scillas amidst *Asperula odorata*, and both like shade, and this is a good cover-crop for *Hyacinthus amethystinus*.

Other plants and creepers which may be suggested for use over small bulbs are the following: *Acaena glauca* and *A. inermis* (sun); Aubrietias; *Bellis rotundifolia caerulescens*; *Cotula squalida* (shade); Drabas; *Erythraea diffusa* (half shade); *Herniaria glabra*; *Hypericum repens*; *H. olympicum*; *Linaria aequitriloba*, *L. pilosa*, *L. origanifolia*, *Linum alpinum*; Mazus; *Stachys corsica*; *Veronica pectinata rosea*; *Raoulia glabra*; many creeping Thymes and the smaller Sedums; numerous Violas.

Low bushes among which bulbs may be grown are the Callunas, Ericas, *Leiophyllum buxifolium prostratum*, *Teucrium chamaedrys*, Origanums and Aethionemas.

In situations where bulbs have died away and blank spaces are left, annuals may well be sowed over their heads. Suitable for this purpose are the following; Anagallis, *Asperula azurea setosa*, *Eschscholtzia caespitosa*, *Gypsophila muralis*, *Ionopsidium acaule*, *Leptosiphon hybridus* and several other Leptosiphons, *Nemophila insignis* (shade), *Omphalodes linifolia*, *Sanvitalia procumbens*, *Saponaria calabrica*, *Sedum caeruleum*, numerous Verbenas.

The bulbs may be planted as I have suggested among the herbaceous plants or in drifts at the base of the rock garden, where annuals may be sown over their heads for later bloom. In all cases, their placing should be a matter for some thought, both from the standpoint of their physical well-being, and in the interest of the beauty of the rock garden as a whole.

Throughout the body of the book, directions for growing the bulbs mentioned in this section will be found under their proper heads.

Earliest to flower in the spring are Galanthus (Snowdrops) and Eranthis (Winter Aconites). *Galanthus nivalis* and the Winter Aconites like shade; *G. Elwesii* and some of the other tall kinds prefer sunnier conditions. Scillas of most kinds like shade and grow well on the north side of the rock garden, or beneath the little shrubs. The brilliant blue *S. sibirica* will thrive even in the shadow of small evergreens. They flower very early, as does *S. bifolia,* while *S. hispanica* and *S. nonscripta,* the Spanish and English Bluebells, hold off until May. *S. chinensis,* flowering in the autumn, seems to prefer a sunny, well drained spot. Scillas are not only bright blue but white, and mauve and pink, as well.

Chionodoxas of several kinds are among the earliest comers and may be had garbed in brightest blue, in pure white, or in pink, as well as a soft lavender. They like full sunshine and make a better showing after a season or two in the garden. The bulbs increase rapidly, and there are few prettier subjects for the rock garden. Leucojums are like immense substantial Snowdrops. *L. vernum* flowers in March, *L. aestivum* in May. Both like partial shade.

Crocuses are of many kinds and seasons; spring and autumn performers alike love sunshine. A good selection for spring would be *C. aureus, C. biflorus, C. chrysanthus* vars. (very early), *C. Imperati, C. susianus* and *C. Tomasinianus.* For autumn, *C. cancellatus albus, C. longiflorus, C. pulchellus, C. speciosus* vars. and *C. zonatus.*

Little Daffodils are many and lovely and none too plentiful. The rock gardener will want *Narcissus minor, N. minimus, N. nanus, N. triandrus, N. cyclamineus,* N. Queen of Spain, N. W. P. Milner, and the quaint little Bulbocodiums. Of Anemones, which are also scarce in this country, there should be *A. blanda, A. apennina, A. nemorosa* vars., especially the double kind, and the flaming *A. fulgens.*

Hyacinthus amethystinus for shade and May blossoming, and *H. azureus* for sun and March blossoming, should not be omitted. They are both blue. *Fritillaria meleagris alba* is the best of this race, and likes a dampish spot. The native *F. pudica* with yellow bells, may also be tried.

A selection of Grape Hyacinths is indispensable. Try *Muscari latifolium, M. moschatum* (for scent), *M. neglectum* (blackish), *M. botryoides album*, and M. Heavenly Blue. All like sun. A few choice Tulip species for sunny, well drained situations, include *T. australis, T. Batalinii, T. Clusiana, T. dasystemon, T. Kaufmanniana* vars., *T. linifolia, T. persica,* and *T. praestans. T. Sprengeri* is the latest of all Tulips to flower. *Iris reticulata* and *I. persica* are most exciting when they appear in the early spring weeks. They want sunny, well drained positions.

The western American Erythroniums (Trout Lilies), are among the most delightful shade lovers. Some of the best are *E. grandiflorum, E. Purdyi, E. Hendersonii, E. Hartwegii, E. californicum,* and *E. revolutum* vars. The Calochortus, also from the West, are difficult, but their extraordinary beauty warrants any trouble that is taken in their behalf. They must have full sun, perfect drainage, and summer drought.

The Brodiaeas are only a little less demanding along the same lines. *B. ixioides* is a beauty. Alliums are many, and do well in any situation. *A. Moly* has yellow flowers in June, *A. cyaneum* blue ones in August, *A. stellatum* rosy ones until the snows fly. Colchicums bloom in August and September, and like rich soil and partial shade. The best for the rock garden are the pink and white forms of *C. autumnale. Sternbergia lutea* bears golden Crocus-like flowers in September and October. It likes a warm rock at its back, and well drained soil. *Cyclamen europaeum* and *C. neapolitanum* are also among the rarities in this country, but are lovely for late flowering, the one in sun, the other in partial shade. Among Lilies for the rock garden are *L. tenuifolium* and its golden variety, Golden Gleam. Numerous Oxalises and Sisyrinchiums belong in the rock garden, and add much to its interest and beauty at both ends of the year.

NATURALIZING BULBS

HOWEVER much we may love trim garden ways, most of us have a sneaking fondness for Nature, what Plato called God's art. Even Bacon, prince of fine gardeners, felt the need for "a window open, to fly out at, a secret way to retire by," a prospect that at least appears uncontrived, simple, reposeful.

There are times when the well schooled, smiling face of the garden seems a little smug and unfeeling and we long for open spaces, for the blithe, untutored impulses of trees and flowers following their own devices. And so we make wild gardens, naturalizing plants in them as nearly in Nature's manner as we can compass.

On every place, of whatever size, there should be some such region of escape from decorous restraint, even if it be only a little hidden path along which wild things may grow, a rough bank or an out-of-the-way corner. There will be times when such a spot will mean more to us than will any garden, however fine and finished its beauty. If it may be done on a wider scale, so much the better.

Among plants to naturalize, none are more willing and appropriate than bulbs. In its narrow sense, to naturalize bulbs means merely to plant them in an informal and unstudied manner in contradistinction to their use in formal beds; but in the broader and more accepted sense, it means to broadcast them on a generous scale in woods, in meadows, by pond and streamside, along winding paths, on rough banks or about the outskirts of the garden, to suggest, as best we may, Nature's handicraft, not man's. It is a charming way to plant, but it is far from easy to bring about a perfectly natural and spontaneous effect in which the plants appear as if they were really on their own, leading a free and undirected life, away from all garden trammels and the anxious guidance of the gardener.

In the first place, we must clear our minds of the idea of boundaries, forget the girdle of the garden hedge, get right away from the memory of straight lines or of beds. The space we have to deal with may not be large, but we must try to think of it as more or less boundless; else we cannot approach it with complete naturalness, and will find ourselves treating it as we should a bed in the garden.

A common mistake in naturalizing plants is to overdo it—filling the whole space so that there are no quiet reaches for the eye to rest upon, and the beauty of the flowers crowded so closely together is confused, their personalities lost. Nature knows well how to plant simply and reposefully—man can seldom let well enough alone.

But, as a great landscape gardener has said, we must not stereotype imperfections; we may toy with Nature, but must not wilfully exaggerate what is ordinary. "Only Nature may exaggerate herself—not Art." It takes a real familiarity with Nature's manner to be able successfully to imitate it, and the restraint of a Spartan. But bulbs are fairly easy to manage, whatever has been our ineptitude in their bestowal, for, if the soil is fertile and the situation suitable, they will soon take things into their own hands and do their own colonizing in a way that is far more satisfactory than anything we, with our garden-trained eyes, can bring about.

And they are particularly happy grown in this free manner, for in woods, or meadows, or out-of-the-way localities generally, they may live out their life span, ripen their foliage and go to rest, secure in the knowledge that they are not offending the sharp eyes of the tidy-minded gardener, or going in hourly fear of the man with the scissors who will chop off their heads while they are still actively at work.

Of course, if we can do our part of the planting with some skill, there will be less for the bulbs themselves to correct. Perhaps the best way is to put our bulbs in a basket, one kind at a time, and throw them out in handfuls, planting them just where they fall, sowing thinly toward the center of the area or toward the edges, as we please, avoiding a uniform distribution and trailing away with a few bulbs here, a few there, sometimes only one, as if the wind had had a hand in the business. If you try just digging holes here and there, you will find it impossible to get anything but a stilted effect.

A wide variety of bulbous things is suitable for naturalization.

Even garden Tulips, so long trained to garden ways, are quite astonishingly beautiful when planted naturally. I remember once seeing a mass of scarlet Tulips in England growing at the top of a hill in grass. There must have been hundreds of them blowing against a windy sky. The flowers were not large, but the effect they made of wild and untaught beauty was perfectly satisfying.

Tulips grew in the orchard grass of my old home in Rockland County, New York, and against the line fences, coming up here and there in the most unexpected manner. These, too, were red —perhaps red Tulips are the most enduring—and quite small. They had evidently been there for many years, but when we began to mow the orchards early, and to clean up generally, they gradually disappeared.

In a lovely garden near Poughkeepsie, I once saw a plantation of the Lily-flowered Tulip Sirene, pink and sleek and lovely, growing in the grass as if they had been dumped down casually against a bank of evergreens. Such highly civilized flowers would be expected to look out of place in such a position, but oddly they did not.

The native Lilies, of course, naturalize perfectly—*canadense*, *superbum*, *philadelphicum*; and there are many sections of the country where *Lilium tigrinum* and *L. croceum* have taken to the great open spaces, and display their ruddy wares prolifically along the roadsides and in fence corners and meadows.

Daffodils are perhaps the supreme flowers for naturalizing. They are exquisite sweeping down a hillside, or forgathering by streams or ponds in irregular drifts and patches. The pale *Leedsii* forms make a gay gladness of color amidst the burning stems of the red-twigged Dogwood, *Cornus sibirica*, and a copse of white Birches is, of all places, the loveliest place in which to naturalize Daffodils. The Poets Narcissus is perfect for dampish locations, or lovely (how that word "lovely" just must be used!) beneath Apple trees, for they flower at the same time, and a canopy of pink blossoms over the gleaming white Narcissus would cause the most hard-boiled to catch his breath.

Snowdrops and Winter Aconites may be planted in hundreds, in thousands, on shaded springy hillsides, or in copses where they may spread about among the bare-twigged bushes. They will sow their seed widely, eventually finding their way to all sorts of situations that suit them. Also for woodland places are the Spanish and English Bluebells, *Scilla hispanica* and *S. nonscripta.* These make pools of soft color in the dim light, and increase prodigiously.

Scilla sibirica burns its blue fire in sun or shade, in grass or bare earth; it will even endure beneath the shade of evergreens, and it, too, sows its seed and spreads apace. But look out for the seedlings! They look like stripling Garlics. The Leucojums naturalize well in half-shaded places in light soil, as does the pink-flowered *Lycoris squamigera. Fritillaria meleagris,* the little Checkered Lily, naturalizes happily in damp places out in the sunlight. Camassias also do well in such places. I've not tried them in grass, but they would be lovely topping the "long and pleasant grass." The Little Star of Bethlehem thrives in grass in sun or shade, and it is there that it appears most perfectly at home. Nor need any scorn it for its commonness. Erythroniums, our eastern kinds, and those from the West, look charming on lightly wooded slopes. *Tulipa silvestris* has naturalized itself with me in many situations, in sun and in shade. Colchicums seem to like part shade and a rich soil.

For definitely sunny regions, there are Crocuses, spring- and autumn-flowering, the Muscaris, Puschkinia, Chionodoxas, the Blackberry Lily, *Belamcanda chinensis,* Alliums of many sorts, *Bulbocodium vernum,* Hypoxis, Sisyrinchiums and Zygadenus, and the quaint blue-pointed *Hyacinthus azureus.* Its sister, *H. ame-thystinus,* is better off in light shade.

Where there are no wide spaces to be planted, there are doubtless trees beneath which bulbs may be planted naturally, and low shrubs under which the smaller fry may play about in complete freedom. It is losing a great opportunity not to give a floor of bulbous plants to such flowering trees and shrubs as Dogwoods Almonds, Forsythias, Crab-Apples, Japanese and orchard Cherries, Witch Hazels, Magnolias, Peaches, Laburnums, Lilacs Mock Oranges, Thorns and Azaleas. The shade of most of these is not too heavy for even the sun lovers to survive.

TENDER BULBS IN THE ROCK GARDEN

ROCK GARDENERS who scrupulously follow a horticultural Hoyle in their selection of plants, look askance at practitioners who admit annuals to the austere company of their alpines. What, then, will be their opinion of one who now and again slips in a few tender bulbous things among them?

But here, it seems to me, is an end that justifies the material. Some years ago in the fever of late winter list-making, I ordered a few tender bulbs as an experiment. When the rush of spring planting was over, it was discovered that they had been overlooked and that all suitable situations in the borders had been filled. There was, however, a newly constructed bit of rockwork quite empty and tempting. And so there they were planted, and there they flourished and made bright color while the leisurely alpines destined to people this region were getting their growth in the frames.

Since then it has seemed to me very sensible to make use of some of this tender bulbous material in the rock garden when occasion serves. Every year I put in a few where they will do the most good, and the results are admirable. Some of them, as a matter of fact, are mountain plants and so seem to have a sort of right of entrance, while others are quite shamelessly lowland; but most of them look none the less suitable and behave as if to the mountain born.

The two European Anthericums are mountain plants. Correvon refers to them as "among the glories of our mountain meadows." They belong to the Lily order, and are commonly known as St. Bernard's Lily and St. Bruno's Lily. The first is *Anthericum Liliago* and is found on grassy hills in southern Europe and low in the Alps and Pyrenees. It is more strictly a hill plant than is St. Bruno's namesake. In "Among the Hills," that wholly delightful book, Reginald Farrer describes a walk he once took in the Cottian Alps when, as he neared the base, he passed over a steep slope that was all spiry with the snowy delicate plumes of *Anthericum Liliago*.

In the rock garden the plant grows little more than a foot high; in less hungry soil it would grow taller. The leaves are tufted and narrow, and from their midst arise slender stems carrying a loose raceme of starry "Lilies," each an inch across in early summer. It has been grown by gardeners since 1596, and so is an old hand at making garden beauty, and it is so light and graceful in effect, and so floriferous, that none need hesitate to plant it among his choicest treasures where a little height is wanted.

South of Philadelphia, St. Bernard's Lily may be planted in the autumn in little groups in the rock garden, or along sunny sheltered borders; but in cold regions it must be set out in spring, and the bulbs taken up in the fall and stored over the winter in a frost-proof place.[1]

Much like it, but altogether of more circumstance, a little taller, a little less careless of port, the flowers a little larger, appearing indeed like small slightly disheveled Madonna Lilies, is St. Bruno's Lily. This was once known as *Anthericum Liliastrum*, but answers now to the name of *Paradisia Liliastrum*. Though sometimes found growing with its one-time brother, it is a more strictly alpine plant, often climbing the mountains, to a height of more than six thousand feet.

According to M. Correvon, it "haunts the fresh meadows of the mountain regions all over Europe, and especially in the south, where it covers large spaces in such abundance that at flowering time the soil seems to be covered with snow." Also it floods the thin air, as it does the less rarefied atmosphere of lowland gardens, with a scent that is strong and sweet. The flowers are borne in a loose raceme on slender stems that arise from amidst grassy recurving leaves. They are pure white save for a green spot at the tip of each segment, and of an almost transparent texture.

This, too, is an old plant in gardens, for it is said to have been grown since 1629. St. Bernard's Lily was named for the gentle founder of the famous hospice, highest habitation in the Alps. St. Bruno's Lily commemorates the name of the founder of the ancient and austere order of Carthusian monks who dwell in the lonely valley of Chartreuse, in the French Alps, La Grande Char-

[1] I find St. Bernard's Lily lives over the winter with a light covering of litter.

treuse, out of whose "agreeing spirit of uncommunicativeness" was born, among other things, the pale green and aromatic seduction of that "amiable temptation," green Chartreuse.

Like St. Bernard's Lily, it may be grown in the rock garden where height is wanted, or along sunny, well drained borders, the bulbs planted a few inches apart. Both are delightful plants.

Zephyranthes is an American genus belonging to the Amaryllis family and consisting of about sixty species that have been described, and doubtless many more that have eluded this distinction, but very few of them are in general cultivation, or easily procurable. They are found in the southern part of the United States, in Guatemala and Mexico, and in many parts of South America and the West Indies. The flowers are funnel-shaped, borne on slender hollow stems, and are of two general types. Some have a good deal the appearance of Crocuses; others look more like small Lilies. The foliage is narrow and grassy, and springs from small tunicated bulbs.

In cold climates the bulbs may be planted out after danger from frost is past, and are charming in little close groups in the rock garden, or used to edge borders of summer flowers, as most of them bloom off and on throughout the summer and autumn, being especially active when hard rains follow periods of drought. A well drained sunny, but not too dry, situation suits them. I have grown eight kinds, and all save one have proved easy and amiable.

Since childhood I have known the white-flowered Atamasco Lily, *Z. Atamasco*, for it grew in masses in our old Maryland garden, where it was hardy in a warm border against a grape arbor, the foliage remaining green over the winter. We also grew a pink kind in pots indoors. This may have been *Z. carinata* or *Z. rosea*. The common name, Flowers of the West Wind, always has seemed to me among the prettiest of flower names, and these little Lilies wear it with grace. They are also known as Zephyr Flowers and as Fairy Lilies. The rock gardener who does not make use of them to brighten his late summer and autumn landscape is missing a real opportunity. The bulbs are not expensive and may be stored over the winter and used again and again.

Z. Ajax proved to be bright yellow and of the Crocus type, its pretty flower hoisted on a long slender tubelike stem. *Z. Atamasco* (*B.M.* t. 239) is of the Lily type, larger and more substantial than the foregoing, and this is probably the hardiest of the clan. It grows wild from Virginia to Florida and westward through Alabama and Mississippi. The flowers are produced singly, and are pinkish in the bud but open to almost pure white. They are about three inches long and are borne on stems five or six inches in height. As are all the Zephyranthes, they are quite scentless, though they look as if they should be fragrant. The Atamasco Lily haunts woods and meadows in the wild and flowers in the late spring. In the garden it is the earliest to bloom. Local names for it are Swamp Lily, Stagger-grass, and in some districts Easter Lily.

In *Z. candida* we have a pretty little Crocus-like flower hoisted on a tall tubelike stem (*B.M.* t. 2607). It opens white from rosy buds, making its appearance in the late summer amidst bright green roundish leaves, and blossoming industriously into the fall. It is reported to be abundant in the marshes along the Río de la Plata.

Harold Hume in the *National Horticultural Magazine*, July, 1935, says: "It is said that when the river was discovered by Juan Díaz de Solis in 1513, the name Río de la Plata (The River of Silver) was given because of the abundance of the silvery flowers of *Z. candida* along its banks." Late summer visitors to Kew may remember being delighted with these pale "Crocuses" thickly starring grassy places or edging borders with thick green leaves and masses of their pretty flowers.

Z. carinata (*B.R.* t. 902, 2594) is a dainty species with soft pink funnel-shaped flowers about two inches long borne on green tubes. The narrow bright green leaves are reddish at the base. It is a Mexican species and blooms in summer. *Z. longifolia* has small bright yellow, bronze-coated blooms. It is found wild in Texas, New Mexico, Arizona, and Mexico. *Z. rosea* (*B.M.* t. 2537) is small-flowered and very pink, the slender stems raising the flowers well above the narrow green foliage. It is found in mountainous regions of Cuba, and flowers here late in the summer and well into the autumn.

Z. texana (*B.M.* t. 3596) is another small-flowered sort, this time with golden blooms deeply flushed on the exterior with copper-red. It is a native of Texas.

Z. Treatiae, a large-flowered type, has so far evaded my advances. It belongs to Florida and Georgia, and I believe grows under damper conditions than I have thus far given it. The flowers are said to be pure white turning pinkish as they mature.

In back-country neighborhoods, the Flowers of the West Wind are prime favorites. They are used as exchange flowers among the housewives, and often may be found in every garden plot within a radius of several miles, edging beds in the rough grass, or grown in battered pails or tin cans to ornament the front stoop, or stand upon a tree stump in the front yard. I have more than once seen these rude receptacles bursting with bloom in the steamy atmosphere of country kitchens, where they shared the window ledges with flourishing Begonias, Geraniums, and Christmas Cactus plants, or in summer standing upon the narrow graves in lonely rural churchyards.

Much like the Fairy Lily is *Cooperia Drummondii* (*B.R.* t. 1835), native of Texas and Mexico. It is commonly called Rain Lily from its propensity to spring up after a hard shower; and it has another pleasant idiosyncrasy—it flowers in the cool of the evening, and when the small, salver-shaped blooms open from pink buds at the ends of slender scapes some five inches high, one becomes aware of a delicious spicy sweetness pervading the air.

A few clumps of Rain Lilies add much to the interest and sweetness of a rock garden or sunny border. The small bulbs should be planted in spring when danger from frost is past, about three inches deep and as much apart, in warm situations where the soil is somewhat gritty. The foliage is narrow and scant, but the flowers are of good texture, and last several days.

Chlidanthus fragrans (*B.R.* t. 640), the Delicate Lily, was, it seemed to me, a grand find. Like Cooperia, it is of the Amaryllis family; but it is much more showy and is, in truth, too large in scale for the moraine into which I hastily tucked the large ovoid bulbs last spring. It is a native of the Andes of Peru, and most energetic and masterful in its behavior. It began to shoot up foliage almost as soon as it was underground, and in a surprisingly short time had materialized gray-green linear leaves and the most gorgeous yellow funnel-shaped flowers at least four inches long. These are carried in a cluster on stoutish stems, three or four to the stem, about six inches high, and are richly fragrant.

For this, alone, they would be worth growing. Even in the

starved moraine they flowered gloriously for several weeks in the early summer, and there I have left them, covered well with salt hay to see if under these conditions they may not possibly weather a northern winter.

Rex D. Pierce in the "Year Book of the Amaryllis Society," 1934, says of them: "The bulbs store well in a dry cool cellar, but start into growth early and must be planted just as soon as the ground has stopped freezing a crust in spring. Only well grown fairly large bulbs will flower, and it needs high fertility and ample moisture. It is hard to get the soil too rich." How nobly, then, my bulbs comported themselves in the barren and thirsty moraine! They never faltered or failed, and it is just one more instance of the fact that though we may disappoint a bulb, it seldom has the heart to disappoint us.

Mr. Pierce goes on to say that the bulbs make offsets profusely, and that these should all be taken off before replanting; otherwise one will simply have clusters of bulbs too small to bloom.

Of course the Chlidanthus is too large for the rock garden. I grew it there in an emergency, as I did some bulbs of the flaming *Sprekelia formosissima*, the Jacobean Lily (*B.M.* t. 47). These were set on a little plain in front of a bush of *Berberis verruculosa* with its lustrous foliage, and looked very well despite their size.

According to Linnaeus, the Jacobean Lily has been known in gardens since 1593. It is a native of Mexico and Guatemala, and must surely have been among the first plants to take the eye of early voyagers, and brought from the New World to the Old. Parkinson figured it in 1629, but curiously enough placed it among the Daffodils, calling it the Indian Daffodil with a red flower. The flower is somewhat spidery-looking. The three upper segments are clawlike, the central one being the widest and slightly reflexed; the three lower segments droop, and against them the yellow stamens show conspicuously.

Mrs. Matschat says: "On the *estepas*, in the barrancas, the Sierra de Guadalupe, and other sections of the country, *Sprekelia formosissima, amacayo*, glorifies the landscape with its vivid crimson flowers. Listed in the catalogues as the Jacobean Lily and closely allied to Amaryllis, this plant enjoys immense popularity as a pot plant for early spring bloom. When set out in May, after danger from frost is past, the bulbs will usually flower in about four weeks. In cold climates, the bulbs must be stored over winter." [2]

More fitting in size for the rock garden is the pretty little African Irid, *Acidanthera bicolor*, said to grow wild in the rugged fastnesses of Abyssinian mountains, about which we are today hearing so much. Its corms are roundish, small, and rather flat, and if planted in spring, should be held until after frosty weather is past, and then given a rather stiff soil. The leaves are linear and veined, and from their midst arise slender stems to a height of about fifteen inches, carrying delicately fragrant starry flowers. These are white, and each segment has at its base a chocolate-colored splotch.

The Spring Star Flower, too, is charming in the rock garden, and though usually grown in a pot, has lasted well in this garden out of doors over the winter and flowered in early May. And Mr. T. H. Everett says in *Horticulture*, October 15, 1932, that a plantation made by him in a rock garden in a more northerly locality than this has lasted over three winters, and the quantity and quality of the flowers have improved with time.

The Spring Star Flower is usually catalogued as *Triteleia uniflora*, and is sometimes known as *Milla uniflora* (*B.M.* t. 3327), but I believe it is now correctly *Brodiaea uniflora*. By whatever name it is known, it is a most appealing and sprightly flower, a six-pointed star, white palely washed with lavender, and a tiny golden "eye" formed by the anthers just showing in the mouth of the tube. The flowers open out flat, and on the tube and the undersides of the segments are distinct purplish green lines. Each is borne singly amidst grassy leaves, and though these leaves when bruised have a distinct odor of onions, the dainty flowers are quite fragrant.

The Spring Star Flower comes from about Buenos Aires, and is a member of the Lily family. As far south as Washington, this pretty bulbous plant may be regarded as quite reliable for outdoor planting, and should be freely used among other spring-flowering things that are regarded as permanent fixtures in the garden.

The Mexican Tiger Flowers, or Shell Flowers, Tigridia, are brilliant bulbous plants that may well now and again be used in

[2] *Mexican Plants for American Gardens* (Houghton Mifflin, 1935).

the rock garden, as well as, more often than they are, in the borders. They were formerly known as *Ferraria Tigridia* (*B.M.* t. 532), and they have been grown in gardens since the middle of the seventeenth century. When Hernández was sent as a physician to Mexico by Philip II, King of Spain, he reported it growing wild about Mexico and much cultivated because of its excessive beauty, and for the medicinal virtues of the roots.[*]

Mrs. Matschat says of the Tiger Flowers:

"While their blossoming season lasts, they are the most spectacular sight in the garden, reminding one of the triangular, translucent shells found on coral reefs among southern seas. And such a variety of color combination! Pink, white or lilac, yellow to apricot, orange to scarlet, all deeply blotched and speckled with crimson and maroon!

"*Tigridia Pavonia*, the El Cacomite of the ancient Aztecs, is the probable origin of the exquisite Tiger Flowers of our gardens. Its bulbs, with the flavor of chestnuts, are an important article of diet. It is found in the valley of Mexico, both wild and cultivated, and in the states of Hidalgo, Morelos and various other parts of the country, as well as extending, it is claimed, into Guatemala."

The bulbs may be planted out of doors in the North in early May, being set three to four inches deep in rich sandy soil in a sunny location. They like plenty of moisture during summer, and if this is forthcoming, the blossoms, though individually fleeting, will maintain a steady succession for many weeks, each day bringing a fresh and seemingly more brilliant supply. In mild regions, they may be left in the ground.

The Tiger Flowers grow from a foot to fifteen inches tall. Well grown bulbs produce as many as four stems, at the joints of which appear the plicated, oblong-lanceolate leaves, rather thick and deeply veined. The flowers commonly open at night and do not always outlast the day, especially if the weather is hot, but new ones may be counted upon to greet the new day.

Like the Fairy Lilies, the Tiger Flowers are often cherished by rural women, procured, I suppose, in the first place, from itinerant peddlers of horticultural wares.

---

[*] Francisco Hernández, physician to Philip II of Spain, wrote the first Natural History of North America, while he was employed by the Spanish Government to examine into the "virtues" of the plants of the New World.

I have often seen bright clumps of these vivid flowers in narrow farm dooryards, those little oases maintained with so much difficulty and real sacrifice by hard-working farm women in their scant spare time. It is indeed astonishing what unusual flowers one comes upon in these back-country gardens. The last Tigridia I saw flowering was in a garden in the mountains of Rockland County. Its bedfellows were dusty-cheeked Bouncing Bet and round-eyed Periwinkle. It looked strangely exotic and out of place—but it was flourishing.

PART II

PART II

ALLIUM *LILIACEAE*
ONION

ALLIUMS are not so popular in gardens as on many counts they deserve to be. Some persons do not know of the qualifications of certain of them as garden decorations; others shy away from them because of their Onion-like odor. This, however, is apparent only when the stems or leaves are bruised; it is not given off spontaneously to the air, and, as a matter of fact, the blossoms of some of them have the fragrance of Violets and other cherished blooms which they give off voluntarily. Moreover the race—outside its purely esculent members and a few undesirable weeds such as *A. canadense*, the almost ineradicable Wild Garlic, *A. tricoccum*, the Three-sided Leek, and *A. vineale*, Crow Garlic, an unlovable gift to us from Europe—offers to the gardener a quantity of valuable and varied and easily grown material that it is a mistake to ignore.

It is a vast race, so vast that I hesitate to attempt to number its members, but they run into the hundreds and are distributed over Europe, North Africa, subtropical Asia, and North America, including Mexico. They vary in height from little fellows a few inches high to great stalwarts of several feet, and in their blossoming cover the months from May onwards into the autumn. I have had *A. stellatum* still flying a few rags of color when the first snows began to fly. Certainly not all are of equal merit— some indeed are suitable only for the rubbish heap, but others are good enough for any society in the rock garden, or showy in the borders, or useful and bright in the wild garden or waste places. In any case, it is a race not to be passed by without further examination. Among their merits is the ease with which they may be grown; among the drawbacks of at least some of them, their uncontrolled increase.

Some persons may object to a too great prevalence of "rosy-purple" in their coloration, but there are also lovely blue ones among them, good yellows, desirable mauves and lilacs, and a few pure white ones. Sometimes the small flowers are gathered into a perfectly round head at the end of the naked stem, sometimes into an umbel, which may be formal or informal in its arrangement, with the individual blooms held erect or drooping; and the leaves may be flat, sometimes very broad, again narrow, or round and hollow. The root is usually bulbous but occasionally rhizomatous.

All this is matter of fact and plain sailing, but one setting out to make a collection of Alliums which he would like to address by their proper names, will encounter trouble. The confusion in their nomenclature is, well, stupendous and on the increase. Botanists, gardeners, dealers, have all contributed to it, and it is a wise gardener indeed who knows his Alliums.

In the *New York Times* (August 19, 1935), a gentleman from Stamford, New York, addressed to the editor an impassioned complaint against Cornell scientists who, he claimed, proposed to eliminate not only the "tears" but the "odor" from the onion. "It is depressing," he wrote, "to think of an onion without that delightfully appetizing something which to its friends, conveys that it is about to become one of the components of that joy of joys, a rich meat dish. Why, one might just as well drop in a piece of turnip or a chunk of squash, or something else, to fill space. There will never be anything to take the place of an onion."

I am quite in agreement with this gentleman, and strongly recommend that the Cornell scientists cease to tamper with that grand gustatorial reek, without which many a dish would cease to be an achievement and become a mere flat futility, and turn their attention instead to the elimination of the confusion in the nomenclature of the race. Many would rise and call them blessed.

The only monograph on the race that I can find was published in 1826, by Mr. George Don, A.L.S., in the "Memoirs of the Wernerian Society." It is very narrow and inadequate in its scope, and throws little light on the exact identities of the great number of Alliums now known. Mr. Don himself admits it to be a most difficult genus of plants to investigate. "In the prosecution of this object I have met with considerable obstacles arising from . . . the intricacy of the whole genus, for although many of the species afford good and permanent marks of distinction, it must be admitted the limits of others are not so easily determined."

I have been collecting Alliums more or less assiduously for about fifteen years. At the present time there are in the garden some sixty or seventy species, many of which I cannot name with any certainty. Whenever I see an Allium listed whose name is strange to me, I send for it; but too often it turns out to be a repeater, and an undesirable one. I have made an effort to follow every clew that might lead to identification but with, I must confess, indifferent success, for there seems to be no highest authority for the humble onion tribe; so what is given here, while an honest effort, is not intended as a final word, and I shall welcome contradiction, or at least correction.

Let me say, however, that I have found all the kinds I have tried, hardy and partial to warm, rather light loam, and I have transplanted them successfully at all seasons, whether in or out of bloom. Propagation is effected by offsets from the older bulbs, and they are readily raised from seed; some self-sow with far too much enthusiasm, but this may be frustrated if the flower head is cut off as soon as it loses color. The most recent to come to the garden are those made available by Carl Purdy, Ukiah, California, and these western Alliums, many of them, are very pretty and useful, especially in the rock garden.

Generally accepted as edible species are the following: *A. Cepa*, the most commonly used for cooking, Western Asia; *A. ascalonicum*, the toothsome Shallot; *A. Porrum*, Leek; *A. Schoenoprasum*, the invaluable Chives; *A. Scorodoprasum*, the Sand Leek or Rocambole; *A. fistulosum*, Welsh or Spring Onion, that so titillates our winter-jaded appetites in spring; *A. sativum*, Garlic (beloved of Homer). We shall not want any of these in the flower garden, but all of them should be present in the vegetable plot for the glorification of the salad and the stew.

A. acuminatum Hook   Pax. *Fl. Garden* vol. II, t. 48
Pink Wild Onion

Paxton thought so highly of this species that he said it was scarcely inferior in beauty to the Guernsey Lily [1] itself. It is a native species found in rich soils on prairies and rocky hillsides from British Columbia to California, Arizona, Montana, Idaho, Colorado, and in other sections of the west country. The bulb is

[1] *Nerine (Amaryllis) sarniensis*, South Africa.

almost round with a thick outer coat; the leaves are scant and rushy, and almost, if not quite as tall as the flower scape, which is about a foot high. They die away early. The flowers are gathered into a loose umbel; they are bell-shaped and, when wide open, quite starry, the segments sharply pointed and carried erectly, not drooping. Half the segment is white, of a curiously transparent quality, the other half a bright rose-pink.

This is a very gay and pretty species, flowering here at the end of May or very early in June, and lasting a long time when cut or in the garden. The flowers gradually become papery as they mature, but they also lose some of their bright color, and seem mere ghosts of their former selves. There is very little of the "loathly stink" about the plant, and colonies of it are cheerful in the borders, freely planted in the wild garden, or even in the less choice positions in the rock garden.

A. albo-pilosum C. H. Wright   *B.M.* t. 7982
    Giant Allium

This is the much coveted species, which, though I have received from several sources what purported to be the genuine Giant Onion, has always miserably failed to come up to specifications. It is a well defined species, and there is no excuse for sending out in its name various kinds of Chives and allied forms. It is a comparatively new species introduced from the mountainous regions of northern Persia, and is heralded as one of the best and most striking of the race.

It made quite a sensation when first exhibited in England. The name means "white and shaggy," referring to the pale hairs on the leaves and the downy stem. The stout stem grows two feet tall and carries a head that is said to be sometimes a foot across, made up of a vast number of starry lilac flowers having a sort of metallic quality. "The individual flowers are borne on slender stems about six inches long, all radiating from a common center and composing a huge globular head . . . as large as a full-sized football." The strap-shaped leaves are nearly two inches across and about eighteen inches tall. The Giant Allium flowers about the middle of June, and a group of the plants is said to make a handsome show in the border or shrubbery, where they are best seen against a dark background. It is quite hardy.

A. amplectans

A slender, rather fleeting little species a few inches high which I had from Mr. Purdy, who says it is only of interest to collectors; but I found its close heads of white pink-tinted flowers pretty enough for a position in the rock garden. It flowers the first week in June, and a pink form of it is now offered. This species is found in open fields and on hillsides from Washington to San Diego County, California.

A. atrorubens   King. *U. S. Geol. Expl.* V.

A little western species growing only three or four inches high that flowers here toward the middle of May. The bulb is small and sends up only one leaf, which is longer than the flower stalk. The small, many-flowered umbel is composed of reddish flowers crested with a deeper or purple color. It is found on dry hillsides in northwestern Nevada to the base of the Sierra Nevada, south to Owens valley, Inyo County, California. Good in the rock garden.

A. Austiniae
Austin's Onion

Another little western species that is distinctly worth a place in the rock garden. Its height is four to six inches, and the slender scape carries an umbel of from fifteen to thirty-five starry flowers of a dull reddish pink with green centers, surrounded by bands of dark color. The leaves number usually only two and are narrow, and scarcely equal the scape in height. It bloomed here on May 3rd. Gravelly soil at high elevations in the Sierra Nevada, extending from Plumas County to Tehachapi Mountains, California. It is said to propagate by bulblets borne on the ends of slender rhizomes sometimes several centimeters long. Appears as if it might be a spreader, but I have not had it long enough to know. Hardy.

A. Beesianum W. W. Smith   B.M. t. 9331
Mountain Garlic. Blue Leek

This species, which may be called one of the real beauties of the race, was collected in 1904 by Forest in western China, where he found it in full flower in September growing in stony pastures on the eastern flank of the Lichiang range at a high elevation. F. Kingdon Ward records that he met with it in the mountains of Tibet.

It is a very distinct as well as charming species—an exalted Onion, it has been called. A tuft of sparse glaucous leaves makes a setting for the slender stems, nine to twelve inches high, which bend over at the top, allowing the clustered flower head to droop gracefully. The cluster is composed of a number of narrow rather long bells, each on a little stalk nearly half an inch long, and of a distinctive china blue. Flowering at a season (August and September) when bulbous plants are scarce, it is a valuable acquisition for the rock garden or narrow border of choice plants. Its unusual color also adds to its value at this season. Seeds of *Beesianum* are often offered, and will flower the third year, sometimes the second.

A. Bidwelliae S. Wats. (A. campanulatum)

This is a species about which some confusion exists, for it is variously described as two feet high, and as "one of the dwarfer kinds, suitable for the rock garden, growing only a few inches high, with few flowered umbels of bright rose-colored blossoms in July."[1] Perry[2] describes it as an extremely pretty early-flowering species from Sierra Nevada, light green foliage, graceful umbels of *pure white* flowers, fifteen inches. Lester Rowntree[3] offers seed of it, and says she collected as this species, 8,500 feet up in the central Sierra Nevada, a kind with a round bulb, six inches in diameter, bearing a many-flowered umbel of deep strawberry-pink flowers with purple markings. And a portrait in *Gardening Illustrated* seems to bear out this description, showing fluffy globular heads of starry flowers on strong stems two feet high, with two very narrow leaves, shorter than the flower scape, the flowers described as soft pale rose. It is probable that it is not a dwarf but one of the taller kinds, as nearly all the descriptions I can find of it give the flower head as large—thirty- or forty-flowered.

[1] *The Garden*, Jan. 5, 1924.
[2] Catalogue of Hardy Plant Farm, Enfield, Middlesex, England.
[3] Carmel, California.

It is said to grow in open coniferous forests in the Klamath Mountains, south in the Sierra Nevada, and the higher altitudes of the inner Coast Ranges to the Mt. Pinos region, Ventura County, California.

A. Bolanderi Wats.

A pretty and slender little species growing some four to six inches tall, with two narrow leaves, shorter than the flower stalk, and a small open umbel of dark rose-red flowers. It bloomed here about June 10th. Found usually in heavy, clay soil in the Siskiyou Mountains in southern Oregon down into Humboldt and Mendocino counties in California.

A. brevistylum S. Wats.

This is an early native species flowering here about May 13th. It came from Mr. Andrews of Boulder, Colorado, who describes it as a subalpine from Wyoming, requiring much moisture. It grows here at the base of the rock garden, and is a slender plant with narrow leaves shorter than the flower stalk, which is about ten inches high. The flowers are borne in a small umbel, and are rose-pink in color, but a good deal of depth and richness, not washy.

A. caeruleum Pall (*A. azureum* Ledeb.)   *Bot. Reg.* XXVI t. 51
Blue Garlic

The Blue Garlic, as I had it from Mr. Van Melle, of Poughkeepsie, New York, is a handsome and desirable kind with a dense, nearly spherical, head of small deep blue flowers carried at the top of a slender stem, between eighteen and twenty-four inches tall. The leaves are triangular and not as tall as the scape, and in time it makes an attractive clump. It has flowered here twice, once about the 1st of May, and the next year nearly a month later. Weather doubtless had something to do with this rather inconsistent behavior.

Nicholson makes a difference between *A. caeruleum* and *A. azureum*. The first was introduced from Russia in 1840, and he gives its height as eight inches; the other, which he describes as a deep sky-blue with a dark line through the middle of each division, was introduced from Siberia in 1830, height one to two feet.

"One of the handsomest species known." The Kew Hand-List recognizes no difference between the two.

A. carinatum L.　　　　　　　　　Sowerby's *Eng. Bot.* t. 1658

A fine species from Europe, growing something over a foot tall, and bearing loose umbels of bright rosy crimson flowers made conspicuous by the long protruding stamens. It flowers in midsummer. The seed of this I had from Mr. Cleveland Morgan's garden, in Montreal. It is said to be one of the non-bulbous species.

A. cernuum Roth.　　　　　　　*Gardening Illus.* Nov. 4, 1933
Allegheny Onion

This is a widely distributed native species ranging from New York to West Virginia, Colorado, Washington, etc., usually found on sunny banks and hillsides. It was the first Allium to find a home in my garden, and was sent to me many years ago by Professor Edgar T. Wherry, of the Department of Botany, University of Pennsylvania. It is a charming species with narrow leaves and flower stalks, about eighteen inches tall, well topping the leaves. The flower head is loose and graceful in shape, for each pale lavender-pink flower is carried on a long curving stalk of its own, which gives the head a sort of shower effect, and this is accentuated by the very long stamens. It flowers here toward the end of June, is perfectly hardy, and seeds somewhat too freely. Does well in sun or shade.

A. Chamaemoly L.　　　　　　　　　　*B.M.* t. 1203
Bastard Garlic

Undoubtedly this is the smallest and most curious of Alliums. My hope of securing it has been so long deferred that I now despair of ever entertaining this midget in my garden. Several times I have been on what seemed a warm trail to seeds, but so far nothing has materialized. It belongs to the Mediterranean region, is found in Provence, the neighborhood of Tunis, Seville, Naples, and Rome, has been reported from Plage d'Hyères off the south of France, and the neighboring island of Porquerolles, growing in sand. Its bulb is said to be the size of a hazel nut, covered with a soft membranous coat, or sometimes by a brown crustaceous shell. The leaves are "radical, of a dark green, faced broadways to each other in pairs of unequal lengths." The flower scape of about an inch and a half in length, is "almost wholly within the ground, and sheathed by the cowled-convolute bases of the leaves." The little umbel that is made up of a few starry green and white flowers is almost on a level with the ground. In its natural haunts it makes its appearance in January and February. It is said to have little or no Onion odor.

Whether this small southerner would be hardy in our gardens, I do not know. Mr. Bowles grows it in his garden, Middleton House, in England, and I find a note of its thriving in Yorkshire, England, not so gentle a locality as it is accustomed to. It would, of course, require a sheltered place in the rock garden in full sun and sandy soil. I should be glad to meet with it in the flesh.

A. cyaneum Regel   *B.M.* t. 7290
   Blue-bell Garlic

Many years ago I raised *A. cyaneum* from seed. The resulting little tufts of narrow leaves, only about five inches high, just topped by dainty hanging heads of soft true blue flowers with yellow anthers, were quite enchanting. They flowered in early August, and were a real addition to the late summer display in the rock garden. Gradually I lost this first lot, and, wishing to replace them, procured more seed. This time my reward was something quite different. The little plants were alike as far as I could remember, but the flowers were poor indeed, pale and washy, and altogether lacking the charm of the first lot. And Mr. Farrer in the appendix to "The English Rock Garden" makes it plain that there is more than one plant going about under the name of *cyaneum:* "I greatly suspect that this name embraces several of the lovely blue-bell Garlics that so abound all over the Alps of South Kansu and Tibet dotted freely in the hot alpine herbage, or forming mats on the edges of cool limestone cliffs. . . ." In his "On the Eaves of the World," he often refers to the Blue-bell Garlic, and always with admiration: "At last we came to the entrance of the gorges, close to the shadow of titanic cliffs, from which the blue-bell garlic floundered in delicate flufferies of blue," etc. I am sure this must have been the form I first had, and not its poor little pale shadow. It is worth while trying to get the best form. The one is lovely, the other worthless. (See also *A. kansuense.*)

A. *Douglasii* Hook. (*A. unifolium*)

Nat. Hort. Mag. July 1930

A pretty early-flowering species from the Northwest with flowers "of the palest pink with a flush of rose at the base of the petals, and a deep rose line down the center of each, giving a pink and white beauty much like that of the Spring Beauty of the Eastern woods. As the flowers wither, they become papery and last like ghosts of themselves long after the leaves have disappeared." [4] I have not grown this Allium, but Mr. Morrison, whose notes are quoted above, says it has, despite its name, several leaves which appear so early that they are sometimes nipped by late frosts. The flower heads on their twelve- to eighteen-inch stalks, are developed in time to bloom with the true *Phlox amoena*, just after the familiar *Phlox divaricata* has passed.

A. *falcifolium* H. & A.
Scythe-leaved Onion

A quaint little species, distinct and interesting and well suited to the rock garden, for it grows only a few inches tall. The dark, rather wide leaves, make their appearance early and lie about on the ground in a strangely contorted manner, rather, as some one said, like a mass of writhing snakes. They are about six in number. The stem is flat as is the sheath that contains the flowers. When it breaks, the rather large flowers, twenty or more in an umbel, appear something like a paintbrush. They are strong purple tinged with pink, not at all magenta, and they reflex slightly. They are held erectly, and have prominent white anthers. The leaves disappear before the flowers are mature. It blooms here about May 27th, and has so far thriven at the top of a small mountain in full sunshine.

Usually found on serpentine outcrops in the Coast Ranges from the Siskiyou Mountains, Oregon, to Sonora County, California.

[4] *National Horticultural Magazine*, July, 1930, p. 167.

A. flavum Salisb. B.M. t. 1313
  Golden Onion

A pretty and slender-growing species with yellow, somewhat drooping flowers in a loose umbel borne on a scape about a foot tall. The leaves are roundish but not hollow, and it flowers here about the 1st of July. Mr. Morrison says that in Washington it blooms with *Heuchera sanguinea,* and that the two are nice in combination. It is an old kind in gardens, having been introduced from Italy in 1759. The leaves are almost evergreen, lasting until it is nearly time for the new growths to make their appearance. In milder climates they would doubtless last quite through the winter.

The Kew Hand-List makes no difference between this and *A. Moly,* but they are quite different as I have them here, and a kind growing in the New York Botanical Gardens and labeled *flavum* appears to me still different, stronger-growing, more erect, and with larger umbels of flowers. All three are very good, and the one I have as *A. flavum* is quite pretty, and slender enough for use in the rock garden. This may be a form sometimes known as *minor.*

A. Geyeri Wats.

A not very common species found near watercourses and in mountain meadows from British Columbia to the Blue Mountains, eastern Oregon, and Wyoming. It flowered here about May 28th, bearing a small erect umbel of flowers of a very nice pink tone on a stalk about ten inches high. The leaves are thin and narrow.

A. giganteum Regel B.M. t. 6828

This is one of the tallest of the genus, growing when well suited four and a half feet tall. The leaves are two inches broad and apt to lie about the ground. From among them arises the tall strong stem carrying a ball of bright lilac flowers, appearing, says Mr. Hamblin, like an Eremurus gone globular. It is a handsome and stately species, and obviously belongs in important positions in the borders among the perennials, or in front of shrubs against which its great balls of lavender bloom would show to advantage.

It flowers in July, a month that is too often poorly furnished, and in no great time forms showy clumps. It will also thrive in partial shade, and is a handsome addition to fern borders or the wild garden. It comes originally from the Himalaya Mountains.

A. kansuense Regel   B.M. t. 7290

This is one of the charming Blue Garlics about which confusion seems to cling. It is sometimes known as *A. cyaneum dasystemon*, and I suspect is the one Mr. Farrer knew as *A. c. macrostemon*. In any case, it is close to *cyaneum* in its dwarf stature, its little hanging head of blue bells, its grassy leaves and leafy stems, and its midsummer blossoming. H. S. Bothman, writing in the *National Horticultural Magazine* for August, 1932, says: "In *A. kansuense* the leaves are flat and channeled and the stamens do not protrude beyond the mouth of the bell, whilst the leaves of *A. cyaneum* are rolled and the stamens do protrude. *A. cyaneum* is not so tall and flowers a little later." Obviously a gem for the rock garden by whatever name we may have it, and especially important because of the sparse-flowered season at which it blooms among our small hills. It is a native of Kansu in China.

A. karativiense Regel   B.M. t. 6451

This rather astonishing plant is said to have been a discovery of Russian explorers in the mountains of Central Asia east of Samarkand; a little later (in 1876) Dr. Albert Regel found it in the Alatau Range and sent the bulbs to his father in St. Petersburg, and from thence it reached the rest of the world. It is a curious plant for an Allium, as it discards the usual narrow-leafed habit of the clan and produces instead broad glaucous leaves—two, occasionally three, to a bulb, broader than those of a Tulip—that arch over to touch the ground, almost oblong in shape and thick in texture. The leaves are perhaps of more value than the flowers which, though forming a round ball, are rather poor and unconvincing in color. They are supported on stout stems just above the leaves, and appear in the late spring. It is a perfectly hardy species, but likes a sunny situation in the rock garden or at the edge of a warm, well drained border. It remains a feature for rather a long time, for its seeding is decorative, and its blue-

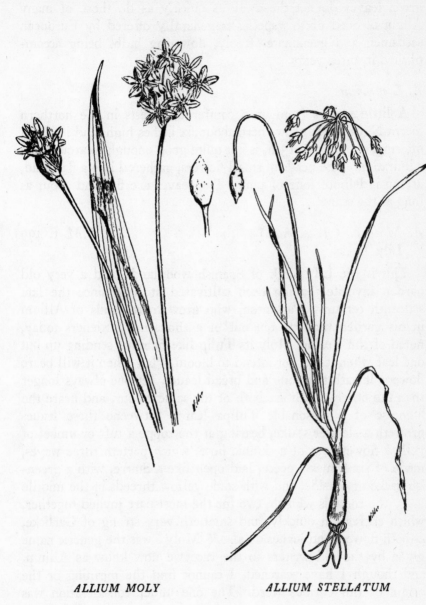

ALLIUM MOLY   **ALLIUM STELLATUM**

green leaves do not die away as quickly as do those of many Alliums. Seed of this species is generally offered by European seedsmen and germinates freely, flowering bulbs being accomplished in three years.

A. Lemmonii

A little species from open coniferous forests in the northern Sierra Nevada. It grows here about six inches high, and its floral offering, about May 13th, is not quite good enough to arouse real admiration. The heads of small flowers, gathered into a flat head, are an indefinite tone of pink. The leaves are flat and about as long as the scape.

A. Moly L. (*A. aureum*)   B.M. t. 499
Lily Leek

This is the Lily Leek of Spanish woodlands, and a very old garden favorite, having been cultivated at least since the late sixteenth century. Parkinson, who grew more kinds of Allium in his garden than do ten out of a thousand gardeners today, noted of the Yellow Moly its Tulip-like habit of sending up but one leaf when it did not intend to bloom; "but when it will beare flowers, it hath two long and broad leaues, yet one always longer than the other, which are both of the same colour, and neare the bignesse of a reasonable Tulipa leafe; betweene these leaues groweth a slender stalke, bearing at the toppe a tuft or umbel of yellow flowers out of a skinnie hose, which parteth three wayes, made of six leaues a peece, laid open like a Starre, with a greenish backe or outside, and with some yellow threeds in the middle . . . the roote is whitish, two for the most part joyned together, which encreaseth quickly, and smelleth very strong of Garlicke, as both flowers and leaues do also." Moly [5] was the generic name given by the old writers to the race we now know as Allium, and though I have searched, I cannot find the meaning or the origin of this curious word. The one under consideration was

<hr />

[5] Moly, the name of a plant in Homer's *Odyssey*, and occasionally introduced into modern poetry, as in Milton's *Comus*, line 636, but not identified with any known species, and probably meant by Homer to be understood allegorically. *Popular Names of British Plants*, by R. C. A. Prior. Moly, in Homer's time and before, was endowed with magical properties. Ulysses walked, under its protection, unharmed into the sties of Circe. In dictionaries it is dismissed as a fabulous plant.

called by Parkinson, *Moly montanum latifolium lutea flore.*
Imagine taking your neighbor around your garden and spouting
such cumbersome names. Small wonder that simple common
names sprouted like—well, like Garlics, in that early day. How
grateful we should be to Linnaeus, the great Swede, who invented
the binominal nomenclature, or two-word designation, which we
use today!

Well, the Yellow Moly was popular in an earlier day, chiefly
doubtless because of its yellow flowers, when all the then known
members of the race ran so monotonously to rosy-pinkness or to
white; but perhaps its vogue was due, also, somewhat to the belief
voiced by Alfonse Harr, botanist and poet, that you can spill salt,
meet a spider, a hare may run across your path, a crow may fly
past on your left hand, you may sit down thirteen at dinner, you
may do anything on a Friday that you like, and snap your fingers,
if you have *Allium aureum* in your garden. And he goes on to
say that many persons who have it in their gardens do not know
that it is to this "assiduous vegetable" that their astounding good
fortune and prosperity may be ascribed.° Then, of course, the
world progressed and anxious persons began to depend on Holy
Water, Abracadabra, Rabbits' feet, or the stock exchange to pro-
tect them from evil, and the Yellow Moly was discarded. But it
lingered on bravely in certain old gardens, and now is coming
back to notice; and perhaps in "these pinching times" its infalli-
bility may again be credited. Miss Jekyll admired it and
grew it, and that in itself is enough to give it place in the best
society.

My bulbs came to me long ago from my old friend, the late
Clarence Lown, who said, "Here is something nice that will give
you no trouble, and you won't notice the odor if you don't break
the stems or leaves." I have handed on bulbs of it to many
persons, so that it has never increased greatly in my garden, but
remains a nice tidy clump, with wide gray leaves and heads of
starry flowers that appear in early June. It flourishes in full sun
as well as in moderate shade, growing something more than a foot
tall. The *Botanical Magazine* says it is found wild in Hungary,
on Mount Baldo, about Montpellier, and in the Pyrenees. It is
offered by a few dealers in this country.

° E. M. J. in *The Garden*, Oct. 10, 1925.

A. narcissiflorum Vill. (*A. pedemontanum*)   B.M. t. 6182

Farrer calls this the glory of the race. It dwells "in the steep earth pans and stony screes far up in the most awesome shelves of the limestone Alps of Piedmont (and far away into the Caucasus). Here it runs underground, forming a huge ramifying mass of rootstocks below in the unnegotiable stony hard earth, and the surface of that barren place is covered with a waving green jungle of upstanding strap-shaped leaves, up among which come shooting, in August, springy stems of eight to ten inches, each hanging out a loose head of some six or eight flowers, very large and lovely indeed, great pendent bells of glowing vinous red. Unfortunately an evil godmother has dowered this beauty with a commensurate drawback in the form of an exaggerated stench, a stench so horrible that one can hardly bear to collect it."

I quote thus at length from Mr. Farrer because, though I have several times thought I had this species, it either has failed to come up, or has come up as something quite different. Stephen Hamblin, in his *Lexington Leaflets*, says: "The roots creep something like those of Lily of the Valley. The leaves are strapshaped, very erect, very many, very unlike most Onions." He says it is very distinct, wholly hardy, not a foot tall, and well suited to the rock garden. Seeds are offered, so it may be experimented with, and it sounds a most desirable species.

A. neapolitanum Cyr. (*A. lacteum*) Sweet's *Brit. Fl. Gard.* t. 201
Daffodil Garlic. Naples Onion

The Naples Onion may at once be given a good mark because it has not the usual Onion stink; but it has the drawback in our climate of not being quite hardy. I have lost it more than once, but also kept it over more than one winter; and it is most attractive, with large white flowers of great purity, save for the rosy stamens, gathered into loose heads "like a bunch of Pear blossoms." The leaves are few and flat, and rather like those of a Daffodil. It flowers in spring, and has been recommended as a becoming companion for *Scilla nonscripta* (*S. nutans, S. festalis*). If it is to be grown in cold climates, a warm and sheltered place should be chosen for it, and covering given in the winter. Mr. Farrer says the fine white flowers are gathered in stacks and exported to England for decoration. It is probably the finest white-flowered sort, and worth taking a little trouble to keep. It grows wild in southern Europe.

A. *Nuttallii* Wats. (*A. Helleri*)

A slender little species from the plains and prairies of Kansas, Arizona, Idaho, and thereabouts. It grows about a foot tall, and the individual flowers that make up the umbel are borne on rather long pedicels, and are pale pink or white. It has lived in this garden only a year, so I do not know if it will prove a colonizing nuisance or not. The leaves are few and flat.

A. *odorum* L.

A number of years ago, a bulb was sent me nameless from the Cambridge Botanic Gardens. When it blossomed in the late summer, it proved to be a very handsome white-flowered Allium. An Onion, its narrow foliage when crushed had proclaimed it to be, but the flowers exhaled the perfume of Heliotrope. Through the years this bulb has increased until now there are numerous good clumps occupying a knoll at the back of the rock garden which, at the time of their blossoming, scent a wide area with their delicious Heliotrope fragrance. The Onion odor is noticeable only if the stem is crushed, and is then not very strong. The flower scape grows to a height of about eighteen inches or two feet, is slender but very strong; and the umbel is nearly flat and is made up of many small white flowers marked with green on short pedicels. These stand erect and are closely set. It flowers throughout the late summer and early autumn, and is nice to use as a cut flower combined with other blooms of its season. The flower heads last long in good condition, and even when in seed, the erect heads are handsome enough to call forth a good deal of admiration.

Now as to its exact identity I am not quite sure. I have given away many bulbs, and have inquired of botanic gardens and other authoritative sources without receiving confirmation of my belief that it is the *A. odorum* described in *Hortus,* a plant said to come from Siberia and Japan. Mr. P. J. Van Melle of Poughkeepsie, in whose nomenclatural zeal I have great faith, agrees with me; so, for the time being, it may rest beneath that label. In any case, it is one of the best of the Alliums and, because of its late season, extremely valuable. It seeds rather freely, but not so rampantly as to become a nuisance. Its progeny are easily taken care of, and while it breathes that rich fragrance into the summer air, it is a welcome guest. Plants of *Verbena venosa* set about it, made a good association both in the garden and for picking.

A. Ostrowskianum Regel   B.M. t. 7756

A good and comely kind to grow in the rock garden, that was introduced from Turkestan in 1883. The leaves are commonly only two or three, flat, limp, and bluish. From among them arises a stem less than a foot high carrying a head of large flowers of rather a rich tone of reddish violet with darker marks on the segment. An unusual charm is the very pleasant fragrance of the flowers; but do not bruise or crush the leaves or stem! It blooms about mid-June, and as the flowers age, they grow thin and papery, as do many of their kind, remaining sightly while the seeds mature. The leaves die away early in July.

This is said to be closely allied to, and frequently confused with, a kind that I have sought and not found: *A. creophilum*, a very low-growing kind described as native in the Caucasus, Siberia, etc. Of it Mr. Farrer says it has "two narrow flat recurving little leaves, and sends up a stem of only three inches or so, with clustered domes of big purple blossoms. This beautiful mountain jewel comes from the screes of alpine Caucasus and Dagestan at some 7,800–9,000 feet." Perfect, obviously, for the rock garden, but if it is in this country I have not found it, though I have more than once purchased a stalwart under its name. These masqueraders are most annoying.

A. oxyphilum Wherry
Acid-soil Onion

This species came to me many years ago from Dr. Edgar T. Wherry. It is, he writes, allied to *A. cernuum*, but is found commonly in acid-soil regions, whereas the latter is usually found on limestone ledges in alluvial soil. It is a pretty kind, but belongs distinctly to the wild garden as it is a somewhat too assiduous seeder. The flowers have the same pretty drooping habit as those of *cernuum*, are pure white or pale lilac, and are borne from mid-July to late August.

A. Purdomii

If this species is "a pretty little Tibetan with heads of clear blue flowers," three inches, as described and recommended for scree or moraine by W. E. Th. Ingwersen, then I have it not. On the other hand, if it is the plant I have from Mr. Andrews,[7] which seems to agree with several other authorities, then I may pat myself on the back. It is agreed by all that it comes from Tibet. My plant has very short foliage in a tuft out of which arise the stems to a height of something over six inches, carrying a large umbel of erect flowers, a nice lilac in color. The whole is neat and compact and very good in the rock garden, flowering early in July.[8]

A. *platycaule* S. Wats.

A pretty little Californian species that flowers here about the middle of May, bearing between the two rather flat and wide leaves a compact head of silvery pink flowers with very narrow petals on stems less than six inches high. This came from Carl Purdy, and is said to be found in subalpine meadows of the Sierra Nevada, etc.

A. *pulchellum* G. Don

I have, most confusingly, several quite different flowers labeled *pulchellum* in my garden. Mr. Morrison describes it as an evergreen pushing up into new and vigorous growth in the early spring, and flowering in mid-July. The foot-high stalks rise with graceful curves through the slender tufts of leaves; indeed, the whole plant is so delicate that one needs a considerable clump in order to get an effect, or else one should plant them in small groups among some lowly perennial of earlier or later blooming through whose leaves the onions may arise. (Mr. Farrer says it blooms at midsummer, and has a special charm if planted among similar graceful things, such as fine grasses, *Campanula rotundifolia*, and white Linums.) "The color of the flowers is a tender

[7] Boulder, Colorado.

[8] Stephen Hamblin in *Lexington Leaflets* describes it as having small narrow leaves and little blue flowers, deepest blue, like a Grape Hyacinth that forgot to lengthen its stalk, and bloomed all in one bunch. Mr. Andrews' species is quite evidently not this. With Alliums, things get "curiouser and curiouser."

pinkish lavender made remarkable by the fact that the little stalks of the individual flowers are almost white, tinted with almost pure pink. This tendency to have almost colorless flower stalks appears in other Allium species even in the cultivated Leek, and gives a very unique effect when there are well developed flower heads, as if the whole were illuminated from within."

A. pulchellum is said to be native to southern Europe and parts of the Orient. Another year must elapse before I can positively identify it among my masqueraders.

A. recurvatum Rydb. (*A. cernuum obtusum* Cockerell)

This species, which has a wide range through South Dakota, New Mexico, British Columbia, and the Rocky Mountains where it is found on dry hillsides, grassy slopes, etc., flowering in June, is a very good sort for the wild garden. It has narrow grasslike leaves that persist and form a tangled mat on the ground, out of which the stems arise to a height of about fifteen inches. The flowers are borne in a spraylike head, the individuals about a quarter of an inch long, nodding on thin pedicels, and of a nice rose-pink tone, each with a darker mid-vein and pale yellow anthers. They flower here early in July. There is a pure white-flowered form that is rare and very lovely. Under the name of *A. recurvatum superbum,* and called by Mr. Durand the Pagosa Onion, which he collected near Pagosa Lake in the Rocky Mountains, I have a more robust form, taller and altogether more showy. This Mr. Durand gave me from his original collected stock. He thinks it unsurpassed by any other Allium, and it is quite good enough for a prominent position where there is room for it. I have had it for several years and do not find it a too aggressive spreader.

A. senescens glaucum L.   B.M. t. 1149

After considerable searching about in Garlic literature, it seems probable that the plant received here as *A. glaucum* is more properly named as above, but by any name it is a good kind, especially valuable on several counts for the rock garden. It makes a tuft of short gray quaintly twisted leaves, numerous and pointed, out of which arise the sturdy flower stems to a height of about a foot. These bear flower heads that are a flattened round made up of many mauve flowers with yellow anthers. The balls of buds remain closed for a long time, and are darker in tone than the opened flowers, and very decorative at this stage. When they unfold it will be noticed that they are very fragrant, but if any other part of the plant is crushed, the old Adam in them is distinctly noticeable. In this garden it comes into flower late in the season, about the first week in September, so it may be added to the list of plants that flower in the rock garden in autumn. It is nice in combination with *Sedum Sieboldii*.

A. serratum

Another nice species for the rock garden, this one blossoming in early June. It is a native Californian found in the inner Coast Ranges in rather heavy soil. It is a neat, attractive little species, the leaves shorter than the flower scapes and fading away before the flowers are mature. The small umbels are made up of some twelve or fourteen flowers, purple at the pointed tips, but fading to almost white at the base. As they fade, they turn papery, and so their life and usefulness are prolonged.

A. sikkimense Baker   *B.M.* t. 8858

This is a newcomer to the garden, and I have not much to say of it that is matter of fact. It is said to be a native of alpine Sikkim, and to like a position that is not open to the sun for the whole day. It has proved hardy here over its first winter, and gave its small nodding heads of clear lavender-blue flowers in June. It is compact and neat and ideal for the rock garden; indeed it is too small for any less protected situation, growing only about six inches tall. The leaves are few and grassy.

A. sphaerocephalum L.   *B.M.* t. 1764
Globe-headed Garlic

A tall, rather coarse species for the border or wild garden. It bears round heads of densely packed flowers, large and rosy, the buds purple at the top and greenish at the base, the leaves narrow. It is native of parts of Europe and the Orient, and seeds of it are usually to be had in the catalogue of the Floraire Nurseries, near Geneva, Switzerland. It flowers at midsummer, but these giant Chives are rather tiresomely ubiquitous.

A. *stellatum* Fras.

This is a widely distributed species found on rocky banks in Illinois, Missouri, Kansas, and parts of the Northwest. My bulbs came from Mrs. Fanny Manhood Heath many years ago, from about Grand Forks, North Dakota. She described it as "lovely on the dry sandy ridges where it grows in patches of hundreds of plants." It is the last of its race to be found flowering, at least in this garden, bravely showing bits of glowing color late in the autumn, though it begins to flower in early August as a rule. The bulbs are finely reticulated, the leaves bright green and flat, and the stem longer than the leaves. The flower head is in the form of an uncrowded umbel, the individual flowers borne on long pedicels. It is a rampant seeder here, and has had to be segregated in a part of the garden where its activities are a boon rather than a bane.

A. *stenanthum*

A very pretty little species that came from Mr. Purdy's rich store, and that finds a welcome place in the rock garden. It grows little more than six inches high, and bears a head loosely set with long bell-shaped white flowers in early May.

A. *textile* Nels. & Macb. (*A. reticulatum*)
Early White Onion

Though this little Onion came to me many years ago, it has been content to keep to its corner in a sunny section of the rock garden, increasing almost not at all. It belongs to dry plains and hills from the far North to New Mexico and Arizona. It is not conspicuous, but I always welcome its few-flowered umbel of white flowers when it appears early in May. It grows about eight inches tall, the leaves narrow and channeled and few. The bulb is said to be densely and coarsely fibrous-coated. A pink-flowered form is reported.

A. *triquetrum* L. ⸱⸱⸱⸱⸱⸱⸱⸱⸱⸱⸱⸱⸱⸱⸱⸱⸱⸱⸱⸱⸱⸱⸱⸱⸱⸱⸱⸱⸱⸱⸱ *B.M.* t. 869

I like this little Onion for several reasons, chief among them that it grew in Parkinson's garden. He calls it the three-cornered Moly, and gives a figure of it on page 143 of the "Paradisus,"

and a nice description, calling attention to the "skinnie huske" out
of which come "diuers white flowers, somewhat large and long,
almost bell-fashion, with stripes of greene downe the middle of
euery leaf, and a few chiues tipt with yellow in the middle about
the head . . . both roote, leafe and flower hath a smacke, but
not very strong of Garlicke." And then I like it because it is a
really lovely "Garlicke," having larger flowers in a looser head
than most, "as crisp a dead white as any Narcissus or Snowflake,
with smart lines of vivid green down the backs of each petal." [*]
It is a favorite generally when known. Besides Mr. Morrison's
description, just given, Mr. Farrer also praised it, saying, "The
plant has great attractions and is always to be known by its fat,
three-sided stems of some six inches or so, each carrying perhaps
six large pendulous flowers of a diaphanous white, looking like
the ghost of a dead white flower drowned long ago in deep water."
The figure in the *Botanical Magazine* shows its charm, and suggests its use more frequently as a spring-flowering bulb among
the many that bloom in May. The leaves are quite wide and flat,
but I am not sure of its hardiness north of this region. It is found
naturally at the edges of fields, and on cool shaded banks in Spain
and France, and it has become naturalized in Cornwall, England.
I have had my bulbs only a year and am protecting them. Mr.
Morrison says they have shown no tendency to spread underground or by seeds.

A. ursinum L.
Bear's Garlic

The "Dictionary of English Plant Names" gives so many by-
names for this little British wild flower (it is also found in many
parts of Europe and Asia) that at once we know it has long been
both notable and notorious. Some of these names are Bucrammes
or Bucrames,[10] Ramsons, Devil's Posy, Gypsy Onions, Hog's
Garlick, Ram's Horns, and Stink Plant.

This species, which is found in moist woods and beside hedges
in great abundance, though somewhat locally, is by way of being
a joker. Its two wide leaves might well be mistaken by the
unwary wayfarer for those of the Lily-of-the-Valley, and even

[*] *National Horticultural Magazine.*
[10] *The Names of Herbes*, by William Turner, 1548.

when the umbel of starry white flowers appears, he is still minded to gather it as something precious. And then the cat is out of the bag, and the Gypsy Onions laugh loud and long in the only way they can laugh, by letting loose their fetid odor and defiling the hand that has gathered it. Anne Pratt says, "Sometimes this garlic grows among grass, and after a shower the odour arising from it is so insufferable that we are glad to escape from the meadow." [11]

But for all its evil ways, it is very pretty, growing a foot tall, and opening its clusters of white stars in the spring, each on a long pedicel. And once poor folk turned to it to give relish to their dull diet of bread and meat. A corner might well be found for it in some by-place where its spring grace could be displayed without our coming to grips with its less attractive attribute. The old books all have something to say about it. Bears especially were thought to fancy it (and are there not still occasionally bears in gardens?), and it was reputed of great medicinal value for various ills:

> Eat Leekes in Lide, and Ramsins in May
> And all the year after Physitians may play.

But the fine taste of English milk and butter is often spoiled where cattle have eaten it, and the flesh of calves is sometimes flavored with it. (Rather nice, that!) The more fastidious sheep, however, will not touch it.

A. validum S. Wats.
   Swamp Onion

This stalwart Onion, found in alpine meadows of the Pacific region, from Mt. Rainier to the southern Sierra Nevada, and in the Coast Ranges to Lake County, California, and east to Nevada, is very handsome, but unfortunately has a rather stronger odor than is acceptable in gardens. From the abundant grassy foliage, the stems rise to about eighteen inches in height, carrying in summer a head of dark rose-colored flowers, which last a long time in good condition. I would not call it choice, but it is sufficiently decorative to fill a place in the shrubbery, or the less special borders. I do not know yet if it is a dangerous spreader, but it looks as if it might be.

[11] *Haunts of the Wild Flowers,* by Anne Pratt.

As I go about examining the forest of my Allium labels, I find among them *A. fallax, A. galanthum, A. Huteri, A. Helleri, A. japonicum, A. ledebourianum, A. Libanii, A. macranthum, A. nigrum, A. Pallens, A. Pikeanum, A. roseum, A. senescens, A. tibeticum* (at least three distinct kinds bear this name), *A. Victorialis, A. yunnanense;* but as none of them come up to any reliable specifications that I can find of them, any description of them must be omitted here. Many of them are simply like overgrown Chives, and have no distinctive characteristics. Collecting Alliums is at the present time simply a game of chance—it may bring rewards or it may not—it may indeed multiply trouble, but it is very amusing. One never knows.

ANEMONE *RANUNCULACEAE*

WINDFLOWER

OF all the flowers that flicker briefly across the worn brown garment of the early spring, none are more tenderly beguiling than the Anemones. They do not charm by splurge (save *A. fulgens*) but by far gentler arts:

> Anemones, which droop their eyes
> Earthward before they dare arise
> To flush the border . . .

And I know of no more wholly enchanting experience than to come upon a wide group of them in animated dance beneath the pale green veil of the early year's weaving before the snow feel has gone out of the air.

We have our native Anemones, or Windflowers, and they are pretty enough, though inconspicuous in comparison with some of the foreign-born kinds. There are Anemones in Asia Minor, in many parts of Asia, and in many parts of Europe. Some climb the mountains to a great height, but more are subalpine than alpine.

They may be roughly divided into two types: those with fibrous roots, and those with tuberous roots. The latter are the only ones treated here. All have finely divided leaves springing directly from the root, and so far as I know them, are hardy and not too fussy about their board and room.[1] Nearly all, however, in our climate, prefer some shade, though not dense woodland, and the majority like an open gritty, humus-filled soil with, save in the case of the Americans, a little lime in it. Shelter from high winds, despite their common name, is a consideration that is appreciated.

The tubers commonly look like bits of dry stick, and it is sometimes difficult to know which side is right side up. When in doubt,

---

[1] Forms of *A. coronaria* have occasionally lasted over a winter, but cannot be termed reliably hardy.

lay them lengthwise, and they will manage the rest. Plant them two or three inches below the surface of the soil, and the same distance apart. Planting should be done as early in the autumn as the tubers may be secured, for they quickly dry out and lose vitality. Bad luck with them is commonly simply bad management. They are willing and easy if their perfectly reasonable needs and necessities are considered, and I have more than once transplanted them in full flower without loss. Set in congenial surroundings, they increase generously, both by means of the tubers and by seeding, and there is no more gratifying sight to a gardener than those tiny little, finely divided leaves that are Anemone seedlings, though they are slow to arrive at flowering strength.

Anemones may be raised from seed if one has a handsome equipment of patience. The seed must, in the first place, be fresh, if prompt germination is to take place; otherwise one might as well prepare for a year's wait, sometimes more, guarding the pans all the while from weather and pests of one kind and another. Gather your own seed if you are so fortunate as to have Anemones in the garden, and sow it at once in a cold frame, or in pans of light soil. It takes about three years to obtain flowering plants. The wait and the trouble are worth while, however, and the only way, unless one is a plutocrat, to secure these exquisite flowers of the spring in any quantity. The few dealers who offer them charge a high price for them, as why should they not? The Quarantine Law sees to it that these innocents are not admitted to the country. Abroad they may be purchased for a few pence each; here we must pay as much as forty or fifty cents a tuber, and it takes many to make even a modest show. I have heard of no disease which makes them dangerous to us, but still we keep them out! The tuberous-rooted Anemones die down and disappear after flowering, and are no more seen until another spring calls them forth. So mark well their stations.

A. apennina L.

The Apennine Anemone is normally a woodland and often a mountain plant. In our country it thrives in light shade beneath high-branched trees, or in the lee of little bushes in the rock garden where the sun can reach it for a part of the day. Its range is wide through southern Europe; it is found in Italy, Corsica, Dalmatia, Herzegovina, Montenegro, and Corfu, and in parts of Great Britain it has naturalized itself. It is a many-sepaled blue flower with a brush of golden stamens at the heart. Its hue of blue is what might be termed atmospheric, and at a little distance a plantation has the appearance of a delicate haze upon the earth. The leaves are the usual finely divided type, and a bright soft green. The height is from four to six inches. It flowers in April.

There is a pure white form and a variety called *rosea;* these I have not seen, but I have long possessed an Anemone like *apennina* in all respects, save that it is white with the reverse side of the sepals tinged lilac-rose. I do not now remember whence this came to me. I understand that there is also a double form which I cannot but think must be a little penny-dreadful, though the double-flowered *nemorosa* is a flower of indubitable charm.

A. baldensis L.

A little plant that has not yet come my way, so I quote Mr. Clarence Elliott as to its charms and qualifications: It is "a high alpine, found in screes of the primary rocks, at eight or ten thousand feet, where it threads about through the stony soil, with long running fleshy strings of root, and sends up little tufts of parsley-like leaves, and pale flowers, white, with sometimes a pinkish lilac wash. It makes little show in the rock garden, but it fascinates the Alpine purist with its shy ways in the non-lime scree." [2] It is said to be found in the southern Alps, including the Dolomites. The solitary flowers appear in May, and have from eight to ten oblong oval white sepals, hairy outside and reddish, with a blue cast. Mr. Farrer recommends growing it in a very earthy moraine with a few large coarse boulders buried in it, and water flowing below. He also says, however, that it is difficult to cultivate, and that he has not solved the riddle of its necessities.

A. blanda Schott. & Kotschy

Though a Daisy in form, it none the less manages to be one of the loveliest of flowers, "this starry purple flower of eighteen points," a tone of bland purple or lavender not often achieved by flowers, and varying to white and rose in different forms. A touch

[2] *Rock Garden Plants.*

of the sun is enough to bring it forth in spring; one day it is not there, the next you are enchanted to find it swaying in your path, a bright, ingratiating harbinger. It is much in the way of *apennina*, but neater, more compact, and the flowers of somewhat more substance, less ethereal in color and in texture. Happy those who have seen it decking "all the Islands and coasts of the Eastern Mediterranean with sheets of color with the first breath of spring."

The "blue" forms are far the prettiest, and with me are more vigorous of constitution, sowing themselves readily in well limed situations at the edge of the shady portion of the rock garden. It wants to be where the sun can reach in and touch it into life—sun for a little more than half of the day is better than shade. In Mr. Lown's Poughkeepsie garden were lovely plantations of the Greek Anemone that were of long standing. They always set my feet in that direction with the first spring days. They were something to see, and my "tubers" came originally from that beloved and accomplished gardener. The root is a fattish, almost bulbous tuber, not the elongated affair of *apennina* and *nemorosa*.

The variety *scythinica* has pure white flowers with a blue reverse. It is not, to my knowledge, offered in this country at any price, and is even somewhat dear across the water. I cannot think it could approach the blue forms in beauty.

A. *fulgens* Gay
Scarlet Windflower

This bright "intemperate glory" belongs to Asia Minor and Greece. Maurice Hewlett called it the truly typical Greek Anemone. "It is a wonder of the woodlands," he says, "as of those between Olympia and Megalopolis, or of the yet denser brakes about Tatoi, where the late Constantine used to retire and meditate statecraft." One flower coming up amidst the herbage in the rock garden rivets all eyes upon it. Could anything be redder? A colony is simply dazzling when the sun shines upon them. The hue of the flowers is heightened by the central boss of blue-black stamens.

Its hardiness is under suspicion, but it has lived in this garden for a number of years. Its residence, however, was carefully chosen. It is in a slightly raised portion of the rock garden with a good-sized rock on the north side, and the soil is gritty and well drained (it would never stand wet feet in winter), and it receives a covering of salt hay in the late autumn after the ground is frozen. There is some shade on its western side from tall trees at a little distance, which gives it relief during the hottest part of the day. It grows happily among other plants, Crocuses, Corydalis, and the like. The roots should be put into the ground as early as they may be procured.

There is a double-flowered form, said to have a multiplicity of narrow sepals, but I have not seen it. I have a few bulbs of *A. hortensis*[a] which seem to be very close to it with slight variations of the color tone. All are fine for cutting, and last well in water.

A. nemorosa L.
Wood Anemone

The lovely Wood Anemone grows wild in woods and copses all over Great Britain and in many parts of Europe. It is hardy and long enduring, increasing with a good deal of generosity. The large flowers droop and swing from their slender five- or six-inch stems in a charming manner above the soft, five-parted leaves. The color varies from white to many tones of violet and "blue." They flower here soon after the 1st of April and seem, with their delicately swaying grace, true flowers of the wind.

The collector of Wood Anemones will be enchanted with the many different forms to be had. *A. n. Allenii* boasts the largest flowers among them, and perhaps the sturdiest habit. Its sepals are broad and overlap, their upper surface a pale rosy-lilac, with the backs distinctly rose-colored. It soon spreads into nice thrifty clumps, very bright and smiling on a spring day. *A. n. Robinsoniana* in color is a clear and limpid blue-lavender, the flowers smaller than the foregoing, but large enough to make a fine showing when gathered into little groups on the shady side of the rock garden, or at the edge of light woodland places. Blue Bonnet has large soft blue flowers, almost as large as *Allenii*, and it flowers later, and is of a dwarfer habit. Royal Blue has very bright blue flowers. Blue Beauty, pale blue with a silvery reverse side.

[a] *B.M.* t. 123. Said to have abounded in gardens in the time of Parkinson.

A. nemorosa alba plena Maund's *B.G.* t. 80
Double Wood Anemone. Jack-in-the-Green

Though one may not care for double flowers generally, one cannot fail to be pleased with this fairy powder-puff of a flower. There seem to be two forms of it. Mine is the one figured in Maund's *Botanic Garden*, Plate 80. Mr. Bowles says this is a very old inhabitant of gardens, "with six well-formed and regular sepals, and then the whole center filled up with a rosette of petaloid bodies, beautifully neat and regular, looking like a small double Daisy." The other, which I have not seen, but which may be come upon by some lucky American gardener any day, is described by Mr. Bowles as "that eccentric Mad Hatter and March Hare in one, the variable *bracteata*, which in some seasons may be nearly single, then in another, the green bracts will be mixed among the white sepals, or they may be striped with green, or at other times, stained with a dull purple." This is doubtless the kind known as Jack-in-the-Green.

My powder-puff kind came as did so many of my treasures from Mr. Lown's garden in Poughkeepsie many years ago. In shaded places its root has run about until there are wide colonies of it carpeting the ground. Where I have transplanted it to sunnier areas, it has gradually died out. It undoubtedly likes cool conditions of soil and aspect, rather damp than dry, and it forgathers happily beneath small shrubs in the rock garden, and even presses in under the small evergreens. It is important to get the roots into the ground early; otherwise the life will have gone out of them and there will be no sprouting in the spring. A dressing of leafmold every autumn helps to keep the tubers plump and cool.

A. quinquefolia L.
American Wood Anemone or Windflower

A much more fragile appearing and smaller flower than the European Wood Anemone, is our American representative. A little solitary flower, less than an inch across, pure white or tinged very palely with pink or blue on the reverse of the petals, that grows from a horizontal, elongated rootstock on stems two or three inches high. The leaves are very frail and are borne in a whorl of three to five below the flower, each leaf divided and cut several times. Later a leaf appears at the base. It is a lovely pure little flower that bears the most minute scrutiny, but it is a difficult plant to establish under man-made conditions. Where it grows naturally on wooded hillsides and in hollows in the woods, it is so plentiful that to find it such an unwilling guest in gardens, is a surprise. Buy it; do not dig it from the woods; it is more easily transplanted when it has first been established in a nursery. It is found from Canada south to Georgia and west to the Rocky Mountains. Like all Wood Anemones everywhere, it folds its petals in cloudy weather, and hangs its delicate head in meek protest.

A. *ranunculoides* L.
Wood Ginger. Yellow Windflower

A free-flowering, free-spreading, and jolly little subalpine plant from southern Europe, where it grows in woods and meadows and dampish places, especially on limestone. It is not showy but is a neat and courteous small Windflower, running about among fern fronds or out in the sun, and never interfering with its betters or becoming a nuisance. It may be plumped down almost anywhere and will thrive. It commonly bears two bright yellow flowers on a stem, and as these do not open simultaneously, the plants keep up their show for quite a time.

There is said to be a double form which has "nice little button-like flowers," and is as free with them as the single sort. Mr. Farrer calls the color of the Wood Ginger a shrill canary-yellow, and does not think much of it. The mind of that great gardener was so engaged with aloof rarities that he sometimes neglected to bestow praise upon the small, deserving commoner plants. Any one who has the Wood Ginger will enjoy it, I am sure, and he will suffer no disappointments on its account.

A. *thalictroides* (*Thalictrum Anemonoides. Syndesmon Anemonoides*)
Rue Anemone

Often confused with the true Anemone is the little Rue Anemone; but the observant eye will see differences at once, and the gardener will find it as easy-going, and as readily established in

ANEMONE RANUNCULOIDES

woodsy places or the shaded side of the rock garden, as the true American Wood Anemone is stand-offish. The little pale pink or white flowers usually grow in a cluster of three, the central one opening first, and the whorls of thin, three-lobed leaflets are a pretty setting for them. The leaves are much like those of the Meadow Rue, which accounts for its common name, and also for the fact that it is sometimes classed as a Thalictrum; indeed, it is one of the plants whose names have been constantly changed by botanists. In "Hortus," Dr. Bailey names it *Anemonella thalictroides*. The plants grow four to six inches high from a tiny bunch of Dahlia-like tubers. In the East, it is one of the most abundant of spring flowers, found from Ontario to Florida, and somewhat less frequently in the Central West. It is frequently found disporting itself about the roots of old trees, dainty and crisp and gregarious, often crowding the true Wood Anemone, and always outclassing it in beauty.

Those who love Anemones should grow not only these tuberous-rooted kinds, but the fibrous-rooted ones as well: the lovely, easily grown Pasque Flower, *Anemone Pulsatilla*, in its different forms, and the American Pasque Flower, *A. Nuttalliana*, not so easily grown, the Lady of the Snows, *A. vernalis*, the virginal *A. sylvestris*, *A. narcissiflora*, and several others.

ARUM *ARACEAE*

A. italicum Mill. B.M. t. 2432

In Mr. Lown's famous Poughkeepsie garden, in the low shaded section, were large clumps of this curious plant which drew attention to itself at more than one season. It is said to be a native of the Channel Islands, southern England, and southern Europe, but it is quite hardy in these parts.

My plants came from Mr. Lown's garden and are grown in the same sort of situation, a little damp and partially shaded, where the soil is rich and deep. It grows from a thickened tuberous root, and in the spring the queer Jack-in-the-pulpit flowers appear. They are creamy white or yellowish inclosed in a greenish yellow or whitish spathe, or hood.

These are followed in autumn by scarlet berries on naked stems something under a foot tall which are very ornamental and showy. The shining leaves, arrow-shaped, large, and shining, appear in the autumn and last over the winter. When we take the winter blanket off the garden, there they are, lustrous and splendidly green, unharmed by winter's rigors.

The variety I have here, has leaves marbled with yellow, and I believe this is called var. *marmoratum;* and if there is one time when we are able to tolerate variegated foliage, it is in the spring. This species is sometimes grown indoors in pots, as are so many of the Arums.

BELAMCANDA *IRIDACEAE*

BLACKBERRY LILY

B. chinensis (*B. punctata, Pardanthus chinensis*)

B.M. t. 171 (under *Ixia chinensis*)

Blackberry Lily, Dwarf Tiger Lily,
Chinese Ixia, Leopard Flower

THE Blackberry Lily is, of course, a Lily only by trivial usage. It is an Irid, a hardy tuberous-rooted perennial from China and Japan, with leaves much like those of an Iris, swordlike and erect and about ten inches long. The flowers are borne on branching stems from two to three feet tall in forked clusters in summer. They are a warm tawny orange in color, spotted and barred on the interior with purple-brown and nearly two inches across.

The individual flowers open late in the morning and close about sunset, and these have finished their stint and do not open again; but they are followed in quick succession by other flowers, so that the plant has a long period of bloom in summer. They, in turn, are followed by curious fruits which, when mature, resemble exactly a ripe blackberry. In rural neighborhoods these forked branches of shining black berries are used in the winter bouquets of dried grasses and everlastings that countryfolk depend upon to brighten the best parlor or the kitchen shelf during the flowerless season.

This showy plant was once much prized in gardens, but it fell on evil days; in many localities where are old gardens, it has shaken the dust of inhospitality from its feet and taken to the open road where, in the company of Rampion, Bouncing Bet, Toadflax, and other outlawed spirits, it makes merry in fence corners, along old walls or in thickets, from Connecticut to Georgia and westward to Missouri and Indiana, and it is said to be common in the Southwest. At the present time, it appears to be experiencing a renaissance, for it is again being offered, with encomiums, in catalogues and opening its leopard-coated blossoms in the best border

68

company; and it is, indeed, an excellent plant for massing in the wild garden or shrubbery, or to hold the outposts of the rock garden where its long and bright display is most welcome.

It thrives best in good sandy loam, in sun or in partial shade, and while it is hardy in most of the northern states, it is the happier for a covering of leaves in exposed situations. It is easily propagated by seeds or division of the roots in early spring or autumn.

Nicholson gives the date of introduction of the Blackberry Lily as 1823, but on page 171 of Curtis' *Botanical Magazine* is a fine figure of the plant and the information that seeds received through the Admiralty germinated and lived out in pots over the winter of 1790–91 and flowered profusely during the following August and September.

The Blackberry Lily is said to grow spontaneously in India, where in sandy soil it attains a great height. In that country the natives consider the root as an antidote to poisons in general, particularly efficacious in curing the bite of the serpent called cobra de capello.

BRODIAEA *LILIACEAE*

THESE attractive native cormous plants have never reached anything like popularity with the general gardening public, at least beyond the Pacific states, where they are found growing wild between the Coast and the Sierra Nevada and Cascade Mountains. So distracting is the chorus in praise of the so-called Dutch bulbs, so loud the plaudits, that a not inconsiderable number of persons who garden for pleasure in this country do not even know that there are bulbs born and bred of our own soil that are well worth growing. We still love a foreign title, and are a little suspicious of what is labeled "native."

There are many kinds of Brodiaeas, some dwarf, some quite tall, the scapes and narrow scant leaves rising from a small flattish onion-like corm. Many of them are valuable because they flower in summer after the great spate of spring-flowering bulbous things has run its course. If they have a fault, it is that, in the case of many of them, the stem is too tall and slender, the foliage too scanty to balance the generous cluster of flowers.

One has the feeling that they should always be seen above waving grasses, for not infrequently their own foliage dies away entirely before the flowers come to maturity. This leaves them looking a little shorn and forlorn. The flowers are borne in a loose umbel, each flower on a slender pedicel, which gives the flower heads a charming informal appearance, particularly as the pedicels vary greatly in length. The individual flowers are usually tubular, sometimes long and narrow, again more starry, and in color they are chiefly in tones of blue and lavender and violet, occasionally white, and there are a few fine yellow-flowered species, and at least one scarlet. The flowers as they mature have a papery quality which causes them to last a long time in good condition, whether cut or in the garden.

Unquiet botanists have been unable to let the genus Brodiaea (named for J. J. Brodie, a Scottish cryptogamist) alone, and as you search them out in various publications, such names as Milla, Triteleia, Hookera, Stropholirion, and Brevoortia crop up; but

Dr. Jepson of the University of California, in his "Manual," groups them all under Brodiaea, as does Mr. Purdy in his catalogue, and it is more convenient to follow their lead here, giving the alternative denominations in parenthesis.

All but one of the Brodiaeas I have grown here have proved quite hardy in the gritty soil of the rock garden in sunny positions. Some kinds have been in the garden for many years, increasing slowly. The corms were planted from three to four inches below the surface of the ground according to size, and they were given the usual blanket of salt hay as a winter protection. In planting it must be remembered that they are slender things, and the corms should be set rather close together in little colonies, or they will make little show.

Of their growth in the wild, Mr. Purdy has this to say: [1] "It is to be noted that in all of the regions where they grow, there is a midsummer period when there is little moisture in the soil, and when the foliage dies and the bulb ripens hard. Rains come in September or October and root growth begins. There is no leaf growth until growing weather comes, which may be as early as February and as late as May in the higher country. In the wild they are to be found in many soils, varying from the stickiest clay, which dries as hard as bricks in the summer, to sands and gritty soils. More often they are in loose, woodland loam. Doubtless the soil is acid in some of these regions, but without question sweet or neutral more generally. . . . While some species are found where the ground is wet all winter, they do as well with ordinary moisture, and good drainage is by far safer. They like moderate moisture until about a month after flowering." September is the best time to plant them.

Brodiaeas are commonly known as Fools Onions, but though the corms do somewhat resemble Onions, there is no hint in taste or odor of the humble esculent so far as I have been able to note, save in the leaves of *Brodiaea uniflora* (*Triteleia uniflora*), a species from South America.

B. Bridgesii S. Wats. (Triteleia Bridgesii)

A handsome species with an open head of reddish violet flowers, wide open and starry, at the top of a slender scape about

[1] *National Horticultural Magazine*, Oct., 1933.

fifteen inches high. The leaves are shorter than the scape, and the cluster is composed of from ten to twenty blooms. It flowered here about the 10th of June.

It is widely distributed through the Coast Ranges from Curry County, Oregon, south to Lake County, California, and in the foothills of the Sierra Nevada to Mariposa County, usually in heavy soil in open woods or Chaparral.

B. *californica* Lindl. (*Hookera californica*)
Harvest Brodiaea

This is one of the taller species, growing sometimes fully two feet tall, but the hungry soil of the rock garden tends to keep its height down. Those in my garden did not reach a greater height than eighteen inches. It is a very slender plant, and tends to throw itself about, leaning into near-by bushes as if it sought support. It blooms here about July 1st, and the tubular flowers in umbels of a dozen or so are of a delightful tone of pinkish lavender, and very showy. I had from Mr. Purdy a form with bluer flowers, but I thought it less effective than the other.

This species is found on dry grassy hillsides in the Sierra Nevada foothills from Shasta to Nevada County, California.

B. *capitata* Benth. (*Dichelostemma capitatum. Milla capitata*)
California Hyacinth, Grass Nuts, Blue Dicks, Covena, Cluster Lily, Hog Onion   *B.M.* t. 5912

This is a very common and apparently much loved species, to judge by the many common names that have been bestowed upon it. It is found in one or other of its several forms on dry ridges and in fields from southern Oregon to Lower California, and as children in the East gather bunches of Violets and Columbines to offer the passing motorists, California's children gather bunches of Blue Dicks for the same purpose. The corms are said to be edible, though rather tasteless.

Ira Gabrielson calls this "the least attractive and therefore the most frequently offered" of the Brodiaeas. Perhaps familiarity has bred contempt. It seems to me very pretty and in every way attractive, a variable species, as would be expected of one with so wide a range. My plants grow under a foot tall. The poorer the soil, the shorter the stem; under generous conditions, it lengthens out. The leaf growth begins early, but the lavender-blue flowers are not fully open before the middle of May. They are gathered at the top of the slender scape in a rather close head, each tubular flower carried erectly, and lasting an amazingly long time in good condition. Their texture is thin, and as they age they assume the papery quality that is characteristic of many of their kind. The corms should be planted three times their own depth in soil that is on the heavy side—clay with a little humus.

B. *coccinea* S. Wats. (*Brevoortia Ida-Maia* Wood)
Floral Firecracker. Crimson Satin Flower

This is one of the most fantastic of flowers, and certainly the showiest of the clan Brodiaea. One might choose to grow it as a curiosity, but not, I think, for the sake of its beauty. It does look quite amazingly like a bunch of firecrackers. The flowers, which are long and narrowly tubular, hang in a one-sided bunch from the top of the scape. They are bright red with green corolla lobes encircling the creamy white petal-like stamens that show just below the red tube, like the fuse of the firecracker. It has the usual ineffectual foliage flopping about the base of the stem. There has been some suggestion as to a lack of hardiness in this species, but my bulbs came through fourteen degrees below zero in the winter of 1933–34 with only a light covering of salt hay, flowering about May 24th. They did not, however, appear the next year.

The Firecracker Plant is said to grow naturally on grassy hill-sides and in open forests of the Siskiyou Mountains in Oregon, south to Marin and Contra Costa counties in California. Its height is said to vary from nine inches to as much as four feet. My plants grew about sixteen inches high.

Thomas Meehan in "The Native Flowers and Ferns," tells this tale about the origin of one of its names: It seems that the first botanist to notice the plant was Alphonso Wood, to whom it was pointed out in 1867 by a stage driver in the Trinity Mountains. The flowers had long interested this non-botanical mountaineer, and he had gratified the sentiment of his heart by naming it Ida May, after his little daughter, with whom it was a favorite. Wood realized that the plant was new to science, and believing it also a new genus, described it under the name of *Brevoortia*

Ida-Maia, the specific terminology commemorating not only the paternal affection of the stage driver, but also the fact that the plant had been collected on the "ides (15th) of May." It seems rather too bad that the plant should have lost this romantic name, but I suppose the entirely prosaic one had a prior claim.

B. *crocea* Wats. (*Triteleia crocea*)
Yellow Triteleia

This is an early-flowering and a very pretty species, growing about nine inches tall with me. The flowers are gathered into a small umbel at the top of the slender scape, and are warm yellow in color, with a prominent greenish brown mid-vein down the center of each pointed segment. They have something the appearance of Freesias but lack, unfortunately, the delicious scent. It flowers here about May 10th, and because of its low stature is very nice in the rock garden.

It is found growing wild in open woods in the Siskiyou Mountains and in northern California. I grow it in full sun.

B. *Douglasii* S. Wats. (*Triteleia grandiflora*)   *B.M.* t. 6907
Indian Hyacinth

Of this species Margaret Armstrong writes: [2] "It is wonderful to find these lovely and exotic-looking flowers, deliciously scented, gleaming in the shadow of a dusky oak thicket or a deep canyon. They last a long time in water, becoming papery as they wither." Usually we see the flower without the leaves, for these wither away before the flower buds are open. The flower head is large, many-flowered, and flat, each tubular blossom held upon a fairly long pedicel. They are lavender, growing paler as they mature, and of an almost translucent quality. In the rock garden this species grew only fourteen inches high, but in its natural surroundings it is said to reach a much greater height. It flowered in May. Mr. Purdy says it is found east of the Cascades, as far as Utah and Montana.

B. *Eastwoodiana*

A new species to me, found, according to Mr. Purdy, plentifully in California from southeastern Lake County to eastern

* *Field Book of Western Wild Flowers.*

Mendocino and north Sonoma counties. The flowers are white in a many-flowered, rather close, umbel. It flowered here about June 10th.

B. *grandiflora* Sm. (*Triteleia grandiflora*)   B.M. t. 2877
  Harvest Brodiaea

This Harvest Brodiaea is one of the commonest species, and is found in its several forms from British Columbia to Lower California. It is a showy beauty with clusters of almost Lily-like flowers carried erectly on pedicels of unequal length, which gives a gay flyaway effect to the cluster. The flowers are deep purple within and paler without, and they have a sort of sheen which adds to their handsome effect. There is rather more foliage than is common to Brodiaeas, and this makes its appearance early, though the flowers do not open until late June in this garden. The stems are sturdy and about twelve inches tall, and altogether it is a very good sort and lasts well in the garden and when cut. Mr. Purdy says that the stems cut in the haying last fresh for many weeks. The haycocks filled with purple Brodiaeas must be charming! It appears not to be particular as to the quality of the soil, and it is one of the species that last well in eastern gardens.

B. *Hendersonii* S. Wats.

A very pretty species with slender scapes about a foot high carrying a head of from eight to twelve open tubular erect flowers of a soft yellow with a purple line down the center of each segment. It is especially nice in the rock garden, flowering here toward the end of May. It is found on canyon slopes and rocky hillsides in the Siskiyou Mountains of Oregon, and in the extreme north of California.

B. *Howellii* S. Wright (*Triteleia Howellii*)   B.M. t. 6989

This species, which I have not grown, is native to the west country from Puget Sound to the Columbia River, east of the Cascades in northeastern Oregon. "The umbels bear from few to fifteen flowers. The flowers are rather tubular and a deep violet purple." Mr. Purdy notes that there is a large-flowered form with blooms "of an exquisite porcelain tinge. Always found in moist ground, and one of the prettiest Brodiaeas." This is known as var. *lilacina.*

B. *ixioides* S. Wats.   *B.M.* t. 3588
    Golden Brodiaea. Golden Star. Pretty Face

If I had to choose one, this would be my choice among the Brodiaeas. First, perhaps, because it has stood by me for many years, the original corms coming from the garden of Mr. Clarence Lown in Poughkeepsie. Then it has, indeed, a pretty face. It is one of the rare yellow-flowered kinds, a charming tone of yellow enhanced by the brown line down the center of each segment, and here it grows little more than a foot tall, which makes it nice for the rock garden. The flowers are borne in a loose umbel, many-flowered, each flower open wide like a star on a short tube. It blooms here about May 20th. The variety *splendens,* which I grew last year, had larger and more flowers to a head, and the stem was somewhat taller. There are other forms, some much dwarfer, some taller, but all showing those pretty yellow faces upturned toward the sun. It is common in the foothills of the Coast Ranges and Sierra Nevada.

B. *lactea* S. Wats. (*Triteleia hyacinthina. Hesperoscordum hya-cinthinum*)   *B.M.* t. 1639
    White-flowered Grass Nuts

This is another short-tubed starry-flowered species, easy to grow and very pretty. The milky flowers are borne in a loose, irregular umbel, and each is set off by a green band down the outside of the segments. It grew with me about a foot tall, and flowered early in June. It is said to be common in low moist ground in the Coast Ranges and Great Valley. There is a lavender-flowered form, var. *lilacinum.* These last well in the garden and increase with some freedom under congenial conditions.

B. *laxa* S. Wats. (*Triteleia laxa*)   *B.R.* t. 1685
    Ithuriel's Spear. Grass Nuts

A strong stem upholds the beautiful wide irregular umbel of this species above the waving grasses of the open hillsides and valleys where it grows naturally in the Siskiyou Mountains, south

through the Coast Ranges and the Sierra Nevada to Los Angeles,
especially in adobe soils. In the rock garden my plants have not
grown much taller than a foot; but the flower head is most
showy, each long tubular blue-purple flower being marked on
the outside with greenish lines, and they are carried on pedicels
of unequal length. The plant flowers in this garden toward the
end of May, in its native haunts somewhat earlier. Mrs. Rowntree says it is to be seen in fine masses along the road to
Yosemite Valley in May or late April.

A form sent me by Mr. Purdy as Blue King had flowers of a
much darker blue tone; and at one time I had a variety *candida*
that was very pale, almost white in color, and all the flowers curiously faced in the same direction. *Laxa* and its forms are undoubtedly among the finest of the Brodiaeas, and they endure
well in eastern gardens.

B. *multiflora* Benth. (*B. parviflora*)   *B.M.* t. 6598

I have not grown this kind, but it is said to have a close-set
umbel of deep violet-purple flowers on tall stout stems.

B. *pulchella* Greene (*B. congesta, Dichelostemma pulchellum*)

This is another unknown so far as I am concerned; but it is
said to be much like the last named, with a close-set head of small
violet flowers on stems one and one-half to three feet high. Sierra
Nevadas northward to Oregon and Washington.

B. *Purdyi* Eastw.

This species, named for Carl Purdy, flowered in my garden
for the first time last year, opening its charming short-tubed
starry flowers about June 24th. Its color is unusual, being a soft
pinkish lilac, and its dwarf stature makes it especially suitable for
use in rock gardens. It did not, with me, reach a greater height
than eight inches. The segments of the flowers are very pointed
and recurve a little at the tips; the flower head is loose and open.
Sierra Nevada foothills from Butte to Eldorado County.

B. *stellaris* S. Wats. (*Hookera stellaris*)

Flowering a few days before the last-named species, this rather
rare Brodiaea made a very pretty show in the rock garden at the

base of a little cliff where the soil is rather rich and not quite bone-dry. It has an open irregular head of purple flowers, starry in shape, and each carried on a long pedicel. It is found wild from Mendocino to Humboldt County in California.

B. volubilis Baker (*Stropholirion californicum*)   B.M. t. 6123
    Twining Brodiaea. Twining Hyacinth or Saitas

The twining Brodiaea does not like my garden; at least in the two trials of it I have made, the result has been negative. Mr. Purdy's description is here given: "It has a bulb like several other species, but soon after the very slender stem comes up, it begins to encircle anything which will support it, and climbs just as a honeysuckle does. If it is near a bush, it will climb up to a length of as much as eight feet; if no such support is at hand, it will climb over grass or plants, or if there are several of the flowering stems near, they will encircle each other, and in thick patches, I have seen regular cables made of many such encircling flower stems." Obviously, it is no plant for a rock garden. Where my error in its treatment lies, I cannot say. Mr. Purdy goes on to say that the flowers are small and a very pretty pink. "I have seen stems which have become detached from the bulb go on flowering in the air." It is found in the mid-foothills of the Coast Range close to the interior valley. Surely this is the most curious of bulbous plants. Margaret Armstrong describes it as a grotesque-looking plant with a compact cluster of papery flowers sometimes six inches across.

BULBOCODIUM *LILIACEAE*

Bulbocodium vernum L.   B.M. t. 153
Spring Meadow Saffron

THERE flowers in our garden soon after the Snowdrops, sometimes indeed catching them up, a flower that we know familiarly
as Raggedy Ann. Some visitors mistake it for a pink Crocus,
others for a spring-flowering Colchicum. But it is neither. It is
Bulbocodium vernum, sole member of its genus in cultivation. It
differs from Colchicum, says Mr. Bowles, in that the segments of
the flowers are divided right down to the top of the ovary instead
of being joined to form a perianth tube, though at their first
coming forth the flowers sit so low on the ground that the absence
of a tube is not noticeable. It differs from Crocus, says Nicholson,
in having a superior (free from the calyx) ovary and six stamens.
It differs from both, to the non-botanical eye, in wholly lacking
the trimness of figure and pristine crispness that are characteristic
of both Colchicum and Crocus; in fact, in being a most untidy-
looking little individual altogether, appearing as if it had almost
certainly slept in its clothes.

Yet there is a most engaging quality about the Spring Meadow
Saffron. One is so enchanted to see a pink—well, almost pink—
flower so early in the year, among all the chaste whites and
greenish yellows, that one is not at all critical of its careless port.
That little pink point appearing between its three pointed, en-
closing leaves is somehow *drama,* and we give it an ecstatic
welcome.

There are usually two flowers to a corm, and they are larger
than any Crocus. The color, if one must be perfectly honest, is
somewhat more purplish than would be whole-heartedly admired
later in the year; but, as I say, in March one is at one's most
tolerant, horticulturally speaking. The leaves develop fully only
after the flower has faded, and they then rise to a height of five
or six inches. It is quite hardy in our garden, though the small

brown ovoid corm is covered with a sort of wool, which indicates its dislike of too much moisture, and therefore its preference for a sunny situation in gritty, well drained soil, in which medium, asserts Nicholson, it multiplies rapidly from offsets.

I have not found this to be exactly the case, for my corms have been slow of increase, though I have rigidly observed the dictum that transplanting every few years to fresh, well drained soil is necessary to its health and happiness. There is a nice, reassuring drawing of it, however, in Curtis' *Botanical Magazine*,[1] showing it in the very act of increasing from an offset. And it does increase, though very slowly. Mr. Bowles grows it most successfully in the sand moraine which has running water beneath it.[2]

It seems to have grown in Parkinson's spacious gardens, for he gives a most exact description of it and a nice drawing under the name of *Colchicum vernum*, the Meadowe Saffron of the Spring. The Kew Hand-List names a variety *versicolor*, but this I have never seen.

Bulbocodium vernum is said to be fairly plentiful in the high mountains of central Europe, in the Pyrenees, and in the Caucasus, where it thrusts up its little pink points along the hem of the receding snows. It appears also to be plentiful in Continental and English gardens; but in the severely protected gardens of the United States it is sadly scarce, for we may not import this small, harmless mountain tramp. What it might infect us with (other than unseemly pride in its possession), is known only to an omniscient Department of Agriculture.

But you may come across it in some pre-quarantine garden, and the kindly (all gardeners are kindly) owner will doubtless part with a corm or two if you hint a little. Take it at any time you can get it, but the best time to plant it is in August. Set it three inches deep and, if there is more than one, about four inches away from its fellow or fellows.

[1] Vol. V.
[2] *A Handbook of Crocus and Colchicum.*

CALOCHORTUS *LILIACEAE*

GARDENERS are accustomed to thrills, not the kind with which they are confronted in the press or on the screen, but those none the less authentic stirrings of the blood caused by the recognition of uncommon beauty or by unexpected success in some field of horticultural endeavor. Amazing and lovely things happen daily in even the littlest garden. But to him who grows successfully for the first time a collection of Calochortus, may confidently be promised surprise and delight such as he has not heretofore experienced. These natives of our west country, it seems to me, stand virtually alone among flowers in their strange and fantastic beauty, their amazing diversity. I can call up no words that will give an adequate idea of their pure and brilliant hues, the exquisite brushwork on the satin petals, the startling "eyes" that ornament them, the breadths of Persian embroidery, the silken fringes, the velvet-like pile that is the embellishment of many. The doubting Thomases must see them to believe in their reality. They will prove a veritable revelation.

The Calochortus belong to the Lily clan. There are something like half a hundred species, perhaps more, scattered chiefly along the Pacific coast, from Washington to Mexico, but some species range as far east as Colorado. They inhabit such widely differing localities as the summits of mountains, deep valleys, meadows, wooded areas, and burning deserts. Of the thirty-six kinds I have grown here, all save one (*C. catalinae*) have proved perfectly hardy, surviving below-zero temperatures without loss of life or diminution of vigor, and with only the light covering of salt hay that is given to the rest of the garden. Nevertheless, it must be admitted that these plants are not easy to grow or to keep in eastern gardens. I do not pretend to have solved the problem of just why this is so, but the idiosyncrasies of climate, chiefly of rainfall, are among the factors to be blamed. Perhaps we shall solve them all some day.

In the meantime, these flowers may be grown in eastern gardens with a fair degree of success if preparation is made for them. A year's trial proves nothing; almost any bulb will do what is expected of it the first year under almost any conditions—it is the second and the years thereafter that tell the tale. One thing the Calochortus seem to require is a complete rest in the late summer and autumn, and the incitement to growth to which they are subjected by our frequent summer and autumn showers, and the watering they receive in the natural care of our gardens is bad for them. They should be kept as dry as possible all through the autumn; otherwise they are apt to start into growth, and this young foliage is fatally injured by the first frosts. In any case, they are not recommended for use in ordinary garden borders. In a well built sunny rock garden, with its deep, well drained gritty soil, they are more than apt to thrive for several seasons; or an exclusive border may be made for them. This should face the south, be protected on the north by hedge or wall, and be raised a few inches above the surrounding ground. The soil should be dug out to the depth of at least a foot and replaced by a coarse mixture of grit, humus, stone chips, and a little ordinary loam. Thus will heat and light and drainage be assured them. They want moisture during their spring growth; but if we refrain from watering this border after the flowers have faded, the droughty conditions so dear to their hearts during their resting period will be at least partially maintained. To grow them under such conditions is perhaps the most certain to bring success, and it is a very good way if one wants them for cutting (they are lovely for this purpose) or for observation.

But the rock gardener will not be able to resist scattering these lovely things over his hills and in his valleys, and here, of course, they must take their chance with the treatment that is given the other plants there grown. It is in the rock garden that I have chiefly grown them, and a trial of three years has surprised me by its many happy returns. The longest-lived, however, have been among the Cat's Ear type. These have persisted in my own garden and in other gardens that I know of for more than twelve years, though they have shown little, if any, increase.

Mr. Purdy has advised digging up the corms after the foliage has matured, and storing them in a dry place as is sometimes done with Tulips; but this is a chore that most busy gardeners will shirk, and it seems to me that the surest way to enjoy these flowers is to devise the best possible conditions for them, and then not to expect too much of them in the way of longevity. We may experience happy surprises, but on the other hand, we shall not be cast down by failure. The bulbs are inexpensive, and even if we replant them every few years, the cost will not be excessive. They are well worth their price even for a single season's delight, but it is safe to say that if they are given the maximum of sunshine, drainage and late summer and autumn drought, more than a single season is assured.

Because of their tendency to make an early fall growth, the corms should be put into the ground as late as possible. I like to wait until after Indian summer, in November, in this New York neighborhood; thereafter the cold will keep them in bed, and after the ground is frozen a light covering of salt hay or oak leaves will prevent their starting up too early in the spring, which they are inclined to do with the first warmth. Altogether, they are fidgety things, and their restlessness must be circumvented. The corms, Tulip-like, should be put into the ground at about twice their own depth, and if you want to cover them with sand it will do no harm, and perhaps some good. Remember that when they begin to grow in earnest in the spring, they want water—if the heavens do not supply it, the hose must be resorted to—and do not be tricked into taking the winter blanket off the moment you see the little impatient tips piercing the ground; remove it little by little, hardening them off by degrees and protecting them from their own impetuosity.

The Calochortus fall naturally into three groups and a fourth group that is less well defined. These groups are felicitously called Cat's Ears, or Owl's Ears, because of the soft pile of hairs that lines the ear-shaped segments; Fairy Lanterns, because of the suggestive shape and delightful swinging grace of the flowers; Mariposa Tulips, by the Spaniards, because of the brilliant markings on the segments; and the fourth group Mr. Purdy calls the *nitidus-Lyallii* group. These come from more northerly regions, and have shorter and stouter stems than the other Mariposas.

If representatives from all the groups are planted, these most amazing flowers may be enjoyed in the neighborhood of New York from late April through June. And there are not many June-flowering bulbous things. As I write, July 3rd, *C. macrocarpus* is in magnificent bloom; but this will be the last of the splendid pageant.

To David Douglas, a young Scotch botanist, we are chiefly indebted for calling attention to the beauty of the Calochortus. He introduced them into England round about 1826 and wrote an account of the genus. What a sensation they must have made, though the British climate would go hard with them! (Farrer says they are not fitted for general outdoor culture in England, and calls those who would possess this "precarious beauty" bold heroes.[1]) Before Douglas, many seeing eyes must have feasted upon them, and the Indians of the regions where they abound feasted upon them in a different sense. They were regarded, according to Mr. Saunders, as a gift of the gods to be eaten, and throughout the range of the plants the bulbs were the most desired of foods.[2]

Fairy Lantern, Globe Tulip, Satin-bell

The beauty of the Fairy Lanterns is hardly to be described. The flowers are globular and possess a delicate, pearl-like sheen, and though appearing almost of the fragility of a soap bubble, yet they have a certain crispness of texture that reassures us. They are more leafy than others of the race, a long leaf clasping the slender stem at the base, and other shorter ones appearing along it at intervals. The stem is very slender and bends under its weight of little lanterns, so that it is a good plan to insert among the bulbs, as inconspicuously as possible, a few twigs to support them so that the flowers may be displayed to the best advantage. Mr. Purdy says these "are natives of woodlands, delighting in loose soil and liking leaf-mold and light shades." They grow

[1] *The English Rock Garden.*
[2] *Western Wild Flowers and Their Stories,* by Charles F. Saunders.

here on a western slope of the rock garden where they receive in the afternoon the shade of tall trees at a little distance. They have done exceptionally well, all the kinds blossoming freely in the third season after planting.

C. *albus* Douglas
White Fairy Lantern or Satin-bell

This is the plant that John Muir thought the most beautiful of all the Lily family, which so moved him that he wrote of it as "a spotless soul, a plant saint, that everyone must love and so be made better. It puts the wildest mountaineer on his good behavior. With this plant the whole world would seem rich, though none other existed." The flowers are white with a faint greenish tinge, and appear almost translucent, and they swing from delicate pedicels with a rare grace. The stems are about nine inches tall, and each bears many flowers. The bulbs should be planted about four inches apart so as to give each stem space to swing its lanterns freely. Found in open woods in Mendocino and Butte counties, southward through the Coast Ranges and Sierra Nevada to San Diego County, California.

There are two lovely forms of *albus;* namely, White Pearl and Pink Pearl. The first has pure white flowers with soft, fawn-colored shadings; the other is a lovely, clear rose-pink. Both are highly desirable.

C. *amabilis* Purdy
Golden Lantern

This species grows somewhat taller than the above, and the flexuous branching stem is hung with clear golden yellow flowers marked externally with a brown patch. It is found growing wild in California in open woods and grassy slopes of the Coast Ranges, through Humboldt and Trinity counties, south to Sonora and Solano counties.

C. *amoenus* Greene

This, and a giant form of it recently discovered by Mr. Purdy, and growing twenty-four inches high, are most beautiful plants. Their color is a soft and melting mauve-pink, and the slender,

CALOCHORTUS AMOENUS MAJOR   *CALOCHORTUS AMABILIS*

branching stems bear many globes that flutter in the wind. They come from the western slopes of the Sierra Nevada, Fresno and Tulare counties.

Cat's Ears, Owl's Ears, Star Tulips

The members of this group are more suitable than other Calochortus for use in the rock garden because of their dwarf stature, but it must be admitted that they are less showy. They are fragile things with delicate slender stems, each carrying a number of upturned flowers whose interior is lined with a soft pile of silken hairs. The leaves are narrow and tend to lie about upon the ground as if the stiffening had been left out of them. The colors are pure and clean but not bright. They are woodland plants, but like the Fairy Lanterns, while they do well enough on a half-shaded slope of the rock garden, they do not thrive in woods in eastern gardens. They must have the sharp drainage and the summer baking that is necessary to them all. They bloom in late April and early May.

C. Benthamii Baker   *B.M.* t. 6475
   Yellow Owl's Ears

This is a pretty species growing from four to eight inches tall. The flowers are pure bright yellow with a brown patch on the segments, and the narrow leaves are bluish green. It is common in the foothills of the Sierra Nevada. It flowers early and is a good stayer in the garden.

C. Maweanus Leichtl.
   White Pussy's Ears

This charming and delicate flower is perhaps the prettiest of its group and bears the most minute scrutiny. The flowers are an inch across, with soft lilac sepals and a pile of lavender hairs laid upon the white petals. The general effect is more silvery gray than white or lilac. It is common in grassy places in northern California. There is a form of it with larger flowers called *major*, and another called *roseus* that is a delicate lilac-pink in color. All are exquisite.

C. lilacinus Kell.   *B.M.* t. 5804

This kind and the next, perhaps, do not belong in this group, but I do not know just where to place them. They are not woodland plants, and they are almost hairless. *Lilacinus* has grown in my garden for twelve years and seems a hardy and long-suffering species. The fragrant flowers are pale lilac, of a satin-like texture, and are slightly hairy at the base. It grows naturally in damp meadows; that is, damp until after blossoming time is over, then very dry. It grows here in sandy loam in a partially shaded situation. It is the first of all the Calochortus to flower.

C. nudus Wats.

A Sierra species with white, or almost white, flowers, brushed lightly with green or sometimes with pale lilac. It is a low species, the stems no more than four or five inches high. It likes a cool exposure.

Mariposa Tulips

These are the most brilliant of the race, the tallest and the latest to flower. *Mariposa* is Spanish for "butterfly," and the aptness of this name is obvious to all who observe the amazing markings on the petals of the flowers. The plants have a fault in their lack of foliage, which consists of a few narrow green wisps set at long intervals along the wiry stem, and another fault in their height, which in the rock garden is excessive. They should properly be seen above a waving sea of grasses when their sparse foliage is not noticeable. In the rock garden or raised bed, they must be staked with the slenderest of Carnation stakes, or planted among dwarf shrubs that will serve to clothe their naked stems and keep them upright; and they are more difficult than the others to keep in eastern gardens. But they are California's most sensational wild flowers, and no language is too extravagant to use in their praise. They like the sunniest situations in sharply drained soil, and a warm covering over the winter, and when they are uncovered in spring, it is wise to keep a bit of the rubbish handy in case cold threatens the precocious growths. They bloom in May, June, and early July.

C. *catalinae* Wats.

So far I have failed to keep this inhabitant of Santa Catalina Island off southern California, over the winter. It is described as flowering a month earlier than others of its group, with the Cat's Ears, and having an erect stem, one to two feet tall, and a lovely open cup-shaped flower of large size, white to lilac in color, with a large round dark patch at the base of the petals.

C. *clavatus* Wats. B.M. t. 7606

This is one of the largest-flowered of the Mariposa Tulips, and the flowers are borne on a stout-branched stem. They are bright yellow bowls at least four inches across, the interior base lined with dark hairs below a band of dark color. *Clavatus* comes from wooded cañon slopes in Los Angeles and Mariposa counties in California and the Santa Monica Mountains. It has not proved very enduring with me. It flowers in mid-June.

C. *Gunnisonii* Wats.

From the Rocky Mountains, from Wyoming to New Mexico, comes this handsome Butterfly Tulip. It grows a foot tall and carries from one to four flowers in a terminal cluster. They spread broadly, the petals fan-shaped, white tinted mauve or very pale pink, running into green at the base, and ornamented with many green hairs over a purple band. It is hardy and fairly easy to keep. It flowers here just after the middle of June.

C. *Howellii* Wats.

A graceful branched stem, a foot high, carrying white bowls lined at the base with greenish crisp hairs. The petals reflex a little or roll back. The buds are very narrow and pointed. It is found in southern Oregon to the Siskiyous. It has proved a good stayer, flowering here the middle of June.

C. *Kennedyi* Porter B.M. t. 7264
Desert Mariposa

Vermilion is the brightest color name I know, but the Desert Mariposa is vermilion raised to an extraordinary pitch. It is the most vibrant and intensely colored flower I have ever seen, and makes everything in its neighborhood appear pallid and ineffectual. Its open cup is burnished and blazing, the interior vermilion, the exterior clouded bright yellow, and there is a darker zone deep in the interior. The texture of the flower is firm. A startling flower, and not easy to keep in eastern gardens. It is said that the form common to Arizona is a rich yellow, while that belonging to southern California is the more brilliant vermilion. It is found on dry, gravelly hills and mesas of the desert regions, Mt. Pinos, Ventura County, and the desert slopes of the Tehachapi Mountains in southern Nevada and Arizona. In the garden it requires the dryest conditions that may be given it, and a thorough summer baking is an absolute necessity; but despite our efforts, this vivid apparition will hardly become common in cultivation. It flowers toward the end of May, is superb as a cut flower, lasting long in water.

C. *Leichtlinii* Hook. — B.M. t. 5862

This is a high mountain species, usually growing no more than eight or ten inches tall, which makes it especially suitable for the rock garden. The flowers are a curious dim white hue, sometimes described as smoky, but washed at the base with greenish lilac or greenish yellow, and ornamented by striking patches of dark purple. It is found from eastern Oregon to the Sierra Nevadas, eastward to South Dakota and New Mexico. It flowers here in late May.

C. *luteus* Douglas — B.R. t. 1567

The yellow-flowered Mariposas are particularly lovely and show many variations in tone. This one usually bears many flowers on the much-branched stems. They are Chinese yellow in tone, and their cups are rather shallow and ornamented on the interior with soft hairs and dark, faint veinings, and a dark patch toward the base of each petal. The variety *citrinus* is lemon-yellow with the usual dark markings. This is sometimes considered a form of *venustus*. Numerous hybrids have been developed from it in various tones of yellow and buff, "no two alike." The stems are nearly two feet tall and branching. *C. luteus* is a central

Californian species, and belongs to dry, gravelly ground in the Coast Ranges and Sierra Nevada foothills.

C. macrocarpus Douglas   *B.R. t.* 1152
Sagebrush Lily

This is the latest of the Mariposas to flower here, and is, perhaps, my favorite. Its immense lavender satin flowers are carried on tall, stiff stems that are almost leafless. Its dignity and poise are pronounced, and the wide green bands on the reverse side of the petals add much to the beauty of the flowers. They last well in the garden and in water, and it is altogether a hardy and satisfactory kind. The corm is very large and was once, and probably still is, regarded as an important and delicious article of diet by the Indians. It was first collected by the Scotch botanist Douglas in 1825, who must have been surprised to find its beautiful flaring blossoms lifting above the waste of gloomy Sagebrush, where it elects to grow. In its native country it is called the Surprise Lily, which seems very apt, for, as a writer in the *American Botanist* says, "It blooms on the Sage-brush Plains in late May or June when all other flowers have been literally scorched away and the ground is baked hard." The Surprise Lily is then at its best, and one may gather great armfuls of the beautiful flowers. It inhabits the Sagebrush regions of the Great Basin.

C. Nuttallii Torr. & Gray
Sego Lily

The Sego Lily is the state flower of Utah, and in times of hardship furnished the pioneering Mormons with food, the corms being much relished and cooked in various ways. It is a variable species. As I have it here, the stem is slender and rises to a height of about eighteen inches. It bears several rather fragile flowers, the petals white and delicately fluted, with dark markings and short hairs around the gland. The foliage is very scant and distinctly ashen in color. It is the most widely distributed of Calochortus, extending through Dakota, Nebraska, Colorado, Utah, California, and New Mexico, commonly haunting arid localities, such as the Sagebrush plains of the Great Basin. It is said to be very variable in color, showing pink, lilac, and yellow forms as well as the white. The flowers are rather delicate and fragile, and the stems need to be artificially upheld. It flowered here in late May. "In the Grand Canyon they begin to come out early in May, among the dry grasses half way down the Bright Angel trail, and are a lovely shade of clear lilac. The slender stem, about a foot tall, bears a small bulb near the base." [8] I have not found it easy to keep in the garden, though it is quite hardy. Apparently one appearance in this alien land suffices it.

C. obispoensis Lemm.

A rare species from California that I have seen only once. It is perhaps more curious than beautiful, as the sepals are very long and somewhat oblong, and, as Mr. Purdy describes them, reduced to mere remnants on which are crowded all of the hairs, typical of the *Weedii* group, to which this and *Plummerae* belong." The color of the petals is a low-toned orange-yellow, washed with red at the tips, and the curiously long sepals are reddish brown. It is found on rocky hillsides in San Luis Obispo County.

C. Plummerae Greene (C. Weedii var. purpurascens Wats.)

A handsome species of a warm tone of lavender, the petals flared and fan-shaped, with the long silken hairs characteristic of the group filling the interior almost to the apex, and in this case of a rich orange color. It is found on dry gravelly hillsides from Los Angeles to Riverside, and in Orange County. I have not found the two foregoing species very easy to keep in the garden. They are southerners, and while they usually come through one winter, their vitality then seems exhausted and they appear no more.

C. splendens Douglas

This flower is, indeed, well named. The color is a warm pinkish lilac, the texture that of silk, the petals fan-shaped, the interior flushed with purple and covered with silken hairs. The beautiful flowers are distinctly cup-shaped and carried on tall much-

[8] Margaret Armstrong, *Field Book of Western Wild Flowers.*

branched stems. The anthers are blue. There is a pinker form called *rubra*. It is found on dry, gravelly hillsides, usually in Chaparral, in central and southern California, the Coast Ranges, Santa Clara County to San Luis Obispo. It flowers here toward the end of June and is handsome for cutting.

C. *venustus* Douglas   B.R. t. 1669

This is the splendid flower that suggested to the Spaniards the name of Mariposa; it is brilliant and varied in its colors and markings, and the flowers are of great size and carried on very tall stems. The ground color may be white, or it may be some tone of yellow, pink, lavender, rose, or wine-red, but always there are the exquisite contrasting brushwork on the petals and the striking "eyes" ornamenting them. Often a single colony will show a perfect riot of colors; again one kind will predominate.

C. *venustus citrinus* is a most satisfactory yellow-flowered form with black markings. It is hardy and long-lasting in the garden. What are known as the Eldorado strain choose their colors from a well furnished palette—while there are many white ones, variously "eyed" and otherwise marked. Among them will be found all tones of soft rose to claret, mauve, lilac, and purple, always with the rich interior markings. The flowers are cup-shaped, two to four inches across, the edges of the petals a little rolled over, and are borne on tall branched stems. The buds are pointed and very beautiful in themselves. The *oculatus* strain abounds in creamy tones and in white varieties, all with brilliant "eyes" and other markings, and the flowers are of immense size. These, while they grow well in the loose, gritty soil of the rock garden, are too tall to look well there. The raised bed is the best place for them. They flower toward the end of June, and they certainly are happiest, at least in our eastern gardens, in full sun. *Vesta* is a superb variety in this group, with flowers sometimes measuring five inches across. "It is," says Mr. Purdy, "a species of my own, found on heavy clay soils, is the best grower of all Calochortus, and will succeed in almost any ordinary soil." The great bowl of the flower is white, played over by soft flushes of mauve that deepen at the center to claret, and the reverse of the petals is violet.

Nitidus-Lyallii Group

There are five species placed by Mr. Purdy in this group. They are found in the northeastern corner of California, in the Great Basin, extending into Montana and Canada, and are quite different in appearance from other Mariposa Tulips. The region where they grow is a cold one, and they are commonly found in grassy meadows. All have a single ovate-lanceolate basal leaf and a slender stem. Such of them as I have grown here have proved very satisfactory and entirely hardy, and as they have shorter and stiffer stems than Mariposas generally they are satisfactory for use in the rock garden.

C. apiculatus Baker

This is an uncommon species, not often found. It is said to grow a foot tall, the stem sturdy and erect, and to bear a soft yellow flower, about an inch across, filled with fine hairs. I have not grown it.

C. Erycarpus (C. eurocarpus)

This handsome species grows here and has proved very satisfactory, flowering the first week in June. The flowers, borne in a cluster of three or four, on erect stems six to nine inches high, are great white bowls exquisitely shot with lavender, and with a rich patch of violet on each segment. It is said to be found in open meadows of the Blue Mountains in eastern Oregon; also in Montana and northern Nevada. It is a very hardy kind.

C. Greenei Wats.

Greenei grows a foot tall; its stem is stout and erect, and the flowers are open bowls with oblong green sepals and lilac, fan-shaped petals, barred with yellow and ornamented with a tangle of yellowish hairs on the interior. It is not a common species, but has now lived in my garden for three years, so may be accounted fairly reliable.

C. nitidus Douglas

With the exception of *C. macrocarpus*, this is, I think, the handsomest of the Mariposa Tulips. It is very distinct, with a strong, self-supporting stem, twelve to fourteen inches tall, carrying the usual wispy outfit of narrow leaves and a cluster of large flowers. The segments are fan-shaped and rather widely separated, of a clear lilac color overlaid with short soft hairs; and at the base of each is a brilliant "eye" like those on a peacock's tail. It blooms here about the middle of June, and is splendid to cut, lasting well in water, or to leave in the garden to receive the admiration of all who behold it. It is found in meadows in northeastern Nevada, eastern Oregon to Montana. "The Standard Cyclopedia of Horticulture" states that specimens found near Yellowstone Lake are yellow.

CAMASSIA *LILIACEAE*

THAT Camassias are not more frequently grown in gardens can only be because they are not known. There are few more decorative bulbous plants, and they are as easily managed as Daffodils and Scillas. They belong wholly to North America, and are found in the eastern states in certain localities, in western Pennsylvania, Minnesota, Texas, and Georgia. This is the species *C. esculenta,* now more correctly known as *C. Fraseri* Torr., a slender plant looking somewhat like a tall Scilla; but it is inferior to the western species, and it is not until we cross the Rocky Mountains that we need take special note of them. There we see them forming blue lakelets amidst the waving grasses of damp meadows, as does *Iris versicolor* in eastern meadows.

The name Camass or Quamash was bestowed upon the plants by the Indians of the Northwest, who made use of the onion-like bulbs as a food. The members of the Lewis and Clark expedition were regaled by the hospitable Nez Percé Indians on buffalo meat, salmon, and Camass roots. The Camass grounds were carefully guarded by the Indians, and it is said that bitter and bloody wars were fought over their possession.

Now dedicated to more peaceful occasions, the Camass furnishes a beautiful garden ornament. The long leaves come directly from the bulb, and are about an inch wide. High above them arises the flower stalk to a height, sometimes of four feet, carrying many starry flowers in an elongated raceme, opening from the bottom up, and in color from white or cream, through many tones of pale to deep blue with green bracts. These starry flowers are further set off by conspicuous yellow stamens and by lines of darker blue (on those of blue coloring) on the narrow segments. The blending of blue and green in the unexpanded flowers of the deep blue forms, is one of the loveliest color effects I know in Nature.

While growing naturally in damp meadows, Camassias take kindly to any good garden soil in sunny places, and during May add their spirelike grace to many situations, in sun or shade, grouped in the borders, naturalized in thin woodland or along stream and pondsides, if there is no standing moisture, or set in wide colonies in the wild garden. In any situation where they are used, they show to better advantage when massed, that is, in colonies of from a dozen to a thousand or so. One plant makes little effect. They are the most delightful companions for May Tulips, with which they bloom, their soft uninsistent hues blending equally with the most flashing or strident or offish of the Tulip tones.

When the flowering is past, the foliage dies away with a neat expeditiousness for which we are grateful. There is no long drawn-out and unsightly flopping about in all stages of unlovely decay. The bulbs may be planted in September or October about four inches below the surface of the soil, and six to eight inches apart, and once established, need not be disturbed as long as they continue to flower well. Apparently they are very hardy, and will endure without protection very far north. They like liberal moisture during the growing and flowering season, but it seems to make no difference how dry they are after that. Winter wet, in our climate, with much freezing and thawing, is bad for the bulbs.

Not to grow Camassias, is to forgo the opportunity to possess unusual beauty, both for garden decoration and for cutting.

C. Cusickii S. Wats.

This is a somewhat scarce species, but well worth searching out and planting in the garden borders in bold groups. I first saw it in the beautiful garden of Mrs. Wheeler Peckham, in Westchester County, and could not rest until I could enjoy it in my own. Finally Mr. Purdy sent me a few bulbs. These are very large and look somewhat like potatoes. From them arise the leaves, wider and more numerous than in other species, and the tall flower scape is strong and erect and bears a long inflorescence. This has almost the appearance of an erect plume. The flowers are very numerous and with narrow segments, and in color they are a very pale blue-lavender, almost what might be termed a lively gray. The pale green stem and the green tracts show through the mist of gray-blue blossoms with lovely effect. *C. Cusickii* was discovered by an Oregon botanist, and named for him; it does him credit, for it is a beautiful plant and should be more easily available. According to Carl Purdy, it is a native of a very limited region in the high mountains of Oregon and northern California.

C. Quamash Greene (old name *C. esculenta*)   B.M. t. 2774

This is the species most favored by the Indians of the Northwest as a food. It is found from British Columbia down the coast to San Francisco and in the Yosemite valley district, climbing the mountains to a height of four thousand feet. It grows from a foot to eighteen inches tall, and its long raceme of starry flowers is very showy. Usually they are of a deep "Aconite-blue," but individuals with paler flowers are not uncommon. The petals of the flowers are of unequal length, which gives the spike a careless, informal appearance, especially as they begin to wilt and fall forward over the seed pod. This species is lovely for cutting, and its color blends well with any hue that is combined with it.

C. Leichtlinii S. Wats.   B.M. t. 6287

This handsome species keeps green the name of the noted plantsman of Karlsruhe, Max Leichtlin. It was first discovered in British Columbia, and as this happened to be a white-flowered form, it became the type, instead of the much more common blue forms. It is a tall species, often reaching a height of four feet under auspicious conditions, and seems just made to lend distinction to the spring borders, where it should be grown in clumps of a dozen or more. The flowers are large and starry, and symmetrically spaced, but from the standpoint of color it is less effective than the Quamash. There are the cream forms and the blue ones of varying strength, with now and then one that verges toward reddish purple. As the flowers fade, they give themselves a little twist about the seed pod. It is stated that as many as a hundred and twenty flowers have been seen on a single stalk, but nothing like this has ever happened in my garden.

In Europe named varieties of Camassias are offered; some of them are Blue Star, Mauve Queen, Royal Purple, Silver Queen. Whether they are superior to the natural kinds that are available here, I cannot say.

CHIONODOXA *LILIACEAE*

CHIONODOXAS are formidable rivals of Scilla, Hyacinthus, and Muscari. They are as blue, as early, as easily grown, and their general utility is as great. They are, comparatively speaking, newcomers. Their names will not be found upon the full roster of Mrs. Loudon's "The Ladies Flower-Garden of Ornamental Bulbous Plants" (1841), so they are really of yesterday; but they have made good use of their time since they came before the public, spreading rapidly by seed and by offset, and pushing their advantage to the limit by captivating all who see them by their gay beauty and friendliness. In parts of England and on the Continent, they have even found their way out of gardens to the uncultivated fields and woodlands, colonizing vigorously.

It is a small genus, inhabiting the mountains of Asia Minor and Crete, where at great elevations their sheets of blue starry flowers press hard upon the receding snows. George Maw, when looking for Crocuses in Asia Minor, found them thus on Nymph Dagh, a mountain east of Smyrna, and described them as forming one of the most sumptuous displays of floral beauty, a mass of blue and white resembling *Nemophila insignis*, but more intense and brilliant.

Nearly all the kinds grown in gardens today are generally considered as forms of *Chionodoxa Luciliae*, and so they are regarded here.

Chionodoxas require little in the way of special culture. They prefer a sunny situation in soil that is a little gritty, and it is important to leave them alone year after year to increase their lovely kind in peace. Every few years a top dressing of good soil or very old rotted manure will serve to keep up their vigor and increase the number of flower spikes. The bulbs should be planted three inches deep and two or three inches apart. Recent plantations make little display; it is only after several seasons have passed that those sheets of inimitable blueness are produced that so richly reward the planter.

99

To derive the greatest effect from Chionodoxas, they should be planted closely and in great numbers. They are lovely for underplanting the golden-boughed Forsythias, *Magnolia stellata*, the early Azaleas, and other forward-flowering shrubs, or they may be naturalized in grassy places, thin woodland or in close colonies in the rock garden. They make a brilliant show as a foreground to a plantation of *Tulipa Kaufmanniana*. The main point is to leave them to themselves once they are planted; they will do the rest, increasing yearly until the reward is far greater than we could have envisaged.

"Be the frost never so keen," wrote Sir Herbert Maxwell in "Flowers," "the wind never so bitter, the rain never so ruthless, these little flowers never bow their bright heads." No wonder we love them!

C. Luciliae Boiss.   *B.M.* t. 6433
  Glory of the Snow

So impressed was the French botanist Boissier at the spectacle of thousands of sky-blue flowers against a background of dissolving snows when he came upon *Chionodoxa Luciliae* near the summit of Boz Dagh, the Tmolus of the ancients, east of Smyrna, that he at once coined the generic name Chionodoxa, which means Glory of the Snow; but it remained for George Maw[1] to introduce them to cultivation, and for Mr. Elwes to give them their start toward the great popularity they enjoy today.

There is a tale told that when Mr. Elwes exhibited the little plant at a London show, he was scoffed at for taking such pains and care with a thing so inconsiderable; but Mr. Elwes knew a fine plant when he saw it, and, moreover, he had seen it growing in masses, and he knew of what it was capable, given a chance. In the *Gardeners' Chronicle* (1879, p. 379), he wrote: "I can say with confidence that it is one of the best, if not the very best of its class, far surpassing any of the Squills, and apparently as hardy and as easy to increase as *Scilla sibirica*."

It was not long before the little blue flower had "caught on"

---

[1] In that delightful book, *Of Gardens and Woodlands* (1881), Frances Jane Hope tells of Mr. Maw's sending her a few bulbs of *C. Luciliae*, which she, fearing to intrust such rarities to the open ground, planted in a cold frame. It was not until she saw them growing out of doors in the Botanic Garden at Edinburgh that she knew they were quite hardy.

and was making its way in gardens where the new and beautiful are always ardently welcomed.

The bulbs are small and pear-shaped, the leaves rather broad and recurving, about four to a bulb, and contemporary with the flowers. The flower scape is about four inches high, and carries from four to six or seven starry blooms of a pure sky-blue that pales to a white central zone and throat. Three or four will be open at one time, and they do not droop as do Scillas, but look boldly at the sky whose color they repeat. The variety *alba* is a lovely frosted thing, not often seen, and the pink form *rosea* is a most delightful little plant, with buds of raspberry-red opening to almost white, but flushed on the reverse of the segments with rosy color. These forms of *Luciliae* flower in this garden about the 1st of April; but *C. L. sardensis* is more enterprising, and I always look for the first gentian-blue flowers soon after the middle of March. They are smaller than those of the type and deeper in color, while the white portion is hardly more than a pin-point. Even when massed closely, they do not produce the brilliant effect made by the blue form of *Luciliae*. *C. L. gigantea*, sometimes known as *Allenii* (*Addisonia*, Vol. I, t. 33), is a large edition of the type. Bulbs of it were first collected in the mountains above Allah Cheir (the ancient Philadelphia), by Edward Whittall, in 1887. It differs from the type in its greater height, five or six inches, and the size and number of flowers it bears. These are usually but two, occasionally three, and are about two inches across.

I have had forms that were of the typical sky-blue hue, with white throat and zone, and others that showed a decided lavender cast. And there is a fine and vigorous white-flowered form. They gaze skyward, as do the others of their kind, and when massed in quantity produce an almost dazzling effect. This kind flowers here a little later than the common *Luciliae*. The leaves are tinged with red. *C. L. Tmoli*, named for Mount Tmolus, has not proved a very satisfactory kind with me. It is reported as being found in deep mountain gorges that all winter, and into the spring, are filled with deeply drifted snow. Perhaps in our lowland gardens it misses the severe conditions and the ready supply of moisture to which it is accustomed; but it is a handsome sort with large flowers, the buds dark blue with a white base, the segments narrow, and it does not flower with me until the middle of April, so that it serves to draw out the Chionodoxa season appreciably. It is said to require damper soil and more shade than are liked by the race generally.

C. nana Boiss. & Heldr.   *B.M.* t. 6453

I have not yet come across this rather rare species from the mountains of Crete. Coming as it does from an altitude of some five or six thousand feet above sea level, it would doubtless be perfectly hardy, but from its portrait I should judge it to be a species distinctly inferior to *Luciliae* and its kinds; and we need not bewail the fact that it is not easily available. The flowers are small and vary from lilac to white, the stem somewhat weak, the whole plant dwarfer than those we have been considering. I think we can well do without it. It was discovered in 1820 by an Austrian traveler named Sieber, and so is the oldest known species.

There is also a species named *cretica* Boiss. & Heldr., but of this I can get no news at all.

CLAYTONIA *PORTULACEAE*

SPRING BEAUTY

C. virginica   *B.M.* t. 941
Good-Morning Spring, Grass Flower

THIS gay sprite of the early spring days is widely distributed from Nova Scotia to Saskatchewan, south to Texas and Georgia, in all suitable places; that is, in low woods, and along the banks of streams where are overhanging trees. It shuns the prairies and open places generally. The simple stem arises from a small, deep-set tuber or corm, bearing a pair of slender leaves and a cluster of pretty flowers, pale pink, or white veined with pink, very fleeting and wilting at once if gathered.

Brought into the garden, it establishes itself quickly and, where conditions are congenial, spreads rapidly. I have a plantation among Snowdrops which is very effective, and the two get on admirably together. The Snowdrops (of the *nivalis* section) flower in late February and March, and before they have gone the Spring Beauty literally springs up all about them, hiding the yellowing foliage of the Snowdrops, and giving me a second crop of beauty on this single little woodland strip. Later, ferns arch over the section, and it again commands admiration.

The genus Claytonia, named for one of our earliest botanists, Dr. Jules Clayton, will bear investigation by the rock gardener. I think it will yield a number of delightful plants for this special region or for not too wild gardens. I once had a plant or two of *C. asarifolia*, with large fleshy leaves and pink flowers in spring. It came from the West, and I believe is native in springy ground in Utah, Montana, California, and as far north as Alaska.

C. megarrhiza, the Alpine Spring Beauty, is offered by D. M. Andrews, of Boulder, Colorado, and other western dealers. It sounds a lovely thing, and is said to be one of the few plants that bloom among the rocks on the very tops of the highest peaks of the Rockies. "It often appears to be spread out in mats upon the bare rocks, but closer inspection shows that the large tap-roots are growing in the crevices and pockets through which they writhe and twist to great depths. The fleshy long-petioled, root leaves are rounded in outline, and they spread out from the crown in large rosettes from which ascend many one-sided racemes of delicate white pink-veined flowers. . . . In spite of the delicate appearance of the flowers, and the succulent character of the plant, snow and frost do not harm it. It is often in full bloom close to the melting snow, and emerges from the occasional summer blizzard even brighter than it was before." [1]

This species is said to have a superficial likeness to a Lewisia. A dampish, deep, porous soil is recommended for it, and light shade. Thus considered, it is said to be a satisfactory plant, not at all difficult to grow.

C. lanceolata is another which sounds alluring. It comes from moist mountain slopes up to a height of nine thousand feet in the Northwest, and is said to resemble its eastern relative, growing only three or four inches high, with juicy reddish stems, and thinly succulent leaves, the flowers the usual pale pink tone, or white veined with pink. I see *C. nivalis* offered by a western dealer; *C. aurea*, a yellow species, *C. multicaulis* (Yellowstone Park and Colorado), *C. parvifolia* (frequent in the Selkirks); and there are still others, among them *C. Sweetseri*. Surely here is a trail leading from our pretty little spring native into untracked regions. I think it would pay to set out upon it.

[1] *American Botanist*, Nov., 1920.

COLCHICUM *LILIACEAE*

Meadow Saffron

Few flowers are more floriferous than Colchicums, and as this bounty is vouchsafed the autumnal season, and they come blowing out of the earth with all the verve and enthusiasm that we associate with spring's manifestations, when most other plants are making their valedictory gestures, it is astonishing that they do not command more notice from gardening folk in general.

To the casual eye they look like giant long-tubed Crocuses; but as a matter of fact they are not even members of the same family. They belong to the Lily tribe, while Crocuses belong to the Irids, differing, as Mr. Bowles explains, in three main characters, the position of the ovary (which is inside the perianth tube), the number of stamens (of which there are six), and also of the styles, of which there are three distinct ones arising from the top of the ovary.

And they could be used in the same situations and associations as we use the Autumn Crocuses, save for one thing. In the spring they make a lush and lusty leaf growth, so coarse and heavy that it must be placed where it can do no harm by flopping over other smaller plants. Moreover, this foliage ends in a most unseemly orgy of yellowing dissolution, long drawn out and unlovely; therefore they must be placed where this phase of their activity may be hidden or ignored.

No one looking at the slim trim vases emerging naked from the earth in the autumn could suspect them of such overindulgence in the matter of foliage, or such a lack of dignity in passing on. The best place for them is in the shrubbery borders, or in herbaceous borders that are especially planned for autumn display. They make a lovely foreground planting for such things as Japanese Anemones, Michaelmas Daisies, tall and dwarf, *Chrysanthemum arcticum,* and the sky-blue Plumbago. The colors are all tones of pinky-lilac to almost purple and pure white. They like a rather rich soil, not bone-dry, and partial shade. We grow them on the north side of the rock garden in a situation given over to such things as Lungworts, Mertensia, *Anchusa myosotidiflora* and Dicentras, plants that are well able to hold their own against the extravagant performance of the Colchicums in spring.

We are permitted by the Agricultural Department to import Crocuses, but Colchicums are denied us; so it takes some hunting about to acquire anything like a representative collection. This may explain the fact of their being so little known. Let me here mention that Chautauqua Flower Fields, Greenhurst, New York, has the largest selection that I know of.

Like the Autumn Crocuses, they must be planted early. They begin to bloom in late August, many of them, so should be ordered in June with a request for early August delivery, and planted as soon as they arrive, else the flowers will be born in the paper bags, which is an unnecessary strain upon the vitality of the corms, and the fall show is missed besides.

Colchicums increase rapidly in congenial surroundings, and replanting is necessary every few years. It is always surprising and gratifying to find how many new corms we have when we dig them up. This operation may be carried out any time during the resting period, that is, after the foliage has ripened. Colchicums do not like deep planting. Place the corms just under the soil—but the soil itself should be deep and well tilled. They are natives chiefly of Asia Minor, the Caucasus, and southern Europe.

C. agrippinum B.M. t. 1028

This is a supposed garden name for an undetermined member of the tessellated group, or those forms whose flowers are checkered. I know of only one other genus of plants whose flowers show this neat checkering, the Fritillarias, where in the Checkered Lily, *F. meleagris,* it is most pronounced.

Agrippinum has not proved very reliable in this garden, and I think it probable that it requires dryer and sunnier conditions than seem to suit the other kinds. It is very effective; the large flowers arising, many from each corm, on their long slender pale tubes, are faint pink checkered over with deeper color. It is one of the first to flower, usually at the end of August. Other definitely

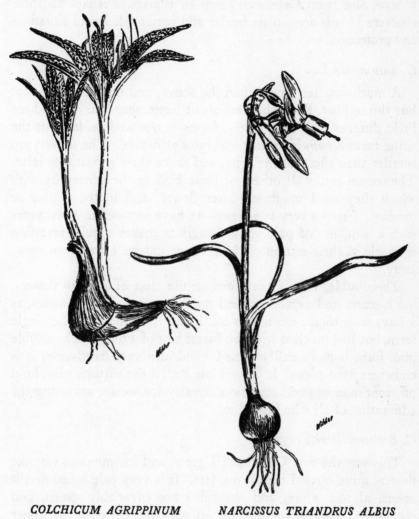

COLCHICUM AGRIPPINUM   *NARCISSUS TRIANDRUS ALBUS*

checkered forms, which I have not had, are *variegatum*, flowering late, a Greek (the same, I believe, as *C. Parkinsonii*), and *Sibthorpii*, also from Greece and near-by islands. Perhaps all these checkered kinds are a little tender and require sheltered situations and protection.

C. autumnale L.

A much smaller flower than the above, and of a soft rose-lilac hue throughout, flowering here about September 8th. I could see little difference, if any, in the forms *major* and *minor*, but the white form *album* is distinct and most attractive. The flowers are smaller than those of the type, and make their appearance later. The corms outdo all others of their kind in the generosity with which they send up flower after flower, and in the matter of increase. From a very few corms, we have acquired in a few years such a company of pale ghost flowers as makes a quite arresting spectacle in their section of the garden, and we have given many away.

The double white form is among the elect of autumn flowers, but is scarce and expensive (and worth its price). The flowers, as I have seen them, are not as coldly white as those of the single form, but just touched with the barest hint of a blush. The double pink form is more easily come by and also very handsome; it is known as *flore-pleno*. It flowers late and, if the autumn rains hold off, continues in good condition literally for weeks, attracting the admiration of all who behold it.

C. Bornmuelleri Freyn.

This was the first Colchicum I grew, and its immense vaselike flowers quite carried me off my feet. It is very pale when first it opens, almost white, and the tubes are invariably green, and remain so, never becoming flushed with the color of the upper flower, which increases and deepens with maturity, and even becomes slightly mottled. They have a light springlike fragrance. *Bornmuelleri* flowers early in September, and continues almost throughout the month. Before the flowers have quite faded, the observant gardener will notice the tips of the leaves and spathes peeping above the soil, forerunners of the two-feet-tall whorls of leaves that so embarrass us in the spring.

C. giganteum Baker

As I have it here, this species is not so large as *Bornmuelleri,* and it flowers later. Its form is gracious, swelling gently from the greenish tubes to form a lovely deep mauve-pink vase, pale or yellowish in the throat, and with the scent of honey. It comes from Asia Minor, and is sometimes considered as a mere form of *speciosum.*

C. speciosum Stev.   B.M. t. 6078

Speciosum flowers late in September and early in October. It appears to have several forms, and from different dealers I have received quite different-appearing plants under the same name. The one I have finally accepted as the true plant has beautiful large bowl-shaped flowers hoisted on tall slender tubes. The color hints of raspberries, and it is very floriferous, as well as fragrant. It comes from the Caucasus, Macedonia, and as far east as Persia.

The white form I have not yet been able to secure, but Mr. Bowles says it is one of the most beautiful of hardy bulbous plants. "The snow-white goblets, of good form, equal to that of a Tulip, standing on soft emerald-green tubes, cannot be equalled for beauty in the late autumn by any other plant so easy to grow well in the open. Its only rivals among white flowers are *Romneya Coulteri* and *Crinum Powellii album.*" *Speciosum* requires replanting every second year, as it increases rapidly.

Of late years there has been considerable activity among hybridists in producing new forms of Colchicums, and happily a good many of these we have at our disposal in this country. One of the most beautiful, however, a product of van Tubergen genius, is not yet, so far as I know, obtainable; this is a double lilac flower known as Water Lily. But I have here a number of hybrids that add greatly to the gaiety of the autumn. Premier has satin-like flowers of large size opening starrily. The tube is creamy-white, the body of the flower lilac-pink. Eight flowers came from a single corm. Lilac Wonder, pinkish violet; Conquest, light violet; Violet Queen, deep purplish violet with a white center; Autumn Queen, bright amaranth checkers on a pale ground, base of segments white, and tubes green, enormous flower, and many born of a single bulb. I have also Mr. Kerbert, Disraeli, and the Giant, fine, but their labels have been lost, so that it is impossible to tell which is which. Many of the hybrids are faintly checkered, many slightly fragrant.

No enemy animals, it seems, have a taste for Colchicums, not even, says Sir Herbert Maxwell, "the clandestine slug or the rapacious rabbit." This immunity may be explained by the fact that the plant is supposed to have poisonous qualities. All the early writers knew of this danger and wrote of it. Mr. Bowles quotes Lyte in his translation of Dodonaeus (1579): "Meadow or wilde saffron is corrupt and venomous, therefore not used in medicine." It is now regarded as a valuable remedy in the treatment of gout, and in modifying pain.

There are many other species, some flowering with the leaves, a few in late winter or early spring. There is a yellow-flowered kind, *C. luteum,* from Kashmir, that we should like to try, and there are others that should be within our reach. Among these are *C. alpinum, C. byzantinum, C. cilicicum, C. libanoticum, C. croaticum, C. montanum, C. umbrosum.* All would seem to be definitely worth while. It is hard to be content with a half-loaf.

CROCUS *IRIDACEAE*

ALL the world loves a Crocus. There can be no two opinions about this. Few flowers are so fresh-looking, so jaunty, and withal so appealing, yet many good gardeners are satisfied with a mere bowing acquaintance with the genus, and have no urge to plumb the Crocus wealth that is so readily at hand.

In too many gardens the Crocus season begins and ends with the flowering of the so-called Dutch varieties, a matter of two or three weeks in March and April. These for the most part are hybrids of *Crocus vernus* that have been developed in great numbers, chiefly by the industrious Hollanders, and while they are showy and altogether delightful, as any Crocus is, they furnish only the barest hint of what the race can be.

Let any one who is at present satisfied with his drifts and patches of Kathleen Parlow, President Lincoln, and Grand Yellow, seek out in some library Maw's great monograph on the genus, superbly illustrated in color, or buy a copy of E. A. Bowles' "Handbook of Crocus and Colchicum," and he will feel desires not hitherto experienced sprouting within him, and find himself scanning the bulb catalogues with new discernment and a rapidly rising pulse of acquisitiveness.

Instead of a few weeks of Crocus bloom, that is all the average garden boasts, these flowers may, in fact, be enjoyed during many months of the year. In this cold garden, we frequently have them flowering in September, October, November, and December; in February, March, and April. January we nearly always skip, and it must be understood that it is only during spells of ingratiating weather that they are lured forth in December and February, but it does happen now and again, even here in New York State. The months of March and October, however, show them at the height of their celebration.

The Crocus "bulb" is, properly speaking, a corm; that is to say, it is "a solid body and not one formed of scales." Each year a new corm is formed, nourished by the life blood of the old one, which gradually shrivels up and disappears.

Sometimes several new corms will grow from the stored vitality of the old one; these will be found adhering to various parts of its perimeter, not by any means always directly on top. The young corm is at first innocent of covering, but a mature corm is wrapped in what is called a tunic: a fibrous covering of varying thicknesses and "weaves" that may be brown or reddish. Directly from the corm spring the sheathing leaves and the narrow keeled leaves which enfold the tube and the flowers until they are safely through the earth; then the leaves arch away, setting the amazingly long tube that bears the gently swelling flower free to reach upward. I have sometimes thought that in all Nature there is no line more lovely than the long slow outward curve of a Crocus. Vaselike, we say in an attempt to describe, but no vase made by man can approximate its pure grace.

Crocuses are to be found in many parts of the temperate world, in Europe and Asia and a few in North Africa. Spain and Portugal, France and Greece, and Italy have their Crocuses, and they wander eastward through Palestine and Turkey and the Caspian region to Asia Minor, where are found the greatest number of species, and Persia, with points of call at the Balearic and Ionian Islands and the Cyclades. They climb the Pyrenees, the Alps, the mountains of Armenia and the Caucasus, and by far the greater number of them are hardy and may be grown out of doors in cold localities of this country.

The best soil for them is one that is deeply tilled, nourishing, and fairly light, a little gritty, and neither wet nor clayey nor overrich with manure; and they thrive in the full eye of the sun, not craving even gentle shades, though they will put up with light branches far above them. If they are given some shelter on the north from scourging gales, so much the better; but the sturdy little Crocus girds up its tender loins and does very well without this provision when necessary.

Personally I have not found that they thrive especially well in grass, but this is not the invariable experience. Where turf is not heavy and coarse, they endure and increase. They are charming planted in swirling masses about the skirts of the shrubs, winding in three- or four-ply ribbons among the herbaceous plants in borders, or used as edgings, and they are delightfully and happily situated in the rock garden.

It must be borne in mind, however, that their foliage must ripen and turn yellow before it is removed, and they should not be placed where this will prove a serious drawback. A sunny bank where it is difficult to grow grass, may be converted from an unsightly feature to a lovely one if it is planted with spreading mats of *Phlox subulata* and thickly strewn with the stronger-growing Crocuses.

We plant them about four inches deep in August, September, and October, and leave them to increase until they show by their congested growth and failing bloom that it is time to give them more space. Then the bulbs are taken up after the foliage is thoroughly ripened, usually in July, cleaned and sorted out as to size, the autumn-flowering species replanted at once and the spring bloomers stored until it is convenient to plant them in the autumn. The larger bulbs are given prominent places, the smaller set in rows, where they may come to full maturity at their leisure.

A lightly rooting annual may be sown over the heads of Crocuses where they are grown in the rock garden. Such delicate things as the dwarfer Alyssums, *Eschscholtzia tenuifolia, Gypsophila muralis, Ionopsidium acaule,* or *Leptosiphon hybridus* serve to cover the blanks that are left when they die down, but they are probably better off without this competitive growth that robs the soil, and may retard their growth.

Crocuses are gregarious creatures and do not mind being planted close together, and it is so that they show at their best. When they have died away, we usually treat them to a thin top dressing of rich sandy loam to increase the calories in their diet and keep them up to standard size and floriferousness.

For purposes of the garden, Crocuses may be divided into two groups—the late winter- and spring-flowering kinds, and the autumn-flowering species. Many persons who give generous space in their gardens to spring-blooming Crocuses know nothing about those that flower at the other end of the year; yet there is something about a Crocus blooming in the autumn that reaches beyond the mere pleasure of the eyes and touches the heart.

From amidst the coarse growths and strident hues characteristic of the season, amidst the signs of hurry and farewell all about it, its flowers arise cool, serene, unafraid, a lovely gesture of the waning year, foretelling future burgeoning and blossoming.

Who, looking upon a colony of these crisp young flowers, can doubt that spring will come again, that winter is but an interlude for rest and renewal? In spring we are accustomed to such floral freshness, such jaunty cocksureness, the youth of the year personified in flowers; but when the year is old and tired, we are grateful for such an eloquent earnest of regenesis. Often they are to be found blowing their fragile-seeming bubbles in the very teeth of autumnal gales and inclemencies, even after freezing weather.

One point is of especial importance in growing the autumn-flowering species. They should be put into the ground *early*. Order them in July with the request that delivery be made in August, at the latest. Then they should be put into the ground as soon as received, and not allowed to sprout in the paper bags. In this way, satisfactory blossoming may be enjoyed the current autumn.

If autumn Crocuses are planted in grass, it has to be remembered that the tender little points will be peeping up in August, and that the lawn mower will injure them, and where spring-flowering kinds are planted, the grass must not be cut until their foliage is mature. This, it seems to me, rules them out of any save out-of-the-way grassy places; they should not be planted in lawns, or where the turf must be kept shorn and tidy.

Certain autumn species come out of the ground innocent of foliage, the leaves developing later in the autumn, or in some cases not until spring; others have the foliage partly developed at flowering time, while still others bloom with a full equipment of the dark narrow leaves.

It is a sad fact that Crocuses are beset by numerous enemies. Birds, mice, rabbits, and squirrels all devour them. In a single night a foraging bunny will eat your Crocus patches clean, ignoring utterly the fresh lettuce leaves that have been left temptingly about. Right before your scandalized eyes, squirrels will dig up the bulbs and sit unconcernedly munching while you rave. Mice work more secretly, but just as effectively, and birds pick the blossoms to pieces, seemingly out of a love of wanton destruction, and they also pull up and eat the smaller corms.

Many preventives and distractions have been suggested; fresh green food placed conveniently, naphtha flakes sprinkled among them, poisoned halves of apples offered, pans of water set about, a covering of black netting. But who wants to look at his Crocuses through a haze of black netting!

Cats are a help, but here, unhappily, we have been obliged to resort to a rifle after losing our Crocuses for several seasons in succession. Spring is the most dangerous season for the Crocuses, but as Mr. Bowles points out: "Mice need fighting in all months and by any means. Breakneck traps baited with Brazil nuts are very useful weapons. Nor should one neglect the aid of cats, poison, virus, sunken jars or any other method of destroying the Bank Vole which nibbles off leaves and buds, and the Long Tailed Field Mouse which digs up and devours the corms." It is easy to see to what a rabid state of mind the gentlest and most humane of persons may be brought by the destruction of his beloved Crocuses. The gun in a sure hand is the most unfailing weapon.

LATE WINTER AND SPRING-FLOWERING CROCUSES

C. aureus Sibth. & Sm.   Maw t. 35
                                            B.M. t. 2986

This glowing species has warmed the cold spring days for many generations of gardeners. It grew in the London gardens of Parkinson and Gerard, and there is abundant evidence that it was known long before their day. Gerard says that it was sent to him by "Robinus of Paris, that painfull and most curious searcher of simples," and that it "hath floures of a most perfect and shining yellow colour, seeming afar off to be a hot glowing cole of fire."

It is a fine, easily grown Crocus, and the most brilliantly colored of all the species. The hue is pure unmarked orange-yellow, and Mr. Bowles says that it is the most western of the yellow species, ranging from western Asia Minor and the Dobrogea on the east, as far west as Serbia, occurring generally at low elevations. It flowers here about the middle of March. *C. Korolkowii* and *C. susianus* are yellow Crocuses blooming earlier, but neither has quite the unsullied hot brilliance of *aureus*. It makes fine trails of color in the shrubbery borders, or may be grown in clumps in the rock garden. It is hardy and enduring, and increases freely.

C. aureus sulphureus concolor (*B.M.* t. 1384) is a pale form, individually lovely, but too delicate in color to make a show in the garden. There is a white-flowered kind, *C. aureus lacteus,* said to be singularly beautiful and refined, but I have not come across it. Mr. Bowles says: "The white has a gleam of yellow in it, yet is clear and in no wise muddy. It flowers later than the other *aureus* varieties."

The Crocus we know as Dutch Yellow is said to be a form of *aureus,* a large-flowered and very resplendent form. This is probably the most frequently planted of any Crocus, and when left to itself in sunny places, gradually forms close masses that make clots of burning color against the dark earth and last year's withered leaves. It flowers a few days later than the true *aureus,* and considerably earlier than the other so-called Dutch varieties, and it differs from *aureus* in having fine gray lines veining the outer segments. The foliage lies close to the ground, the goblet-shaped flowers rising above it as if on a little standard. This Crocus likes good rich soil and full sun. It does not make seed but increases surely, though deliberately, from offsets. No garden should be without it.

C. banaticus Heuff.   Maw t. 24

A species which is allied to *C. vernus,* but which flowers earlier. It has not appeared happy here, and I am piqued to new efforts in its behalf when I see the few charming bowl-shaped flowers of a soft reddish lilac color that yearly make their appearance. It seems not to be a robust species, though it haunts alpine pastures up to an altitude of six thousand feet. It is found from Slavonia throughout southern Hungary and Transylvania to western Podolia.

C. biflorus Mill.   *B.M.* t. 845
Scotch Crocus

This is one of the most reliable and satisfactory of early-flowering Crocuses. It begins to bloom here, if the weather is at all reasonable, at the end of February, and is one of the few kinds that for me hold their own in grass. There are numerous forms of it, but that most generally grown "is an old garden form, called Scotch Crocus, which most likely originated in some Scottish garden, and was introduced from thence into England and Holland. Nothing very closely resembling it is found in a wild state, and like other old garden varieties, it is sterile and increases rapidly by corm division." [1]

If I have the true old garden form here, it is larger than any of its varieties and is most floriferous, white with distinct reddish purple lines on the outsides of the segments, and a yellow glow in the throat. The buds are beautifully formed, and the flowers open out wide and flat in the sunshine.

C. biflorus Adami Baker (*B.M.* t. 3868) is a variable form said said to come from the easternmost range of the species. My corms, that were sent to me by van Tubergen of Holland, display flowers of several tones of lavender, some verging toward blue, others more pinkish and only faintly buff-colored at the base of the outer segments, which are lightly feathered with deeper color. The flowers are not large but are neat in shape, and I should be glad if they showed more enthusiasm for my garden. The first year they bloomed well, but subsequently they have languished and appeared anything but robust.

C. biflorus pusillus is a little Italian form, with white flowers that are lightly feathered on the exterior. It opens starrily under a warm sun, displaying the orange throat. It flowers here rather late in March and belongs in the rock garden, as it is too small to make a display in a wider sphere. *C. biflorus Weldenii* (*B.M.* t. 6211) is a beautiful Dalmatian species, as large as the type, hardy, free-flowering, and of "massive gourd-like shape." The flowers are pure white within, and lack the yellow glow in the throat. The outside of the segments is flushed with soft blue-purple. It flowers early, and is altogether a grand flower.

C. chrysanthus Herb.   *B.M.* t. 6162
                                                 Maw t. 62

This Crocus as described by Herbert is a beautifully rounded flower of a fine orange-yellow, but it is a most variable species,

[1] *A Handbook of Crocus and Colchicum,* by E. A. Bowles.

exhibiting such different hues as yellow, white, cream, orange, lilac, with every imaginable ornamentation on the outer segments in the way of veinings, featherings, flushes, and freakings, these in strangely contrasting hues, such as brown, gray, or purplish blue; and some of the forms are quite unmarked.

A distinguishing feature of the species is the black-tipped barbs of the anthers, though not all the forms show this characteristic, and in some the "anthers are more or less suffused with a smoky brown, and the flowers striped or freckled with gray or brown on the outer segments. Baker placed these as the varieties *fusco-lineatus* and *fusco-tinctus* of *chrysanthus*."

The range of *C. chrysanthus* is wide. It is found in Asia Minor, near Smyrna, on the Bithynian Olympus, in Turkey and in Greece, ranging in altitude from near sea level up to five thousand feet above it. Its various forms are among the loveliest and most floriferous of Crocuses, and they rush valiantly into bloom any time after the new year if the cold and snow hold up at all. In 1934 certain of them made an attempt to stage a display in December. The result was sad, but their gay impetuosity warmed the heart.

C. chrysanthus has been a prolific source of seedlings, and many fine ones have been raised. Mr. E. A. Bowles is responsible for a charming series to which he has most felicitously given the names of birds—Snow Bunting, Golden Plover, Yellow Hammer, Golden Pheasant, Silver Pheasant, Bullfinch, White Egret, and the like. Few of these, unfortunately, are at present on the market. From van Tubergen's workshop also comes a delightful string of seedlings, all characterized by their medium size, their gently rounded form, and their generous and early flowering.

Some of the seedlings which I have been able to procure are the following: Canary Bird, orange-yellow flushed or feathered with bronze; E. A. Bowles, soft butter-yellow, tinged at the base with brown, and of a strong, durable texture; E. P. Bowles, orange-yellow with outer purple featherings; *fusco-tinctus*, warm orange-yellow with outer brown suffusion; Large Warley, lovely white flower with a yellow throat and purplish exterior; Moonlight, soft yellow paling to cream as it matures; Snow Bunting, a fragile-looking flower, pure white with a yellow throat and purple featherings on the exterior; Zwanenburg Bronze, fine deep yellow with bronze exterior markings. Mixed seedlings may be purchased and yield many a rare beauty.

C. dalmaticus Vis.   Maw t. 34

I once had this pretty early-flowering Dalmatian Crocus, but it has disappeared from my garden; and I do not now see it offered. There are several forms of it; the one that grew here was a soft dove-lavender in hue faintly tinged with rose.

C. etruscus Parl.   B.M. t. 6362
                                                        Maw t. 22

A pretty and shapely Italian Crocus, large and rather blunt, belonging to the same general group as *Imperati*, and somewhat resembling it, though it flowers considerably later; in this garden, not before March 20th. The color is soft lilac, and the outer segments are rather richly feathered with reddish purple. The anthers are yellow, and the three-branched stigmata, orange. It does not open flat here save under a very warm and persuasive sun. This Crocus was discovered by Professor Palatore in the Oak woods by the roadside as he ascended the Salita del Filetto, in Tuscany, and I believe is confined to that general locality. The tunic of the corm is very coarsely woven. In this garden it has made a most satisfactory increase.

C. Fleischeri J. Gay   B.M. t. 6174
                                                        Maw t. 66

This quaint and engaging little Crocus is usually referred to as winter-flowering, but it has never bloomed here, even in sheltered locations, before early March. Its fine grassy leaves are very prompt to appear, however, and presently between them the narrow buds push upward, opening to display a white flower with long narrow segments that cause it to have an especially starry appearance. The segments are feathered violet on the outer sides, and the stigmata are scarlet. Close examination will show them gleaming through the closed flower. Though frail in appearance, and sometimes injured by inclement weather, this is a hardy and satisfactory species. The bulb is yellowish and covered with a complicated network of fibers that are plaited at regular intervals. It was brought by Mr. Elwes from Asia Minor.

C. Imperati Tenore

Given a sheltered position in the rock garden, or against a warm wall, this beautiful Italian Crocus comes into bloom very early in the year. I have known it to be lured forth by ingratiating weather in January, but in any case it may be depended upon to make a delightful display from the middle of February well into March, and it is better to wait a little than to have the brave show extinguished by sudden freezing weather.

This is a most lovely Crocus, large and vaselike, and deliciously fragrant. The furled bud is buff in color, richly feathered with reddish violet. The open flower is soft rosy lilac in hue. It usually blooms without the leaves, but these push upward before the flower fades.

An unfeathered form is sometimes received with bulbs of the ordinary kind, and this, too, is very lovely, but I have not found it as ready of increase as is the ordinary kind. It is commonly known as *C. Imperati unicolor*. There are also white-flowered forms; but I have not seen them, and I believe they are very rare.

C. Imperati belongs to a group of species that includes *C. suaveolens, C. minimus, C. versicolor*, and *C. etruscus*, and one or two others of which I have no first-hand knowledge that are not found outside the Italian district; and though they are southerners, they seem to be very hardy and enduring. *C. Imperati* is said to be very profuse in the mountains around Naples.

C. Korolkowii Regel & Maw
Maw t. 56
B.M. t. 6852 a

All the yellow-flowered Crocuses are welcome in the cold spring garden for the sake of their warmth of hue. This one is so impetuous that it is often frozen back by cruel February weather, and it is best to plant it where it will not be encouraged to rash flowering. The flower is not large but is very starry in form, opening out flat when the sun shines brightly. Its gold is tinged faintly with green, and the backs of the segments are feathered with brown, the whole having a shining varnished appearance. The leaves are many and lie upon the ground, making a setting for the bright little flower. The corm is rather flat and of large size.

C. Korolkowii is named for its discoverer, the Russian General

Korolkow, who found it growing in stiff soil near the river Kly in Turkestan. It is rather pleasant to think of a Russian general, perhaps big and fierce and bearded, showing his softer side by thinking it worth his while to notice and collect a little starry yellow Crocus.

While less showy than *C. aureus*, it is a member of the same general group, and is very hardy and floriferous.

C. minimus DC.   *B.M.* t. 6176
                                                      Maw t. 19

Though not the smallest Crocus known, it is quite the smallest that I have seen, a quaint goblet-shaped little flower with rounded segments, the cup not much more than half an inch deep. It grows here on a little sunny slope in the rock garden, and seems to be variable in color and markings. Some individuals are almost pink in color, the outer segments pale unmarked buff, while others verge toward garnet and are strongly feathered with reddish purple. The stigmata are yellow and conspicuous in the shallow goblet, and I have not noticed that the flowers open very widely, even under a hot sun. It is a sturdy and attractive little species, well suited to the smallest rock garden. It flowers late and long; indeed it is the latest species to bloom here, and remains in good condition for several weeks. There is a white form, but it has not come my way.

C. minimus belongs to the Italian group, which includes *Imperati*. It is said to be frequent in the islands of Corsica and Sardinia, growing at low elevations.

C. Olivieri J. Gay   *B.M.* t. 6031
                                                      Maw t. 53

A member of the *aureus* group, this species has flowers of rather small size, but very warm and bright in their orange hue. The segments are somewhat narrower than is usual, and the leaves, which are produced at the same time as the flowers, are unusually wide. Massed, it produces a brilliant effect, and is well worth growing. It flowers here later than *aureus*.

The French traveler, M. Olivier, discovered it growing on the island of Chios in the Aegean Sea, and it is found also in the Cyclades, in Greece, Roumania, Roumelia, and about Salonika.

It was very fine in my garden for a number of years, and then died out. I do not know if this is its usual habit, or if something was not to its mind. It is not often offered.

C. Sieberi J. Gay   B.M. t. 6036
                                                           Maw t. 33

This is the first wild Crocus I ever grew. It has been in my garden for twenty years, and will always be one of the most beloved. When closed, the bud has a demure and dovelike appearance, for the color of the outer segments is curiously lifeless; but when it opens all is changed. It seems to laugh, displaying the bright pure lilac interior, orange throat and scarlet stigmata. It is a trig little flower, and has the air of knowing that it is well turned out. It is usually in flower before the end of February, and snows often fall about it, when its color looks almost brilliant against the white carpet. The leaves are wide at blossoming time, but shorter than the flower. The white line down their center is very strongly marked.

It is a common flower in Greece and found at elevations of from one to seven thousand feet above sea level, disporting itself at the edge of the receding snows. Forms of it are also found in the islands of the Archipelago. It is a sturdy and robust species and increases in the garden, though not rapidly; and it is one of the best and most reliable of the race and a good species to begin with, for it requires little attention and never disappoints.

C. stellaris Sabine   Maw t. 15

A slender, not very vigorous little flower, pale yellow with brown featherings on the outer segments. It has apparently been long in cultivation, but no natural habitat for it is known, and it is probably of garden origin. Baker suggests it may be an old hybrid between *aureus* and *susianus,* but it is less sturdy than either of these two strong-growing kinds. It flowers in mid-March with the leaves.

C. suaveolens Bert.   B.M. t. 3864
                                                           Maw t. 15

This delicately fragrant Crocus has not proved constant in my garden. Unlike *Imperati,* to whose group it belongs, it endures for a year or two and then disappears. Nor need one sorrow over-much for it. It is far less lovely than *Imperati*, paler in hue, thinner in texture, and with stripes instead of featherings on its buff outer segments. Its form is starry, and in the sun it opens wide and flat, but always looks as if it needed a little stiffening. It is said to be plentiful in the environs of Rome, found on the Campagna and on calcareous hills and in Pine woods even growing thickly by the roadsides.

C. susianus Ker-Gawl.   *B.M.* t. 652
   Cloth of Gold Crocus   Maw t. 36

This small brilliant Crocus has been splashing sunshine in cold spring gardens since before the time of Parkinson and Gerard, in both of whose gardens it grew. Its hue is of the richest orange, and the segments are feathered with burnished bronze on their outer sides. Under the eye of the sun, it opens perfectly flat and even turns back a little, so that where it is planted in numbers, it appears as if color had been spattered over the ground.

It is recorded that Clusius received this species at Frankfort in 1587. It is a native of southwestern Russia and the Crimea. No garden would be complete without this dashing small thing. It endures in grass and, if left to its own devices, increases rapidly. It is as hardy as iron, and may be used freely in the borders or in clumps in the rock garden. It flowers any time after the middle of February, and as the flowers are of sturdy texture, it weathers the gales and the showers, even the snows, with equanimity.

C. Tomasinianus Herb.   Maw t. 26

This exquisite Dalmatian species has become almost an embarrassment in my garden. More than any other Crocus, it has increased until in certain parts of the rock garden it forms a thick turf. It seeds freely and also increases from the corms. It is very hardy and is one of the very early bloomers. The buds are long and pointed, and narrowly furled, the color as pale as silver; but when the sun has warmed them, they open wide to show a soft amethyst interior.

Among my lavender forms, a few with pure white flowers have appeared, and these are cherished. *C. Tomasinianus* is distributed in the country east of the Adriatic, in Dalmatia, Serbia and Bosnia. It is allied to *Crocus vernus*, but is of a slenderer build than any *vernus* I ever saw. It appears fragile but is able to stand a good deal of hardship in the garden.

C. vernus All.   Maw t. 26

A variable species with the widest distribution of any Crocus save *biflorus* and *sativus*, from the Pyrenees to the Carpathians. It is found in alpine pastures seventy-six hundred feet above sea level. In these alpine heights, Mr. Bowles says, he has "often seen the Crocus flowers pressing upward against a thin layer of almost transparent snow, and a few hours afterward, widely open in the sunshine which melted away their last film of winter covering. On the St. Gotthard the myriads of their white flowers imitate the last drifted patches of snow, and on the slopes of the Little Mont Cenis, I have seen an endless variety of white, lavender, and striped forms that resemble Lilliputian counterparts of the well-known garden favourites."

Of the true *Crocus vernus* types I have here only *albiflorus*, a small white flower with a yellow throat; but a vast number of *vernus* progeny are scattered about the garden. These are what we know as Dutch Crocuses. To choose among them is difficult, but a lovely round dozen would include Enchantress, Amethyst, Excelsior, Gladstone, Edina, Margot, Maximilian, President Lincoln, Remembrance, Paulus Potter, Kathleen Parlow. All these are splendid for massing about shrubs or planting thickly in the borders among the perennials. They have large flowers with finely polished surfaces, and embrace many tones of lavender, reddish violet, purple and white, some with striped flowers. Among them Maximilian is my favorite. It is a rather small flower of a most lovely pure lavender color, said to have the blood of *Tomasinianus* in its veins. Unfortunately it is also the favorite of the sparrows that infest the spring garden.

C. versicolor Ker-Gawl.   *B.M.* t. 1110
                                                    Maw t. 16

A most beautiful and wholly reliable Crocus, it has grown in gardens since the time of Parkinson and Gerard. It is extremely variable, some individuals being pure white with deep purple featherings on the outsides of the segments (these called Cloth of Silver). Others have delicate markings on the inner segments, and the ground color varies from white to deep lavender.

The variety *picturatus* is very fine and free-flowering. In this garden it flowers as late as the Dutch Crocuses, and has increased freely. "It is abundant east of the Rhone River to the western extremity of the French Department of the Alpes-Maritimes and the Italian frontier. It extends northward as far as the mountains about Grenoble, and has a range of altitude from sea level to four thousand feet. It occurs near Mentone at an altitude of three thousand feet."

To one who wishes to choose a half-dozen of these winter- and spring-flowering Crocuses, I would suggest the following: *C. aureus, C. biflorus, C. Imperati, C. Sieberii, C. Tomasinianus,* and *C. versicolor.*

AUTUMN-FLOWERING CROCUSES

C. asturicus Herb. Maw t. 7

We are told that this Spanish Crocus is known in its native mountains as "Espanto Pastores," "Terror of Shepherds," because appearing, as it does, just after the autumn rains, it heralds the coming of winter. In this garden it flowers about October 20th. It is a pretty, rather shallow flower with pointed segments, darker toward the base, and with a few dark lines, not feathers, streaking the throat. The stigmata are yellow. The ground color varies in different forms from pale to rather deep lavender, and there is a white form with a purple flush at the base of the segments. My patch is almost the exact color of the tumbling mass of *Verbena venosa* that grows near it. At flowering time the leaves just show above the ground, but later they develop a considerable length. This is an easy free-flowering sort said to be abundant in the Asturias and the Sierra de Guadarrama.

C. cancellatus Herb. B.M. t. 6103
Maw t. 31

A lovely Crocus that flowers before its leaves appear, in this garden toward the end of September. The flowers are pure white with faint gray lines on the outside of the segments, which give it a curiously transparent look. It is extremely floriferous and increases rapidly, soon forming close colonies of pallid ghost flowers on sunny ledges in the rock garden.

Cancellatus cilicicus has pale lavender flowers feathered with deeper color, and with me a less robust habit. Both have slashed and somewhat fringy stigmata, and lack a basal spathe. *Cancellatus* in its several forms has "a wide range from Greece to Persia, is found in Armenia and parts of northern Asia Minor, and abundantly around Palestine, where it is one of the species collected for food and sold in the Markets of Damascus with *C. Gaillardotti* under the name of Hursinein." In the Taurus it is found at an altitude of eight thousand feet above sea level.

C. hadriaticus Herb.   B.R. t. 16
                                                         Maw t. 30

This species, which is a native of Albania and the Ionian Isles and the Morea, does not live over the winter with me. It is said to be a near relative of the Saffron Crocus, but is white with a yellow throat and purplish lines at the base of the segments. I shall try it in a sunnier, more sheltered location.

C. hyemalis Boiss. & Blanche.   Maw t. 43

Hyemalis is called a midwinter species, but it flowers here in November. It cannot be considered a reliably hardy Crocus but, given a sunny, sheltered position in well drained soil, may linger, as it has done here, for a few years. Its range is limited to Palestine and the borders of Syria, and Mr. Bowles says it grows plentifully in the Campo di Pastori near Bethlehem, "and one likes to think that the shepherds of Bethlehem listened to the first Christmas carol while resting in a field full of the flowers of *C. hyemalis*." As it grows here, it is a slender flower, white with an orange throat and a few purple lines on the segments. The anthers are black. It opens wide and starrily when the sun is ardent. It flowers with the leaves.

C. iridiflorus Heuff. (*C. byzantinus*)   Maw t. 1
    The Iris Crocus

It is difficult to imagine a more enchanting Crocus than this. It looks like a tiny Iris flowering out of its turn so to speak. The outer segments, which reflex slightly, are of a warm purple hue, and considerably longer than the pale lavender, pointed inner segments. The stigmata are light purple and thready. Visitors frequently exclaim, "Oh, what kind of an Iris is *that?*"

I have trouble with this unique species despite the fact that it is acclaimed easy and sturdy. My colonies of it are always skimpy, however many I plant, even though I bear in mind and heed the fact that it is a native of woods and requires more shade and moisture than is usual with a Crocus. "I find," says Mr. Bowles, "it thrives in soil that is chiefly peat or leafmould in a position that one would choose for a choice Hellebore or Ferns, that is, on the northern, or northwestern side of a boulder in the rock garden, or under some small deciduous shrub."

It blooms without its leaves, which do not appear until the following spring, and are then seen to be uncommonly broad and of a dark, shining green hue, devoid of the white central line characteristic of Crocus leaves in general. It occupies a limited area bordering on the Carpathians in Hungary and Transylvania, a lowland plant, growing on chalky alluvium in wooded thickets of the lower hills. It flowers here in early October.

C. laevigatus Bory & Chaub.   Maw t. 56

This is the latest Crocus to flower in this garden. Last year the variety *Fontenayi* was in bloom on December 2nd. It flowers with the leaves, which it seems to need at this cold season, and it is a very lovely flower. It is a variable species found in the Morea, the Cyclades, and the Greek mainland, but seems quite hardy, and it is so fragrant that standing above a colony in the late fall sunshine, one catches the Freesia-like scent distinctly. Smaller than *Imperati, laevigatus* is yet a good deal like it in appearance, its outer side tinged with buff, its interior rosy lilac. The type is more lavender in hue and heavily feathered with rich purple. It flowers earlier than the variety *Fontenayi*. The corm is notably hard and smooth.

C. longiflorus Rafin. (*C. odorus*)   B.R. t. 3
Maw t. 28

Next to *C. pulchellus*, this is my favorite autumn Crocus, a bright, gay flower that adds to its warm pinkish lilac coloring,

yellow throat, and scarlet divided stigmata, a delicious scent. One
has, at the late season when it flowers, almost given up expecting
sweet scents, so one bends gratefully above this little Crocus, or
gathers a handful to place in a low glass bowl indoors.

Though a southerner, native to Italy, the islands of Sicily and
Malta, it has proved quite hardy here, and increases in a most
satisfactory manner. And I do like a Crocus to be accompanied by
its leaves, exciting as the naked bubbles rising from the stark earth
undoubtedly are. They always look to me as if they had forgotten something, and as if they must have that nightmarish
feeling of having arrived without their clothes in some public
place.

There are several forms of *C. longiflorus,* and I think I must
have at least two, for my two groups flower several weeks apart,
though they both face south in a warm section of the rock garden.
The first flowers in late October, the second in late November,
lasting until the rosy blooms of *C. laevigatus Fontenayi* make
their appearance. It is a very free-flowering species, several
blooms being produced from each set of sheathing leaves.

C. medius Balb.   B.R. t. 21
                                                           Maw t. 27

This is a bright and delightfully easy species that flowers early
in October. The flowers are a deep rich lavender-purple, and the
conspicuous forked scarlet stigmata remind one of those of the
Saffron Crocus. It increases rapidly, and always, barring the
attentions of rabbits, blooms prolifically. It is one of the naked
ones, the leaves with a wide white central line developing later,
and holding over until spring.

My bulbs lie beneath a mat of Aubrietia, whose dark foliage
serves as clothing for their lower parts. It is said to be limited in
distribution to a narrow belt of the Riviera in the neighborhood of
Spezia, and for the most part is found on the spurs of the mountains up to an elevation of about three thousand feet. "Near Mentone it has been found in the Holly wood on the northeast side of
the ridge beyond the cemetery and chapel of St. Lazarus." Commonly the flowers have a purple star in the throat formed by radiating lines, and the rare pure white variety, which I have not seen,
retains this distinguishing mark.

C. nudiflorus Sm. Maw t. 6

Parkinson, I believe, was the first to describe this species, in 1629. It is his "purple mountaine Crocus" or "purple Saffron flower of the Autumne," *Crocus pyrenaeus*, so it has been long an inhabitant in gardens; and it is said that in parts of England, chiefly in the midland counties, it may be met with growing wild in hilly pastures and meadows. It is one of the earliest of the autumnal species to flower, the new growth starting just after the corm has ripened and the vernal leaves have died away, its large warm purple flowers with scarlet stigmata appearing in this garden about the first of October. Mr. Bowles describes its curious and un-Crocuslike method of increase, by underground stolons so curiously shaped "that anyone seeing them for the first time might be pardoned for mistaking them for some evil form of stoloniferous grass, or even for the pupa of an insect." These stolons go wandering about at a considerable distance from the parent stock, and because of this roving disposition, it is important to plant them where they will not meet obstructions. For this reason the rock garden is a less happy home for them than the edge of some warm, sunny border. Newly planted corms do not always flower the first season, so disappointment should not be felt if there are no results for a year.

This is a Crocus of the Spanish group, occurring on both sides of the Pyrenees, and also in southern France about "Bayonne, Biarritz, Saint-Jean-de-Luz, the Landes and Pau. In Spain it occurs in the Asturias, near Gijó and Santander."

C. ochroleucus Boiss. & Gaill. *B.M.* t. 5297

Save for the rare Caucasian Crocus, *C. Scharojanii*, that flowers in August, there are no bright yellow-flowered autumnal Crocuses. *Ochroleucus* is a pale substitute, being a delicate cream-color, the throat stained with orange. The texture of the flower is thin, and altogether it is not very striking, but because it blooms late, almost as late as *laevigatus*, it is worth including in a collection. It is a southerner found "in Syria in very rocky places on the Phoenician coast, on Lebanon and Anti-Lebanon and in Galilee"; but it has proved quite hardy here, and I hear of it enduring much farther north.

C. pulchellus Herb.   B.R. t. 3
                                                             Maw t. 65

Though it comes leafless from the ground, this little Crocus
seems to need no embellishment. The segments are rather broad
and rounded, giving to the cup a most graciously rounded form.
The color is pure lilac of a lovely satin texture, almost invisibly
veined, with a deep yellow throat, white anthers, and orange-
colored stigmata. A neat and beguiling flower, one of the petti-
est, and it is as sturdy and satisfactory as it is pretty. This would
seem enough, but it adds to its other charms a delicate fruity
fragrance.

In this garden it begins to flower usually toward the end of
September, and is still going strong nearly a month later. It is
said to be abundant in heathy places and woods in the environs of
Istanbul, on both sides of the Bosporus, on Mount Olympus above
Broussa, in the hills behind Salonika and on Mount Athos, occur-
ring near sea level and up to four thousand feet above it.

C. Salzmannii J. Gay   B.M. t. 6000
                                                             Maw t. 9

Though it forms the largest corm of any Crocus, which gives
rise to hopes of something extra splendid, the flower is a disappointment, large but rather poorly colored, and thin in texture as
I have it here, and with narrow segments. It is hardy and enduring, but decidedly not one of the best. It flowers here about the
1st of October. Its native land is southern Spain, and it is found
also in Tangier, the only autumnal species, I believe, that is common to both Europe and Africa.

C. sativus L.   *Red. Lil.* t. 173
  Saffron Crocus   Maw t. 29

In "Hortus Floridus" [1] there is a beautiful drawing of the
Saffron Crocus, showing a wide-open flower with the long,
branched pistil lolling over the edge of the flower, and also a
bloom in the bud, showing the lovely cupped form. This is the
flower that has been cultivated since most ancient times for the

  [1] Crispin de Pass, 1614.

sake of the dried yellow stigmas, which were put to all manner of domestic uses, medicinal, culinary, as a dye and as a perfume. It was the *Karcom* of the ancient Hebrews, and was known to the ancient Greeks and Romans. "To the nations of Eastern Asia, its yellow dye was the perfection of beauty, and its odour a perfect ambrosia," [2] and one writer says that "not only saloons, theatres, and places which were to be filled with a pleasant fragrance, were strewed with this substance, but all sorts of tinctures retaining the scent were made from it, and the perfume was poured into small fountains, which diffused a highly esteemed odour. Even fruit and comfitures placed before guests, and the ornaments of the rooms, were spiced over with it." In the Song of Solomon we read, "Thy plants are . . . spikenard and saffron."

It is still widely grown commercially in Persia, as it was in the tenth century; also in Spain. When I went to South America, many of the dishes served us were flavored with Saffron, and very unpleasant I thought it. A dingy neighborhood of London still is known as Saffron Hill, and the town of Saffron Walden, in Essex, commemorates the flourishing Saffron industry once carried on there.

And so the Saffron Crocus is one of the most famous of flowers; but it is sadly disappointing in the garden. In the first place, it is indifferent to your best efforts in its behalf, flowering sparsely and seldom. Then its color is a poor reddish lilac and, though veined with deeper color, lacks character. If it were not for the flaming branched pistil, one would not notice it. It likes a good drying out in the summer, and when the weather is exceptionally hot, one may in the following year get some sort of display from the Saffron Crocus. There are numerous forms of it, but save for the sake of its antique interest, so to speak, it seems to me the Saffron Crocus is not worth growing.

C. speciosus Bieb.

B.M. t. 3861
Maw 64

This, on the other hand, is infinitely worth growing, all its ways are seemly, all its forms lovely. It has an extended range from northern Persia through eastern Asia Minor, the Caucasus, and

[2] *A Modern Herbal*, by Mrs. M. Grieve.

the Crimea to the province of Podolia, and into southern Russia. The flowers of the type are distinguished by their remarkable (for a Crocus) blue tone—it is the bluest of all the Crocuses—and they are very large, both the inner and the outer segments marked with fine veinings, while the stigmata are conspicuous for their size, and the fact that they are divided into a mass of orange-scarlet threads.

It is the first autumnal species to flower, and it is always startling when it comes bubbling through the earth, innocent of leaves, usually after a warm rain in late September. It is perhaps the most satisfying and satisfactory of autumnal Crocuses, hardy and enduring from year to year in a way to warm the heart, and increasing freely.

It has many forms and varieties, and all that I have seen are eminently desirable. We have Mr. van Tubergen to thank for the exquisite white form which, as I have it here, is not always quite white, but has sometimes the faintest flush of ashes of roses which serves to make it look even more ethereal. Fragile these flowers appear, as if a rough wind would cause them to dissolve, yet my group of them remains in good condition for quite three weeks, and always assiduously attended by bees.

The variety known as *Aitchisonii* is the largest of all the wild Crocuses. It opens starrily in the sunshine, and makes a fine effect despite the fact that it is paler in color and less strongly veined than others of the *speciosus* forms, and it blooms later than most of them. Last autumn they were still flowering after several hard frosts in late October.

Speciosus Atabar flowered a few days before the type, a large flower of soft "blue" coloring, deeper inside than out, and darkly feathered on the outside of the segments.

Speciosus Cassiope has a large flower that appears late. It is very blue in tone, with a faint yellow base, and altogether one of the best. *Speciosus Pollux*, that begins to bloom about October 7th, is perhaps the most showy of the group. It has immense flowers with bright blue-lavender outer segments with widely spaced lines of a deeper tone; the three inner segments are almost white, reticulated and veined with blue-purple. The stamens are bright orange-yellow. *Speciosus globosus* I have not grown, but it is described as bright blue and very late.

C. vitellinus Wahlenb. Maw t. 50

This bright native of Syria and Asia Minor has not proved constant in my garden, nor is it easy to procure. It flowered here for several seasons and then disappeared, and I have not since been able to find it listed. It is chiefly valuable for its late flowering and for its warm yellow color; nor must its fragrance be forgotten. Its leaves are contemporary with the flowers and are exceptionally narrow. Between them appears the small pointed bud, yellow with brown veinings, early in November, each corm producing from one to five flowers. Lovely for a sheltered nook in the rock garden.

C. zonatus J. Gay Maw t. 4

A few days after *speciosus* begins to flower, *C. zonatus* follows suit. Though fragile-appearing, it is quite stout and hearty in reality. It has lived in my rock garden for more than fifteen years. It flowers before the leaves, and when the little furled bud makes its appearance, it is of the palest silvery pink color; but as the sun warms it, and it gradually opens, the color deepens to a warmer pinkish lilac, and it will be seen by the observing that the segments are faintly veined and that there is a circle of gold spots in the throat. The anthers are cream-colored. It is a most satisfactory species, for it multiplies rapidly under cultivation, soon making broad patches that give much pleasure in the autumn garden. It is an alpine plant, found high in the mountains of Cilicia and on Lebanon and Hermon in Palestine.

If half a dozen autumnal Crocuses are to be chosen, they might inclue *zonatus*, *speciosus Pollux*, *pulchellus*, *longiflorus*, *medius*, and *cancellatus*. Herbaceous plants to grow with the autumn Crocuses are Japanese Anemones, *Chrysanthemum arcticum*, Plumbago, *Verbena venosa*, *Sedum Sieboldii*, and low mat-making plants with gray foliage.

CYCLAMEN *PRIMULACEAE*

SOMEWHERE in his writings I remember that Mr. Bowles says, "I have an insatiable desire for Cyclamen." Many persons in this country echo this sentiment, but because of the quarantine against the importation of plants, this desire is in a fair way to become a dangerous repression. Because of this ban, the little hardy Cyclamens are as scarce as the proverbial hen's teeth in the United States, and as expensive as rare gems, which, indeed, they are.

The quarantine took us unawares. Thousands of gardeners had no idea of what was afoot, or if they knew, had no realization of the crippling effect it would have upon the happy and innocent course of horticulture in the United States. It caught us, too, just when we were emerging from our horticultural adolescence, so to speak, when we were breaking away from the leading strings of old practices and beginning to sense the wide realms of delight that lay within our reach. Then the door closed, shutting innumerable treasures on the other side.

And so we are hobbling along behind the rest of the world, but patting ourselves on the back in the sturdy American way, because of our artistic arrangements and table decorations, instead of growing and showing the new and rare plants that are occupying the attention of the rest of the flower-growing world.

Now as I have done a good deal of complaining in print and out about Quarantine 37, it is only fair to say that there is something more than "meanness" and thoughtlessness behind it in this as in all other cases. Mr. B. Y. Morrison, who, as all the gardening world knows, is a collector and grower of rare plants, and who is in a position to know of the workings of the quarantine and what lies behind it, writes me that "the diseases of Cyclamen have already cost commercial growers a great deal of money." The commercial grower is, of course, chiefly concerned with *Cyclamen indicum*, and very big and bloated, and altogether horrible, he has made it; and presumably the little alpine species would be subject to the same diseases, and might act as carriers.

But how does the rest of the world combat this danger? Is it only under the Stars and Stripes that pests flourish, or do other countries maintain some sort of efficient examining boards at the ports of entrance so that infected material is not admitted? Doubtless all this will be set down by those in the know as what some one has called "my cedar chest of eminent misjudgments," but it does seem that a reconsideration in the case of some of the species of plants now excluded is in order.

When we read in English periodicals and books of the great charm and usefulness of the hardy Cyclamens as rock plants, and that "they are beautiful, too, for naturalizing under trees, in half open woodland, and in such shrub-shaded parts of the garden as produce a thin under-herbage," [1] and then contemplate our hard-won, stingy groups, if any, the sour dregs of envy are apt to be stirred. The one ray of light is that they may be raised from seed, and seed is easily procurable; but the process is a slow one. In the first place, fresh seed must be procured; even then, it germinates slowly.

A. J. Macself in "Plants from Seed" says: "The mountain species should be sown as soon as ripe, pressing the seeds half an inch deep, singly, an inch apart, in pans of peaty compost with an abundance of sifted porous rubble. Use charcoal to keep the soil sweet, and allow seedlings to form two leaves, then pot them in small 60's." The little tubers must be kept potted until they have reached the size of a five-cent piece, and always shaded and protected from pests of one kind and another. Then they are best planted out in their permanent quarters, and "permanent" is the right word. They hate being disturbed. Then we must wait until the tuber is of sufficient size and strength to produce flowers. It is worth while, all this trouble, but it does involve patience. I have seen it stated that a seed will produce blooms in a year. This simply cannot, I am sure, be true. Three years is more like it.

Once planted out in a snug shaded position, they should never be disturbed save for a reason so good as to be irrefutable. Daffodils and Crocuses increase by making other bulbs and corms, but the Cyclamen simply sits tight and gets fatter and wider and more prolific world without end. It may also sow its own seed. Tales of the size of Cyclamen tubers abound, like fish stories.

[1] *Rock Garden Plants*, by Clarence Elliott.

Mr. Bowles is said to have in his garden a tuber of *C. neapolitanum* which he knows to be more than sixty years old, the root so large that, according to his own testimony, it would not go into the crown of his hat. M. Correvon, in speaking of the ultimate of which a Cyclamen tuber is capable states, "I have one of the rare *C. Rolfsianum* from the Cyrenaic Desert weighing nearly a pound and measuring twelve centimeters broad and nine centimeters high." Mr. Stapely, of Staplehurst, England, has a *C. europaeum* forty years old which gave more than five hundred flowers! One exclamation point seems entirely inadequate.

For this reason, when and if you procure a few Cyclamen tubers, prepare a comfortable place for them in a shaded situation and leave them strictly alone. In their native haunts, they grow in light woods and thickets. The rock garden, on the shaded side, makes a good home for them, or they may be planted beneath small shrubs or deciduous trees.

As there is a period when they are not visible above ground, their stations should be marked. These little tubers are too precious to be left unguarded where injury from prodding fork or trowel is possible. The soil should be porous, a good loam with some humus and sand added, and a little lime. Set the tubers about two inches deep and four inches apart. An occasional top dressing of sandy loam mixed with a very little well rotted manure, is beneficial.

And now we come to the little plants themselves. It is a surprise to find them belonging to the Primrose family, for there is little likeness to the lay eye between the Cyclamens and the true Primroses, but to this family also belong the Shooting Stars, our Creeping Jenny, the Androsaces and other familiar garden flowers.

Nothing more unlike their gorged relatives of greenhouse and show bench could be imagined than the little mountain species with which we are here concerned. They are little and low, and beautiful leaves are the common possession of them all alike. The flowers appear in early spring or in late summer and autumn, in some species with the leaves, in others, without. The buds are carried singly on naked scapes, and have a funny little twist. The opened blossoms reflex. Their colors are in tones of pale to deep rose, and there are white kinds. Certain of them are richly fragrant for such small things. It is a small genus comprising only a few species, and restricted in range to southern Europe and western Asia. There is some confusion as to just how many kinds deserve specific rank, certain of them being regarded as mere forms of the others.

C. Atkinsii

This kind is generally believed to be a hybrid between *C. coum* and *C. ibericum*. The flowers are soft pink or may be white, and the leaves are indefinitely mottled with pale color. It flowers in spring, and is not hardy in my garden. The only time I was able to secure bulbs, they did not live over the first winter.

C. balearicum Willk. B.M. t. 8989

Described by Clarence Elliott as a most beautiful small species, with heart-shaped marbled leaves and pure white fragrant flowers. It grows only in the Balearic Islands, and is especially profuse in Majorca, where it is found throughout the island from the lower levels to near the summits of the mountains, usually in rich soil among rocks. Mr. Elliott says he has not found it hardy in his garden, so that it is suitable in this country for use only in the southern states.

C. cilicicum Boiss. & Heldr.

A form from the Cilician mountains and the pine forests of Asia Minor. It is said to bear in the autumn pale fragrant flowers with a purple blotch at the base of the petals, and rounded leaves with a silver zone.

C. coum Mill. B.M. t. 4

This is a dour little harbinger of the vernal season, appearing loath to give way to high spirits even when buds are forming and birds singing all about it. Its leaves are round and fattish and of a sombre unmarked green color, their darkness not much relieved by the small crimson-magenta blossoms that appear above them very early in the spring, almost as early as the Snowdrops. The leaves make their appearance in the autumn and last over the winter.

There is considerable difference of opinion as to the hardiness of this species. I have not been able to keep it here though I have twice had tubers of it, nor did it prove hardy in Mr. Lown's garden in Poughkeepsie; but Francis Lazenby of the Cambridge Botanic Garden, in an article in *Horticulture,* lists it among "Cyclamens hardy in the north," and again in *Horticulture* (February 1, 1933), W. Marshall Mackay of Ingersoll, Ontario, says, *"Cyclamen coum* has been a source of joy in the early spring."

Another instance of the advisability of trying things out for oneself. *Cyclamen coum* is an old plant in gardens. Parkinson calls it casually, "the common round-leaved Sowebread, named in the Apothecaries shops where an ointment is made from the juice, *Panis Porcinus."* Parkinson describes ten kinds of "Sowebread," including a double one which he says comes from Antioch. There is a white variety of *C. coum* which I have not seen.

C. europaeum L.   *B.R. t.* 1013

This is a wholly enchanting member of the genus. The leaves are in evidence for the greater part of the growing year. They are firm in texture and nicely marked with gray-green. The little rosy-red flowers smelling of Violets, and with their petals turned skittishly back, appear any time after the middle of July and often continue to appear well into October, though never many at a time.

It is widely distributed in central and southern Europe, and it is nice to read that instead of being known as the Bread of Sows, it is at least in some sections called more suitably, if it must be known as a food at all, *Patata della Madonna.* It is said to be very common in the mountains of Switzerland, and there it is known to children who gather fragrant bunches of it to offer tourists, as *Alpenveilchen* (Alpine Violet). It is perfectly hardy and enduring, given the right soil and a shaded situation. Recently a white form has been discovered, but that still hovers in the sphere beyond my wildest dreams. A fine little plant, the common rosy kind, to make a patch of color in the late summer rock garden.

C. graecum Link.

A species I have not seen, but it is described by Mr. Lazenby as being hardy in the north. It is said to be a native of northern Persia and southeastern Europe, and to have large, irregular tubers and leaves developing after the flowers are past. They are obscurely mottled and tinged with red on the undersides. It blooms in September, and the flowers are light to deep lilac, rarely white.

C. ibericum Goldie.

This species is of the spring bloomers, and has not proved hardy with me. It comes from the Caucasus, and is sometimes regarded as merely a form of *C. coum*, though the foliage is more or less obscurely silver-zoned, and the flowers white or various tones of lively rose. It is an altogether more cheerful-looking species than *coum*. I should like the chance to try it again.

C. neapolitanum Tenore
Ivy-leaved Cyclamen

Of all the species, this has the most beautiful leaves, far more beautiful than those of any Ivy. They are large and quite luxuriant in a small way, dark and rich and zoned with silver. They spring up in autumn after the little naked flowers have disappeared, and last over the winter, making a beautiful ground cover, and into the spring, a decoration in themselves. The dartlike buds of the flowers push through the earth in September and, opening, make the gayest small show, pink and rose and white. They are more exciting and amusing even than the autumn Crocuses.

Once I had a really fine plantation of them in the lee of an upright Yew, but the Yew broadened out and covered the Cyclamens, causing them to dwindle so that there was nothing for it but a new home. I dug them up with care, and gave them what seemed to me perfect conditions. But alas for poor human endeavor! This was three years ago, and since then they have done nothing but lift an occasional accusing leaf at me as autumn draws on. Never a blossom!

C. hederaefolium seems to be exactly the same as *neapolitanum*. It occurs to me that some of the tiny Daffodils might be planted among the tubers of the Neapolitan Cyclamen, *minimus* or *juncifolius*, for instance, to provide bloom in the spring, though perhaps the leaves of the Cyclamen might prove too great a handicap for these small and early venturers.

The best species for northern gardens are certainly *europaeum* and *neapolitanum*. The latter is said to grow on limestone hills in western and southern France from the eastern Pyrenees to Haute-Savoie and in Corsica and Italy. It is reported rare in Switzerland.

No account of the Cyclamens would be complete without a description of their ingenious manner of seeding, and no one could have these flowers in the garden without noticing their clever maneuvers to perpetuate their kind. When the flower fades, it drops off and seed is formed. "Nature then performs one of her miracles. The stem proceeds to coil itself up. Day by day another coil is added to the spiral until the seed capsule is brought close to the ground and, in fact, is often forced into the soil." This, suggests Reginald Malby in that delightful little book, "The Story of My Rock Garden," is a provision of nature to ensure the next generation, as, flowering late, or very early, the seeds would be exposed to all the inclement weather.

ERANTHIS *RANUNCULACEAE*

WINTER ACONITE

AMONG the most venturesome of late winter- or early spring-flowering plants are the Winter Aconites. They are a small genus of dwarf-growing perennials that spring from most unpromising looking small dark irregular-shaped tuberous roots that often, when received, resemble bits of old dried wood. The stems of leaves and flowers arise directly from the little tubers.

Often one sees the round, tightly folded flower bud protruding just above the soil while frosts are still bitter and snows fly in the air. I always want to push them back or cover them up, but somehow they seem able to weather whatever vicissitudes are sent them by the grim mother. As soon as they feel it to be safe, and long before we are so sanguine, up pushes the flower stem carrying its single round gold ball, which presently opens wide to look like a buttercup, with just below it, and forming a very pretty setting for it, a frill-like green involucral bract, which has been compared to an Elizabethan ruff. The palmately cut leaves are slow to make their appearance, usually hanging back until the flower is well developed.

After the flower has withered, and while seed is forming, the leaves make a charming ground cover where they are seen in quantity; but as soon as the work of seed-forming is over, the whole plant quickly and quietly dies away and is not seen until a mild spell in winter or early spring again sets its little green pulses to beating.

One hears of many disappointments where plantations of Winter Aconites have been attempted, and the reason is almost invariably that the tubers have been kept too long out of the ground. It is of the first and most imperative importance to secure them early, in July or August, and to put them into the ground at once. If planting is delayed until the usual September or October bulb-planting season, virtue will have gone out of them and few will sprout.

They may be naturalized in any shaded places, preferably beneath deciduous trees, though I have several plantations doing well under some white Pines where the soil must be quite acid, and this in spite of the fact that they are said to have a taste for lime. They grow well on shady banks where the soil is loose and friable, and where they are happy, self-sow freely after a time, and bright little colonies—those precious garden gratuities— spring up in the most unlikely places. I have several such that contend successfully with ramping Periwinkle. Once they are planted, they should not be disturbed—they do not like removal —but if it is necessary or desirable to change their place of residence, it is best to dig them up in sods with a spade while they are in bloom, and to place them immediately where they are wanted.

In new plantings, set the tubers about three inches deep and about four apart. Snowdrops are their boon companions and flourish under the same sort of conditions, and while they may be planted in the borders about the skirts of early-flowering shrubs, they are happiest when allowed to run wild in some spot that does not have to be too well ordered. Snowdrops and Winter Aconites and *Scilla bifolia* make a pretty effect when strewn together beneath the branches of the early Witch Hazels [1] or in the neighborhood of Pussy Willow bushes. [2]

E. *cilicica* Schott & Kotschy

As I grow it here, this species has reddish stems and the green "ruff" is composed of more finely divided sections than is that of the ordinary kind, and they are tinged with bronze, while the flower is a little larger and a little paler in color, but it seems to me a more delicate plant. My colonies increase slowly and flower a little later, seeming to hold back for better weather. It is nice for a succession, but it cannot compare to the common kind as a satisfactory garden plant. It comes from Asia Minor, and was introduced about twenty years ago.

E. *hyemalis* Salisb.

This is the commonest and best known of the Winter Aconites, but even so, it is absent from many a garden, despite the fact that

[1] *Hamamelis mollis.*   [2] *Salix discolor.*

it is far from being a newcomer. In 1633 Gerard wrote, "we haue great quantitie of it in our London gardens."

For centuries it has flashed its yellow cups in the face of tumultuous weather, kindling a responsive glow in the hearts of those who have ventured forth in search of signs of spring, and proving again and again old Gerard's assertion that "the colder the weather is, and the deeper that the snow is, the fairer is the floure and the warmer that the weather is, the lesser is the floure, and the worse coloured." The few times when a mild December has tempted this little flower forth in this garden, it has certainly been both small and poorly colored. Apparently hardship is its pleasure.

Parkinson called it the Winter's Wolfsbane, and noted its frequent custom of thrusting upward with a powdering of snow upon its head. Early writers generally assigned it to the genus Aconitum, to which belong the tall Monkshoods of our gardens. There is a lovely drawing of the Winter Aconite in the "Hortus Floridus" of Crispin de Pass.

It is a quaint little flower, neat and chipper, but it needs to be planted in quantities to make much of a show, and even then it takes years of self-sowing to bring about a really sensational display. Then begin with it at once in some shaded corner while your garden is young, so that when it is mature, you may go out on a late winter's day to view brave spreads of yellow beneath the bare branches of deciduous trees.

The Winter Aconites come into bloom at about the same time as the Snowdrops of the *nivalis* section, and as both like the same kind of situations, they may well be planted together. The Aconites grow only some three or four inches tall, and I have noted a curious thing about them. Often a warm interval will get them started into growth so that the yellow heads will appear just at the ground level; then cold again grips the world, and the yellow heads will remain sometimes for several weeks in exactly the same position and quite unharmed until another softening spell of weather allows them to edge upward a little farther.

Eranthis hyemalis is found growing wild in damp shaded locations in the Vosges, Jura, and the Alps of Dauphiny and Provence, and in central Europe as far east as Serbia. It is sometimes found at five thousand feet above sea level.

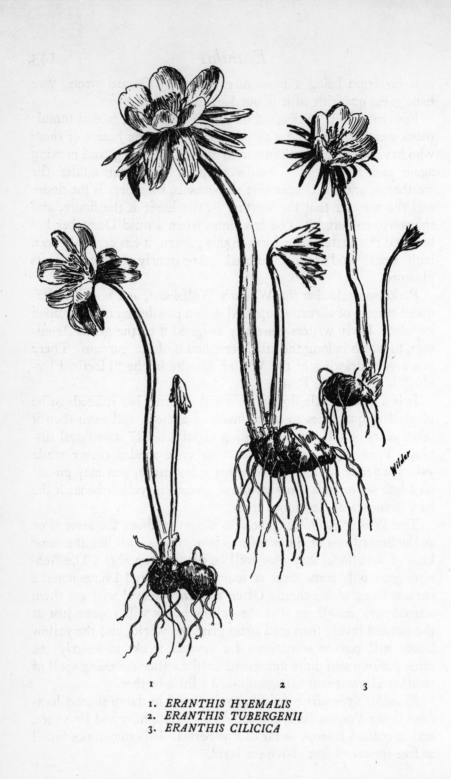

1. *ERANTHIS HYEMALIS*
2. *ERANTHIS TUBERGENII*
3. *ERANTHIS CILICICA*

E. Tubergenii   *Addisonia* Vol. XVI, t. 519

This is reputed a sterile hybrid between *E. hyemalis* and *E. cilicica,* and was raised in the nursery of the brothers Hoog, successors to their uncle, C. G. van Tubergen of Haarlem, Holland. When exhibited by the late Sir William Lawrence in 1924, it received an award of merit from the R.H.S., and created quite a sensation. Though it has grown in this garden only a few years, it has already asserted its superiority over the older kinds in size and richness of color.

The flowers are almost twice the size of *hyemalis* and look, before they are expanded, like yellow silk balloons balancing on their taller and sturdier stems in the shifting winds. Also they have a pleasant scent. The "ruff," or involucre, is bright green and sharply reflexed, and its parts are not so finely divided as in the other kinds. It is quite hardy, and if it proves fairly generous in increase, it will add much to the gaiety of spring, for it is certainly far more showy than either of its parents, and it lasts in perfection for several weeks.

ERYTHRONIUM *LILIACEAE*

Troutlily, Dog's-tooth Violet

The Erythroniums are among the most prepossessing plants belonging to the great Lily order, though they are small and modest in comparison with some of its members. They appear, indeed, like little Lilies, with their airy nodding reflexed flowers, but Lilies that have put off their traditional dignity and aloofness, and assumed, in the interest of true charm, a most seductive gaiety and sportiveness. I know of no more captivating group of bulbous plants, none more easily satisfied in the garden, none easier on the pocketbook. They are hardy in all parts of the United States and far to the northward, and surely deserve greater attention than is at present accorded them.

The leaves are almost as lovely as the flowers. They are wide and taper to a point, and while occasionally bright fresh green, they are more often handsomely mottled with various tones of brownish red. The flower stalk carrying one or more flowers rises between the broad twin leaves, usually topping them by several inches. They bloom in the early days of spring, and for a considerable period. Erythroniums may be naturalized on a wide scale in shaded, not too dry situations, or they may be scattered at the base of shrubs, or grown in small close colonies on the shaded side of the rock garden where they nod at one another with charming affability in the keen spring weather. They are, of course, most effective when seen in large congregations, fluttering and dancing in the breeze, like the Daffodils. A lightly wooded slope where the soil is deep and rich in humus, and slightly gritty, is ideal for them. The bulbs dry out quickly and deteriorate, so it is of the utmost importance to keep them out of the ground for as short a time as possible. They should be ordered in August and planted as soon as they arrive, which should be shortly after the 1st of September. If there must be delay, they should be stored in a cool place where they will not readily dry out. The long bulbs should be planted five inches below the surface of the ground—that is, there should be about three inches of soil above the top of the bulb—and from two to three inches apart, in irregular colonies. Collected bulbs are not always of a size to give a satisfactory result the first season, but successive springs will retrieve their reputation. They need not be replanted if flowering well. They are said to flourish in grass, but I have not so tried them. After flowering and setting seed, the whole plant dies away until another spring awakens it to life.

There is one European species, *E. Dens-canis*. The rest belong to North America, and one kind or another is to be found in almost any section of the United States and into Canada. The bulbs are long and white, and look remarkably like a dog's fang, which doubtless gave rise to the name of the sole European species, which means "dog's tooth," and thus to the common name by which it is almost universally known in this country. But why Dog's-tooth *Violet*, instead of Lily, is not clear, for there is no resemblance in any part of the plant to the Violet. The name was undoubtedly brought by the settlers from Europe, and applied to the species they found growing so plentifully here. In various parts of the country, they have acquired other trivial names—Troutlily, Adder's-Tongue, Fawn Lily, and the like.

THE SOLE EUROPEAN SPECIES

E. Dens-canis   *B.M.* t. 5

This species was introduced to cultivation about the year 1596. It grew in Parkinson's garden, who described it as appearing "after the winter frosts are past," and turning its petals back "after it hath felt the comfort of the Sunne," very much in the manner of a Cyclamen flower. The blooms of the typical form are a purplish rose and, as I have seen it in the garden of the late Clarence Lown in Poughkeepsie, rather smaller and less effective than any of the American species. But Stephen F. Hamblin of the Lexington Botanic Garden had some time ago a note in *Horticulture* which disagrees radically with my impression. "With all due respect," he writes, "to our two or more native species of troutlily, and the many good and showy species from the Pacific states, for ease of culture and amount of bloom, the European species, *E.*

dens-canis, has no equal. The bulbs are large, and may be moved in summer or in spring while in bloom, if kept moist. The leaves are mottled, the flower, one on the stalk, rose, purple or even dull red. It is the first to bloom, coming very early in April." There is a white-flowered form that was noted by Parkinson, and European catalogues offer named varieties.

The European Dog's-tooth Violet is found growing naturally in thickets and on wooded hills in the south and central sections of Europe, a lowland and subalpine plant distributed in the Apennines, southern Alps, Cévennes and the central plateau of France, Corbières, the Pyrenees, as well as in the Caucasus, Siberia, and Japan. In Switzerland it is found wild only in Tessin, though it has become naturalized about Geneva and in a few other localities.

It is propagated by offsets from the root, or may be raised from seeds. I do not know of its being offered in this country at the present time.

The Eastern American Species

These are found growing east of the Rocky Mountains. They all have one flower to a stalk, and the leaves may be mottled or plain.

E. albidum Nutt.

The white Troutlily of the East is a much rarer plant than the common yellow species next described. It is found in rich soil and partially shaded locations from Ontario to New Jersey, but more frequently in its western range to Texas and Minnesota. The leaves, though they may be indistinctly marbled, are as often free of such ornamentation. The flowers are white, usually delicately tinged with lilac, and have a yellow base. They are lightly fragrant. It grows in the well stocked garden of my neighbor, Herbert Durand, but I have never had it in mine. It is not often offered.

In the *American Botanist,* July, 1926, Willard Clute wrote of a double-flowered form of *E. albidum* that had been sent him from the neighborhood of Shelbyville, Illinois. The sender reported a colony "of about an acre in extent in which the flowers are completely double, in some cases with as many as twenty-four petals. Not only have all the essential organs turned to petals, but additional petals have appeared also. The ground in which the plants were growing is a hard black soil with little or no accumulation of leaf-mold." I wonder if this fat travesty on the winsome white Troutlily still exists. It sounds as stodgy as a double-flowered Lily-of-the-Valley.

E. americanum Ker-Gawl. *B.M.* t. 1113
   Adder's-Tongue

All spring wayfarers in country districts are familiar with the mottled leaves and fluttering yellow flowers of the Adder's-Tongue. They crowd every dampish copse over a wide range of country from New Brunswick to Florida, and westward to Ontario and Arkansas. Wherever it is found at all, it is usually in vast numbers, for it increases rapidly by means of offsets on slender underground runners, and also by seeding. The flowers in these aggregations are, in comparison with the leaves, unfortunately few, which is a pity, for they are sprightly and pretty. So prolific is their increase that they are not among the wild plants requiring protection, but because of their assiduity in the matter of leaf-making and their stinginess with blooms, they are not worth bringing into the garden. They are better left to the spacious countryside, where their fluttering blossoms and handsome foliage are always a welcome sight. The flower is sensitive to light, and toward night almost closes, while during the day it will be seen to turn upon its stalk in order to keep within the sphere of the sun's warmth. It has a faint, earthy fragrance which is quite manifest if a large bunch is placed in a warm room. Their companions in the wild are Spring Beauties, Bloodroot, Violets, and other early friends.

E. mesachoreum Knerr.

This is a species found on the prairies of western Iowa, Missouri, Kansas, and Nebraska. The leaves are not mottled and it makes no offsets, spreading, I read, by means of seeds only. The flowers are purplish lavender, and the petals are only slightly turned back at the tips.

E. propullans Gray

Found from Ontario to Minnesota, the flowers of this species are rather pinker in tone than those of the above plant and are yellowish at the base. The leaves are uncommonly narrow, and only faintly marbled, and the increase is made by means of offsets formed near the middle of the underground stem. I do not know of these two central western species being offered by the trade, though they must be well known in their respective localities.

WESTERN SPECIES

Well enough as are our eastern Erythroniums, those who know the race only by these representatives can form no idea of the grace and charm and colorfulness of these flowers when they cross the Rocky Mountains and make toward the Pacific Ocean. The far western species are infinitely superior to the eastern—larger of flower, more floriferous, taller of stalk, handsomer of leaf, while their colors range brightly from pure white through cream and yellow almost to orange, and from blush to bright waxen pink to mauve, often zoned with contrasting colors like a band of Persian embroidery. Many years ago, when my first plantation of western Erythroniums flowered in a bit of woodland at the edge of my garden, I was quite breathless with excitement. Nothing I had read had prepared me for their gentle beauty. It seemed, indeed, as if fairyland had materialized under my bungling touch; that the exquisitely tinted elfin flowers swaying before me were creatures of some fabulous land:

> Aerial spirits, by great Jove designed
> To be on earth the guardians of mankind.

And each spring I am enchanted anew. With but two exceptions, they have proved, moreover, to be the most friendly and reliable of garden citizens, and given the consideration of the shade of deciduous trees, and a deep humus-filled soil, quite as ready to add to the glamour of the spring in the conditions prescribed by eastern lowland conditions as in the high valleys and on the mountain slopes of their native west country. Of all the western bulbs, they are the most easily grown in eastern gardens, and they are quite hardy in all parts of the United States, and probably in Canada. They are so wholly bewitching that I would urge all gardeners to make a trial plantation in some shaded place without delay.

With few exceptions, the western Erythroniums increase by means of seeds only and not by offsets from the bulbs. Thus the increase will be slow, for it takes about four years for a seedling to reach blossoming strength; but it will also be sure, for under congenial conditions, seed is produced and scattered freely, and given a little time, fine plantations will result.

Two kinds, *E. Hartwegii* and *E. Purdyi*, have heavily coated bulbs that enable them to withstand the drying conditions above ground for a longer period than the others; but it must again be urged that the bulbs be ordered early and planted as soon as received, for the longer they are exposed to the air, the poorer will be the display, if any, of blossoms in the coming spring. If there must be delay in planting, keep them in a cool place covered with slightly moist moss or earth. Mr. Purdy, who has been responsible for introducing these bulbs far and wide in our own land and abroad, enjoins us, also, that they must not be planted when the ground is dry: "I have lost many bulbs by planting in dry ground, or by planting in moist ground which, during a long fall drought, lost its moisture." Thus we learn to plant when the soil is moist, and to keep it artificially moist if the natural rainfall fails. Once the bulbs are established, they are able to take in their stride, and without harm, such droughts as Heaven sends.

Let me here urge that no one try to save expense by buying Erythroniums from department stores or from any shop where they have been exposed to the drying air in open bins and boxes. Such bulbs will be no good at all, and why court disillusion and disappointment? The bulbs may be purchased at an amazingly low cost from reliable dealers who will send them in good condition for planting.

Over a period of many years I have collected all the kinds of western Erythroniums I could find, and in only two cases have I met with a lack of ready coöperation on the part of the bulbs. *E. montanum*, the Avalanche Lily, is notoriously difficult away from its mountain slopes, and has refused even to make a first appearance in my garden, and I have not been conspicuously successful with *E. parviflorum*. But by no means am I discouraged to the point of giving them up entirely.

E. californicum Purdy
California Fawn Lily. Easter Lily

This is an extremely handsome species found in open woods and on shrubby hillsides of the Coast Ranges, from Mendocino to Lake County in California. Its color is that of rich cream deepening to yellow at the base, and it bears from two to several flowers on a stalk. The leaves are showily mottled and of firm texture. A lovely form of it was discovered by Carl Purdy in 1930, and is known as *E. c. bicolor*. The outer portion of this flower is cream-white, but within, it is a soft glowing yellow with bright golden stamens. This was found in the southernmost section of the range of the species and may, Mr. Purdy thinks, prove to be the finest Erythronium in cultivation. It is indeed a lovely flower, and has as an added charm, a very pleasing fragrance. There is also *californicum* White Beauty, *pure* white only in contrast with the creamier forms, and made to appear even more candid in contrast with the maroon band in the throat. "In the wild it only grows in very rocky places, and even in the fissures of rocks. At one point I saw fine flowering bulbs in the fissures of an almost perpendicular cliff. It takes to ordinary soil wonderfully well, and van Tubergen, one of the best European authorities, considers it the best garden erythronium."[1] It is found in the extreme northern range of the species, in Humboldt County, California. Flowers in mid-April.

E. citrinum S. Wats.

This is a local species found only in the Siskiyou Mountains of southern Oregon and in Tuolumne County, California. It is somewhat dwarfer in stature than the last-named species, but very upstanding and sturdy. The flowers are cream-white deepening to yellow at the center and strongly reflexed. The leaves are handsomely marbled. As the flower ages, it turns pinkish at the edges. An easy species if given cool conditions and drainage, flowering here just after the middle of April. Propagated by seeds.

[1] Carl Purdy, in *National Horticultural Magazine*, July, 1931.

ERYTHRONIUM CALIFORNICUM   **CHIONODOXA TMOLI**

E. grandiflorum Pursh.
    Snow Lily. Easter Bells

This is always the first species to blossom in my garden, often opening its bright yellow, pleasantly fragrant flowers before the end of March, and always very early in April. It is an arresting plant with a most elegant and imperious carriage, seeming to droop its bright, Lily-like flowers with some condescension from the tall erect stalks. The leaves are shining, unmottled green. Although it maintains itself year after year in this garden, making its appearance punctually with the earliest flowers, its increase has been very slow, if any. Mr. Purdy is of the opinion that the form named by him *robustum*, which was found at low elevations along the Columbia River, is easier to handle in the garden. I have not had the bulbs long enough to prove them. *E. grandiflorum* is a true mountaineer, always found at high elevations. It is frequent on slides and mountain slopes from the Rockies in Colorado into Canada and westward to the summits of the Cascades. In its native haunts, it blooms along the skirts of the melting snows (hence its vernacular name), and the individual flowers are almost as fleeting as snow under a warm sun. The white form of *E. grandiflorum*, known as *album* or *albiflorum*, I have never seen. It is said to haunt the plateau regions of northern Idaho and eastern Washington. The flower is reported to be white with a faint greenish cast. If it has the proud poise and early-flowering habit of its yellow sister, it would be a real acquisition. I do not remember to have seen it offered.

E. Hartwegii S. Wats.   *B.M.* t. 7583

Found on hot, shrubby hillsides of the Sierra Nevada in California, this species will endure more sun in the garden than most other Erythroniums; in fact, where planted in quite dense shade, it died out with me; and because of the heavily coated bulbs, this species, with *E. Purdyi*, is less sensitive to the drying air before being planted than others of its kind. Its keeping qualities, according to Mr. Purdy, are about equal to those of the Tulip. It also has the distinction, rare in western Troutlilies, of increasing by means of offsets borne on slender underground stems, so that in a short time it makes nice colonies. In appearance it is something in the way of *californicum*, creamy-white running to orange-yellow at the base. The flowers are borne in a cluster, each one hung from a long pedicel, which creates a misleading appearance of solitariness. The effect of a mass in flower is very blossomy and showy. The leaves are strongly mottled, and it is a good doer in the garden.

E. *Hendersonii* S. Wats.   *B.M.* t. 7017
    Pink Troutlily

This is one of the friendliest and most captivating of the race. It is found in grassy valleys and on low hills "on either side of the Oregon-California border for perhaps fifty miles and well back from the ocean." In eastern gardens it is a reliable plant, appearing every year with increased vigor, the strongly reflexing flowers forming veritable fountains of bloom. To the casual eye the flowers appear to be pinkish lilac in color, but closer inspection reveals the band of "Persian embroidery" in the throat, surrounded by a narrow gleaming white zone. It flowers here just before *Hartwegii* gets under way, and the two make good companions if the situation is not too sunny.

E. *Howellii* S. Wats.

The differences between this and *E. citrinum* are very slight and are not important to the horticulturist. They are found in the same localities, and save that *Howellii* is more quick and thorough in turning from cream to pink, I can see little difference between them.

E. *montanum* S. Wats.
    Avalanche Lily

A perverse beauty, this Avalanche Lily of the "timberline parks on Mount Rainier, where it pushes up almost through the snow, to cover the meadows with dancing myriads of dainty, clear white orange-centered lilies of comparatively huge size." [2] I have seen photographs of it behaving in just this manner, and one would think that a plant that grows in such riotous profusion at home would at least be tolerant to the point of staging a small show in other localities. But my experience of utter failure with the Ava-

[2] *Western American Alpines*, by Ira Gabrielson.

lanche Lily is borne out by growers far more capable than I can claim to be. It is seemingly an incorrigible wilding. Mr. Purdy says: "My experience is that it is utterly intractable in cultivation. Instead of starting growth with moisture in spring as all others do, it lies dormant until its usual growing season, which is July or August when it meets (in lowland gardens) utterly hopeless growing conditions." It meets no conditions at all in my garden, for it does not so much as what we used to call "stir a stitch"; but one day some horticultural sorcerer will make this maddening Circe change her habits, or will find a way of getting round them. In the meantime, we may dream of the high valleys of the Olympics described by Ira Gabrielson, thronged with the pale Sirens, and every peak and volcanic cone in the Cascades boasting its own fairyland when the Avalanche Lily is blooming. The leaves, I believe, are broad and of an unmottled clear bright green.

E. parviflorum Goodding
Glacier Lily

The Glacier Lily is by some botanists considered as a form of *grandiflorum* from its easternmost range in the Rocky Mountains, and by others as a distinct species. It is dwarfer with me than *grandiflorum*, but the blossoms are of the same unblemished yellow, the leaves clean unmottled green. The anthers are russet color, but Mr. Purdy avers that this is not by any means the invariable case. It flowers early in its chosen Rocky Mountains close to the forbidding rivers of ice, hence its common name. Its behavior here is the reverse of enthusiastic, whatever I do for it. It lingers on for a season or two, usually blossoming down its throat, so to speak, or when it is only half out of the ground, between the two green leaves, as if it could not get up the energy to face the awful conditions of my garden; then shortly there comes a spring when it does not make even this slight effort. I am not, however, by any means through with the Glacier Lily, though it has every appearance of being through with me. The Avalanche Lily I have almost given up, but those little throaty appearances of the Glacier Lily keep me spurred to greater effort. But I sometimes think how presumptuous we are to call a plant from those high, snow-haunted fields to our muggish lowland gardens and expect it to live. When it does, we have not been skilful—we need not swell with pride. It is merely that the gentle god who watches over the prayerful activities of earnest gardeners, thinks it time they had a break. Let us call it a miracle, for such it is.

E. Purdyi

When Mr. Purdy's lovely Troutlily, sent to me by this generous and accomplished gardener, first flowered in my garden, I was enchanted; and I still am. It is a beauty, a friendly beauty this time, ready to do its best far from its native foothills of the Sierra Nevada in California. Its range is the same as that of *Hartwegii*, and it belongs in the same group, a group of two with coated bulbs that increase as do the eastern species and the European *Denscanis*, by offsets. Its pure white flowers faintly yellow in the throat are very lovely, and exceptionally graceful. It thrives in the garden, and as in its natural habitat there are no shades, it may be brought out from beneath the trees and given a place in at least half sunshine. The leaves are richly mottled. I think it decidedly one of the most valuable.

E. purpurascens S. Wats.

Though named by Abrams the Purple Fawn Lily, as I have it here, it has not color enough to justify this description. It is a curious little flower—a sort of gnome among Troutlilies—much smaller and dwarfer than any of the others, and of a sort of light greenish yellow with only a hint of purple manifest in an indefinite livid suffusion. There are from one to three flowers on a stem, and they open to wide bells in the sunshine, reflexing very little. The leaves are light green and unmottled save for a reddish patch at the base where they clasp the stem, and they are very much fluted or waved along the edges. It came to my garden in 1934, so is not an old friend; and if it disappears I shall not mourn. It is said to grow naturally high up in the Sierra Nevada, a region of heavy snowfalls and late springs, and is usually found in moist granite soil.

E. tuolumnensis

A distinct departure among Erythroniums, this species was discovered, according to Mr. Purdy, by Professor Applegate of Stan-

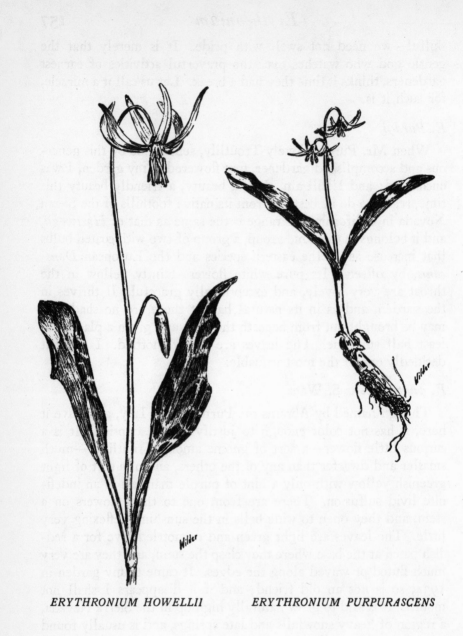

ERYTHRONIUM HOWELLII   **ERYTHRONIUM PURPURASCENS**

ford University in 1930, "and is limited to a very small area in Tuolumne County in the Sierra Nevada region of California at about three thousand feet elevation." It is more curious than beautiful, and lacks the winsome grace of the race generally. The bulbs are remarkably large and cone-shaped and, again according to Mr. Purdy, offset like a Tulip with the offsets inside the covering of the mother bulb. I have not had it long enough to know what its behavior will be under prolonged lowland conditions, but it has come through the past three very cold winters safely, and blossomed almost as early as *grandiflorum*, remaining in good condition for several weeks. The leaves are large and of rather thick texture, unmottled, broadly fluted, and almost erect. The flowering stem is from twelve to fourteen inches high, and three smallish flowers of a deep orange color, nodding to horizontal and bell-shaped, are carried by each stem. They have much the appearance of a Fritillaria. It takes a very warm sun to cause the flowers to lose their belled form and to flare more expansively. A collector would want this species, but one who grows flowers for their beauty alone would not, I think, give it space.

The Revolutum Group

The types of Erythroniums that come under this head are without doubt the aristocrats of the clan. One has but to observe the taller and stouter stems, the large firm-textured flowers, from one to four to a stem, their proud bearing and the opulent, superbly mottled leaves, to know that here is something special. They are the latest of the Troutlilies to blossom, beginning here toward the end of April; and as they offer something special in the way of beauty to the eye of the beholder, so they ask something rather special in the way of culture. Yet they are not difficult. They merely expect to have their perfectly reasonable necessities satisfied.

In Mr. Purdy's very comprehensive article, "Erythroniums" (in the *National Horticultural Magazine*, July, 1931), which I have had occasion to quote several times, he describes their home surroundings in this wise: "The forms of *E. revolutum* have quite different habitats from any other western species. They are found in decidedly moist soils, and prefer a rich loam. In the rainy season the soil is often quite moist and wet. I have seen beds over which a little stream flowed for months in the early season, and often have dug them when ripe in soil which was so wet as to be sticky." In this garden they have flourished for years in rather heavy soil at the north side of the rock garden. The soil in summer is apt to be on the dry side; but in winter and spring it is moist almost continuously. There is also a small plantation in my tiny wood which is dryer, as it is also shadier, but these too have remained in a satisfactory condition and flower well. In moist locations they are better off when the ground remains frozen over the winter so that they are not subjected to the brutal experience of alternate freezing and thawing.

The forms of *E. revolutum*, while very distinctive in appearance, vary in color in the different localities where they are found. The range begins less than a hundred miles north of San Francisco, and about twelve miles inland from the Pacific Ocean, "a region of heavy rainfall and many summer fogs," and continues northward through Oregon and Washington, never very far from the sea, well into British Columbia.

The kinds that I have grown here are the following: *E. revolutum*, the type. This is the form found farthest south, in Mendocino County, California. The stems are strong, and occasionally reach a height of eighteen inches, though they have not done so here. The flowers, usually several to a stem, are large and very pale, almost white, upon opening; but, as they mature, become suffused with a delicate lilac flush.

Pink Beauty is indeed well named. The color is a soft lilac-pink, a most gentle and tender hue, and the flowers are of fine form and texture. This comes from Humboldt County, California. Rose Beauty is new in my garden, and a recent introduction. Its form and habit are those of Pink Beauty, but its hue is a much purer pink, and it flowered here almost ten days earlier. The leaves are darkly marbled, and its range begins almost a hundred miles farther north. *Johnsonii* is a species from the near-coast region of Oregon. To me it is the most beautiful of the group, and as it has endured the not too perfect conditions offered in this garden for nearly ten years, I am inclined to pronounce it a very reliable kind. The flowers are pure pink and almost waxen in texture with a contrasting yellow center. Purdy's White has

lost itself among the other forms in my garden, but it is said to be
a large bold flower, almost pure white and richly marked at the
base with dark color. *Praecox* is one that has lived in this garden
for many years. It flowers considerably earlier than the other
forms. The leaves are handsomely mottled, and the flowers are
creamy-white, richly banded with dark color at the base. Both
Purdy's White and *praecox* are said to be forms of *E. Watsonii*,
sometimes and erroneously known as *E. giganteum*. Mr. Purdy
is of the opinion that this kind should be considered a separate
species. "It has," he says, "the mottled leaves, the stout stems,
the large auricles and the broad based filaments of the type, yet it
is not nearly so stout a plant, nor so erect." It has numerous forms,
and is said to be a most graceful plant. I have not grown it. Its
range begins fifty miles south of the Oregon-California border,
and extends north "in the moist interior, west of the Cascades section, far into British Columbia." All these Erythroniums are
quite hardy in any section of our country as well as in Canada.

Though the group name *revolutum* indicates a markedly Lily-
like form, this is not the fact when the flower opens: it is then
more bell-like. But as it matures, the segments turn backward
until the name is justified.

FRITILLARIA *LILIACEAE*

FRITILLARIA is the problem child of the Lily family. I was on the point of saying the bad child, but bad children are not recognized in modern child psychology—only unadjusted ones.

So in the plant world. If the Fritillarias do not act as we think they should—and they almost invariably do not—it is not because there is an inherent venial streak in their characters, but because we have failed to provide the environment proper to bring out the best that is in them. But there are few guides to success with these flowers, and a burning and ever present question is, what *is* the proper environment?

Whenever I contemplate the genus Fritillaria, the trenchant words carved upon the beam beneath which Montaigne wrote, come to mind:

I do not understand;
I pause; I examine.

But I go further. I almost give up, but not quite, for there is something extraordinarily provocative about the members of this wary, sad-hued race. One pursues them almost without volition, and in the face of discouraging and long continued lack of success, and with no apparent coöperation on the part of the Fritillarias.

I have been fussing about among them for more years than I care to count; yet all I have to say is that, while they still intrigue me, they seldom do what they ought to do, what I hope they will do, what I am told they will do, even when I, myself, have done all I can possibly do to make them comfortable. Their ways are altogether unpredictable; indeed, what follows is rather an attempted analysis of failure than a success talk, yet I have had my golden moments with Fritillarias, as when the pale green bells of *F. armena* flowered in an amazing likeness of my mental picture of them, or that other time when our western *F. recurva* gave a magnificent exhibition of flaming youth.

Of course one can nearly always depend upon the *meleagris*

group, and often upon the Crown Imperials, and for these two we should be thankful and take heart in our efforts to please the others.

Another obstacle obtrudes itself in the path of the would-be grower of these plants. It is extremely difficult to acquire anything like a representative collection for study and comparison. Fewer than half the known species, I read, are in cultivation, and of the thirty or so that appear from time to time in catalogues, very few are known save to a narrow group of obdurate gardeners with a yen for conquest.

There are thirty-two species enumerated in the Kew Hand-List, but very few of these are readily available, and very little exact information concerning their needs is obtainable. Leafing through the "Lily Year Books" of the Royal Horticultural Society yields some valuable information concerning them, and in *The New Flora and Silva* for April, 1931, is an interesting discussion of them by Mr. A. Grove. Mr. Grove says that Max Leichtlin in his day and Henry Elwes in his, both ardent bulb growers, gave much attention to Fritillarias, and met with some success; but the genus still awaits a gardener "more clever and determined than the rest who will rise up and prove himself at once the master and the monographer of the race, who will take the genus in hand and do for it what has been done for Crocuses, Irises, Lilies and the rest." Mr. Grove compares them to birds of passage in British gardens. It is barely possible that we, with our dry hot summers, may in time learn to please them better than can our accomplished cousins across the water, for a summer baking is what most of them undoubtedly require.

Mr. Farrer in "The English Rock Garden" is discouraging. "Many of the race," he says, "are very miffy or mimpish, or both, and the family all round has a bad character. Not to mention— a fact which catalogues rarely do—that an enormous number of Fritillarias have more or less stinking bells of dingy chocolate and greenish tones, which often appear transfigured by the enthusiasm of those who desire to get rid of them as rich purple or amaranthine violet."

Can it be that Mr. Farrer was a poor loser, and that he could see no beauty in plants that resisted his blandishments? He allows beauty to a few members of the race, but quite fails to emphasize the curious elegance that is the character of nearly all of them, even those of the gloomiest coloring. Garb themselves as they may in tones of brown and mulberry and green, often mottled, streaked, or checkered—toad-colored, says Jason Hill—none that I have seen (and I have seen a good many in passing) could be called dowdy, and all have been remarkable for an indefinable distinction of bearing—a look of race. They may be gloomy, but it has to be admitted that they "do their gloom awfully well."

The flowers are bell-shaped, and many of the kinds have an unusual square-shouldered or rectangular form, and the pointed buds of some species suggest the head of a snake. They have a curious darting pose as of a reptile about to strike. The foliage is often silvery or pale green in lovely harmony with the strange-hued blossoms. When a single radical leaf is sent up, it means that, as in the case of Tulips, they do not intend to flower.

Fritillarias are native to the north temperate zone, so they may be assumed to be pretty generally hardy. "The genus begins," says Mr. Grove, "on the Atlantic side of Europe, crosses Asia and ends on the Pacific side of North America." There are something over a hundred species known.

With all the Fritillarias, early planting is desirable. Deterioration soon sets in if the bulbs are left long out of the ground; and at least with the Asia Minor species, and those that stand sunshine, it is desirable to have a good percentage of lime in the soil. During active growth, all should have ample supplies of water at the roots, and it is for this reason, rather than for the desirability of shade in itself, that so many will do well in a north border in lighter soil which do equally well under a south wall in more retentive loam.[1]

The bulbs are increased by means of offsets taken early in autumn, but frequent disturbance, if they are doing well, is not to be recommended. If replanting is necessary, it should be done quickly, the bulbs lifted and reset immediately, before they have had long exposure to the air.

Certain species ripen seed freely; but the process of raising the bulbs from seed is a long one, most kinds requiring from four to six years to reach blossoming strength. Altogether, these plants

[1] R. W. Wallace.

tax one's patience in many ways, but they are occasionally very rewarding and always interesting.

Some of the species belong in borders, some in the rock garden, a few in the wild garden and naturalized in grassy places, and certain of them are usually grown in pots under glass. September is the best time to plant them out of doors. The roots then have time to form before winter. All are spring-blooming, flowering before the middle of May.

The soil most generally recommended is a good sandy loam. Some of the kinds are woodland plants, and these should be given shade; others that come to us from hot countries will stand full sun.

Alien Species

F. acmopetala Boiss. *B.M.* t. 6321

This is one of the more tractable members of the foreign group and, given a limy soil, free drainage, and partial shade, may settle down contentedly to long residence in the rock garden. It is said to have been introduced by Mr. Elwes from western Syria in 1874. The bulbs are composed of fleshy scales, like those of a Lily, and from these the grayish stems arise to a height of about a foot, ornamented with linear alternate leaves of the same glaucous tone, and surrounded by a solitary bell with pointed, slightly reflexing, petals. The color scheme is somber, an indescribable blend of blackish purple and low-toned green. Mr. Elwes is quoted as having said, "If only the colour of the petals were more distinguished, it would be one of the best plants in the garden . . . another good perennial Fritillary for limy and calcareous soils, and most obligingly lavish of seeds."

F. armena Boiss. *B.M.* t. 6305

The flowering of this species gave me a distinct thrill. What is there about a green flower that is so arresting, other than its rarity? And the green of *armena* is so lovely, both of the leaves and of the flowers, which are almost of the same silvery tone. The slender stems arise to a height of about nine inches clothed with narrow leaves, and from the top dangles the cone-shaped bell, the green segments having a yellow selvage. Filaments, stigma, and ovary are green, the anthers yellow and arranged compactly about the style, which protrudes a little below the flaring bell. It is a really enchanting flower, one of most unusual grace and distinction, Lily-like in its obvious, if modest, pride of bearing.

I planted it first in a cold frame and there it flowered. Then I removed the bulbs to the rock garden, where it flowered again; but the next spring it did not appear. Probably I gave it too sunny and dry a situation. According to Mr. Farrer this species, sent me by van Tubergen of Haarlem, Holland, as *armena*, should rightly be *F. Sibthorbiana* (*armena*, according to him, being a "dingy, lurid purple-flowered plant, of low stature."

F. Sibthorbiana seems to be a Greek, and Johnson's *Gardener's Dictionary* gives its height as six inches, its color as yellow. Thus I am confused as to its true identity, and must grow it under the name of *armena* until I can get more accurate identification.

F. askabadensis Micheli. B.M. t. 7850

This Caucasian species is mine only in the spacious realm of the imagination. I have never seen it in the flesh. It was introduced in 1902 by the late Miss Ellen Willmott, author of "The Genus Rosa," and owner of a most enchanting garden. It is described as "a refined and fragrant edition of the Crown Imperial." Ralph Arnold in comparing it to the Crown Imperial says: "It is quite as tall, and with more charming port than that well known plant. The stem is more slender, the leaves narrower, and the flowers smaller. From a strong specimen, as many as eighteen flowers are produced, varying in color in different plants from white or almost white to sulphur. They exhale a distinct and delicious scent." [2] It is said to flower early, to be quite hardy, but likes shelter from the cold winds of spring, as well as from the hottest suns. It sounds like a good sort, and one that would make an admirable border plant, especially for those who cannot abide the strong odor of the Crown Imperial.

F. aurea Schott.

In case the inquiring reporter should approach me, I should have to admit that here is another species that I cherish in the mind's eye. Though I did get as far as planting the bulbs. It is

[2] *Gardening Illustrated*, Apr., 1933.

not considered a difficult species, and the bulbs seemed sound; but I got nowhere with it—the bulbs did not even sprout. Probably some of its crotchets were not considered. *F. aurea* should be hardy, for it comes from the alpine pastures in Cilicia.

It was first introduced by Max Leichtlin, and it is obviously one that would be useful in the rock garden. Mr. Farrer was moved to say that it is "perfectly beautiful . . . of a soft canary yellow, faintly checkered with more or less brown," and Mr. Grove describes its habit of growth as curiously like that of the common Snowdrop, and says that when it is planted, as it should be, in colonies, it is the most effective of the dwarf Fritillarias, and rather more sure of its color than most of the yellow-petaled species. It is not always offered, but is worth shopping about for. There is a good photograph of it in *The New Flora and Silva* (April, 1931).

F. camschatcensis Ker-Gawl.
Black Lily

The Black Lily is a strange somber flower with a roving foot. Across Kamschatka, Siberia, Mongolia, Japan, it wanders, and turns up on the other side of Bering Straits in Alaska, where it is by some botanists considered as a form of the North American species, *F. lanceolata*. Its dark bells dangle on stems from nine inches to a foot and a half tall, the lower leaves whorled about the stem, with a narrower extra leaf or two toward the top. They are shining and of good texture. It is not a difficult species to please if given a somewhat moist soil, or a good deal of shade, but the dark bells hang gloomily in the face of smiling May. It looks an ill tempered flower and out of tune with the gay season in which it elects to bloom.

I have read that this is quite a common plant in old European gardens, where it is known under the name of Black Seranna, and where it plays a sort of game, disappearing from time to time only to come up again greatly to the surprise of the owner of the garden. It is also recommended for the moraine.

A. citrina Baker

This is an altogether delightful little species from Asia Minor. The slenderest of gray-green stems, embellished with narrow gray-green leaves, reaches a height of some six or eight inches, and then dangles a dainty bell, sometimes a pair of them, flaring and soft yellow, save for a few greenish spots on the lower part of the petals. The petals are neatly rounded so that the little bells are evenly scalloped. This is a small choice plant for a sheltered, partially shaded nook in the rock garden. It needs to be seen in little close colonies to be effective. It flowers in early May. It may commonly be had of van Tubergen, of Haarlem, or of R. Wallace, The Old Gardens, Tunbridge Wells, England.

F. imperialis L.   *B.M.* t. t. 194, 1215
    Crown Imperial

This "jocund herb," this super-bulbous plant, has been at once the splendor and the despair of my garden experience. True to the traditions of its race, it pleases when it pleases, and withholds when it feels that way. It has the honor of being the first plant mentioned in Parkinson's "Paradisus." It is there called *Corona Imperialis*. How sonorously the syllables roll from the tongue—how perfectly the name fits the plant! Parkinson, the grand old gardener of the early seventeenth century, says it deserves to be "entreated of" before all other Lilies, "The Crowne Imperiall for his stately beautifulness, deserueth the first place in this our Garden of Delight."

A native of the East, probably of Persia, it was introduced, according to Dodonaeus, into the gardens of the Emperor and of some of the nobility at Vienna in 1576. It speaks eloquently of the rapidity with which plants got round from one enthusiast to another in that far day when transportation was slow and difficult, and news was transmitted chiefly from person to person, that in a scant fifty years or so after the Crown Imperial had entered the gardens of the Emperor, Parkinson could write of it as being "so well knowne to most persons, being in a manner euery where common," that it was necessary to give only a brief description of it. It must, indeed, have taken the eye of those gardeners of old, and one wonders if ever before (or since, for that matter) a more arresting plant had been introduced. The modern meaning of the word "stunning" might well have been devised to describe the stout and leafy green column and gorgeous crown of rich-hued flowers of this plant. Nor were the splendor of hue and pride of size and port all it had to offer. It displayed an altogether amazing and almost terrifying impetuosity.

Long before the calendar or the thermometer (if such a thing had then existed) hinted of spring, the red noses of the Crown Imperials thrust belligerently through the crusted soil were proclaiming it; and they still, more surely than the bluebird and the singing hylas, proclaim it in the face of all signs to the contrary.

When I was a young and fearful gardener, many a bitter night saw me, lantern in hand, draping hay about those reckless headlong shoots, for they do not remain reconnoitering noses long, but begin to rise at once and quickly, disdainfully bidding the frosts hold off, not as King Canute bade the rising tide to go no farther, that he might show himself before his subjects in humbleness, but apparently with a conscious sense of their own immunity to such elemental forces. And, as a matter of fact, I never knew the impetuous shoots of the Crown Imperials to be injured. And I sleep o' nights instead of stalking abroad with hay and a lantern.

Very poor in horticultural experience is he who has not grown these splendid liliaceous plants, but I have spoken of them as being at once the splendor and the despair of my garden, and for this reason: Newly planted bulbs flower magnificently for several years; then they begin raising a leggy family, and they appear to give their whole mind and all their vitality to the business and cease to flower. Many young green shoots do not compensate for the superb flowers.

Of course in my garden many things go undone that should be done, for lack of man power and because I am only one person with a multiplicity of horticultural interests—for there is no doubt that, while it is best not to meddle with the bulbs as long as they are flowering satisfactorily, they should certainly be taken up and replanted in freshly enriched soil when bloom falls off; and this I frequently neglect to do. They are heavy feeders, and exhaust the soil. Too often, moreover, the bulbs are thrust into crowded shrubbery borders where the soil is impoverished by the roots of the hearty shrubs. They will bloom once, perhaps twice, and then no more under these conditions.

The soil they prefer is sweet and limy, fat, deep, and rich. In this the bulbs should be set from four to six inches deep and at least five inches apart, in groups of five or seven, or more; and two points in their cultivation seem to be universally recognized as vital: They should not be kept out of the ground a day longer than is necessary. Order them early and plant them immediately, and when they have put on their show and finished, the stems must not be cut off. However embarrassing these may be to the tidy gardener, they must be allowed to die down naturally.

If the bulbs must be moved, it is best to do it just after the foliage has ripened fully—this will probably be in June—lifting the bulbs with care, separating the large from the small ones, and replanting at once.

They bloom well either in full sun or in partial shade; but in the latter situation the blooms will be later and more prolonged. If you set your bulbs as I did long ago, beneath a pink-flowered Dogwood, your esthetic sufferings will be extreme, for the two flower together in noisy and furious disagreement; and to decide whether to move a thriving clump of Crown Imperials or a flourishing pink Dogwood, is one of those quite agonizing emergencies that gardeners must meet as best they may. Many will compromise as I did, by letting them be. Let them shout. "The life of man is stronger than good taste," his peace of mind more valuable.

When the leafy stem of the Crown Imperial has reached perhaps three feet in height, it hangs out a crown of great bells, "ruddy or lemon yellow as may be, surmounted by a defiant plume of leaves, each bell containing five nectaries like large pearls, charged with tears of honey, which for my part, I have never seen any British insect so venturesome as to approach." From the whole plant, bulb, stalk, leaves, and flowers, emanates a strange pervading skunkish odor, so that while it is called *Corona Imperialis* in some quarters, it is also to the less poetic-minded known as Stink Lily; but I am inclined to agree with Parkinson, who regarded this odor, which is at its most extreme in the early spring, as "not unwholesome." Old Gerard said the astonishing flowers were used to adorn the bosoms of the beautiful, and a modern defender compares the odor to that of coffee!

The Crown Imperial flowers in April. There are numerous

kinds on the market: the common red, whose hue an early writer likened to that of a boiled lobster; the common yellow, a lovely rich tone; *citrina,* green shaded yellow; Aurora, blood-orange; Orange Brilliant, somewhat tawny in tone; Crown upon Crown, with its flaunting second tier of crown leaves. There are double-flowered forms, but these are decidedly stuffy and congested-looking, and moreover do not flower freely. And there are some with variegated foliage, gold or silver, which are said to be effective.

F. karadaghensis   *B.M.* t. 9303

This species I had from van Tubergen's a few years ago. It flowered in the rock garden for two successive seasons late in April, an amusing solemn little plant some five or six inches tall, with gray-green leaves curiously twisted along the stem, and little angular bells in which brown mingled with apple-green. The first year, it was quite jaunty and spruce, the second somewhat subdued. I think it is preparing to depart to a better world. It is planted in a low part of the rock garden in sun and gritty soil. Perhaps the soil is not damp enough, perhaps too damp. Who can tell? In any case, I shall try the species again in another situation. It is pretty enough to make an effort for.

F. meleagris L.
Snake's Head Fritillary, Guinea Hen Flower, Checkered Lily

Among gardeners who are concerned with growing Fritillaries, the Checkered Lily, in its various varieties, is the white hope. If any may be said to be amiable, it is this one. Given a damp situation in sandy loam, it nearly always endures and increases, and where it grows in generous colonies, is a most charming thing. The bulb is small, roundish, and composed of several thick scales. The stem arises to a height of about a foot, the leaves which appear along its upper portion might be termed incidental. They are few, narrow, and pointed, grayish in color. The flower is quaint and engaging, not bright, but decidedly attractive.

And its development from the bud stage is interesting to watch. Usually there are two flowers to a stem, but at first the two buds appear to be united. Presently they separate, and the large bud

FRITILLARIA MELEAGRIS ARTEMIS

develops a faint checkering, garnet upon a pale ground, and this checkering becomes more distinct until, in the fully expanded, square-shouldered flower, it is very marked. The second bud then follows suit. The buds droop, but the open flower raises its head somewhat, while the narrow leaves, as the stem lengthens, change their position from a slanting one to almost vertical. Each of the six petals that make up the bell is rather narrow and bluntly pointed, and about one and one-half inches long.

The Checkered Lily was called by Dodonaeus—the sixteenth-century botanist of Flanders, whose writings are said to form the basis of Gerard's "Herbal"—*Flos Meleagris, meleagris* then being the name of the guinea hen, for the reason that the whole flower is checkered over like the wings and breast of that curious fowl. "Nature, or rather the Creator of all things, hath kept a very wonderful order, surpassing (as in all other things) the curiousest painting that art can set downe. One square is of a greenish yellow colour, the other purple, keeping the same order on the backside of the flower as on the inside, although they are blackish on one square, and of a violet colour in another: in so much that every leaf seemeth to be the feather of a Ginnie hen, whereof it took its name."

This species is found from Norway throughout the whole of central Europe to the Caucasus. It is said to grow thickly in the smiling meadows about lovely Azay-le-Rideau in Touraine; and in parts of England it is so abundant—as in the valley of the Thames and its tributaries, especially "in Christ Church Meadows, at Oxford, at Minety, on the border of North Wilts, in the neighborhood of Aylesbury, and formerly between Kew and Mortlake" —that it has come to be regarded as a native Britisher, though the early gardeners and botanists, up to the time of J. Blackstone, a botanizing apothecary of the eighteenth century,[3] did not recognize it as such. Even today there are skeptics who persist in regarding it as an escape from gardens, though its freedom is of long standing. It was the abundance of these flowers in the Oxford Meadows that caused Matthew Arnold to write the well-known lines:

[3] J. Blackstone wrote the little known work, *Specimen botanicum . . . Anglaea* (London, 1746), "the last book issued in England before the adoption of Linnaeus's system." Miller, writing his dictionary in 1768, however, did not refer to *F. meleagris* as a native of Britain.

I know what white, what purple fritillaries
The grassy harvest of the river-fields,
Above by Ensham, down by Sandford, yields.

An exquisite form, *meleagris alba*, abounds in some localities, and is the prettiest to grow in the garden. Its checkerings are faintly greenish yellow on the almost white ground, and each segment is marked by a green ridge. It is said that this white form is more readily raised from seed, and comes more quickly to flowering strength than the common one.

The Dutch have raised numerous pretty forms of *meleagris*, and most of them are a real improvement over the natural kinds, the colors more definite, the checkerings more distinct. Shirley Hibberd in "Familiar Garden Flowers" (written toward the end of the last century), stated that he had seen at least sixty varieties in one garden in Haarlem, and these varied so much that their specific identity was a matter of question with a party of experts until Mr. H. Krelage himself gave the assurance that they were veritable seedlings of *meleagris*.

No such number is available to my knowledge today, but there are several very fine ones to be had, among them Aphrodite, a very fine large-flowered and strong-growing white form; Cassandra, a delightful silvery pink flower checkered with lilac; Orion, very splendid and dark, with handsome claret-colored blooms mottled with a deeper tone; Artemis, perhaps the finest, lovely and large in two tones of wine color, the ridges of the segments green. This is a strong and thrifty grower.

A double form has long been known, though it has always been scarce. Parkinson called it wordily *Fritillaria flore duplici albicanti*, and it has been cherished from the times of Queen Henrietta Maria and Parkinson, being handed down from gardener to gardener as old lace and rare china are handed down through the years in families. I have not seen it, and it cannot be very pretty, for Mr. Bowles describes it as looking like "a bunch of fragments of the marbled cover of the exercise books we used in our school days."

I have never tried naturalizing the Checkered Lily in grass, though it is strongly recommended for this purpose, and it certainly thrives in meadows in England and on the Continent.

Those who have grassy orchards or damp meadows might do well to experiment with it thus.

F. pallidiflora Schrenk. *B.M.* t. 6725

Another species which I have enjoyed only through the words of others more fortunate than myself. It is mentioned here because it appears to be well worth searching out for use in our gardens, for it is described not only as "of sound perennial temper," but as very attractive, and flowering for a long time in April. A stout stalk carries one or two, or in the case of large bulbs, seven or eight, square-shouldered bells, soft straw-yellow without, and faintly checkered within. The leaves are few, thickish, and glaucous. It is said to thrive in sun or partial shade, and is a native of Turkestan. I do not see it offered at the present time.

F. pyrenaica L.

This Pyrenean species lived in my garden for several years, even making a modest increase, but there came a spring that knew it not, and I have no idea what caused it to die away. It is, however, offered by Dutch and English firms, and so can be replaced, though I have to admit it is not among the most attractive sorts. The outside of the bells is a trifle liverish in hue, but if you take the trouble to raise them and look within, you will see a satinlike finish of texture, and an intricately checkered pattern of green and brown and purple; however, the bells have a curiously unpleasant odor, and so are not to be held to the nose. The plant blooms just after the Checkered Lily and is a little taller, the stem carrying a few glaucous, fleshy leaves and a reflexing bell. It is said to have been grown in gardens since the first part of the seventeenth century.

F. verticillata Willd. (*F. Thunbergii*)

A small Japanese species also found in Siberia, and not often grown in gardens, though it is quite pretty. My bulbs came to me from van Tubergen in Haarlem, and have not been here long enough for me to judge of their character or behavior over any long period. They did, however, live over the first winter, which was a cold one, and flowered in the spring. The plant's habit is quite graceful, and its deportment modest; the broadly bell-shaped flowers are a pale, indeterminate hue, faintly reticulated with green on the outside and marked with maroon within. According to R. W. Wallace, it belongs to a distinct section, which has slender leaves with curled hooklike tips, and the little masses of gray foliage that it makes are really more ornamental than the flowers, which are rather lacking in character.[*]

NATIVE SPECIES

By many persons, the North American Fritillaries are considered finer than those from other lands. Certain of them are of very real beauty, but none, I think, eclipse in quaint charm the white-flowered Checkered Lily, or in splendor the Crown Imperial. They do, however, keep us guessing quite as successfully as do their cousins from across the water.

Mr. Carl Purdy of Ukiah, California, to whom we are chiefly indebted both for our knowledge of these shy natives and for their distribution among gardeners, has been kind enough to write me the following concerning their range, and the natural conditions under which they grow. This is invaluable information from an expert:

"Most of these charming bulbous plants are natives of California, but three species have a much wider distribution. There are three groups of them, each differing very widely not only in its habit, but in the conditions under which it thrives in the wild.

"The first group is of species which have a single circle of leaves near the base with a few scattered leaves along the stem. Their bulb is composed of large thick scales which separate easily. All of the species in this group grow in full sun in rather heavy soils which are decidedly moist during their winter growing season. Of these *F. Purdyi* is found only for about one hundred and fifty miles north and south in northwest California, and oddly in this hundred and fifty miles they are seldom found more than two or three miles east or west of this line. *F. liliacea* begins about where *F. Purdyi* ends, and travels south another hundred and fifty miles, and was once to be found on the site of what is now the city of San Francisco. *F. biflora* begins where *F. liliacea* ends, and ex-

[*] *The Garden*, Sept. 19, 1914.

tends to the lower California border. *F. agrestis* is found across the center of California, north and east of San Francisco Bay. *F. pluriflora* grows on both sides of the Sacramento Valley, which is north of the last species, and *F. striata* is very local two hundred miles farther south. In this group is also *F. glauca*, which is found only in a very narrow area in southern Oregon.

"The second group has disk-like flattish bulbs covered with small pearly white bulblets, like grains of rice. The stems are tall and graceful, and there are a number of circles of leaves with many in each. *F. lanceolata* has many varieties, and several of them are named as species by some botanists. Away up in Alaska, *lanceolata* starts with an almost black sort, and across Bering Straits in Siberia, is the Asiatic form called *F. kamtschatkensis*, almost black. It extends down the coast of California, growing in open woodlands as far as a hundred miles south of San Francisco. *F. parviflora* is found in the mid-Sierras, from twenty-five hundred to five thousand feet above sea level. It has many small reddish brown bells. *F. atropurpurea* extends from high in the Sierra Nevada Mountains far to the north and east. A dwarf sort. *F. recurva* has two forms, one of which is known as *F. coccinea*. The typical form is found in woods both in the Coast Ranges from not far north of San Francisco Bay to just into southern Oregon. In the Sierras it is found from the central region to about the state line. *F. coccinea*, on the other hand, is found only in small areas of a peculiar soil just north of San Francisco Bay.

"The foregoing species are found either in open woods or in scattering brush, which gives them some shelter. The soils are clayey or gritty, with just a moderate amount of humus. There is not nearly as much humus in Californian woodlands as an easterner would expect to find. This is because from time immemorial, forest and brush fires have been periodic. The bulbs are always much finer the year after a fire.

"The third group contains only *F. pudica*. It has the flat bulbs with ricelike offsets, but it lives in the semi-arid regions east of the central section of California, and extends to British Columbia, Idaho, and Utah. There it is found in a silty sandy loam near or under Sagebrush. This Sagebrush seldom rises over three or four feet in height.

"One might be led to think from the widely differing types of soil to which these Fritillarias are native, that it is necessary to copy these soils in order to succeed with them. This is not true. I have very excellent results with a friable soil which is mostly clay with a very moderate amount of humus. In regions where there are summer rains, I think it good practice to allow the leaves of the plants to ripen and turn yellow, then to dig up the bulbs with care and store them in a dry place. They may be packed in any dry material, such as dry sand or dry peat moss. We use the latter exclusively for packing material."

My personal experiments with the American Fritillarias have been carried on without this digging and storing. I am making an effort to find which, if any, will endure without this arduous process, and under what conditions of soil and aspect they will endure. For the most part, they appear above ground very promptly with the first relenting weather. Many of them are well up and budded early in March, but, after having got so far, they progress more slowly. All, however, have flowered here before the middle of May. In growing the American species, it is important to note to which group they belong, to the shade-lovers or the sun-lovers.

F. agrestis

A neat little species, low-growing, with open slightly mottled bells, the ground color greenish yellow. They have a slightly unpleasant odor. In my garden this species has proved short-lived.

F. atropurpurea Nutt.
Bronze Bells. Brown Fritillary

A quaint and slightly fantastic little species that deserves its common names, though after the fashion of its kind there is some purple and some green in its ensemble. This gives the burnished, bronzy effect. The stem rises to a height of some ten inches among ribbonlike leaves, and bears from one to six flowers an inch or more across, and with pointed segments. The pistil is three-pronged and projects beyond the segments in rather a threatening manner, suggesting, as some one has said, the forked tongue of an adder. "When," writes Margaret Armstrong, "we found this flower growing in the Grand Canyon, half way down Bright

Angel Trail, it seemed entirely suitable to the mysterious place." [5]

F. *glauca*
Siskiyou Fritillary

From the small Lily-like bulb, the slender stem rises less than a foot high. The leaves scattered along the stem are distinctly bluish in tone, and are oblanceolate. It flowers here about the 1st of May, hanging out from one to three small broad bells of the characteristic green-brown-purple color scheme, irregularly mottled with yellow. It has done fairly well, that is, it is in its third year in the garden.

F. *lanceolata* Pursh.
Brown Lily. Mission Bells.

The stems of the Mission Bells rise to a height of about eighteen inches, and are set along their length with two or three whorls of shining leaves. The flowers, which may be few or many in a cluster, are curiously clawlike in shape, the segments being pointed and turning in a little at the tips. They are of the usual brown or purple and green blend, but rather richer in effect than is common among these somber flowers, and they are of good size. The plants are found on shaded slopes and along streams. It blooms here by the 1st of May, and has proved only moderately happy, though quite hardy. A form called *gracilis* is darker in tone throughout and is also of dwarfer stature.

F. *liliacea* Lindl.
White Fritillary

A dwarf species with a strong stem under a foot tall. The flowers are from one to six, funnel-shaped, and whitish tinted with pale green, sometimes spotted with purple. The leaves of the radical tuft are somewhat more broadly oblong than the scattered stem leaves. I have not grown this kind.

F. *phaeanthera*

Under this name a species has been offered from time to time. It lived through two winters here, flowering the first week in

[5] *Field Book of Western Wild Flowers.*

May, and then disappeared. The bulbs are of the rice-grained type, the stem slender; and the small spreading bells, though not showy, have a certain distinction due to the graceful pose of the flowers upon the stem.

F. pluriflora Torr.   B.M. t. 7631
   Pink Fritillary

When this species flowered in my garden for the first time, it came as a distinct surprise, for instead of the gloomy coloring that one had come to expect, here was a flower of soft, rose-wine color, and a long deep bell without checkering. Next to the brilliant *recurva*, it is the showiest native species. My bulbs bore from one to three flowers, but it is said to produce as many as twelve in an umbel; and it must then be a grand sight indeed. Even one-flowered, it is a quite charming plant and very nice for the rock garden. The bells are not quite so downcast in their pose as are most of their kin, but are carried almost horizontally. The stem is stout, and the ample leaves are scattered from the base to near the summit. As it grows naturally in adobe soils, it must be given a dry sunny place in the garden if it is to last; and from my experience with it, it seems to be one that does last unusually well.

F. pudica Spreng.
   Yellow Bell. Indian Rice. Rice-root

This is an ideal species for the rock garden from the point of view of appearance. It looks like a golden Snowdrop that has got out of step with the rest of its family, flowering in the middle of April instead of in February and March. It grows from four to six inches high, with erect narrow basal leaves, and from one to several pure yellow bells about an inch long; one of the few species to come out with a frank statement of color, with no indecisive mottlings whatever. Margaret Armstrong speaks of its fading to a dull red, which my specimens have not done, and it is said that there are several forms of it, one striped with a greenish hue, and another that is flushed with brownish red. I have not come across these, though I have had importations of bulbs from several different localities.

This pretty little species seems inclined to settle down in the rock garden in sunny places, and to become a contented guest, and it is quite easily forced. Visitors to the International Flower Show may recall having seen it growing there in some of the rock gardens.

F. Purdyi

Mr. Purdy's Fritillaria, as I have it, is a most interesting kind, and has lived and flowered here early in April for three successive seasons. I say, "as I have it here," because there seems not to be complete unanimity as to the identity of this species. The kind I have here is a low form, and coming across its buds amidst the low herbage in the rock garden one is almost startled at their resemblance to the head of a snake poised to strike; but the opened bell is reassuring, though the color scheme is somewhat reptilian, whitish green with an overlay of purplish brown. This Mr. Purdy now offers as "*Purdyi* varied." The other, the true *Purdyi*, he says, was discovered and named thirty years ago, and its locality lost; but it has been rediscovered and is again available. It is described as growing from four to nine inches tall with from one to seven lovely large bells, waxy white, flecked with scarlet. I have not had this sort yet, but it sounds attractive.

F. recurva Benth.
B.M. t. 6264
Red Bell

This is a dazzling species. To call it merely Red Bell is an understatement. The flowers are Lily-like in form, ample and reflexed, and from few to many on a stem. It flowers from quite small bulbs, but the stronger the bulb, the more freely it will bloom. The "Lilies" are a brilliant scarlet on the exterior, and yellow streaked with red on the interior. It has seemingly staged a revolt in a big way against the usual sober garb of its family, but though it seems upon first sight so dramatically brilliant, close inspection reveals a curious dimming of its hue by what appears to be an infinitesimal admixture of purple pigment with the red. The leaves are in several whorls from the middle of the stem upward and somewhat coppery in color.

It has been truly said that *recurva* has probably brought more salt tears to the eyes of keen gardeners than any other bulbous plant. To see it is to desire it immoderately, but it is not an easy plant to grow away from its natural haunts. It has flowered here in two successive seasons, and though I am hoping, I am not expecting, a continuation of this complaisant behavior. It stages its spectacular performance about the 1st of May. It is planted here in a sunny position, but where it receives shade in the afternoon. Ira Gabrielson says it is usually found in the shelter of some gnarled and twisted shrub.

The form offered as *coccinea* is perhaps even more brilliant and, if possible, less of a sure thing in eastern gardens. I have flowered it only once, when it wore a distinctly unamiable and dissatisfied expression. The segments did not reflex, and they were narrower than in the type.

GALANTHUS *AMARYLLIDACEAE*

SNOWDROP

SNOWDROPS are winter's flowers. Though they linger into the early weeks of the spring, they belong essentially to the brumous season, are legitimate children of the frost-bound months rather than forerunners of the vernal tide. It is amazing to watch these tender herbs thrusting indomitably through the frozen earth, often through snow and ice; amazing, their ingenuity in holding the two leaves firmly together to form a sort of beak, callous and protective, that bores its way steadily upward, clasping the flower bud "like an oval pearl" between them. As soon as the point breaks through the earth, its function is accomplished, and the leaves separate to let the flower bud through. This, on its slender stem, takes advantage of every softening moment offered by the weather to edge upward, while the leaves arch away to form a modest setting for the pearl they have sheltered. The solitary bud drooping sharply from its erect stem, remains closed sometimes for several weeks after it has pierced the ground, awaiting some elemental tenderness which will cause it to open. At this touch, the spoon-shaped outer segments flare apart, disclosing the notched shorter segments within. Upon each of these is an emerald splotch shaped like a horseshoe to follow the contour of the notch in the segment.

For such small and seemingly fragile things, Snowdrops display the most astonishing endurance and vitality. I have known the little flaring bells to swing blithely in the wind for several weeks, assailed by storms and snows, splashed by mud, washed clean again by snow or rain, and remain unharmed and still sprightly.

To many of us a Snowdrop is just a Snowdrop, but as a matter of fact there are a number of kinds; and while the differences between them are not very marked and lie chiefly in width of leaf and size of bloom, and also in season, these slight differentiations become important when one is making a collection of Snowdrops, especially as not all the dozen or more species recognized, like, or will endure under, the same conditions.

The late Sir William Lawrence, who had a notable collection of Snowdrops at his home Burford, near Dorking, England, pointed out that they may be "divided roughly into two classes, namely, the Snowdrops of Northern and South-Eastern Europe, and those that come from Greece, Russia, Turkey and Asia Minor. The former, of which *Galanthus nivalis*, the Common Snowdrop, is the type, will grow on a slope or on the level. They prefer a shady position, cool and moist without being damp, and while at rest do not mind being grown over as long as the herbage dies down completely in the winter. Of the other group *G. Elwesii* and the Crimean Snowdrop, *G. plicatus*, seem to prefer a stony slope, well drained and dry in the summer. . . . In this group also come the Snowdrops that flower before Christmas, such as *Olgae, Byzantinus* and *Cilicicus*. These require all the sun they can get, both in summer and in winter. At Burford they grow in a bed of river sand, which is always moist under the surface." [1]

This is information from an expert grower and true lover of the race, and as we heed it, so shall our success be measured, though the directions given for the second class may, in our sun-ridden climate, be somewhat modified. We do not need to plan so carefully for a summer baking; that they will get in the natural course of things, and all save the autumn-flowering kinds will be the better for a little shade during the hottest part of the day. But for years I patiently planted and regularly lost after a season or two, bulbs of *Elwesii* and *plicatus* because I was ignorantly of the opinion that they reveled in the same damp and shaded situations that so obviously pleased those of the *nivalis* group.

One point in the treatment of all alike is imperative. They should be out of the ground for as short a period as possible; in other words, the bulbs should be ordered early and planted immediately upon their arrival—not later than August. Not to do this, is to court loss and a poor showing for many years. The bulbs should be put into the ground from three to four inches deep, according to size, and two or three inches apart. Once planted, they should be left severely alone. If happy, they will increase freely by seed and by offset, and disturbance simply upsets their plans

[1] *Gardening Illustrated*, Aug. 30, 1930.

for an increasing display of frosted bells. If it should prove necessary or advisable to move any part of a plantation, the best time to do it is when they are in full flower. I like to dig up little sods of them, so as not to disturb the roots, and replant the sods in the new position without loss of time. If the bulbs must be dug separately, the operation is a nice one, for it is important that the roots shall not be injured nor allowed to dry out, and they must be placed in a hole wide enough to admit of their being spread out in a comfortable and natural manner. But it is to be hoped that a plantation of Snowdrops will not need to be disturbed if it appears happy.

Generally speaking, Snowdrops enjoy companionship. They like to find their roots among those of other plants that do well in the same sort of situation, and whose foliage dies back in winter. Under no circumstances should the leaves of Snowdrops be cut off or broken before they wither naturally.

Rare species of Snowdrop may be grown in little colonies in suitable situations in the rock garden or in select sections of shrubbery borders where their situation is marked and their roots may be left undisturbed. The common and inexpensive kinds (those of the *nivalis* group) should be strewn broadcast by the thousand on wooded hillsides, in low shaded copses, beneath the skirts of deciduous shrubs, along shaded paths. As these flowers attempt almost unaided to brighten the world during the winter months, they should surely be given every assistance. There is a gentle simplicity about Snowdrops as they come into the winter world, "alone and palely loitering," that is very moving. Who can fail to be impressed by this evidence of the eternal resurrection of all things that are?

I was once told a story of a queen of one of the central European countries who came, while walking in the woods one icy day in midwinter, upon a single Snowdrop blossoming in the vast emptiness of the forest. So moved was she that she caused a guard to be set over it to see that no one should trample the intrepid little flower. Years, or perhaps it was only months, afterward, some one walking in the forest saw a sentry standing erectly in a place where there was obviously no reason for a sentry to be. It seemed that the royal order to guard the spot had never been revoked, so the guard was daily replaced, though the reason for his being there had long disappeared. A good story, true or not, and it sounds to me as if it might be true.

The Snowdrop wealth at our disposal today is sadly straitened in comparison to what it was before the war and before the quarantine. When I look over the lists in catalogues issued prior to 1914, I am discouraged and disquieted. And when I read Mr. Bowles's chapter on Snowdrops in "My Garden in Spring" and his many articles on the same subject,[2] as well as those of Sir William Lawrence, and realize what rich collections of both species and named varieties exist at Middleton House and Burford, I am deeply envious. When shall American gardeners again know horticultural plenty and cease to be, horticulturally speaking, among the illiterate? Not, certainly, until we have ceased to be satisfied with the obvious and the commonplace, and not until we win the right to know and possess the vast amount of plant material that is at present available to the rest of the world and withheld from American gardeners.

In the following list of Snowdrops, numerous kinds are mentioned that are not at present easily available, and certain of them I have not grown; but in this case, information concerning them is culled from the most reliable sources.

Galanthus byzantinus Baker

This is supposed to be a natural hybrid between *G. Elwesii* and and *G. plicatus*. It was collected near Brusa, across the Sea of Marmora from Istanbul, in 1893. It is a grand Snowdrop, with long outer segments, and the extra basal green spot on the tube that characterizes the house of *Elwesii*, and the wide plicate, or folded-edged leaves characteristic of *plicatus*. The flower is large and carried on a tall stem. Mr. Carl Krippendorf writes me that in his garden in Cincinnati it always flowers in December. Here, if December is a kind and favorable month, it does likewise, but if the winter is a steadily cold and snowy one, I must sometimes wait for a February softening before these flowers appear. Mrs. Philip B. Howard of South Lincoln, Massachusetts, wrote me that the first year she planted it, though she was late getting it into the ground, it flowered in January. At any rate, it is an eager spirit,

---

[2] Particularly that in the *Journal of the R.H.S.*, Vol. XIII, 1918–19, which see for the beautiful drawings by Mr. Bowles, of different kinds.

just waiting the chance to do its bit. Mr. Bowles finds that "freshly imported bulbs, if planted as soon as received, generally in August, will give a succession of flowers from November to February." The leaves are generally in evidence whatever the weather by December in this garden, but they often remain stationary for a long time because of adverse conditions.

There are those who go so far as to say that this is the finest of all Snowdrops, and it is generally considered the best for forcing. Like all the forward-flowering kinds, this one is happiest in a partially sunny situation, sheltered rather than shaded, protected from north winds and open to the blandishments of the sun.

G. *caucasicus* Baker

This is regarded as a geographical form of the Common Snowdrop, G. *nivalis*, but it appears distinct in having broader and longer leaves, a taller habit of growth, and it flowers considerably later than the Common Snowdrop, thus serving the good purpose of prolonging the Snowdrop season. It is a native of the Caucasus Mountains, in Russia.

A form of this is G. *caucasicus grandis*, called the Straffan Snowdrop. It is, according to Mr. Bowles, one of the most beautiful of Snowdrops. "It is a Crimean form, and like its relations, bears two flowers from each strong bulb, one rather earlier and taller than the other." It was brought to Straffan in Ireland by Lord Clarina just after the Crimean War. It requires a good summer ripening.

See also Green Snowdrops, p. 193.

G. *Elwesii* Hook.   *B.M.* t. 6166

Mr. Elwes' beautiful Snowdrop was introduced by him in 1875 from the mountains of Asia Minor, where it is found at elevations of from two thousand to six thousand feet above the sea level. It is perhaps deservedly the most popular of Snowdrops. The flowers are exceptionally large and globular, and almost always show a second large patch of green upon the inner tube, but it is a variable species, and leaves and flowers are not always what we have been led to expect. In some forms the inner segments are almost wholly green; in others, the two green spots are connected by a narrow green line down the center of the segment. It is a tall bold plant, with leaves more glaucous than those of other kinds, very wide and concave on their upper surface; but these, like the flowers, vary immensely. I have had for many years a form that has narrower leaves than any other Snowdrop I have seen, with flowers much like those of *Elwesii*. In both kinds, the outer segments when fully developed spread out almost horizontally from the slightly recurving inner segments, or tube, thus fully displaying the beautiful green markings. Both flower at the same time—in late December if the weather is favorable, but usually not until January; and the flowers last a most amazingly long time through all sorts of indignities put upon them by the weather. *Elwesii* is not a success in all gardens, and is said to die out after a time. It is certain that none of the *Elwesii* forms require the damp and shaded conditions recommended for the Snowdrops of the *nivalis* group; they like a little shade during part of the day, but the soil must be well drained, and they must be assured of a summer baking. Thus treated, I think they will prove as constant in most gardens as they have been in mine.

There are numerous forms of *Elwesii*, but not many of them are at this time on the market. Two of the best are *Cassala* (*robustus*), an exceptionally large and robust form, and *Whittallii* (named for the late Edward Whittall, who sent it to England from the neighborhood of Smyrna), one of the giants of the race; and there are others, but as we may not have them now, it is not important to describe them.

Snowdrops hybridize easily, and the narrow-leaved form I have in my garden may have originated there from a natural cross between *Elwesii* and possibly *nivalis*. I have seen nothing just like it pictured or described.

G. Fosteri Baker
Giant Snowdrop

Asia Minor is the home of many Snowdrops. *G. Fosteri* was introduced from the mountains of that country, from the neighborhood of Amasia in north central Asia Minor, by Sir Michael Foster, whose name it bears. The flowers are very large and a good deal like those of *Elwesii*, but the leaves are broad and blunt, somewhat like those of a Scilla, and concave on the upper surface

like those of *Elwesii*. It is thought by some authorities to be a
natural hybrid between *latifolius* and *Elwesii*. It is a tall plant,
and the leaves are commonly taller than the flower stem. Max
Leichtlin called this the King of Snowdrops, but it is generally
reported a poor grower, and is certainly less desirable than
Elwesii.

G. *Ikariae* Baker

This species, which I have never seen, was introduced from the
island of Nikaria (the classical Icaria) off the west coast of Asia
Minor by Mr. Whittall in 1893, the only locality in which it is
to be found. It is distinguished by broad glossy green leaves that
curve outward in a more pronounced manner than do those of
other Snowdrops, and very large flowers, less globular than those
of *Elwesii*, the outer segments very long, and the inner ones
marked heavily with green. It is the latest to flower of the spring
species. The bulb is large and requires to be well ripened; thus
a warm situation is indicated. English gardeners recommend the
base of a south-facing wall for it, and as it is thought to be one
of the most beautiful of its kind, it is worth taking some pains to
please. It is now offered by certain Dutch bulb growers, so is
happily within our reach.

G. *latifolius* Rupr.

This species from high up in the Caucasus Mountains is disappointing because its large handsome bright green leaves, nearly
an inch broad, induce one to expect something extra special in the
way of blossoms, but the flowers of *latifolius* are small even for
Snowdrops, and appear meager, not to say stingy, in comparison
with the grand scale of the leaves.

But there is a handsome form of it whose history Mr. Bowles
tells: [*] "It must have been a great day for Mr. Allen of Shepton
Mallet when he first saw the solid round flowers and wide leaves
of the Snowdrop which was afterward to bear his name. It was in
1884 that bulbs of *G. latifolius* sent to him by the Austrian nur-
seryman, Herr Gusmus, flowered for the first time at Shepton
Mallet. . . . Mr. Allen saw that one of them was vastly superior
to the small-flowered form hitherto found in this species with the

[*] *Gardening Illustrated*, Feb. 20, 1932.

wide and glossy leaves. . . . When the flowers first open, the
leaves wrap closely round the stalks and are only about six inches
in length, but when the flowers are fully grown, they are held up
on stalks a foot high, and the leaves are over ten inches in length
and one and three-quarters inches in their widest part." When
I grew this fine Snowdrop in my Rockland County garden, it was
at the base of a south-facing wall where its roots mingled with
those of a Stanwell Perpetual Rose, which gave it some shade in
summer. I lost this with many another fine thing when I left that
garden, and now I do not see it offered; but it is worth watching
for, as it is a good grower and extremely handsome.

G. nivalis L.

Despite the larger flowers, the handsomer leaves, the earlier
flowering, of many other kinds of Snowdrop, this one, the one we
call the *Common* Snowdrop, is to me the most lovely and desirable of its kind. It possesses a gay grace, a sturdy fragility—if
one may couple two such seemingly contradictory terms—a floriferousness which none of the others have, and when it is happily
placed, it flourishes and increases as do none of those others, and
produces for us in time the sheets of living frost that so enchant
us in the early weeks of the New Year.

In my childhood I was familiar with a wooded hillside, near
Baltimore, where the snows of winter were followed by snows of
spring; literally the ground was carpeted with pendent white
flowers above the brown leaves and greening mosses. We do not
often see Snowdrops planted on such a scale in this country, and
this fairylike scene was evidently of their own contriving. They
had escaped from some garden long ago and run joyously wild
in the hospitable wood, increasing year by year by seed and offset,
until the result was a bewildering display to which we looked forward every year as children now do to seeing some famous movie
star. The Snowdrop Wood has long been put under the bondage
of neat gardens and neater dwellings; but before it disappeared, a
good-sized sod was dug from it and sent me by a dear old Baltimore lady, now also gone, and all the *nivalis* Snowdrops in my
present garden have come from this sod. They were set, the whole
sod, on a shaded bank, and from there they have made their way
to all parts of the garden. Every year there is a fresh colony of

Snowdrops in some unexpected place. And what could be more delightful?

Gray does not mention the Snowdrop's having naturalized itself in this country, but I am sure there must be many sections where it has done so, for it is a determined colonizer. In Great Britain it is considered a doubtful native; but it is found covering acres of ground in woods near Edinburgh, on the banks of the river Tees, about Blackwell and Coniscliffe, and in copses of Gloucestershire and Hereford, so that by some it is accounted a true flower of British soil, and it has won for itself many folk names: Fair Maids of February, Purification Flower, Candlemas Bells, and the like. In the early works on gardening, there is no mention that I can find of the Snowdrop as such, but in Johnson's Gerard, p. 147, under the caption "Of Bulbous Violets," there is an unmistakable description of the Snowdrop and two drawings showing the shorter inner segments and flaring outer segments that leave one in no doubt of what they are. Of these "Bulbous Violets" Gerard writes, "These plants doe growe wilde in Italie, and the places adjacent; notwithstanding, our London gardens have taken possession of them manie years Past." He does not speak of them as British natives, but certain later writers, including Mrs. Loudon,[4] so consider them. It is generally thought, however, that they were introduced many centuries ago into England, as were so many plants, by flower-loving, globe-trotting monks, and in support of this theory we are told, "The glens of the Northern foot of the Herefordshire Beacon, where Withering[5] saw them growing a hundred and sixty years ago, are less than a mile from Little Malvern Priory."[6] Nor did the early poets have anything to say about them; Shakespeare, Milton, and Chaucer are all silent as to their gentle charm, which probably would not have been the case if they had been among the commoner British wild flowers. John Keble, the English divine and professor of poetry

[4] *British Wild Flowers.*

[5] William Withering, physician and botanist, 1741-1799.

[6] "Snowdrops are allowed by botanists merely to be doubtful natives near Malvern and Wrexham. They are said to have been introduced for the prosaic reason that the bulbs make better 'salep' than Orchid roots. Salep or Saloop, as a hot drink, is a delicacy unknown to the present generation, but within living memory there still lingered a few patriarchs who remembered the salep stalls which preceded the coffee stalls that now cater for the refreshment of belated Londoners."—*Gardening Illustrated*, Feb. 23, 1935.

at Oxford in the middle nineteenth century, was the first to celebrate it with his apostrophe to "the first born of the year's delight." [7] Later many poets gave it full praise and appreciation, and truly do "they cheer th' ungenial day."

While we call *Galanthus nivalis* the Common Snowdrop, it is in reality a fastidious individual as regards soil and situation. When given a place to its mind, it radiates health and happiness, increasing in the most generous manner; but when not suited, nothing can be more grudging than its performance, or lack of performance. It lingers along unhappily for a few years, hanging out a few dejected bells to greet the first mild days, and then betakes itself permanently to a better land.

Undoubtedly what this Snowdrop must have for its well-being is a cool soil full of humus, a soil that, while not actually damp, is never quite dry, and that is well drained, and the shade of deciduous trees. A shaded hillside suits it well, or a low copse; it is delightful scattered along a woodland walk, or about the skirts of shrubs, or in narrow borders of ferns and shade-loving plants, such as Bloodroot, Dutchman's Breeches, Hepaticas, and Violets. As I have said, it does not object to being grown over during the summer if the accompanying foliage dies down in winter. If the natural fall of leaves is allowed to remain on the ground, it will require no other extra nourishment, but if these must be raked away, a top-dressing of humus should be spread over the plantations every year or two to keep them in good and productive condition.

In my experience, plantations made under evergreen trees have not prospered. One such made in my garden under a Hemlock tree, however, took matters into its own hands, and while the original bulbs dwindled and finally disappeared, the flowers cast their seeds farther and farther afield until a fine colony was established quite away from the baneful Hemlock; and there it still flourishes, while there is no trace of the original colony. Nor do Snowdrops do well with me in grass, though I know they are said to thrive in turf in the British Isles.

[7] The writer in *Gardening Illustrated* from whose little article on February Fair Maids I have gleaned these facts, adds, "Dr. Siddon, the intimate friend of the poet, used to say that the 'river-islet wild' of Keble's poem is Kennington Island, near Iffley, a familiar way-mark to Oxford oarsmen. It was then uninhabited and carpeted with Snowdrops."

G. nivalis Imperatii
  Neapolitan Snowdrop

This is the beautiful wide-skirted Snowdrop from southern Italy which is earlier-flowering than the type and bears larger and finer flowers. It is a little tender and requires a warm and protected situation, but it lived and multiplied sparingly in my cold Rockland County, New York, garden, under a south wall, where it had the heat of the wall and the shade of a brier Rose for its comfort. *G. n. Atkinsii*, a fine form of the Neapolitan Snowdrop, which is named for its introducer, Mr. Atkins, of Panswick, in Gloucestershire, is distinguished by very long and beautifully formed outer segments; but, like *Imperatii*, it must have a sheltered position.

GREEN SNOWDROPS

We are accustomed to thinking of Snowdrops as purely and coldly white, but as a matter of fact, they do not answer this description at all. There is always the emerald patch, sometimes two of them, on the inner segments that serve to make the white portions seem the more gleaming. In certain kinds, the emerald patches are very large and are augmented by green lines on the outer segments; and the kinds having this extra green ornamentation are called green Snowdrops. They are, perhaps, more curious than actually beautiful; yet a few of them gathered and placed in a small clear glass vase are very effective. "Forms with tendencies to these green markings have been found in all four of the distinct races of Snowdrops." [*] The earliest of these to flower, and perhaps the handsomest, is *G. Scharlokii*, a form of *nivalis* found by Herr Julius Scharlock in 1868 in the valley of the Nahe, a tributary of the Rhine. This is available through van Tubergen's in Haarlem, Holland. It has, besides the green spots on the *outer* segments, large twin spathes that are elongated and wave above the head of the pendent flower in a curious, flyaway manner. Another "green" Snowdrop is *G. nivalis viridi-apice*, a handsome large-flowered and tall-stemmed sort with extra green spots. It is to be found in most lists.

[*] E. A. Bowles.

"A very curious plant," says Mr. Bowles, "in which the inner segments are all green except for a narrow white edge, and the outer ones striped for the greater part of their length with a greyish green, was introduced by Herr Max Leichtlin, of Baden, and has been traced to the Vienna Botanic Garden, but no farther. It is a dwarf, late-flowering form known as *G. caucasicus virescens,* but has no resemblance to the other forms of *caucasicus,* and never produces a second flower in the pair of leaves as a *caucasicus* form should." This kind I have not come across.

YELLOW SNOWDROPS

And there are "yellow" Snowdrops, too, in which the ovary is yellow, and the patches on the inner segments are yellow instead of green. These are prettier than one would think, and a little gathering of them is especially effective with the sun shining full upon them. But they should be kept away from their green relatives, else they simply look rather sickly. The two known kinds are both forms of *nivalis,* and were found many years ago in an old Northumberland (England) garden, and are not, so far as I know, at present on the market. They are named respectively *lutescens* and *flavescens,* the latter being the better plant, stronger of habit and more richly marked.

DOUBLE SNOWDROPS

There is a yellow Snowdrop with double flowers which I have not seen, but which is said to be very charming; and, from what I can gather, there is more than one double green Snowdrop. The one I have grown for many years, and about whose charm there is no doubt, is, I think, a form raised by Mr. Allen, and called by him Charmer *flore-pleno.* The three outer segments are very long, very pointed, and slightly incurved, giving the effect of little claws such as might hold a jewel in their clasp; and within these claws are regular whorls of green-striped petals, the inner segments, very exact and neat, so that the flower has something the appearance of one of those bits of enameled jewelry once very popular as lace pins. The flower is large and altogether a very pretty conceit, well worth having to those who have an eye for more than mass effect. My patch of double Snowdrops is growing on the north side of a Hemlock hedge, and has been flourishing for a number of years without disturbance. This may be the *G. nivalis flore-pleno* offered by van Tubergen and others.

Autumnal Snowdrops

From Greece come several forms of *G. nivalis* that reverse the general Snowdrop procedure and flower in the autumn instead of in the new year. They are not easily available at the present time, and I have had no experience with them; nor do they sound too attractive. They send up their flowers before the leaves, and must appear like little lost souls returned to earth, naked and forlorn, amidst the coarse hurly-burly of autumn's preparations for departure. It is said that they are not too easy to please, and Sir William Lawrence grew these autumn performers in what he called the sand garden, that is, a bed of yellow sand about eighteen inches deep, mixed with humus; and they need all the sun and encouragement that may be given them. I have read that the autumnal Snowdrops come from high altitudes, while the winter and spring-flowering kinds are native to lower regions. Some of their names may as well be set down here against the time when they may be within our reach and "curious" gardeners may care to experiment with them. The leaves of these autumnal Snowdrops, according to Mr. Bowles, are all noticeable for the pronounced contrast of a glaucous central stripe with the deep green of their sides.

G. n. corcyrensis is a small-flowered variety introduced from Corfu by the late Harpur-Crewe. It flowers late in November or early in December. *G. n. octobrensis* is a delicate little variety from the mountains of Albania, flowering in October.

G. n. Olgae is generally the earliest to bloom, "coming up as soon as the late September rains moisten the ground. It was found by the botanist Orphanides, on Mount Taygetus. The green is very pale in an old blossom, and fades out entirely when dried. This has resulted in its being described as without green markings."

G. n. Rachelae was collected in 1884 on Mount Hymettus, famed for its honey, and is the handsomest and most robust of the autumnal kinds. The flowers are larger, and the leaves, when they appear, of more circumstance.

G. plicatus Bieb.   *B.M.* t. 2162
  Crimean Snowdrop   *B.R.* t. 545

This is a very distinct species, found in the Crimea and on the shores of the Black Sea. The specific name comes from the fact that when the leaves first appear, they are plicate, or have the edges rolled back to form a sort of pleat. They are broader than is common, glaucous, rather thin in texture, and channeled down the face. The flowers are large, the outer segments narrow at the base and convex on the back. It is a strong grower, and spreads readily in good rich loam and partial shade. It is especially valuable in prolonging the Snowdrop season into the spring.

An aura of romance is thrown about this Snowdrop when one reads that during the terrible winter of the Crimean War, the weary British soldiers in the trenches watched the snows of winter give place to a kinder white blanket as these Snowdrops blossomed about them in thousands.

Several forms of this variable species, it is said, came to British gardens direct from the trenches.

HYACINTHUS *LILIACEAE*

HYACINTH

HYACINTHS, as commonly known, are the obese, fat-stalked, overstuffed, overscented Levantines, varieties of *H. orientalis*, dedicated since 1596, or thereabouts, to pots or lozenge beds upon a suffering greensward, the florist's pride, the window gardener's delight; but even these stout fellows, when left in the ground for several years with no notice taken of them until their starched pride is somewhat subdued, acquire a slender grace and modesty that is most becoming to them, and may then take their place among other spring bulbs, Daffodils, Scillas, and the like, that are scattered freely about the borders in informal fashion.

But there are Hyacinths of quite a different style that all bulb lovers should know, quaint and comely creatures that are seldom seen in American gardens, whatever may be their usage in gardens across the sea. Most of them are listed in bulb catalogues of any scope, but all too seldom do they find their way from the printed page to the waiting brown earth. This is too bad, for they are hardy, easily grown, long-lived, and inexpensive, and, given half a chance, increase with praiseworthy generosity.

These small Hyacinths appear akin to some of the Grape Hyacinths (Muscari), but Mr. Farrer with characteristic lucidity points out the difference—"that wide mouth which is the one, the final differentiation between Hyacinth, the open lipped and smiling, and Muscari of the dark face and puckered lips and constricted pinched expression of bell." The bells of these small Hyacinths, like those of their relatives, the fat oriental Hyacinths, are *open*.

H. amethystinus L.   *B.M.* t. 2425
Alpine Hyacinth

In Sweet's "British Flower Garden" (Vol. II, 1823–1825), is a charming portrait of the Alpine Hyacinth made, the artist explains, from a fine row of them flowering luxuriantly in the old garden of the Apothecaries' Company at Chelsea. Sweet says in the accompanying text that he hopes this "hitherto rare plant will soon become more common"; but seemingly this hope has not been realized, for it is still rare in gardens.

It made its bow to gardening society upon its introduction from the Pyrenees in 1759, and Linnaeus gave it its specific name; but this is misleading, for though its longish, narrow bells are of a somewhat misted blue, there is no trace of the amethyst in their frank hue. The bells hang from curving pedicels along a slender arched stem which may be six, or may even reach a length of twelve, inches and carry from twelve to twenty bells, which, as Mr. Farrer describes them, are "the most glorious clear china-blue bells with a paler streak and that wide mouth."

It was one of Mr. Farrer's favorite bulbous plants, and he praises it thus: "Without legend, or rivalry, or comparison, it stands high among the loveliest bulbs we have, and yet is one of those most rarely seen, although it lives as long, and multiplies as readily as *Narcissus poeticus* itself, the most exquisite of all delights for early summer."

All this will be borne out by any who have grown it. Especially are we grateful to it for flowering in late May and early June when we have about given up expecting flowers from bulbs, and the green of the trees has lost its tentative quality and become less subtle, more obvious. Suddenly there appears a spread of little bell-hung stalks, blue or frosted white. Nothing could be prettier. One could not meet a pleasanter surprise along a woodland walk, or massed by the hundred beneath lightly shadowing trees anywhere.

They will grow in thin grass if the soil is not too heavy, but there the increase will be less satisfactory, or they may be scattered about the small bushes in the rock garden. The bulbs should be planted in September or October, three to four inches deep and about three inches apart each way. Frequent transplanting is not necessary. It makes delightful small bowls for indoor decoration, the blue and the white kinds together. I have a note in my "going-to-do book" to plant it about the skirts of Azaleas, but I have not yet got round to it.

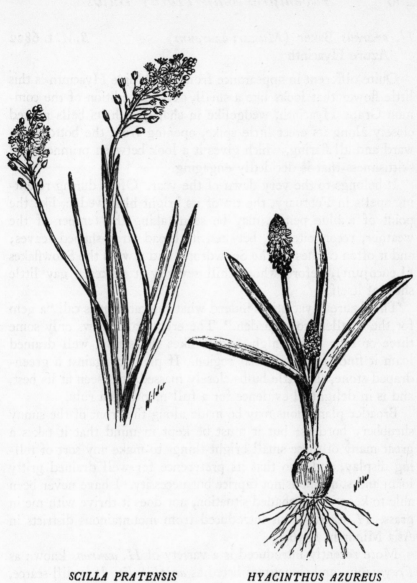

SCILLA PRATENSIS   **HYACINTHUS AZUREUS**

H. azureus Baker (*Muscari azureum*)   *B.M.* t. 6822
    Azure Hyacinth

Quite different in appearance from the Alpine Hyacinth is this
little flower that looks like a small, sky-blue edition of the common Grape Hyacinth, wedgelike in shape, with its bells packed
closely along its erect little spike, opening from the bottom upward and all flaring, which gives it a look between primness and
skittishness that is decidedly engaging.

It belongs to the very dawn of the year. Often during relenting spells in February, the tip of its bright blue wedge, like the
point of a blue pencil, may be seen taking the temper of the
weather, reconnoitering, between its broad strap-shaped leaves;
and it often catches up the Snowdrops, and always the Snowflakes
(Leucojum), before whose chill severity it makes a gay little
show of itself.

The Azure Hyacinth is indeed what the catalogues call "a gem
for the smallest rock garden." The erect stalk grows only some
three or four inches high, and it likes the sandy, well drained
loam it finds in that special region. If planted against a green-
draped stone, the little bulbs closely massed, it is seen at its best,
and is in delightful evidence for a full month as a rule.

Broader plantations may be made along the front of the sunny
shrubbery borders; but it must be kept in mind that it takes a
great many of these small bright things to make any sort of telling display, and also that its preference for well drained gritty
loam and sunshine is not caprice but necessity. I have never been
able to keep it in a shaded situation, nor does it thrive with me in
grass. *H. azureus* was introduced from mountainous districts in
Asia Minor in 1856.

More recently introduced is a variety of *H. azureus* known as
Freynianus, and sometimes listed as *amphibolis*. It is still scarce,
but to be had, and proves a pretty, neat thing, a little taller, a
little paler, a little earlier than the type. Good to have for the
sake of variety, but not a great improvement. I cannot yet tell
about its lasting qualities or its powers of increase.

One has news also of *H. a. giganteus,* from Mount Muris in
northern Cilicia,[1] which doubtless bears out its name for size with

[1] *Gardeners' Chronicle,* Vol. XXIV (1898), p. 190.

a consequent loss of dainty personality—size is no guarantee of charm. And *H. a. robustus* is also reported, but I do not sigh for these Titans when, for so little, hundreds of the ordinary kind are to be had. *H. dalmaticus* appears to be new, or newly brought before the public. I have not seen it. Van Tubergen of Haarlem offers it and describes it as growing four inches high, a light azure-blue with a rosy hue, blossoming in March; but its portrait appears in *Gardening Illustrated* (March 2, 1935), and it is there described as growing five inches tall with amethyst-blue flowers on wiry stems, and again in the same number as pale blue with pink tips.

What is a poor gardener to believe! It appears from its portrait to be a nice little plant with a slightly flexuous stem, carrying a spike of flowers something after the style of *azureus* but not so closely set or so stiff; and from its name, it would seem to hail from Dalmatia, region of many lovely flowers.

H. fastigiatus   B.M. t. 6663

This is a small Hyacinth from the heights of Corsica and Sardinia, introduced in 1882. It has a very small ovoid bulb with several thin tunics, from which arise from three to six leaves, rather weak, and sometimes six inches long, that are contemporary with the flowers. The scape is slender, erect, and a little shorter than the leaves; the flowers in a few-flowered raceme, or sometimes in a congested corymb, are a bright lilac-blue. It is not one of the most conspicuous of the Hyacinths, but it is an early bloomer, and nice to have in a collection.

HYPOXIS *AMARYLLIDACEAE*

STAR-GRASS

H. erecta L. (*H. hirsuta*) B.M. t. 710
Yellow Star-Grass

A SPRIGHTLY if modest little perennial herb found from Maine
to Ontario, Kansas, Florida, and Texas, freely distributed in sandy
soil in meadows, grassy waste places, open woods, and thickets.
The narrow grasslike leaves are somewhat hairy and arise from an
egg-shaped corm of small size to a height of something under a
foot. The slender flower stem is commonly shorter than the
leaves, and carries a three- or four-flowered cluster of bright yellow six-pointed starry flowers, greenish on the undersides. From
a clump arise many stems, and as they are hardly ever out of
bloom from the time they begin to flicker out in May until the
frosts have silenced them, it is readily seen that this little weed-
ling is a valuable plant for the rock garden, or for wide naturalizing in grassy places.

Set five or six inches apart in the rock garden, in a group of a
dozen, nice clumps are soon the result. It is absolutely easy and
reliable, and when more spectacular beauties fail, the little Star-
Grass is on hand to cheer us with its undaunted glint. It is a self-
respecting little soul, too, and does not spread wildly as do so
many wild plants when brought into the garden. The best plantation of it I have seen is in the garden of Herbert Durand, in
Bronxville, and I am sure I have never seen it out of bloom from
May until October.

The genus Hypoxis has other representatives, as many as fifty,
and most of them far more spectacular than is our little *erecta*.
They are distributed over a vast area of tropical Asia, Australia,
South Africa, and tropical America. Many of these are grown in
pots under glass—I have seen a number at the New York Botanical Gardens—and according to Curtis' *Botanical Magazine,* our
small cheerful tramp, the Yellow Star-Grass, when introduced
in 1784 to the solemn surroundings of Kew Gardens, was thought
to be most successfully grown in a pot!

IRIS *IRIDACEAE*

THE bulbous species of Iris are such enchanting plants that it is exasperating to have them so scarce in this country, and when finally come upon, so discouragingly expensive. One does not want a specimen only of any of them; one wants a generous splash, for they are small things, and need to be seen in groups of at least half a dozen, and preferably a good many more, to show their quality.

Their scarcity is one more black mark that must be crossed up against the quarantine. We may not import them, and those who have slowly and painfully raised them from seed, or got them by other means, naturally charge a high price for them. I have known the time when *Iris reticulata* sold (or did it sell?) for two dollars the bulb. It is now happily much less expensive. My own stock is pre-quarantine.

Most of the bulbous Irises are brilliant in color, with gay markings, and many boast a fine fragrance. They flower, too, at a season when many of their relatives are still sleeping snugly with the covers drawn close about them. Under favorable conditions, that is, planted in well drained soil in a sunny position in the rock garden, preferably with a warm rock at their backs, numerous of them will flourish in the "frozen North," and give their welcome blooms in late February and March. Some, of course, are better for the protection of a frame or hand glass, and all, where they are likely to be splashed with mud, are protected from this desecration if a mulch of peat moss or clean white sand is spread about them and later removed.

IRIS RETICULATA GROUP

I. reticulata Bieb.   *B.M.* t. 5577

This lovely and brilliant flower of the early spring has its name from the ovoid bulb, which is covered with a netted, reticulate coat. The leaves are curious, and make their appearance above ground often in the winter; indeed, in mild localities they thrust up their points late in the autumn. They are narrow, four-sided, and are armed at the tip with a horny point. No wonder the hard earth presents no obstacle to their advance.

The flowers open in March, as a rule. They are borne on long tubes, and appear like brilliant insects nestled among the narrow leaves. The color is rich deep violet save where, on the hind part of the claw, there is a bright orange ridge set in a white patch streaked with violet. When the sun shines warm upon them, the scent of violets is clearly perceptible, and a few blossoms brought into the house will perfume a large room.

The seed capsule is borne just above the earth on a peduncle. To find it one must look low down among the leaves. This species has grown in my garden for some twenty years, the bulbs now and then, when they appeared to be crowded, being taken up and re-planted. A warm sheltered place is chosen for them in the rock garden with a rock on the north side. The soil is light and some-what sandy. *Iris reticulata* comes from Asia Minor, the Caucasus, and adjacent regions.

I. reticulata Krelagei Regel   Lod. *Bot. Cab.* t. 1829

This is a variable plant, but the individuals that I have seen have been much less brilliant in color than the type, usually some tone of red-purple, and the flowers are shorter and broader in all their parts, more squat, and have not that poised look that distin-guishes the true *reticulata;* nor have the specimens that have come under my notice had any fragrance, though I hear that this pleas-ant attribute is occasionally present. It flowers here often two weeks earlier than the type, the pointed leaves piercing a mat of *Thymus lanuginosus.* It is said to be common in the Caucasus, spreading into Persia and Asia Minor.

I. reticulata Histrio Reichb.   *B.M.* t. 6033

This is the earliest of the *reticulata* group to flower. It is a bright little flower, distinctly bluer in tone than the type, but with a hint of red in the composition, and ornamented with a creamy region toward the center flecked and veined with bright blue. There is a narrow yellow ridge, and on the claw a yellow streak. It blooms well down among the leaves, which may be a foot tall at flowering time. This form comes from Palestine, Mount Lebanon and Mount Gerizim. A form of it called *aintabensis* is described by Baker. This is said to be a showy and beautiful native of Armenia, where it "hails from the environs of Aintab, haunting the foothills of subalpine regions." I have not come across it.

I. reticulata Histrioides

With this bright form the flowers appear innocent of leaves which, when they finally emerge, are stouter and longer than in any other of the *reticulata* group. It commonly flowers about a month later than *Histrio*, but the flowers are larger, almost five inches across at their best, the falls spreading out horizontally. The color is somewhat variable, but usually a bright blue veined with violet, the falls having the creamy-white area as in *Histrio*, veined and blotched with violet, and the narrow orange ridge on the blade. In a warm room the flowers are distinctly scented. There is a form with larger flowers known as *Histrioides major*. Armenia, district of Amasia.

I. reticulata Vartanii (I. Vartanii Foster) B.M. t. 6942

This Iris, which comes from Palestine near Nazareth, did not prove hardy in my garden on the one occasion when I was able to secure bulbs. It is described as having the usual netted bulb tunic and horny-tipped four-sided leaves that are about four inches or more high at the time of blossoming. The flowers, which are said to appear often in midwinter, are described as of a rather slaty blue color, with yellow and black dots on the claw. Not fragrant. Should I again be so lucky as to receive bulbs of *Vartanii*, they would be consigned to a cold frame. South of Washington, they would doubtless live out of doors.

I. reticulata Bakeriana Foster (I. Bakeriana) B.M. t. 7084

This species also has the ovoid bulb with netted coat of the type, and the horn-tipped leaves that are nearly or quite a foot tall at flowering time. It is some years since I grew *Bakeriana* in my Rockland County (New York) garden against a warm south wall, but there it came through the winter safely and flowered in March, flooding the air on warm days with a rich fragrance. The flower is not large, from two to three inches across; the yellow streak on the ridge is not conspicuous. The color is a medium violet with a white central region on the falls blotched and streaked with color. It comes from Armenia near Marden.

I. reticulata Danfordiae Baker (*I. Danfordiae* Boiss.)

B.M. t. 7140

As described by Mr. Dykes, this sounds like a charming member of the *reticulata* group; and I wish it might come within my reach, for it seems probable that it would prove at least as amiable as the others under our climatic conditions, though it is said to flower in England in February and it might be discouraged by the antagonistic attitude of our weather at that early date.

The color is described as a rich yellow, with variable dark brown dots on the blade of the fall near the ridge and along the claw. The standards "are reduced to a mere bristle, invisible at a little distance." The whole flower is funnel-shaped, the blade of the fall spreading horizontally. It comes, according to Sir Michael Foster, from Asia Minor, Cilician Taurus near Mount Amascha, Amasia, Egin.

Other species in this group are *I. Histrioides sophenensis* Foster, said to follow *Histrio*, and to flower earlier than *Krelagei*, and *I. r. humilis*, sometimes known as var. *cyanea*, said to be a very bright blue in color.

From time to time varieties of *reticulata* have arisen in cultivation. These have been variously known as var. *caerulea*, var. *purpurea*, var. *major*, and the like. The only one that has come my way is a small beauty, var. *Cantab*, which is available in this country.[1] This, which Mr. E. A. Bowles calls "my turquoise treasure," originated in his famous gardens. Of it he says, "I think it is one of the loveliest of spring flowers, and do not believe it is only that sort of paternal pride vented in one's own seedling, that leads me to believe it is of the colour of Delphinium Belladonna, and that the bee guide on the falls is just the right shade of apricot-orange to attract any flying insect and please an artistic eye with its colour contrast, producing much the same effect that you get in the deeper colouring of *Linaria alpina*." Little more need be said save that at flowering time it is just over three inches high.

The *reticulata* Irises are readily raised from seed, though it takes a little time and patience to bring them to flowering strength.

[1] William N. Craig, Weymouth, Mass.

The variety *Krelagei* is particularly generous with its own seeds, and any one having this kind in his garden, will do well to watch for and gather the seed, for the progeny may bring many delightful surprises, varying much in color.

Here is what Sir Michael Foster has to say on gathering and sowing the seed: [*]

"In gathering seed, care should be taken not to overlook the seed-pods, which are often more or less buried in the ground. The seed, if sown as soon as ripe, will to a large extent germinate in the following winter and spring, but some of it may lie dormant for two, three, or even more years.

"Germination is more certain when seed is sown in the open than when it is sown in pots or pans, owing probably to adequate moisture being thus more regularly secured, but the seedlings which appear in December or January from the summer sowing need protection if the winter is severe, and in general, the management of the seedlings is more easy in pots than in the open."

I have found the safest way is to sow the seed directly in the soil of the cold frame, where it may easily be protected over the winter.

I. reticulata, and to some degree, *I. Histrioides*, increase rapidly from offsets or small bulbils, which may be taken up and started on careers of their own. *I. Krelagei* is much slower of increase, though I notice this spring that several clumps seem to have doubled up. All the *reticulatas* make charming pot plants, and may be easily forced in the house.

THE XIPHIUM GROUP

The so-called Spanish and English Irises which compose what is known as the *Xiphium* group, unlike the *reticulata* group which is Asian in distribution, are native chiefly in Europe with an occasional flare-up in Algiers. The bulbs have membraneous, not netted, coats, and the leaves are few, long, and grassy, not foursided. The flowers, usually two, but sometimes one only, are borne on stems varying from a height of sixteen inches to more than two feet. They bloom during the late spring and early sum-

[*] *Bulbous Irises*, by Sir Michael Foster.

mer, and are very beautiful, having the fluttering appearance of butterflies or moths. Under cultivation I have found them, while commonly quite hardy over the first winter, not long-lived. They are apt to degenerate and disappear after a year or two of garden experience at the most.

I. Xiphium L.   *B.M.* t. 686
Spanish Iris

The Spanish Iris is found not only in Spain and Portugal, but in southern France and Italy, Corsica and Sardinia, and across the sea in Algiers. It has been called the poor man's Orchid, so varied and lovely are its colors, so moderate its price—before the ban. It has long been a loved garden flower, for Gerard grew it in 1633. The leaves are slender and grasslike, and usually make their appearance above ground soon after they are planted in the autumn, lasting over the winter.

The flowers flutter forth in late May and early June in this locality. They are exquisite in shape and color, and look, as I have said, like butterflies, their wings, or falls, outspread, seeming to float lazily above the foliage in the gentle summer air. They come in tones of pale to deep blue, to purple, also yellow and white, and often they are parti-colored, the standards bright pure blue or purple, the falls yellow or white; others are mixtures of bronze and gold, or bronze and blue.

The Spanish Iris has been the object of much attention by growers, and many seedlings have been raised. A fine selection is Belle Chinoise, pure yellow and early; Cajanus, fine golden yellow, late; Flora, cream and pale blue; Excelsior, violet and French gray; Hercules, bronze with orange blotch; King of the Blues, clear color and large flowers; King of the Whites, pure and exquisite; Souvenir, light blue; Thunderbolt, bronze and very large; Philomela, blue with white falls.

So far as the culture of Spanish Irises goes, they love sunshine and a dry warm exposure. To plant them in mixed groups in borders or in selected regions of the rock garden, is to secure a most lovely effect; but the bulbs should be set where they will not be pressed upon by the roots of too hungry perennials or predatory annuals. There is a curious scent to the flowers, somewhat like that of Coriander seed.

I. *Xiphioides* Ehrh. B.M. t. 687
English Iris

The English Iris is larger in all its parts than the Spanish Iris, taller, broader of leaf, altogether more sturdy in appearance, less fragile in structure, and to me less lovely, though very showy. The leaves do not make their appearance until spring. They flower later than the Spanish Irises, and are found in nature chiefly in the French and Spanish Pyrenees. The flowers are scentless, large, and handsome.

A good selection of varieties would contain Blue Hesperus, blue with a white patch on the fall; Cornelia, lavender, feathered with dark blue; Grand Lilac, silvery blue, flaked with mauve; Mauve Queen, a rosy tone with darker markings; Mont Blanc, pure white; Princess Irene, white splashed with rose; Sir William Mansfield, claret and extra large. There are no yellow-flowered varieties to be found among the English Irises.

While thriving in ordinary garden soil, the English Irises like distinctly damper conditions than do the Spanish, though they also must have sunshine, and they thrive most heartily in a rich black vegetable loam. They are not easy to suit in most gardens in America where the summers are torrid and dry; most persons will find the Spanish sorts easier to manage, even though copious artificial watering is resorted to in the case of the former.

They have the name of English Irises, by which they are widely known, not because they are native in Great Britain, but because they reached "the Low Countries from England, most probably without any notice of their true habitat," and were presumed by the Dutch to be native in that country.

Clusius, it is said, upon his arrival in England in 1571, sought for it in a wild state until he was informed by Lobel of its being cultivated only in certain gardens near Bristol, where it had been most probably imported from Spain or Portugal. This information is from a magazine article [*] which goes on to state that Gerard included it among British plants, but that Parkinson was aware of its true habitat.

What are known as Dutch Irises are a new race that may be described as a large and early-flowering strain of Spanish Irises.

[*] Curtis' *Botanical Magazine*, Vol. XVIII.

They first saw the light in the van Tubergen Nurseries in Haarlem, Holland. Though larger than the Xiphiums, they have something of the light and airy structure, and are very beautiful. They begin to flower early in May, before any of the Spanish varieties, and they are easily pleased in the garden, preferring a light loam and sunshine.

The range of colors is wide and includes not only the many charming blue tones, but yellow and pure white. They are best planted in October. Both Spanish and Dutch Irises are unrivaled for cutting, and a few rows of them in some suitable by-place will be deeply appreciated for this purpose.

A selection of Dutch varieties would include Adrian Backer, bright violet-blue with line of yellow on the falls; Albert Cuyp, blue and white standards with yellow falls; Rembrandt, two tones of blue; Frans Hals, soft yellow and pale blue; Imperator, soft rich blue with yellow blotch; White Excelsior; Leonardo da Vinci, cream and yellow; Golden Glory; Golden Bronze; Pieter de Hoog, pearly blue.

Other Irises that come under the head of Xiphiums are *I. filifolia*, *I. juncea*, and *I. tingitana*. The first two I have now in seedling stage; with the last, I have had no experience out of doors. But, writing in the *National Horticultural Magazine*, October, 1933, of a trial of various bulbous Irises in Washington, D. C., Charles E. F. Gersdorff states that *I. tingitana* Boiss. & Reut. (*B.M.* t. 6775) from Tangier, which we usually see grown under glass, and its beautiful variety Wedgwood, flowered out of doors in that locality the first week of April, and continued in bloom for twenty days. Any one whose climate will suffer them, should certainly grow these exquisite Irises. The leaves are described as slender and rush-like.

I. juncea Poir.   *B.M.* t. 5890

This species, which is still in the seedling stage in a frame, comes from such warm regions as North Africa, the Riviera, and Sicily. The leaves are described as slender and rush-like, and they "shoot in the late autumn." The stem bears one or sometimes two flowers, not unlike Spanish Irises in shape, and of a warm yellow tone. They are pleasantly fragrant.

I. filifolia Boiss. *B.M.* t. 5928

Filifolia comes from Spain, and is said to flower late in June. The stems are something over a foot tall, and bear flowers of a dark violet or red-purple hue above the narrow leaves. Parkinson, with a fine disregard for space, called this the Purple or murrey-coloured bulbous Barbary Flower-de-luce.

I have thought it not at all likely that I could compose the inevitable quarrel between these heat lovers and our ravaging Westchester County climate, but I mean to try, and my hopes of success are raised by this from Mr. Robert Wayman of Long Island: "In importing it [*I. juncea*], there was a question in my mind as to whether it would prove hardy here, but it came through the winter smiling, every plant bloomed most profusely, and it is apparently quite at home and a rugged strong grower."

When my plants are removed from the frame, they will be given a snug place in the rock garden with a rock at their backs, in soil that is light and well drained, and when winter comes, a warm blanket.

THE JUNO GROUP

Of the Juno Irises I know so little from actual experience that I hesitate to set down my inadequate knowledge at all. I do so only because they are extraordinarily beautiful, very early-flowering, wholly rewarding to those who, having secured them, can supply their not unreasonable needs and preferences. They differ from the two groups just described in several characters.

The bulbs are large and incased in several coats, and the fully ripened bulb, unlike those of the two foregoing sections, which will be found to have no roots at all when mature, is furnished with rather thick "store roots," which, if the bulb is dug, must be guarded from injury, as they are very brittle at first. Also, instead of the narrow and rather scarce leaves, they have many broader and shorter leaves. The flower, too, is larger, and is often borne close to the ground.

"The outer segment or fall, instead of having, as in most Irises, the claw narrower than the blade, is broadest at the claw, which is expanded sideways into two angular flanges or auricles, one on each side. Further, in nearly all cases also, the inner segment or standard is very small, reduced often to a mere bristle, and usually takes up a horizontal position, or is even turned directly downward instead of standing erect. To compensate, as it were, for the smallness of the standards, the crests of the styles are unusually large, and form a conspicuous part of the flower." [4]

It is to be hoped that these beautiful flowers will shortly be more readily available to American gardeners. A search through many Iris lists may turn up a few, but they are still sadly scarce and expensive.

I. persica L.   *B.M.* t. 1

This strangely beautiful and spectacular flower has grown in my garden for many years, not heartily and with good will, but somewhat grudgingly, some years refusing to flower at all, again bursting into bloom suddenly, not waiting for its foliage, and fairly taking one's breath away with its beauty, delighting one with its fragrance. Those are years to live for.

In certain regions of the South, in old gardens, *Iris persica* has long been established and flourishes freely. One would like to know the history of its introduction into these gardens, and why it apparently did not reach northern gardens, though perhaps it did, and simply perished for lack of warmth and a sympathetic understanding of its needs. Mrs. McKinney says that, in one old southern garden that she knows, *I. persica* has grown since the memory of man, and increases to big clumps. Her bulbs came to her from "a generous little girl in the community of which I have spoken. They were a matted clump such as we often see in the Star of Bethlehem." [5]

The full-grown bulb of *persica* is very large, and it has the thonglike roots characteristic of the group. It flowers almost as early as do the *reticulata* group, and without its leaves, which, after the flower has passed, shoot up to a height of about six inches. The flower is large and almost stemless.

To describe it adequately would tax a person far more nimble in the use of words than I. I have often sat down beside it and

---

[4] *Bulbous Irises*, by Prof. Michael Foster.
[5] *Iris in the Little Garden*, by Ella Porter McKinney.

tried to put its strange compelling beauty on paper, but I never have been able to. The best I can do is to say that its color is the palest blue-green, a sort of modified sea-green, or perhaps white, washed with this elusive tint. On the blade of the falls, a purple velvet area surrounds the brilliant orange raised ridge which extends back along the haft. While it flowers, all else seems of small account. *Iris persica* comes from Persia and various parts of eastern and middle Asia Minor.

There are said to be other forms of it, but this is the only one I know, and it suffices. It grows on a southern slope in my rock garden in very gritty soil, and there is a cover crop of *Thymus lanuginosus* to keep the lovely blossoms from being spattered. After a very hot and dry summer, the following spring will often see it bloom; doubtless it needs heat and drought to tone up the bulbs to a flowering state of mind, and I have an idea that it would like a stiffer soil.

Iris sindpers is, I have just discovered with some excitement, offered in this country. This, said Mr. Irwin Lynch, one-time Curator of the Cambridge Botanic Gardens,* is a hybrid raised by C. G. van Tubergen, Jr., about 1899. Its parents were *I. persica* and the much taller *I. sindjarensis*. He describes it as "a charming plant and very floriferous, forming a close-growing mass of blue flowers when well established."

The flower has a fuller color than *sindjarensis* (*B.M.* t. 7145), which is native in Mesopotamia, and is without the conspicuous dark blotch at the apex of the falls found in *I. persica*, its male parent. In the *National Horticultural Magazine,* January, 1932, there is a fine photograph of it, showing its dwarf stature and the accompanying broad leaves. Cold-frame treatment is recommended for it in very cold localities.

In my Rockland County garden, I grew for a short but happy time, under the south wall, two other Juno Irises, but lost them in the moving, and have not been able to replace them.

I. caucasica Hoffm.   Sweet's *Brit. Fl. Gard.*, t. 255

I imported the bulbs of this and the following species from Holland in that gracious time when there were no prohibitions. Though the winters were cold in Rockland County, they were

---

* *The Book of the Iris.*

usually snow-blanketed, and the situation under the south wall, where the soil was light and well drained and limy, was very warm and protected; anyway, they lived out with the protection of a blanket of hay. What they would do in this garden, I am unhappily unable to say. *I. caucasica* is native in the Caucasus to Asia Minor, Persia, Kurdistan, and Turkestan, ascending to six thousand feet above sea level.

After the triumph of bringing it through the winter had subsided, I had to admit it was not very pretty or striking; not in any way to be compared to *persica*. Nor was it in the least fragrant. The flowers, on almost no stems at all, were an indefinite greenish yellow, warming a little on the ridge and in the area immediately surrounding it. I believe there are other and better forms of it.

I. orchioides Carr.   B.M. t. 7111

This species flowered a little later than the foregoing, about the 1st of April, and it was a good deal more worth while altogether. Its yellow flowers were brightly ornamental and set off upon the falls by greenish lines and spots. The stem grew up to a height of something more than a foot, clasped alternately by narrow leaves with three or more solitary flowers produced in their axils. The bulb is large, as large as a hen's egg, and produces roots that persist during the dormant state. *I. orchioides* comes from the neighborhood of eastern Bokhara.

I. bucharica Foster   B.M. t. 7914

Among the should-haves in our gardens is this sturdy Juno Iris from the high mountain slopes of eastern Bokhara. Its portrait in Mr. Dykes' "The Genus Iris," must fill all who see it with longing; moreover, Mr. Dykes says: "This is the strongest grower, and one of the most strikingly beautiful of all the Juno Irises. That it is prolific is proved by the fact that two bulbs planted in the autumn of 1906, gave four flower spikes in 1907, thirteen in 1910, and over forty in 1911. To obtain this result, the bulbs were lifted every second year when the foliage turned yellow in July, and planted again in September in fairly rich soil, in a warm, well drained position. . . . Each stem bears five or seven flowers, of which several are usually expanded at the same time, and the contrast between the pure white of the styles and the golden yellow of the fall-blades set among the glossy green leaves, is extremely pleasing."

There are numerous other desirable Junos which it is to be hoped that a becoming humility, coupled with a determination to put up a stiff fight for them, will eventually bring within our reach. If you secure any of the Junos by whatever means, bear in mind the fact that they like stiffish soil and must be placed where they will receive a summer baking.

LEUCOCRINUM *LILIACEAE*

SAND LILY

L. montanum Nutt.
    Sand Lily, California Soaproot, Wild Tuberose, Desert Lily, etc.

A number of years ago I purchased blind—that is, I knew nothing about them—a half-dozen roots of the Sand Lily from a western dealer. It was in the autumn, and I consigned the little bunches of fleshy fibrous roots to a sandy region (sand seemed to be indicated by the common name) in the rock garden.

In the spring, a tuft of grasslike leaves appeared, and though I watched hopefully, that was all. This was not very satisfactory, but it seemed fair to give them another chance; and in the interval of waiting for another spring, I learned something about them. It seems they are to the West country where they grow what the Hepatica is to us in the East.

In turning the pages of an old bound volume of the always interesting *American Botanist*, I came upon an article by a man who knew and loved the Sand Lily. "It is remarkable," he wrote, "that the first flower of spring on the semi-arid plains should be delicately showy and fragrant. The early flowers are generally inconspicuous, and with no claims to odor. The Sand Lily is the most striking exception. The bright green of the tuft of leaves which often appears before the last snow of winter has disappeared, is prophetic of the spring near at hand; the gleaming whiteness of the six-rayed waxen petals peeping forth from banks of sand and clumps of Buffalo grass in the frosty air of an early spring morning seem, somehow, to remind me of patches of snow here and there on the prairie that have recently surrendered to the benign rays of the returning sun. To me the Sand Lily seems to tie up winter with spring." Later on in the article, this prairie wayfarer says that you are never disappointed when you go out to look for it, that even very early it is to be found on sunny slopes, along the lee of dry arroyos, or in the hollows of prairie trails.

All this gave me a very warm and friendly feeling toward the Sand Lily, and when in the next spring the green tuft spouted white flowers something like Crocuses, I was delighted; but they were not waxen as my prairie author had said, rather they had a sort of crystalline, or perhaps translucent, quality, not at all the opaqueness which the word "waxen" indicates. They were thin in texture, thinner and less crisp than Crocuses, but stemless, slender, and tubelike, and individually fleeting. From a well established clump, I read, may arise in long succession as many as fifty flowers! Nothing like that largess has been thus far vouchsafed me, but last spring several clumps bore a dozen glistening blooms.

Those who plant the Sand Lily must bear in mind that it is little and low, rising only a few inches from the ground, and so must not be placed near enterprising plants that would gradually invade its territory. A little sandy sunny plain in the rock garden, not necessarily completely arid, is nice for it and makes it feel at home.

The whole plant dies away after it has completed its seedmaking (this it does tidily underground), and so its place should be marked. I have not yet tried growing anything over its head to fill the blank that it leaves, but some lightly rooting annual might well be made use of—*Sedum caeruleum* or the small and delightfully gaudy *Leptosiphon hybridus*. I have a few clumps in the moraine, but cannot yet say how they will weather this austere treatment; but I am ready to say that this is one of the most easily propitiated of western plants, and wholly suitable for use in eastern rock gardens, as well as one of the most charming.

As to its range in nature, I gather from Ira Gabrielson's "Western American Alpines" that it is wide—from Nebraska west to Oregon, and southward it is abundant in widely separated localities, and often exceedingly scarce in the intervening territories.

Although clumps of the Sand Lily may be had in the spring from dealers in western plants, early autumn is the best time to plant them. And they are quite hardy. Mr. Farrer says of it, "the apple of the eye should not be more cherished."

LEUCOJUM *AMARYLLIDACEAE*

SNOWFLAKE

THE Leucojums are a small choice group of bulbous plants having much in common with Galanthus (Snowdrop). They both have tunicated bulbs, strap-shaped radical leaves, pendulous and generally white flowers borne on a peduncle rising direct from the bulb; but among the differences readily noted by the lay eye, are the numerous leaves of Leucojum, whereas Galanthus has only two arising from each bulb, the usually two or sometimes more flowers hung from each stalk, and the bell-like, somewhat incurved rather than flaring, form of the flowers, with the six segments of like length and shape.[1]

There are about nine species of Leucojum recognized, but these until recently were not one genus but two, Leucojum and Acis, the latter named for a wandering Sicilian shepherd. Latterly, they have all been enrolled under the one banner, Leucojum, but they remain, nevertheless, distinct and apart, different in habit, habitat, and requirements, the scions of the house of the Sicilian shepherd being small-flowered, low of stature, with threadlike leaves, and tender of constitution, chancy, difficult, requiring warmth, sunshine, shelter, perfect drainage. They inhabit such gentle and alluring neighborhoods as Corsica, the Ionian Isles, Majorca, Morocco, the environs of Mentone. The true Leucojums, on the other hand, are sturdy and easy-going, larger-flowered, more substantial, hardy, and altogether more robust. They own central and northern Europe as their native habitat, and they are doubtful natives of Great Britain.

The name is an old Greek one used by Theophrastus, though it is by no means certain that he had the Leucojum, as we know it, in mind when he used it. It is from *leukos*, white, and *ion*, Violet—which derivation, with its early flowering and sweet scent,

[1] The green spots on the segments of Leucojums are rounded, while those upon Snowdrops are in the shape of a horseshoe.

may explain Parkinson's reason for calling *Leucojum vernum* the Bulbous Violet, for there is no other resemblance between a Snowflake and a Violet. According to William Curtis, founder of the *Botanical Magazine* and author of "Flora Londinensis," it was he who coined the common name of Snowflake for these flowers.

The hardy Leucojums are among the most worth while of spring-flowering bulbous plants. They are strong of constitution, may be transplanted at almost any season, even when in growth, though they should be kept as short a time as possible above ground, and ask little attention once they are settled in well-drained soil, not too dry and devoid of fresh manure.

Leafmold is their delight. They do not require, nor should they be subjected to, frequent disturbance. The clumps may be left alone year after year to make slow but steady increase, unless they show by diminished flowering that they have exhausted the soil, or that the bulbs have finally become overcrowded. Seed should be sown as soon as ripe, and takes three or four years to make bulbs of flowering size. The bulbs are not expensive, and it is hardly worth while to resort to the slower method of seed-raising.

It is important to get the bulbs into the ground as early as possible. They should be planted about three inches apart, and two inches below the surface; they do not like deep planting. They may take a year or so to become sufficiently settled to blossom with freedom. They are invaluable for use in extensive rock gardens, for shaded borders among ferns and wild flowers, for light woodland, springy banks, and the waterside.

L. aestivum L.   *B.M.* t. 1210
    Summer Snowflake. Meadow Snowflake

The Summer Snowflake is a native of central Europe, and is found naturalized in wet meadows and Osier beds in parts of England, especially in the southeastern counties where its distribution is so general as to cause it by some authorities to be considered a native. In the meadows along the little river Loddon, the nodding white bells make a great show, and there they are called Loddon Lilies.

It was first recorded in England from both banks of the

Thames, below London, and it follows watercourses from Suffolk to Oxford, Dorset, and Kent. It is an old inhabitant of gardens, even in this country, and naturalizes readily, so it is possible that it may be found wild with us in long settled neighborhoods, though Gray does not record it.

It is a larger and more robust plant than *L. vernum*, the leaves longer, somewhat narrower, and more glaucous, folding over one another at the bottom where they clasp the stalk, which rises a foot or more high. At the top of the stalk there is a spathe which presently opens at the side and lets out two to six flowers, the buds erect at first but drooping as they expand. Their oval-concave segments, cut almost to the bottom, are pure white with a thickened green tip to each segment. The flowers do not all open at once, but follow one another over a period of several weeks during May. They are followed by triangular seed-vessels. The flowers have practically no scent and secrete no honey. The bulbs are roundish and a good deal like those of the common Daffodil.

The Summer Snowflake should be set where the soil is never bone-dry and where it receives only the morning sun, on springy, half-shaded banks, in low woodland, in fern borders, or naturalized by the waterside. It thrives well even in quite heavy shade. Leaves and flowers used together make charming vases. The species *pulchellum* (*L. Hernandezii* Salisb.) of the Balearic Isles and thereabouts, blooms somewhat earlier than the foregoing but is much like it in appearance; the leaves, however, are narrower and the flowers are smaller. It is especially partial to waterside situations, but it is an inferior plant to *L. aestivum*, important chiefly in bridging the period between Spring and Summer Snowflakes.

L. aestivum Gravetye Giant is an especially stout and vigorous form that originated in the gardens of the late William Robinson, where it is extensively naturalized by the pondsides and in the meadows and borders. It has leaves of heavy texture, flower stalks almost three feet high, bearing snowy, green-tipped bells of large size, and often six to eight to a stalk. It is said to thrive in heavy soil, and I have read that it is a form intermediate between *L. vernum* and *L. aestivum*, though its height and vigor are greater than those of either.

L. vernum L. B.M. t. 46
  Spring Snowflake

Any who have seen this delightful spring flower must surely covet it. In appearance it is much like a Snowdrop, but a Snowdrop that has lost its fragile tentative quality and become more robust physically and altogether more sure of itself. The white buds appear above ground while the true Snowdrops are still flowering; and before they have finished, the Spring Snowflake has hung out its larger green-tipped bells, singly and sometimes in twos, on stalks five or six inches high, between the shining half-inch-wide leaves, of which there are usually four or five. These hold themselves in check until the flowers have had their day, and then accomplish their full length of six to eight inches.

The flowers have a pleasant scent, not unlike that of Hawthorn, and are followed by a pear-shaped capsule containing the seeds. The bulb is much like that of a Daffodil. The soil for them should be a soft sandy loam, and the morning sun is all they should be subjected to. As they are fairly dwarf of stature, they are welcome in the rock garden where in time they make a handsome early display.

The Spring Snowflake has long rejoiced the hearts of gardeners, for it was introduced to cultivation early in the sixteenth century, coming from moist woods in central Europe. It is said to be naturalized in copses in certain sections of Dorsetshire, England; but as it is much slower of increase than *L. aestivum*, it is more difficult to naturalize, and it is more often seen grown in borders. If happy, however, it will sow its own seed, and if the little "garlics" are watched for and protected, the fulness of time will bring about a little colony in which we have had no hand save that of guardian of the babies. The Spring Snowflake is hardy as far north as Ottawa.

Two robust forms of *L. vernum* are procurable and most desirable to possess. These are *L. v. carpathicum* Herbert (*B.M.* t. 1993), a Carpathian form, and *L. v. Vagneri* Borbas (*Gard. Chron.*, XLIII [1908], 131). Both grow in this garden, but I have to confess that I am at a loss to know which is which, the doctors in whom I place my faith not agreeing. Both, as I have them, are more robust and taller-growing than the type, and both

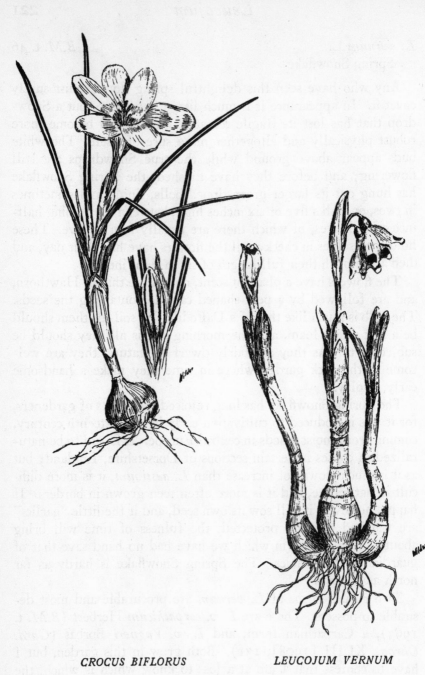

CROCUS BIFLORUS   **LEUCOJUM VERNUM**

have two or three blossoms to a stalk; but one has the characteristic emerald-green thickened tips to the segments, and the other
has canary-yellow tips. S. Arnott and E. A. Bowles declare for
carpathicum as the yellow-tipped kind, but other authorities state
with equal certainty that *Vagneri* has yellow tips. And that is
gardening; in any case, both are desirable.

As I have them, *Vagneri* flowers earlier than the type and is
taller, while *carpathicum* flowers at about the same time as *L.
vernum.* This kind is very pretty when kept away from the emer-
ald-adorned varieties, and should not be grown with them. It
looks a little as if it had spilled its breakfast egg on its snowy bib.

The bulbs of the Spring Snowflakes should be put into the
ground as early as they may be procured, and should be disturbed
as little as possible thereafter. They require a season or two to
become sufficiently well established to make a striking show.

For those who live in mild climates and who like to try the
rare and difficult, there are these other Leucojums, once known as
Acis. They are not at the present time easily procurable in this
country; but seeds are available from European dealers, and the
determined will seek this method of acquiring them.

L. autumnale L. (*Acis autumnalis Salisb.*)   *B.M.* t. 960

This rare little autumn-flowering bulbous plant is found in
Portugal, Morocco, and the Ionian Isles. It sends up a brownish
naked scape to a height of about six inches and hangs out one or
two, or sometimes three flowers that look like delicately flushed
Lilies-of-the-Valley, white with a pinkish base. The threadlike
leaves appear after the flowers begin to bloom in late August or
September. It requires a mild climate, perfect drainage, and a
rather sandy soil. This pretty fragile plant is suitable only for use
on sunny levels of a rock garden, or in a moraine where the small
bulbs should be planted in groups of at least half a dozen. It is
said to ripen seed freely, and this, when sown at once, germinates
readily.

L. hyemale DC. (*L. niacaense* Ard.) (*Acis hyemalis* Roem.)
Mentone Snowflake   *B.M.* t. 6711

This is a fragile little bulbous plant having a very restricted
habitat. It is found only "in the crevices of clefts, and in sandy,

rocky soil on the seashore in the districts around Nice and Mentone." [2] The bulb is small and globose and brown-coated, and sends up several yellowish green leaves that may reach a height of a foot, from between which during the month of April appears the flexuous stem carrying usually one, but sometimes two, pure white nodding blossoms with bright yellow stamens. Like all the Acis group of Snowflakes, it is suitable only for cultivation in a rock garden, and should not be planted where the mercury falls much below freezing. As it does not flower until April, the name *hyemale* is misleading. This species is closely allied to *L. tricophyllum* Schousb. (*Acis tricophylla* Herb.), *B.M.* t. 554, of southern Europe, Morocco, and Algiers. It has very narrow leaves and white flowers in April.

Another very rare and tender species is *L. roseum* Martin (*Acis rosea*), a portrait of which appears in Sweet's *British Flower Garden*, t. 297. It has a small globose bulb, producing in autumn rose-colored flowers on stems about four inches high, followed by the narrow leaves. It is a native of the island of Corsica, and where cultivated in this country, requires all the sunshine possible and a stony, sandy soil.

Persons wishing to try these tender Snowflakes in the North may grow them in pots in a sunny window or greenhouse.

[2] It is also found on limestone cliffs in the Maritime Alps.

LIRIOPE *LILIACEAE*

Lily-Turf

L. Muscari (*L. graminifolia densiflora*)
Big Blue Lily-Turf

Not all plants are born to a distinguished career. Some must fill
the humbler stations of garden life. Of such is the Blue Lily-Turf,
a modest plant that one might easily tuck away in a corner and
forget until one autumn day, mayhap, when casting about for a bit
of color, its spikes of dark blue flowers, not unlike attenuated Grape
Hyacinths, attract one's attention. The habit of the plant is tufted,
the root system a bunch of fattish little tubers, and the leaves
are slender and grasslike, but tough and evergreen, a foot long
and a quarter of an inch wide. The spikes of small blue flowers
rise from amidst the leaves and scarcely, if at all, reach their
height. They appear about the middle of September and are very
durable, lasting a full month whether growing, or placed in water
indoors. The fruit is said to be black and handsome, but it has so
far escaped my notice, or perhaps has not matured here.

There is a form with leaves prettily striped green and yellowish white which have a varnished look, and while I do not as a
rule care for plants with variegated foliage, I like the Lily-Turf;
it appears very cheerful and reassuring in the late garden amidst
all the signs of departure about it.

The Lily-Turf came to my garden, like so many valued plants,
as a gift from a casual visitor who said she had it from a very old
garden, and it is just the sort of prim little plant one would expect
to find cherished in rural neighborhoods, and handed from one
neighbor to another to bind the edges of beds of favorite old-
fashioned flowers. The Liriope comes from China and Japan, and
is named for the Nymph Liriope, obscure and seldom mentioned
mother of Narcissus, and like its modest namesake, is too inconspicuous and retiring ever to achieve celebrity, though it is pretty
enough, and its time of flowering gives it a value that at a more

prolific season it might not possess. Its lateness suggests its use as a companion for Colchicums, autumn Crocuses and the charming pink-flowered *Oxalis Bowiei* in making autumn groups in rock garden or border. In these associations, the variegated form shows up with special distinction. *L. Muscari* is quite hardy and thrives in good soil either in sun or in partial shade. Division of the roots may be carried out in spring, thereby increasing our store.

Close to Liriope and often confused with it are the evergreen, sod-forming perennial herbs known as Mondo (Ophiopogon), natives of Asia, which in mild localities are useful as ground covers, and in the North are frequently used as pot plants.

There is confusion in the trade and in gardens between the genus Mondo and that of Liriope, and both are commonly known as Lily-Turf or Snakesbeard. Under *Liriope spicatus* (see "Hortus"), Bailey describes the same plant that is shown in the *Botanical Magazine* (t. 5348) as *Ophiopogon spicatus*, and Loddiges in his *Botanical Cabinet* (t. 694) so names and describes it. Correvon [1] describes this as a Japanese liliaceous plant with tufts of grasslike foliage and spikes of small white flowers, and he says it is not hardy.

Writing in *Horticulture*, Robert Sturtevant speaks of *Ophiopogon* (*Mondo*) *jaburan* as being used as a ground cover in Italian groves, and "in the Gulf Coast gardens I found one of its relatives (reported as *O. japonicum*) in rich green swaths, a noble substitute for grass in regions where lawns must be sown twice yearly. . . . It is apparently hardy as far north as Nashville, Tennessee."

[1] *Rock Gardens and Alpine Plants.*

LYCORIS *AMARYLLIDACEAE*

L. squamigera Maxim. (*Amaryllis Hallii*)

N.H.M., July 1933, p. 277

Bulbous plants that flower in the late summer and autumn have a special value for us, both because of their comparative novelty, and because, like all late-blooming plants, they seem to renew our hold upon the flowering season, and to postpone the desolation of winter.

Lycoris squamigera flowers in mid-August. In the early spring we have seen the rapid development of the strap-shaped leaves to a length of from fifteen to eighteen inches, resembling those of some exceptionally sturdy Daffodil. By mid-June these have quite withered away, and there is then an interval of some six or eight weeks before the stout leafless flower stalk pushes through the earth and reaches upward so rapidly that often within a week or ten days it has attained a height of two to three feet, and most astonishingly unfurled a great cluster of from six to nine large fragrant Lily-like flowers of a pure Cattleya pink tone, which last for several weeks.

This striking plant has not been long known in gardens. According to B. Y. Morrison,[1] it was introduced into American gardens by Dr. Hall of Bristol, Rhode Island, from his garden in Shanghai, China, where he grew it prior to 1860, and it has not yet become at all well known in gardens, nor is it commonly offered in bulb lists; yet it is a distinctly important plant, and set in groups of five or seven in the borders, either in sun or in shade, it is of immense value in producing a refreshed and unusual effect at the tag end of the summer. The drawbacks to this lovely Lily-like plant are the period when neither leaves nor flowers are in evidence, and the rather untidy dying away of the foliage in early summer. For this reason, as well as because such a situation is ideally suited to it, it is delightful to grow in light woodland, or

[1] *National Horticultural Magazine*, July, 1933.

in borders where ferns and other lightly spreading plants will hide its temporary deficiencies.

My bulbs came to me a good many years ago from Mr. Carl Krippendorf who grows the Lycoris by hundreds and with fairy-like effect along the woodland walks of his estate near Cincinnati. There, in the loose nourishing soil, they increase rapidly and are perfectly happy. "Under these conditions," says Mr. Krippendorf, "these bulbs thrive without cultivation, and do well either in full sun or dense shade, the only difference being that those planted in shade, curiously enough, bloom almost two weeks before those planted in the sun."

The best time to plant the bulbs is soon after they have flowered, and they should be kept out of the ground for as short a time as possible. They should be set five inches below the surface of the soil and a like distance or more apart. Newly planted bulbs sometimes take their time about producing blossoms. The leaves will appear punctually in the early spring, but the expected lovely flowers may be withheld for a season, and I have known my bulbs occasionally to take a rest after they have flowered freely for several years.

When planted in the borders, such plants as Hostas, that have spreading leaves, or the large-leaved Saxifragas, or *Geranium ibericum*, make good companions for them, providing them with "cover" while they are out of bloom, and with foliage when they blossom. A form of deeper hue, var. *purpurea*, has been offered, but I have not seen it. Also there are a few tender species recommended for culture under glass, or for very mild climates. Chief among these is *L. aurea* (*B.M.* t. 611). This has been known as *Amaryllis aurea* and *Nerine aurea*. It is a Chinese species with bright yellow scentless flowers about three inches across, carried in a cluster on stems one to two feet tall. It also flowers in late summer.

MAIANTHEMUM *LILIACEAE*

CANADA MAY FLOWER, FALSE LILY-OF-THE-VALLEY

M. canadense Dessf. (*Unifolium canadense*)

No prettier little plant could be found for use on the shaded side of the rock garden, or for naturalizing broadly beneath deciduous trees where the soil is of a woodsy character. It is a low herbaceous perennial, growing from a widely creeping rootstock, the erect, slender, and often crooked stem bearing from one to three dark green ovate-lanceolate pointed leaves, and above them a dense little raceme of creamy white flowers, rather fuzzy in appearance, with four segments and four rather conspicuous stamens. The little plant grows no more than six inches high and often less. The flowers, which appear in May, are followed in the autumn by a cluster of reddish speckled berries, each containing two seeds.

It is a native plant with a wide range through Canada and the United States, as far south as the mountains of North Carolina, haunting cool woods and thickets. It is easily established in wild gardens. Herbert Durand has established it on a steep rocky bank in his garden, and there in May it makes a most delightful small display.

A European form, *M. bifolium*, is common in many parts of the Old World.

MUSCARI *LILIACEAE*

GRAPE HYACINTH

By the older botanists, this genus was classified under Hyacinthus. Joseph Pitton de Tournefort (1656–1708), the French botanist and plant hunter, struck by the well defined differences in their appearance, made a separate genus of them under the name of Muscari (which came from *muscus*, or musk, alluding to the special type of their fragrance), and his lead was followed by Philip Miller [1] in 1731, when he compiled his monumental and still highly valuable work, "The Gardener's Dictionary." It is strange that Linnaeus should have reverted to the older classification, lumping Muscari and Hyacinthus under the one head Hyacinthus, for we find that Carolus Linnaeus [2] as a young man was a frequent visitor to Miller in his "appartments in the greenhouse" at the famous old Chelsea Physic Gardens, of which Miller was head. There Linnaeus, then at the beginning of his distinguished career, was permitted to roam about collecting and comparing specimens, and to profit by the knowledge of the older man. Botanists of a later day and of the present time, commonly follow Miller's classification of the two genera, but we find them still confused in catalogues. The most readily discerned difference between Muscari and Hyacinthus is that the bells that compose the flower spike of the former are closed, pinched, while those of the latter are open.

But even when we have definitely separated Muscari from Hyacinthus, confusion still remains, for the nomenclature of the Muscaris is in a sad tangle. Some years ago I set out to collect as many of the true Muscaris as I could get together, and to learn something definite about them. From a gardener's standpoint, the enterprise has been highly profitable and altogether delightful, but from that of a botanist, it is worth little or nothing. It will require some one with a blind eye to their charms and a keen one

[1] 1691–1771. [2] 1701–1777.

for their hairbreadth structural differences, some one with a passion for accuracy coupled with botanical knowledge and the ability to follow all the threads to their source, to settle the question for all time. The Muscaris await a capable monographer, for outside a few well defined species like *paradoxum, moschatum,* and *comosum,* who is to say which are bona fide species and which mere varietal forms? Meanwhile let the ignorant whole-heartedly enjoy what the gods, and the bulb purveyors, provide, under whatever name. A low-brow attitude this, but one that nevertheless begets much pleasure.

The Muscaris as a race are found chiefly on the northern side of the Mediterranean, from Spain through Italy, Greece, and on to Asia Minor, Armenia, and the Caucasus. In the garden they are commonly called Grape Hyacinths (by the older writers Grape flowers) from the specific name of one of them, *botryoides,* from a Greek name signifying a bunch of grapes, which the little belled spikes are supposed to resemble. The trivial names of Starch, Plume, Tassel, Feather and Musk, that belong by usage to certain of them, are less well known, though they are in each case most pat and pertinent.

My trials of Grape Hyacinths have been wholly unaccompanied by tribulations. All the kinds that I have grown, under whatever name, thrive with freedom in any fair soil that is not waterlogged, in any situation that is out in the open. They have not in my experience done well in shade. They are undoubted sun lovers, and they appreciate the good things of the earth, though not much manure, unless it is very old and well rotted. They increase rapidly by offsets, and by hearty self-sowing, and all that I have grown have proved perfectly hardy without protection through the severest winters. Many have a richness of color that is a distinct asset in the garden. They garb themselves superbly in blue, and somewhat less successfully in purple, pinkish, and a dull yellow, and when they appear in white they are truly lovely.

In an effort to name properly the Grape Hyacinths in my garden, I have followed the race through the pages of Curtis' *Botanical Magazine* to the older botanists, have studied Dr. Bailey, Baker (author of confusion), and the Kew Hand-List. All I can say of the following list is that *some* of them are correctly named, that they will be found under these names in most catalogues, that nearly all will give you pleasure, and that the wild-haired ones, such as *comosum*, will amuse you.

I wish that Tournefort or Miller had pursued the race a little further, and that Baker had let it alone.

M. Argeai

Confusion begins right here at the beginning of the alphabet. This species I had from van Tubergen in 1916. *M. atlanticum* was given as a synonym, and cobalt-blue as its color. Johnson's *Gardener's Dictionary* gives Greece as its native land, but puts a question mark after it, with the date of introduction as 1883. But Johnson also lists as a separate entity, *M. atlanticum*, "from Spain and North Africa," introduced in 1902. I have grown a kind sent me as *atlanticum* (which see below), but at the present time I can find neither of these species listed, and my plants have gone the way of many another uncertainty—probably merged with others of the Grape Hyacinth clan.[a] According to my note of the time when I first grew it, *M. Argeai* appears not to have greatly differed from the common Grape Hyacinth, *M. botryoides*. It bloomed a little later and was a little dwarfer. The pinched bells were edged with white, and there was a faint fragrance. *M. atlanticum* Boiss. & Reut., as I had it, was a slenderer and taller plant, the leaves narrow and the flower spike narrow and pointed, rather in the manner of *M. polyanthum*, and very agreeably though not strongly scented. The flowers were a good bright blue in tone. So much for my notes, but I cannot be sure of the identity of either of these plants.

M. armeniacum Baker   B.M. t. 9157

This plant, as pictured in Curtis' *Botanical Magazine*, seems without doubt to be the familiar treasure we call Heavenly Blue; but as grown from bulbs sent me by van Tubergen of Haarlem, it seems somewhat different. This is a stronger grower, taller, at least eight inches high, each generous bulb yielding four or five flower spikes. The small bells that make up the crowded raceme, which is fully two and one-half inches in length, are almost spher-

[a] In van Tubergen's 1935 list, *M. Argeai album* is offered, "spikes of pure white flowers, late, flowering a long time."

ical, and a rich blue-violet in color, the "teeth" white but not very conspicuous. The scent is strong and spicy. The leaves, if upright, would overtop the flower spike, but they make their appearance in the autumn, and lie about untidily awaiting the rising of the flower stalk in spring. It is a very desirable kind for use in masses in sunny borders, rich in color, grand in performance. Dr. Bailey fails to list it in "Hortus," which may mean that it is regarded simply as a form of Heavenly Blue (see under *M. conicum*). As its name indicates, it probably comes from Armenia, and it flowers here toward the end of April.

M. botryoides Lam. & DC.
B.M. t. 157
Sweet's *Brit. Fl.*
Gard. t. 15

This is the little graciously common flower that has been an almost universal blessing in gardens since before the time of Parkinson and Gerard, the flower that Parkinson called the "skie-coloured Grape-flower," describing it as looking like a "thinne bunch of grapes" with a very "sweete smell," "a perfect blew or skie colour, euery flower hauing some white spots about the brimmes of them." Miller reports it as growing wild in the vineyards and arable fields of France, Italy, and Germany. So friendly and gregarious is it that, in many parts of the world, it has eluded its guardians and slipped out of gardens to join other cheery frequenters of wayside and meadow. Gray speaks of it as escaped from gardens into copses and fence-rows, and I well remember the fields in Maryland where we went each spring to gather bundles of the fragrant blue spikes. This ability to survive in the wild testifies to its sturdy constitution, and perhaps to its determination to be the friend of man.

The leaves of the common Grape Hyacinth are narrow with the edges incurved, bluntish at the tips, and they stand erect and do not flop about as is the habit of many of their kind. Between the several leaves arise usually two flower stalks bearing toward the top a wedge of tight-lipped, nodding bells that smell of ripe plums. Besides the blue form there is a rather washy uncertain pink one, described in catalogues as "rosy white," and a pure white form. This is one of the most delightful of bulbous plants. The flower spike looks like a wedge of seed pearls. Clumps of it make a charming accompaniment to groups of *Iris pumila caerulea*, or to the deep lavender forms of *Primula denticulata;* and being less of a spreader, it may be admitted without fear to the rock garden. The little common blue form should be rigorously kept out of this special region. As long ago as when Curtis pictured and described it in the *Botanical Magazine* (1793), he sounded a warning against its determined habit of spreading, and recommended that the bulbs should be confined in pots of light soil and plunged in the borders where they are designed to flower, and the offsets removed from the pots each year. Such a to-do! And then it would avail us little, for the Grape Hyacinth knows a trick worth two of that, and scatters its hardy seed hither and yon. The solution of the difficulty, if such blue largess can ever be called a real difficulty, is to let it have its way in shrubbery borders, grassy places, wild gardens, the edges of woodland, but not in shade, and to exclude it from dressed borders and rock gardens—if you can.

M. comosum Mill.   *B.M.* t. 133
    Tassel Hyacinth

    Parkinson calls this "the great purple faire haired Iacinth, or Purse tassel," for "the whole stalke with the flowers upon it, doth somewhat resemble a long Purse tassell, and thereupon diurs Gentlewomen haue so named it." Like so many of the friendly old flower names bestowed by the observant gardeners of times long past, this one had a good deal of point; in fact, it looks considerably more like a tassel than like a flower. It is distinguished more for its singularity than for its beauty, and quite lacks the sleek, well groomed aspect common to many of the Grape Hyacinths. It is altogether a curious-looking individual, tousle-headed and not very prepossessing. The late Rev. Joseph Jacob, who made rather an exhaustive study of the race, classed it among "lunatic flowers," and the fact that the uppermost flowers on the scape, which are long and oval, are gathered into a bunch, and stand wildly on end on long pedicels, while the lower flowers that are cylindrical, droop dismally, does give the plant a somewhat distraught appearance. The upper flowers are sterile, and in color are a sad, indeterminate violet; the drooping lower fertile flowers being of a curious greenish color. It is the last of the race to flower here, usually at the very end of May or early in June. Its natural home is in southern Europe, but it appears to be quite hardy in this locality.

The variety *M. c. monstrosum* (*plumosum*), the Feathered Hyacinth, Parkinson's "faire Curld-haire Iacinth," of which there is a very realistic drawing on page 117 of the "Paradisus," is somewhat better known than the above, because it is frequently grown under glass for winter display; also it is more comely if it can be brought to full flowering in good condition. But this is not always the case by any means when it is grown out of doors. It also is a curious-looking individual, for all its flowers are turned to slender filaments (vegetable hairs, some one has called them) of a soft purplish or "dove color," the whole so delicately divided into "many tufts of threads or strings, twisted or curled at the ends," that it has the appearance of an erect plume. The individual flowers are borne on long foot-stalks, three or four to a stalk. If the weather is kind, the effect of this floral feather is very pretty; otherwise it is well to keep the eyes busy elsewhere, for the soaked and bedraggled plume presents a sorry spectacle. One feels it would rather not be looked at.

The leaves appear before the flowers, and are a half-inch broad at the base, tapering toward a blunt point, and about a foot in height. Between them arises, very slowly, the cone-shaped boss of buds on a scape which reaches finally more than a foot in height, bursting into full flower early in June. It is quite hardy, and the only reason for growing it under glass is to secure the plume in its integrity.

The Feathered Hyacinth is sometimes found in very old-fashioned gardens; it doubtless appealed to the Victorian taste.

M. conicum Baker

After the certainty of identity of *M. comosum*, one is plunged again into uncertainty with *M. conicum*. Just what and which is it? One description says the dense cone-shaped raceme is a deep blue, the little egg-shaped bells composing it having white "teeth," the leaves flaccid and about six to a bulb, and nearly a foot long. There is said to be a scent that is not particularly pleasant. Nicholson gives its habitat as Campagna. I cannot be sure that I have ever had this variety or species, or whatever it is, and the truth about it is hard to come at. There is, indeed, nothing lucid about the clan Muscari. Van Tubergen has described the color of *conicum* as a black-blue; the Kew Hand-List lists it but makes no guess at its habitat, putting a question mark after its name.

In the Century Supplement of Nicholson's *The Dictionary of Gardening* (1900), it is written, "Of this well-known species there is a garden variety, Heavenly Blue, which is one of the finest Muscari in cultivation." Heavenly Blue is a delicious, if somewhat embarrassing, manifestation in most of our gardens today, whatever its parentage, which seems, despite Nicholson, in some doubt. In the *Botanical Magazine* (1926 t. 9157) there is an article on *M. armeniacum* claiming that this is none other than our Heavenly Blue. The author rightly remarks, "There is a flavor of romance in the horticultural history of our Muscari and in the vicissitudes of its naming." And he goes on to relate that when George Maw was preparing his great monograph on the Crocus, he collected material from all parts of the Mediterranean region and the near Orient. For this purpose, he enlisted the sympathies and the help of the British consuls at Trebizond and at Erzerum, so that they would provide him with an ample supply of corms from the neighborhoods of their respective stations. When the corms arrived, as might have been expected, many bulbs other than Crocuses, but mainly of the Liliaceae, were among them. Maw seems to have shared this superfluous treasure with J. E. Elwes and the Rev. H. Harpur-Crewe, both eminent horticulturists of that day, who grew them in their gardens at Colesborne and Drayton Beauchamp, respectively. They, in turn, seem to have shared the largess, and it is told that six bulbs were received by Barr's Nursery from Mr. Elwes of what purported to be *Muscari conicum*, said to have been collected in the neighborhood of Trebizond, and these eventually were decided to be *M. armeniacum*. But these six bulbs, says the author, are the stock from which actually the millions of Heavenly Blues which at present adorn our parks and gardens, were raised. Mr. Barr at first accepted, it is said, the plant as *conicum*, and the bulbs were put on the market as such, and in 1897 received an award of merit from the Royal Horticultural Society. Later Dutch growers sent out an entirely different plant as *conicum*, and Mr. Barr gave his type the name of Heavenly Blue, which, so far as gardeners are concerned, is entirely satisfactory, for heavenly it is in color and in fragrance; but what the final monographer will decide as to the exact origin of Heavenly Blue, I cannot foretell. It has remained in horticultural and botanical literature thus far connected with *conicum*. As I grow *armeniacum* here, it is a taller and more showy plant altogether, and I note that in van Tubergen's 1935 catalogue it is recommended in the place of Heavenly Blue, which is not listed at all.

Heavenly Blue is, in any case, one of the most valuable of hardy bulbous plants. Its blue cones have a svelte trimness which is very attractive, and its Clove Carnation scent, which fills all the garden at its time of blossoming, is delicious where it is grown in masses; and masses of it you are certainly destined to have, for though you may start with a modest handful of bulbs, it is almost embarrassingly free with its increase, both by seed and by offset. But it has infinite uses. One of the prettiest is to scatter it freely beneath the flowering trees, particularly the Japanese Cherries, where it makes a blue carpet for the pale blossoms to flutter down upon. Or it may be grown as a banding for borders or in clumps between the perennials (it is particularly effective blossoming between the fat red shoots of Peonies), along the verge of woodland, but always in the sun. But it is best to keep it out of the rock garden—that is, if your rock garden is at all exclusive. Once entrenched among the rocks, it is almost impossible to eradicate, grub and grovel as you will. When it blossoms there, you are enchanted with its sheets of blueness; when at the busiest season you must cut off the myriads of unsightly seed pods, or later, when it makes its sprawling fall growth, flopping over the most precious and unprotesting midgets, snuffing out their lives, you are greatly annoyed; and when you find that all you have done to curb it has not been of the slightest use, and that the ranks of Heavenly Blues bearing down upon your treasure have been much augmented, you are disgusted. Plant them where they can do no harm and enjoy them. I like a patch close under the windows of the house for the sake of their rich pervading fragrance. This type and *M. botryoides*, the little common kind, are among the few bulbs that hold their own and increase among the greedy heavy grass roots in this country.

M. elegans Hort.

A plant by this name made its initial appearance in this garden in the spring of 1933. It is said by some to be a seedling sent out by Max Leichtlin. In any case, it seems certainly a horticultural variety. It flowered on April 26th, of a good dark blue, darker than *racemosum*, free-flowering and seemingly desirable. The flowers had little scent. The slender leaves appeared in autumn.

M. Heldreichii Boiss.   *The Garden*, XXVI (1884), 136

This species is said to be a Greek. I was long on its trail before I secured a few bulbs. Impatiently their bow to the spring world was awaited, for I had read handsome things of its beauty and elegance. When it finally pushed upward and bloomed, it was in a grudging spirit; it was certainly nothing to write home about; in fact, it looked as if both moth and rust had corrupted it—thoroughly. A weakly uncertain stalk a few inches high bore a few largish bells of a quite undistinguished blue. An altogether niggardly performance. Of course, I may not have had the right thing. A number of Muscaris are attributed to Greece—*graecum, Holzmannii, pulchellum,* and *sartotianum,* as well as *Heldreichii.* It may have been any of these, but I have never been able to find any of them to put them to the test. At any rate, *Heldreichii* never appeared after that initial spring. Perhaps my lack of appreciation withered it at the very root.

Several authors describe it as larger than *M. botryoides;* and larger the individual bells were, but very much fewer. Nicholson says, "Very similar to those of *M. botryoides,* but nearly double the size and arranged in a longer raceme." The usual Muscari mix-up. When I find it again offered, I shall give it another chance on the assumption that the gardener is always wrong.

M. latifolium Kirk.   *B.M.* t. 7843

With this fine plant from Greece and Asia Minor, we are back among the more or less certainties; at any rate, it has distinct features that the hesitant gardener may cling to. While adhering to the general style that is de rigueur among the best Grape Hyacinths—the close, many-flowered cone of blue bells—it is yet something of a departure. In the first place, it has commonly two erect broad leaves clasping the stem, one almost as broad as that of a Lily-of-the-Valley. Occasionally there is only one leaf. The stalk is tall, from eight to twelve inches high. In the bud stage, the wedge of tight-closed little bells is a very dark blue; but as they mature, there is a distinct and immediately striking division between those of the upper half of the two-inch wedge and of the lower. The flower spike becomes distinctly cylindrical, and the bells of the upper half become a soft lightish blue, and these, while hardly opening at all, stand out almost perpendicularly from the stalk; the bells of the lower half are a deep good blue with a sort of bloom upon them, and their mouths are slightly open to display a rather rosy interior.

This is a very erect and jaunty species, and makes a nice show in flower or shrub borders grown in generous clumps. It blooms here about April 13th, and each small bulb is responsible for but one flower stalk.

M. Massyanum Siehe.

This belongs to the Tassel Hyacinth type, and as such is more curious than beautiful. The flowers are a soft rose-color; the stalk, from six to eight inches tall, appears in May. It is from Asia Minor, and in catalogues is variously spelled *Masseyanum* and *Massayanum*.

M. moschatum Willd.   B.M. t. 734
Musk Hyacinth   (under Hyacinthus)

Those who have a fancy to grow in their gardens flowers that have been beloved by gardeners for centuries, should welcome the Musk Hyacinth. It is said by Clusius to have been brought from gardens in the vicinity of Constantinople about 1554, and a little later to have been found growing wild in Asia Minor. Very soon after its discovery, it was to be seen thriving in Gerard's garden in Holborn. He called it the "Yellow musked Grape-floure," and reported that it came "from beyond the Thracian Bosphorus, out of Asia, and from about Constantinople, and by the meanes of Friends haue been brought into these parts of Europe, whereof our London Gardens are possessed." The great gardeners of the seventeenth century admired and loved it for the sake of its strong sweet scent, but critical gardeners of today, looking only for what pleases the eye, are apt to pass it by. It is in no sense a showy plant; it is not even beautiful. The somewhat glaucous leaves, four or five in number, are rather fat, wide, and deeply channeled, and lie about on the ground. Between them arise one or two flower stalks to a height of about eight inches, also fat and somewhat infirm and weakly, set from the middle upward with greenish purple flowers larger than is common with Grape Hyacinths, bottle-like in shape, or, "euerie one made like a small pitcher or a little box, with à narrow mouth, exceeding sweet of smell like the sauer of Muske whereof it took the name Muscari." The flowers turn yellowish as they fade, and the fragrance, while it is, indeed, sweet, is a bit too much of a good thing for most noses, stronger than Poet's Narcissus, and lacking quite the spiciness that is so good in the Heavenly Blue Grape Hyacinth. A few spikes in a glass will scent a whole room. The leaves are a long time dying away.

I have a form here called *M. m. flavum* (*B.M.* t. 1565)[4] which may, with some stretch of the imagination, be called a good yellow in color; it is better, anyway, than the common sort, and the scent is not quite so strongly sweet. I do not know, though it sounds like it, if this is the kind once offered by Dutch florists as Tibcardi Muscari,[5] the scent of which was so much admired that the bulbs of it fell for a guinea each in Holland; or it may be *M. luteum*, spoken of by Nicholson as a clear waxy sulphur color and delightfully fragrant. I do not find this last named kind listed in catalogues today. From van Tubergen has come a form called *M. m. major*, but this seems to me identical with the common sort.

The Musk Hyacinths begin to bloom here toward the end of April. As I have said, they are not showy flowers, but it is pleasant to find a sunny corner for a patch of them both because of their associations, and because of their sweet scent. It is entertaining to read that these strongly scented flowers were once chief among those by which Turkish ladies contrived to correspond in secret with their lovers. Certainly they carried an impassioned

[4] *M. macrocarpum* (Sweet, t. 210).
[5] Miller, in *The Gardener's Dictionary*, assigns this name to a seminal form of *M. racemosum*, of which he says the flowers on the upper and lower portions of the spike are respectively of a purplish cast and yellow, "and have a very grateful odour."

message. The Musk Hyacinth is not particular as to soil as long as it is well drained, but it must have sunshine.

M. neglectum Guss.   *Garden*, XXVI (1884), p. 136
  Starch Hyacinth

This is a handsome, free-flowering sort from the Mediterranean region that continues in bloom for a long time. The raceme is dense and many-flowered (thirty to forty to a raceme), and of the sleek Grape Hyacinth form. The color is a very dark, blackish blue, and the pinched bells show their white teeth distinctly. There is a pleasant scent, but it is quite unlike that of Heavenly Blue. The leaves are linear and deeply channeled and nearly a foot long. Its dark color gives it especial value in the garden borders. It flowers here toward the end of April.

M. pallens Fisch.   Sweet's *Brit. Fl. Gard.* t. 259

This kind I have not grown or seen, but as it is listed in the Kew Hand-List, it must be a distinct species, or pass for one; so I am setting down what I can find about it. It is said to have been introduced from the Caucasus in 1822 by W. Anderson, the then curator of the Apothecaries' Company's garden at Chelsea, and to be closely allied to *M. botryoides*, but with the flowers more cylindrical, much more expanded at the mouth, and more crowded in the raceme. The scape is erect and tinged slightly with red or purple; the flowers, very much crowded or squeezed together, are nodding and "very pale blue or white tinged with blue, and exceedingly fragrant." The leaves are several, smooth, glaucescent, linear, acute, channeled on the inner side, striated at back, with numerous longitudinal lines, at first erect but, as they lengthen, becoming more or less bent by their weight. It is said to flower in April, and sounds a good thing." Where may we procure it?

Of this species, on the other hand, Mr. Joseph Jacob writes in *The Garden*, September 2, 1925: "Totally unlike any other, flowers open-shaped and of a dirty white colour, much crabbed because the bottom flowers are over long before the top ones open, best known as *Bellevalia romana*. Is it a Muscari?" In Curtis' *Botanical Magazine* t. 939 is a figure of this *Bellevalia romana*

" Sweet's *British Flower Garden* t. 259.

with an account of its appearance and introduction, which differs considerably from the above. Curtis calls it *Scilla romana,* and the bells are shown wide open, more like those of a Scilla or a Hyacinthus than those of a Muscari. Parkinson called it *Hyacinthus comosus,* and altogether the confusion seems very general. Curtis says the flowers are *without scent.* The curious may seek out these several authorities.

M. paradoxum C. Koch   B.M. t. 7873

I am very fond of this well defined Armenian species, though it is so dark in hue, a blackish blue with no contrasting white "teeth," that it must be grown in considerable numbers and close together to make any real show; but if you take the trouble to look closely, you will find that those blackish bells are lined with green, which, taken with the dense character of the raceme and its distinctly conical form, gives it a very smart appearance—a handsome and substantial accomplishment. The bulb is large, the leaves generally three and erect, borne in spring; and from between them, very late in the spring for a Muscari, arises the strong, erect flower stalk to a height of about six inches. If you hold a few stalks in your hand, you will detect a delicate Hawthorn-like scent, but it is not strong. The albino form is less attractive, for its flowers are tinged with green; but in the garden dedicated to evening flowers, it is more desirable, for then the dark blue kind is absorbed into the shadows while the white stands out clearly and its Hawthorn sweetness is then more distinct. This is one of the Grape Hyacinths that I should on no account be without. Give it a good, well drained soil in any sunny place.

M. polyanthum Boiss.

A rather uncommon Grape Hyacinth of recent introduction from Asia Minor. The leaves appear in autumn and are very slender and a bright green. The flowers are borne late in April in a slender, somewhat flexuous raceme, each on a longer pedicel than is usual, which gives the raceme a more careless, informal appearance than is common to *botryoides* and its prototypes. The flowers are somewhat larger, too, than is common to this type. They are blue, but of what tone I do not know, as I have grown only the pure white form, which is a very attractive addition to the flowers of the middle spring. My bulbs are growing at the foot of the rock garden just within the shadow of an old apple tree, and seem to be doing well, but the increase has not been as generous as with many of its kind.

M. racemosum Mill. (*Hyacinthus racemosus* L.) B.M. t. 122
  Starch Hyacinth

This little old-fashioned Grape Hyacinth is seldom offered nowadays, though it has grown in gardens for more than three hundred years, and in some parts of England, especially in the southern counties, is regarded as a near-native, having escaped from gardens so long ago and made itself so thoroughly at home in fields and pastures. It is in any case a native of Europe, and, Curtis says, "grows wild in the cornfields of Germany in which it increases so fast by offsets from the root, as to prove a very troublesome weed, and on this account must be cautiously introduced into gardens." Parkinson, long before Curtis, sounded the warning about its spreading proclivities, saying that because of this fault "it will quickly choke a ground if it be suffered long in it. For which cause most men doe cast it into some by-corner, if they meane to preserue it, or cast it out of the Garden quite." He calls it "the darke blew Grape-flower," and draws attention to its peculiar fragrance, which he says is very strong, "like unto Starch when it is new and hot."

The Starch Hyacinth is very close to the true Grape Hyacinth (*M. botryoides*), but there are differences. The leaves, of which there are a number, are narrow and so flaccid as to lie about on the ground, while those of *botryoides* are almost erect. The flower scape is a very dark blue, appearing somewhat faded, and so close-set as to look congested, the upper flowers being almost stemless, the lower ones reflexing slightly at their "brimmes" and edged with white. Many of them grown together scent the air for a long distance, and this scent is by some compared to that of ripe plums. *Racemosum* will hold its own in any soil and under any conditions—no need to pamper it or consider it in any way. It is the earliest of the Grape Hyacinths to appear in spring and, as such, would surely find a welcome in some by-corner in most of our gardens.

NARCISSUS *AMARYLLIDACEAE*

It would ill become me to write of the Daffodil from the standpoint of the fancier or the expert. I can only treat of it as a lover, blind to its imperfections, seeing the race as wholly lovely and lovable.

When spring comes bringing Daffodils "blithe and yellow as canaries," I feel that the high point of the year has been reached, that all that follows is anticlimax; but the space I have to give them in the garden is narrow, and though down the years I have grown a great many kinds, I have not been able to keep abreast of the golden army that marches steadily ahead, lighting successive springs with a gentle glow.

Gerard, who gardened in the time of Elizabeth, named twenty-four kinds as commonly grown about London. There are now something like six thousand!

The literature of the Daffodil began long ago. They brighten the pages of the classical writers, the early herbalists noted the beauty of the flower, and regarded it seriously as a medicinal plant.[1] Poets of all ages have adorned their songs with them; but in 1548 what may be termed the scientific literature of the Daffodil began with Turner's slender treatise, "A Few Narcissus of Dieverse Sortes," describing twenty-four kinds. Then followed the scant information contained in the works of Lobel (1570), and of Crispin de Pass (1615). And in 1629 Parkinson, perhaps the first great Daffodil lover, described in the "Paradisus" ninety-four kinds, figuring many of them.

From then onward, the names of the great Daffodil growers make a chain with links of pure gold reaching down to the present day—Herbert, Haworth, Hartland, Backhouse, Leeds, Barr, Burbridge, Engleheart, Wilson, Pearson, Brodie of Brodie, Wilmott, Chapman, van Waveren, and more, immortal all because

---

[1] "The plentiful roote being administered medicine-like remedieth the serpent's sting." *A greene Forest*, by Maplet, 1567.

they have increased our knowledge of these beloved flowers and added vast numbers to their ranks.

The development of the Daffodil is chiefly due to British gardeners. "A purely British flower," wrote Rev. G. H. Engleheart, "perhaps the only flower of which it may be said that none but English love and care have nurtured it to what it is to-day."

But now, regarding the Daffodil from an artistic standpoint rather than as a mathematical problem, or as an achievement, have they not gone far enough with its development? Should not there be a halt called in this race for bigger and better Daffodils? It is essentially a simple and friendly flower, gay, graceful, appealing, and when it is made bold, and huge, and brazen, it has been called out of character, degraded not improved.

The late Sir William Lawrence, after viewing the Daffodil Show in April, 1930, wrote: "The dead perfection of the Daffodils approaches the mechanized flower; there they stood in well drilled ranks, eyes front, not a button out of place." They might be so many machine-made articles; they do not sound like the flowers that brought song to the throats of so many poets. Let us keep them a little faulty and wayward, wholly enchanting.

A Few Hybrids and Their Culture

There are a vast number of hybrid Daffodils available today, and no flowers are more lovely or useful in the garden. Few require special conditions; a few rules hold good for the majority. For the general run of varieties, it is safe to choose a situation wholly out in the open with shade for part of the day provided by high-branched trees at a little distance, or by the walls of a house, during the hottest part of the day. This light shadowing is especially grateful to the so-called white Daffodils. There is a saying that the paler the Daffodil, the more shade it likes. But even these pallid ones need a little sunshine to keep them in health.

The best soil is one that is deeply worked, is nourishing and gritty enough to be freely pervious to moisture. No Daffodil will long survive the discomfort of a definitely damp bed, though they delight in cool conditions. On hot, starved soils they cannot thrive. If the soil is on the heavy side, it may be lightened by the addition of sand, old hotbed soil, or some coal ashes; if too light, a quantity of good strong loam will be required to put it into prime condition.

If enrichment is needed, on no account should fresh manure be made use of. If manure has been in the soil long enough to become thoroughly decomposed and incorporated with it, there is no danger; and a dressing of old manure in the autumn now and again is repaid in strength of growth and many blossoms, but on the whole bonemeal is the best fertilizer for them. It may be used at the rate of an ounce to a square yard, sprinkled over the ground before planting and worked in, or after planting and gently scratched in with a rake.

The bulbs should be planted if possible in September. It is their nature to root early, and if we are wise we will facilitate them in this matter. October planting is safe, but to put the operation off until November is to court certain failure. The depth to plant will depend upon the size of the bulb and somewhat on the character of the soil. In light soils, deeper planting should be followed than in heavy ones, though the *poeticus* varieties, which prefer a stiffish soil, also like shallow as well as very early planting.

Under ordinary conditions, four or five inches of soil over the round part of the bulb will suffice; very long-necked kinds like as much as six or seven inches, and authorities urge a depth of eight inches for such very large bulbs as those of the *maximus* type. The little fellows, *minimus, minor, cyclamineus, juncifolius,* and the *triandrus* hybrids do very well with two or three inches above their heads. Where the soil is damp, a cushion and covering of sharp sand protects choice bulbs from rotting in wet weather.

On no account should Daffodils be planted too close together. Three or four inches should be allowed each bulb, so that the beautiful form of the flower with its enhancing water-green foliage is clearly seen. Close massing results in an unhappy effect not unlike that of a feast of scrambled eggs set for a giant.

Daffodils lend themselves to the adornment of an infinite variety of situations. They are lovely planted in light woodland, into which the sun penetrates for at least a part of the day, or on grassy slopes where the grass need not be cut until their foliage is well ripened. They always look at home by the pond or stream side, and no prettier setting could be found for them than a copse of white Birches.

Where naturalized on a large scale, or on any scale, they are more effective if one kind to a generous breadth is used, rather than a mixture, and a careless scattered effect should be aimed at, the breadths trailing away irregularly into one another with little gatherings here and there at some distance from the main mass. When used in the borders among herbaceous plants, it is satisfactory to plant them rather far back instead of along the edge, so that the on-coming green of the perennials will arise and hide their unsightly ripening foliage. Their last state is not as lovely as their first.

If careful selection is made among the different types of Narcissus, a gay procession may be maintained over a long period, beginning in the neighborhood of New York late in February, when *N. minimus* may usually be counted upon to flower, and ending late in May with the rush-leaved *N. gracilis*. Among the large trumpet varieties, Golden Spur is invaluable for early flowering, as is *N. obvallaris*. Both are bright self yellows, and the latter is particularly good in partial shade. Alice Knights is a fine early white trumpet, and forward blooming bicolors are Spring Glory and van Waveren's Giant, while in the *incomparabilis* class we have Sir Watkin, John Evelyn, Artemis, Lady Arnott, and Orange Buffer. The earliest of the *Leedsii* group is Mermaid. The old double-flowered van Sion also makes a very prompt appearance, and is fine for naturalizing in grass and beneath the branches of ancient apple trees.

For general planting the following varieties may be recommended to give satisfaction: Large Trumpets: Cleopatra, Cornelia, Moonlight, Emperor, and King Alfred (yellow); Empress, Sir Ernest Shackleton, Vanille (bicolors); Lady Audrey, Peter Barr, Sulphur Beauty (white); Mrs. R. O. Backhouse and Lovenest are "pink" trumpets.

Incomparabilis: Autocrat, Beauty, Bedouin, Bernardino, Glint o' Gold, Gloria Mundi, Lucifer, Marina (very late), Whitewell. *Barrii*: Albatross, Blood Orange, Brilliancy, Cossack, Firebrand (for shade), Masterpiece, Red Beacon, Seagull, Blood Orange. *Leedsii*: Her Grace, Lord Kitchener, Queen of the North, Sirdar, St. Olaf (very late). *Poeticus:* Horace, Epic, Glory of Lisse, Cassandra. Poetaz: Admiration, Antigone, Elvira, Mignon, Orange Cup, Golden Perfection, Thelma.

For naturalizing: C. J. Backhouse, *conspicuus*, Duchess of Westminster, Frank Miles, Mrs. Langtry, Minnie Hume, White Lady, and the two *poeticus* varieties, *ornatus* and *recurvus*.

This is a selection of good varieties, not the largest nor the newest nor the most expensive, but all of high quality and well tried as garden flowers.

MINIATURES AND A FEW OTHERS

The genus Narcissus is not a very extensive one, comprising not many more than forty species all told. The range of habitat is fairly wide, extending "from Scandinavia as far south as the Canary Islands and eastward through Morocco and Algiers to Kashmir, China and Japan." They love the gentle regions about the Mediterranean, and the Pyrenees Mountains and other sections of Spain, Portugal, and France abound in delightful species.

The quarantine against the importation of Narcissus struck a harsh blow at Daffodil lovers, and many kinds have been cruelly scarce during the fifteen famine years, many not available at all. Let us be thankful that it is no more, and that the gardening public in America is once more free to enjoy all that is new and lovely in this race, especially the small species.

As I have said, the space I am able to devote to these flowers is less extensive than I would have it, for one can scarcely have too many; and this lack of space has caused me of late years to specialize in certain types, especially those small enough to be grown in the rock garden, which like the conditions that prevail there, with a few others.

I am here mentioning in addition, however, a few species that have not been available to American gardeners for many years, and that I have not myself grown; but we shall now be wanting to try our hand at them, and in describing them and their needs I have turned for information to acknowledged authorities.

THE LITTLE GREAT TRUMPETS

The miniature Trumpet Daffodils are perfect replicas in little of their larger brethren, and one is amazed that so much character can be compressed within such small compass. When I first saw *Narcissus minimus,* the smallest of them, I had the Alice-in-Wonderlandish feeling that I was gazing through the wrong end of an opera glass at a group of *N. maximus.*

Of course those who cannot divorce their minds from the idea of size as an important integrant of perfection, will not find the elfin Daffodils of interest; but for those who like to find beauty done up in small packages, they will have a most holding charm; and then their early flowering is a delight—no swallow dares dart through the cold air until weeks after the first of the little Daffodils have bestowed their small gold upon the world, and certainly none of their big brothers has the courage to meet the wintry conditions that these miniatures face with such audacious contempt for consequences. They are a hardy little crew and face many degrees of frost without blenching.

N. minimus (*N. minor minimus* Baker)

This is the smallest Trumpet Daffodil known, and the first to flower. If December is mild and the ground bare of snow, the flat leaves of this impatient mite edge upward, and unless conditions are altogether impossible, it will flower in February—perfect, bright yellow, and jaunty, its trumpet delicately frilled, its imposing height all of three inches.

We read that in 1887 *N. minimus* was found by the late Peter Barr, growing freely in the Cantabrian Mountains in Spain, on south-facing slopes among the Gorse bushes. To Mr. Barr we owe its introduction to gardens, though it was known to earlier botanists.

It is a friendly little Daffodil, asking only a gritty neutral soil and, in our hot climate, shade for a part of the day. It seems not to like either manure or lime—just a good wholesome loam made readily pervious to moisture. Thus considered, it increases in a genial and generous manner, and each spring there are more tiny trumpets to usher in the hylas and the bluebirds. It grows here happily in a wedge of woodland where it must fight Spring Beauties and Snowdrops for root room, and it thrives in the rock garden. In the latter situation, I cover the ground over its head with a thin layer of white sand to keep its trumpet out of the mud. English books say it thrives well in turf, but I should not like to entrust these small precious things to the tough harsh stuff that goes by the name in this country.

N. minor L.   *B.M.* t. 6

This delightful Daffodil has grown in gardens for a long time for, according to the *Botanical Magazine*, it is the "least Spanish yellow bastard Daffodil," mentioned by Parkinson in the "Paradisus," the little flower described as having "a short foote-stalke, scarce rising aboue the ground; so that his nose, for the most part, doth lye or touch the ground."

In the "Gardener's Dictionary" (Miller, 1768) it is not mentioned, but Linnaeus describes it in the second edition of "Species Plantarum" (1762) and Curtis chose it for portrayal in the first volume of the *Botanical Magazine* (1787), and there it is shown with all the charm of its short water-green leaves, its quaintly twisted perianth and daintily expanded canary-yellow trumpet.

There is probably some confusion of identity among the small Daffodils indigenous to Spain and Portugal; they might easily cross and produce intermediate forms, but the kind I have grown for many years as *N. minor* is under five inches high and has here proved a very hardy and hearty small thing, eager to please, and thriving and increasing more readily than any of the miniatures. It grows in ordinary loamy soil in partial shade and has increased so much that it must frequently be taken up and given more space, its generosity moving me to be generous, too, to the point of occasionally parting with a bulb or two where I know they will be appreciated and cared for.

It is a pretty and gay thing, its twisted perianth, flanged trumpet, rich color, and nose-dive pose giving it a dashing appearance. It flowers later than *N. minimus,* but it is even prettier and, gathered into small groups in the rock garden, or by the poolside, stages a very nice show any time from mid-March onward, according to the mood of the weather.

There is a white *minor* which, alas, I have never seen. Mr. Bowles, who has been more fortunate, calls it one of the very elect of the earth, and says it was found in a very old Irish garden, and that it has not gone very far afield yet.

N. minor plenus is offered by Barr and Sons, London, and described as "a very rare and charming little double Daffodil of soft yellow color, of elegant form and very dainty." A perfect love of a double, it must be.

And somewhat different from it is another miniature double called Rip van Winkle, of which Mr. A. Wilson, writing in "Daffodil Growing for Pleasure and Profit," says: "It is probably the double analogue of some such species as *nanus, minor* or *minimus*. One would not call it exactly beautiful, but there is a charm in the midget quaintness of the flower, which makes one more than content to see it in the garden foreground with other pigmies of its own race and other genera." Mr. Bowles says its chief feature consists of the repeated whorls of perianth segments with narrow points bent back like crochet hooks which surround the central coronal divisions. It is said to be the smallest of the doubles and to flower as early as any of the *minor* forms. Barr offers it.

To be included among the great little Trumpets, are certain other Daffodils of dwarf stature, chief among them W. P. Milner, which received, I believe, the first award of merit by the R.H.S. as a rock-garden variety. In this garden it seldom grows taller than six or eight inches, but it is said to attain eleven. It is a grand doer, of sturdy constitution and a willingness to spread that almost turns it into a charming nuisance. The flower is sulphur color, and it has a warm scent that makes one think of Cowslips. It flowers here early in April, and is invaluable for use in the rock garden or in narrow borders, or for scattering at the edge of thin woodland, well away from more imposing kinds.

Queen Maya is taller, at best about sixteen inches, and has a lovely flower in two tones of yellow with a beautifully formed and widely expanded trumpet. Barr and Sons offer Santa Maria Seedling as good for the rock garden. They say it grows fifteen inches tall, and has flowers of a deep self yellow and an "elegantly twisted perianth."

N. lobularis Haworth

Some confusion seems to surround the identity of this small and personable Daffodil. Mr. Bowles claims it has no right to the name by which it is generally known, which he says was coined by Haworth for what he called the Tenby six-lobed Daffodil, which was described as yellow in perianth and corona, whereas the plant in question is a bicolor. Another opinion is that it is a natural hybrid found in the Netherlands, and sometimes known as Dutch *nanus*, often being sent out by Dutch firms in the place of the true *nanus*, to which, however, it is inferior. It is pretty, however, and fairly dwarf, about seven inches in height, with a sulphur-yellow perianth and pure yellow trumpet, carried well above the leaves.

N. nanus (*N. minor nanus*)

A trig little Daffodil, dwarfer and less prolific than *minor* but a little taller than *minimus*. It grows about four and a half inches high and is unlike these two in having a slender plaited trumpet and in lacking the nose-dive pose. The foliage is somewhat glaucous and apt to lie about the ground, and the flowers are a very bright yellow. It blooms here about the middle of March, and thrives under the same conditions as suit *minimus*.

N. obvallaris
Tenby Daffodil

Growing a little taller than the above, about twelve inches, it bears a neat symmetrical all-yellow flower as early as Golden Spur. I have not found it long-lived in my garden; that is, after a few years its ranks begin to thin, and there comes a spring when it does not appear at all. It is said to prefer shade, and in England is recommended for use in grassy places.

Glitter belongs to the *Barrii* section, and is a brilliant small thing, valuable for foreground planting or for colonies in the rock garden. It grows a foot tall; the perianth is broad and lemon-yellow, the trumpet shallow and fluted as neatly as if done with an old-fashioned fluting iron, and edged with flaming orange-scarlet. It flowers about the middle of April and is very fragrant. Nanny Nunn, Joan of Arc, Harpagon, and Red Beacon, none of them exceeding fourteen inches in height, are all valuable for narrow borders or the rock garden, and delightful for filling small clear glass vases indoors.

CYCLAMEN-FLOWERED DAFFODILS

N. cyclamineus Baker   *B.M.* t. 6950

Among floral figures of fun, this small and curious Daffy stands with the foremost. A little horticultural joke it seems when first we see it thrusting forward its abnormally long and narrow tube with the perianth turned straight back in a manner that has been variously compared to the ears of an angry mule, a frightened rabbit, a kicking horse. And indeed it does have a startled expression. A group of them makes one think of a bevy of gnomes in agitated conclave.

It is told that when Dean Herbert came upon its likeness in an old work published in Paris in 1633, "Theatrum Florae," he declared that it was an absurdity "which will never be found to exist," and so he wrote in his famous "Amaryllidaceae" in 1836. But exist it did, and does, and it was rediscovered in 1836 by Alfred Tait in Portugal, and a year later by Peter Barr, during one of his explorative tours through the Spanish Peninsula. He found it growing in fair quantities "on the margins of streams or in flooded meadows adjoining, showing its semi-aquatic nature."

Cyclamineus is very forward-flowering, appearing close upon the heels of the small *minimus,* and it grows less than four inches high. The flowers are of the most amazing durability, thick of texture, burnished, and a bright yellow throughout. I have known them to remain in good condition, through fair weather and foul, for six weeks. Small wonder it made a sensation when it was reintroduced by Mr. Barr in 1887, a sensation that was translated into both a Botanical and a First Class Certificate. The leaves are narrow but not rush-like, and they stand erectly.

This little curiosity thrives best in dampish sandy peat in partial shade. It is a neat subject for a cool nook in the rock garden or the miniature pool-side, and if happy, will seed freely. It is quite hardy and seems not to mind how dry the summers are, but it loves a pleasant dampness during the early part of the season.

It is not surprising that *cyclamineus* should have been used to produce numerous interesting varieties. Its unusual character-istics promised unusual results, and where they have grown near other small species, they have brought forth hybrids spontane-ously. I have never seen the tiny *minicycla,* born of *cyclamineus* and *minimus* with the aid of Mr. Chapman, which won an award of merit, but the results of its unions with larger trumpet vari-eties are easily obtainable. They are at first sight disappointing, and one must divest one's mind of the idea of a very small and dwarf flower, for these hybrids at first strike one as too tall and then too stocky for *cyclamineus* progeny, nor does the peri-anth reflex as abruptly as we expect it to do. On the other hand, they flower very early, are of the same long-lasting substantial texture, and make very telling masses of warm color in the early garden. Some of these hybrids are the following:

Beryl (*poeticus X cyclamineus*), raised by Mr. P. D. Williams, received an award of merit as a rock-garden variety. The flowers droop a little, and they inherit from their *poeticus* parent the wide, overlapping segments. These are yellow, paling as they mature, and the crown is lemon-colored edged with bright orange. Neat and charming.

February Gold opens soon after the type. Its flowers are of the richest yellow, appearing to be varnished, and thick in texture. Its color remains undimmed, and its crispness undiminished, as the spring advances. It is a stocky flower on a stout stem, and it increases rapidly. A gem of the first water. Other good *cycla-mineus* hybrids are Flycap, March Sunshine (a little less vigor-ous than February Gold), Orange Glory (larger and taller with a good wet-earth scent), Little Witch (raised by Mrs. Backhouse), Pepys, and Golden Cycle. All are bright and early and invaluable, especially to the gardener who has not great space to devote to them.

Angel's Tears

Daffodils more than other flowers seem to inspire toward poetic nomenclature. Seldom are their names cumbersome or harsh, and nearly always they express a charming thought. What could be prettier than Angel's Tears? An old name for certain members of this *triandrus* group was Ganymedes, in commemoration of the son of Tros, King of Troy, whom Jupiter, in the form of an eagle,

snatched up and made his cupbearer instead of Hebe. The Ganymedes were at one time regarded as a separate genus from
Narcissus.

Every member of this group is lovely in form and color, and
exceptionally graceful, even for Daffodils. They are distinguished
by their curving stalks, from which depend usually several flowers
with fluttering reflexing perianth and exquisitely modeled cups.
They are generally pale in color, white or delicate sulphur, but
in the case of the natural hybrid, Queen of Spain, the flowers are
a rich butter-yellow.

There are now a great many *triandrus* hybrids, many of them
with stronger constitutions than the type, *triandrus albus*. They
will surely be wanted in all gardens where choice things are cherished. They belong in the rock garden, in little protected borders,
in guarded situations everywhere, thriving in partial shade, in a
gritty vegetable soil, damp rather than dry, but not wet. No
flowers are more charming for cutting. Place them in little slender open-mouthed clear glass vases that hide nothing of their
lovely grace and the tender coloring of leaf and stem.

N. *triandrus albus* L.
Angel's Tears

This is a priceless gift from the Spanish Peninsula to the gardening world. It was discovered by the late Mr. Peter Barr,
and introduced by him. Mr. Ingwersen says it is "found most
frequently on steep hillsides, as often as not on limestone forma-
tions, and frequently dangling its charming winged bells from
under rose-flushed bushes of *Erica australis* . . . this occurrence
upon both limestone and granite, should make it one of the most
adaptable in our gardens. . . . Generally it grows in a black peaty
deposit, freely intermixed with stone detritus, and occasionally
we see it in deep limestone fissures on steep cliff-faces in accumu-
lated vegetable soil which has drifted down from Cistus, Broom
and Heather-clad shoulders."

In our gardens it certainly prefers some shade. In the rock
garden, the north side of a stone keeps it calm and cool, or the
weather side of a little evergreen will do. It has grown here for
many years without special consideration, and also without increasing as rapidly as I should like, but it is quite hardy, and blossoms

here toward the end of April. It is a slender little plant not exceeding eight inches in height, the stem arching to let the pale angelic tears drip downwards. There are from two to five blossoms to a scape, creamy white and distinctly other-worldly in appearance. The cup is globular and inturned, the leaves narrow and rushy.

N. t. calathinus

This is perhaps one of the loveliest Daffodils that grow, and it is ours today only by happy chance. Though thought to have come originally from the Spanish Peninsula, it has been found growing wild in only one place in the world—on the small rocky island of Glénan, off the coast of Brittany. Sadly enough it is to be found even there no longer for the sea, carrying its deadly salty deposit, has swept over the tiny island, and all trace of the bulbs has disappeared. Happily it is readily raised from seed, and the stock already in hand enables us to enjoy it still.

Two or three large lovely flowers of firm texture with backward fluttering wings hang from the curving stalk. The cup is deep and ample and delicately fluted, the leaves narrow, dark, and concave, and "they curl back like peeled Dandelion stems." If you secure this beautiful variety, give it half shade and a soil composed of a mixture of leafmold, peat, and sand, with a little bonemeal, a mere pinch, no manure. It has flowered here only once, so I cannot report fully upon its behavior; but it came through a most trying winter.

N. t. concolor

A charming and fragrant little flower thought to be a natural hybrid between *triandrus albus* and the sweet-scented single Jonquil, which is found growing wild in the same localities favored by *concolor*—the Pine woods of Portugal, that land so rich in charming Daffodils. It is slender and a good deal like the Angel's Tears, but a soft pale yellow throughout. Height about six inches.

N. t. pulchellus   B.M. t. 1262

This beauty at once strikes the observer as somehow different, and in truth it is, for it reverses the usual Daffodil color scheme of a deep-hued cup and pale wings. This cup is shallow and very pale, while the perianth segments are the hue of a Primrose. It flowers later than the type and is more vigorous, also a little taller, about eight inches.

N. t. Queen of Spain

This is undoubtedly one of the best of dwarf Daffodils. It is said to be a natural hybrid of *triandrus albus*, discovered by the late A. W. Tait and E. Johnston in 1885 on a mountain slope in Portugal, near Oporto, and named by them *N. Johnstonii* Queen of Spain. It grows a foot tall and its fine butter-yellow flowers make a charming show when massed in half-shaded places, flowering toward the end of April. The crown is long and straight, and the perianth segments reflex gently. The flowers tend to point downward a little. This fine plant has grown in my garden for many years, increasing with reasonable freedom. British gardeners recommend planting it in full sun on sloping ground, but it is said not to be a good doer in that showery land; and I think our warm suns are more to its mind, ripening the bulbs thoroughly. It should be in every garden.

OTHER TRIANDRUS HYBRIDS

The numerous *triandrus* hybrids vary considerably in height, in the number of flowers on a scape, in the shape and length of the trumpet, some being long and straight like that of Queen of Spain, others like little bowls, shallow and incurved. And some are more fragrant than others. Many have the good quality of lasting long in perfection, and they are lovely for cutting. The following are all desirable:

Acolyte, white with shallow crown, usually three to a scape; Agnes Harvey, one to three flowers on a scape, the cup white and fluted and sometimes delicately flushed, a fine long-lasting kind, and fragrant; Alope, two tones of light yellow, the flowers large and appearing late, thirteen inches; Cingalee, a long primrose-colored trumpet and starry perianth, rather tall and flowering early; Dawn, Mr. Bowles's favorite "both for cutting and planting on ledges of the rock garden. It appeared unexpectedly in a bed of Mr. Engleheart's seedlings. Its pure white reflexing perianth and pendent poise proclaim *triandrus* parentage, but what gave it a corona as flat and golden as a guinea, no one knows. Possibly it is *poeticus* influence, but there is no trace of a red rim, and no *poeticus* has so flat an eye. The flowers come in pairs, and their white segments interfere slightly, which causes them to stand out here and there and look like the wings of three white butterflies dancing on a couple of large buttercups." I've not seen this variety.

J. T. Bennett-Poe was one of the first *triandrus* hybrids, and blossoms early, a pale pretty flower with a long trumpet of fine design, fifteen inches; Melusina is very dainty, bearing two or three shallow almost white flowers to a stem, grows eighteen inches tall and is of sturdy habit; Moonshine is a lovely kind, bearing two or three short-cupped flowers on its curving stem which are white and lightly fluted and delicately fragrant, thirteen inches; Mrs. Alfred Pearson, though not new, is exceptionally charming.

The flowers are small and very starry in effect and borne in clusters. The small cups are white, the perianth pale primroses. Rippling Waters, St. Maden, Shirley, Silver Fleece, and Snow Bird, I have not seen. They are well described in English catalogues and doubtless are enchanting.

THE SPANISH PRIMITIVES

The above caption I borrowed from a chapter on old-fashioned Daffodils written by Mr. A. Wilson and included in that bulky and indexless work, "Daffodil Growing for Pleasure and Profit," compiled by A. F. Calvert.[2] Mr. Wilson is disturbed that, though the new *poeticus* Daffodils have retained all that was charming in the original forms, this cannot be said of the modern race of pale Trumpets:

"Undoubtedly fine as these are in their generous amplitude and faultless symmetry, they have, even by virtue of their salient qualities, parted with something desirable which their old fashioned primitives have—something which possibly places the old flowers at a disadvantage on the show table, but which has a singular charm when one sees them in the garden. Such old forms as *cernuus, albicans, moschatus* and the Irish *moschatus*, Colleen Bawn, have a fragile delicacy, a variety of curve and daintiness

[2] Published by Dulan & Co., Ltd., London.

of pose which their more showy descendants would seem to have exchanged for something else—larger size, an imposing stateliness, and a regularity and symmetry of feature more in conformity with show-table canons.

"The great beauty of these latter-day flowers is beyond question, but it differs in kind from the beauty of the Spanish originals, a beauty reminiscent of something too delicate to touch, like a fragile sea-shell or a snowdrop. The moral is this: That while every grower of Daffodils must needs, if he can, grow such splendid flowers as White Emperor, White Knight, Beersheba and other pale Daffodils equally fine, he will miss something worth having if he does not also grow one variety at least of the old Spanish Primitives which were the fashion fifty years ago. Also it may be questioned if hybridists, in devoting their attention so exclusively to increasing the dimensions and imposing proportions of the White Trumpets, and breeding them to hold their heads up and look the R.H.S. in the face, have done wisely in ignoring that other charm—the nodding pose, so graceful and so modest, which led Haworth and Herbert to choose for the flower the distinctive name of *cernuus.*"

N. moschatus of Haworth B.M. t. 1300

This pale beautiful Daffodil has lived in my garden for close on twenty years. The little group has not increased very much, but it has not dwindled. I think (but how can one be sure?) that this is my favorite Daffodil. The solitary nodding pale flower has an infinite appeal, a fragile tender grace that I think is not duplicated in the race. The trumpet is long and exquisitely modeled with delicate flutings, the perianth segments, almost as long as the trumpet, flutter forward over it like protecting wings. The perianth tube is bright green in marked contrast to the purity of the flower. There is a faint spicy scent, and the height seldom exceeds six inches.

The white form from which Haworth chose it, is found high up in the Pyrenees, and from thence it was sent to Clusius in 1604. Parkinson seems to have grown it, or something very like it; and it is believed to be the only pure white Daffodil known in a wild state, and as such is the parent of the whole race of modern White Trumpets, as well as of the lovely pale forms found in old Irish gardens during the last century. No more exquisite flower could be found for a cool, tended corner, among small ferns and Wood Anemones. It likes a soil rich in humus and mixed with small stones and a little grit. No manure, as you value its life. Not to know this Daffodil is to be poor in experience.

The Narcissus known as Dutch *moschatus* is *N. albicans* of gardens, an altogether more substantial and easy-going plant, but it is not in a class with Haworth's *moschatus*. *N. cernuus* is a very old garden form, still procurable and of great beauty and charm. Its silver-white flower is well set off by blue-green leaves, and its height is seldom more than eight inches. The flower droops gently from the stem, and the perianth segments are as long as the trumpet. It has sometimes been called the Silver Swan's-neck Daffodil.

A double form of *cernuus* is offered by Barr and Sons, London, and may be the same as that figured in Mr. Bowles's valuable work, "The Narcissus." I am sending for it, and will plant it as directed in good virgin pasture loam, avoiding manure.

William Goldring is a delightful old white Daffodil that was once in all lists. It grew in a shaded corner of my Rockland County garden, and I always looked forward to its flowering. It was taller than *moschatus* and of stronger constitution. Nowadays I do not see it listed; it has probably been crowded out by the pale hordes of the new varieties, but a search would probably bring it to light, and perhaps some others of the older white forms. They all flower in April and enjoy cool conditions, shade but not dank shade, a good porous soil free from manure. They have a curious fragrance, not sweet, not spicy, but a definitely pleasant scent.

THE HOOP PETTICOATS

The various forms of *Narcissus Bulbocodium* have been given the common name of Hoop Petticoat Daffodils because of the widely flaring trumpet that has much the appearance of an old-fashioned hooped skirt. The perianth segments are very narrow and fly out behind like thin streamers. The foliage is rushlike and shorter than the flower stems, and appears in the autumn. They vary in height from five to eight inches, and the range of habitat of the different kinds is wide, extending from the south of France and the Pyrenees to northern Spain, Portugal and across the sea to Morocco and Algeria—mild climates generally; but all save the African species seem to be quite hardy. Bright fripperies these, with a distinctly frivolous air. Their color tones run from almost white through cream to bright orange-yellow. They are among the quaintest and altogether fetching of bulbous plants.

N. B. *citrinus*
The Sulphur Hoop Petticoat Daffodil

This lovely cream-colored form has larger flowers than the yellow kinds that grow in my garden, and is much less prone to increase. This is disappointing, for it is very charming and one would enjoy wide plantations of it. It blooms somewhat earlier than *conspicuus*, and enjoys low damp situations in the rock garden. In its native northern Spain, it is said to grow in sandy meadows that are subject to periodical inundation.

N. B. *conspicuus* L.

This is a robust high-colored form or species, easily managed and bearing in late April bright orange-yellow flowers that flutter above the narrow foliage as if they were about to take wing. They thrive in several sections of the rock garden, but always in well drained dampish soil that is a mixture of loam, leafmold, and sand, and where there is shelter from the sun during the hottest part of the day. It increases very rapidly here from offsets, and requires to be lifted and divided at least every third year; else the tufts become very dense and the flowering sparse. In the garden is also a tiny copy of *conspicuus*, a few bulbs that came from I know not where. It grows only three inches high, and the perky little flowers are very small—too small to make any show, yet I am glad to see it as successive springs come round. It has not increased.

N. B. *monophyllus* B.M. t. 5831

Of this African Hoop Petticoat I must speak wholly from hearsay, for not even in the most sheltered situations in the rock garden and with a warm winter blanket, does it endure. "The pure white flowers," says Mr. Bowles, "are beautifully crystalline when they are young, and equally admirable when the corona becomes thinner, and portions between the ribs are almost as transparent as the finest lawn." It is generally thought to be the most beautiful of the group, and in mild climates flowers in mid-winter. Photographs show the little "skirt" held upright, that is, flaring toward the sky. Persons who garden in the South would be well advised to make generous plantations in partially shaded places for winter blossoming.

All the Hoop Petticoats make delightful pot plants, flowering on the window ledge after a period of root-making in a dark cool place.

Some Doubles

Since the days when the gastronomic inferences of their names had power to influence my feeling toward them, I have loved double Daffodils. Beneath the ancient Seckel Pear trees in our old Maryland garden grew in clotted abundance such as Butter and Eggs, Codlins and Cream, Eggs and Bacon, and across the road in a meadow now long dedicated to less happy occupation, pure gold was to be found on soft spring days by questing children. There in the rough grass rioted the fat old van Sion, lifting untidy green-gold heads in thousands. We all have childhood memories that we cherish. Going to gather armfuls of double Daffodils in the Homewood meadows is one that is precious to me.

Narcissus van Sion is the *N. telemonius plenus* of English catalogues. Parkinson called it *Pseudonarcissus aureus Anglicus maximus*, Mr. Wilmer's great double Daffodil. According to Parkinson's account Mr. George Wilmer of Stratford Bowe, Esquire, acquired this Daffodil ("as myselfe did also") from one "Vincent Sion, borne in Flanders, dwelling on the Bank side, in his liues time, but now dead; an industrious and worthy louer of faire flowers, who cherished it in his garden until the year 1620." But Wilmer having got hold of it, "would needes appropriate to himselfe, as if he were the first founder thereof, and call it by his own name . . . which since hath so continued." But Wilmer's name has long been forgotten, while that of the worthy lover of fair flowers, Sion or van Sion, lives on. So right has prevailed.

Daffodil fanciers scorn the old van Sion: it has not proper

stance, or whatever it is these worthy folk look for nowadays. But I should not like to look forward to a spring that did not bring these crumpled flowers with their rich scent of damp earth and some other elemental sweetness.

Indeed double Daffodils are not now generally in the mode, and one must turn to old books and catalogues to find out about them. But Victorian ornaments and furniture—and some say Victorian morals—are again becoming the fashion, and with them may come the double Daffodils.

In a catalogue issued by Barr and Sons in 1884 (a rare assemblage of Daffodil lore and now a collector's item) are the names and portraits of many a double that cannot now be found, and admirers of this type of Daffodil might well go off their heads with hankering upon viewing the wealth of these "monstrous" forms described in Parkinson's "Paradisus." "The sea hath bounds but deep desire hath none!"

Alas! Where is John Tradescant's Great Rose Daffodil? Where Gerard's double Daffodil, which is "assuredly first naturall of our owne Countrey, for Mr. Gerard first discovered it to the world, finding it in a poore womans garden in the West parts of England, where it grew before the woman came to dwell there, and as I haue heard since is naturall of the Isle of Wight." And where the double white Daffodil of Virginia—and many more? Probably an expedition organized to explore old gardens in the British Isles and in this country would bring to light many.

In the meantime, exploring the catalogues is not barren of results, for though they are not especially featured, a good many quite enchanting doubles lurk between their pages, and every year sees a few added to the bright flock.

These chiefly belong to the *incomparabilis* group and include those early gastronomic dainties of my youth, with Milk and Honey and Oranges and Lemons added. They are all worth growing, if only for cutting. They make charming vases and bowls, and personally I think they are delightful set in close clumps in the borders or in thin grass. Try a few, and see if you are not won to them.

Some of the best of the *incomparabilis* doubles are the following: Argent, with creamy star-shaped petals and a yellow center, which is lovely for cutting and may be gently forced in the window; Butter and Eggs, the old orange and yellow flower, always free and good in masses; Carnation, immense flowers with pointed petals, pale yellow with orange tones at the center; Codlins and Cream, vigorous and lovely, soft creamy tones merging to sulphur at the heart; Eggs and Bacon, rather tall of stem with a full flower of a light tone of yellow, the center reddish orange; Glowing Phoenix, a beautiful early-flowering double of imposing stature with round symmetrical flowers, soft yellow with a warm orange center; Golden Rose, much like the old Butter and Eggs, but of improved form and greater size; Iphigenia, "a very elegant flower of medium size, perianth white, center golden-apricot margined yellow, a very charming vase flower. Height sixteen inches"; Milk and Honey, distinctive with erect blue-green leaves and white flowers yellow at the center that are remarkable for their lasting qualities; Mary Copeland, tall and lovely, full and fragrant, a pale flower with orange petals at the heart; Lune de Miel, a fine symmetrical bloom of pale color passing to yellow and apricot, carried on a tall stem and splendid for cutting; Primrose Phoenix, handsome large fully double yellow flowers, an old favorite; the Pearl, a charming small flower, pale and starry, nice for cutting; Twink, a new variety with large full yellow petals, bright orange at the center. It is tall and very telling when massed.

These are all charming rose-flowered kinds, some expensive, others amazingly inexpensive, all blossomy and sweet-scented, and of the utmost value for cutting.

There are also a few fine double-flowered kinds in the *Leedsii* group. Silver Rose, with broad white petals and a yellow center, is delightful. Snow Sprite is white throughout save for a faint Primrose flush at the heart, and it is most exquisitely fragrant.

The double Poet's Narcissus, or Gardenia-flowered Narcissus, is a lovely old-fashioned flower, but it is capricious, and I frequently hear of its making buds but not flowering. There is a good reason for this, however, and, treated with consideration, it will always flower after it has become well established. It must be kept cool, and it wants something to get its teeth into in the way of richness; not, however, manure. It grew plentifully in the grass and in the lee of the old shrubs in my Rockland County garden, and I brought it from thence here, where it has increased and multiplied amazingly. The soil it grows in is rich and black, not light, but not clay, and seldom bone-dry.

When the spring is dry, with hot searing winds, I try to water my double Poets so that the buds will not blast, and we seldom have any trouble with them. The flowers are pure white and look like Gardenias, and they have a heaven-born fragrance. Great bowls of them in the house are a delight. They flower late, prolonging the Narcissus season.

Bulbs of the double Poets should be planted early in the fall, as early as you can procure them, and set fully six inches below the surface of the ground. They may possibly require a season to become established before they will flower. After that, if they are not thriving, they may require to be taken up every few years, divided, and given more space and a little new soil mixed with bonemeal to give them a fresh start; but if they are blossoming well, let them severely alone. By the pond or streamside they nearly always thrive, for the cool conditions assured by the nearness of water suit them admirably—cool conditions, a stiffish soil, and deep planting, and the reward will be masses of these exquisitely fragrant flowers for cutting and to give away.

I have somewhere read that Daffodils do not readily produce double flowers, and that no double form has been produced by the ingenuity of man, not at least in modern times. Most of the doubles are believed to be "sports," for they are frequently found among wild single forms; and occasionally these doubles, when transplanted to other soil, go single again. I have noticed that old plantations of Argent and the Pearl in my garden, are less fully rosetted than when young. Perhaps they are reverting to the single type.

Some years ago a box of Narcissus bulbs was sent me by Mr. Carl Krippendorf of Cincinnati. Among them was one whose label was at once lost, and as it did not bloom for several years, I had no idea of the treasure I was harboring.

One spring very early, a fat bud appeared between its two rather broad leaves. It was a very promising bud, but the most deliberate I ever saw. Very slowly the stem elongated until it had reached a height of about seven inches. Then the calyx parted and there unfolded before our astonished eyes a sextuplet star, an astonishing flower, light yellow with six rows of pointed petals neatly arranged, one over another. It was some time before I knew it to be the old Queen Anne's Double Daffodil, *N. capex plenus.*

For years it has been very scarce, even in that land blowing with lovely Daffodils, England, though grown there for more than two centuries. It is sometimes known as *N. Eystettensis.* My single bulb has not increased, nor does it flower every year. I have done all I can for it, giving it a warm corner with shade for part of the day and a nice nourishing soil full of humus and grit. Still it resists my blandishments. It is the spoiled child among my Daffodils.

Mention is made earlier in this section of the small double trumpet Daffodils, and the double Jonquils are listed in the section that follows.

Sweet Jonquils and Campernelles

The name Jonquil, according to Dr. Prior, is a derivative of *juncus,* a rush, obviously because of the rushlike foliage. The Jonquils are old garden plants since certain of them were known to Clusius and figured by him in his "Rariorum Stirpium Historiae," published at Antwerp in 1576. Doubtless in that far day they were thought indispensable, as they are today, for the sake of their bright and animated appearance and rich fragrance.

N. jonquilla L.   *B.M.* t. 15

This is the true sweet-scented Jonquil or Yellow Jack. It is found in a wild state in Spain and Portugal, southern France, and in other mild sections of Europe, as well as in the Balearic Isles, and in northern Africa. The flowers are small but of firm texture, almost waxen, bright yellow throughout, with flat saucer-shaped crowns and flaring perianths. Several flowers are borne on each slender scape, which may be about a foot tall, perhaps more. The leaves are narrow and rushy and almost as tall as the stems. The rich fragrance is altogether unexpected in such small flowers; it is delicious, but those with sensitive noses had best keep the flowers out of doors. Even the Poets do not exceed them in sweetness.

Jonquils like to grow in warm sheltered borders in well drained nourishing soil, or they may be naturalized at the edges of sunny shrubberies, or on the warm side of light woodland. They can stand a good deal of undiluted sunshine. To show for what they are, and thus to give the most pleasure, they should be planted generously, spread in wide breadths when naturalized, or when grown in borders set in clumps of not fewer than a dozen bulbs. They flower in late April or early May, and are invaluable for cutting.

N. jonquilla flore-pleno, the old double sweet-scented Jonquil, is less often seen, and I find it difficult to keep save in very sheltered locations; but it is lovely, the flowers smaller than those of the double Campernelle and of more perfect form. The dark slender scape carries several warm yellow, intensely fragrant blooms in early May—they are true nosegay flowers. They are said to thrive in grass, and to be perfect for pots when forced slowly. There is a fine cut of this double Jonquil in the "Paradisus."

Numerous Jonquil hybrids that add much to the gaiety of the spring borders are now on the market. Some have broader leaves than the rushy foliage of the true Jonquil, and certain of them bear but one flower on a scape; nor have they always the rich fragrance of the parent, though all are sweet-scented in some degree.

Aurelia is finely modeled and of the deepest yellow hue. Its height is eighteen inches; scent, delicate. Buttercup with me has produced but one flower on the scape, deep yellow, the segments broad and overlapping and bluntly pointed, the fragrance light but sweet; it grows about twenty inches high. Fairy Nymph bears two pale flowers on its eighteen-inch stem, the perianth almost white, the crown deeper in hue. Golden Scepter grows eighteen inches tall and here produces but one flower on a stem. It is a rich bright yellow with a flaring cup of medium depth; fragrance, light and sweet but not heady. Tullus Hostilius is more delicately made than the other Jonquil hybrids; the trumpet is long and flaring, the perianth paler than the trumpet, and with narrow segments—a very graceful sort and lasts well when cut. Lady Hillingdon bears two or three flowers to each stem. They have cups of medium depth and short flaring perianth segments, very bright yellow and very fragrant. A showy kind and early to flower.

N. odorus L.   B.M. t. 934

This, the Campernelle Jonquil, is sometimes called the Giant Jonquil. Generally speaking, it and its kinds are taller, sturdier, hardier, and altogether more enduring and satisfactory than the true Jonquils. The crown is bell-shaped and has six rounded lobes. But the plant lacks something of the charming grace of the dwarfer kind, the true Jonquil. But the Campernelles, too, are old garden friends, for Crispin de Pass figures three kinds in "Hortus Floridus." They flower somewhat earlier than the Jonquils and bear from two to four warm-hued flowers to a scape, and they have a pleasing but not powerful fragrance. For very cold gardens they are more satisfactory than the Jonquils.

In southern Europe, the Campernelles are widely naturalized and are generally thought to be natural hybrids between *jonquilla* and *N. pseudo-narcissus*. Several good forms are in cultivation, and should be generally used in borders, on grassy banks, or planted in rows in a cutting garden. Being less heavily scented than the Jonquils, they are perhaps more welcome indoors. The foliage is rushlike.

Orange Queen is a useful variety carrying several orange-yellow flowers on a stem about fifteen inches high. The cups are lightly fluted. Regulosus grows taller (eighteen inches) and carries sometimes as many as four flowers to a stem. It is deliciously scented, and the broad perianth makes a nice setting for the long wrinkled cup. Sweet Nancy is a taller kind, a graceful nymph of a flower. The crown is shallow and of a deeper tone than the perianth. The fragrance is light and sweet, and its long stem makes it fine for cutting. It flowers later than the other Campernelles, and so is nice for a succession.

A double Campernelle Jonquil is often seen, especially in old-fashioned gardens. The flowers are two or three to a stem, like little waxen roses, and are very sweet. They are very fine for cutting.

N. gracilis Sabine   Sweet's *Brit. Fl. Gard.* t. 136

This graceful rush-leaved Daffodil is the latest of all the race to flower, usually well along in May. It is of the Jonquil type, cluster-flowered and fragrant. It has lived in my garden for a great many years, multiplying generously. It is said that *gracilis* is not found in a wild state, and that it is possibly a natural hybrid between *jonquilla* and *biflorus*, or possibly some small form of *poeticus*. Whatever its origin, it is indispensable, for it prolongs the delicious season when Daffodils blow; and it is a slender graceful variety lovely for small vases, and seems to be very hardy. I have flourishing plantations in both partial shade and full sun, in light soil and in heavy. It seems not to be fussy.

Less easily managed is a Jonquil usually considered a form of it, *N. tenuior*, the Silver Jonquil (*B.M.* t. 379), lovely but smaller, dwarfer, paler in color, and less hardy. I once had a good plantation of the Silver Jonquil, but it gradually died out. I miss it.

N. juncifolius Lag.

This tiny Jonquil is one of the smallest of the whole race, so small that it will appeal only to those who have an eye for beauty in miniature and are willing to give it care. It is a perfect rush-leaved Narcissus with the characteristic bright green cylindrical leaves, three to four to a bulb, and one or two vivid flat-cupped little flowers about the circumference of a five-cent piece. They look like forward Buttercups, but the powerful fragrance proclaims them for what they are. It is an enchanting small thing and grows well in the rock garden in well drained gritty soil, opening its bright flowers punctually during the last week in April. Its height is from four to six inches. "*N. juncifolius*," says Mr. Bowles, "is mostly found in the mountains in Spain and Portugal, France and Corsica. It colors meadowland as Buttercups do with us, in some parts of the Pyrenees, especially near Gèdres, and also grows in matted clumps on rocky ledges. In the Bouches-du-Rhône it occurs in stony ground on the limestone hills near Saint-Rémy."

Growing higher up in the mountains *N. juncifolius rupicola* is

---

[²] *A Handbook of the Narcissus*, by E. A. Bowles, 1934.

found, the most alpine of all. Mr. Ingwersen describes finding it on Sierra de Guadarrama, well above the level of the last creeping Pines, pushing its flat tips through the almost frozen granitic soil, "a tiny Jonquil with wide open soft yellow flowers of the most delicious fragrance," that is easily established in sandy loam, granitic scree or on limestone moraine. A valuable addition this to our rock gardens, now that we shall be able to secure it, as will be *N. scaberulus,* found only in Portugal, "high on a granitic mountain near Oliveira do Conde in moist gravel."

In *The New Flora and Silva,* July, 1930, Mr. Ingwersen tells of finding this Daffodil, which he believes to be the smallest of the race, after a rough climb through thickets of Cistus, sticky and aromatic, through waving masses of Broom and tree Heaths until he came to a wilderness of boulders, where, in the short game-nibbled turf, were small colonies of *N. scaberulus.* He describes it as growing only about two and a half inches high, with rich orange-hued flowers, deliciously fragrant. The leaves, he says, were never more than two from a bulb, linear and generally prostrate and longer than the scape, more or less glaucous in color. The bulb is always very small, and is covered with a dark tunic. "The plant is a good subject for the alpine house, and succeeds readily under granitic moraine treatment."

All rock gardeners will surely want these minute sweet Jonquils.

Autumn-Flowering Daffodils

Daffodils that flower at the tag end of the year would seem to have lost their way. That there are such, we know from books and magazine articles, but I doubt if any have thus far flowered in American gardens. Now, however, with the lifting of the quarantine against the importation of Narcissi, we shall doubtless be trying all sorts of rare species, the autumn bloomers among them. These are by no means new to European gardeners. All the old craftsmen seem to have had a go at them, though none seem to have been successful in keeping them in health, or for any length of time. Doubtless in the mild sections of the British Isles, they may survive for a year or two. Mr. Bowles's drawings of them in "A Handbook of Narcissus," were made from living specimens.

There is always the yen on the part of some gardeners to over-come the reluctance of rare plants, and while it is not likely that these small chancy bulbous things will attract the attention of any but "the enthusiastic jardinière-botanist, who happily has ever a hearty welcome and an inch or two of genial soil for plants like the present," some of us will undoubtedly want to try out these curiosities. They are southerners, and in the northern parts of our country must be grown in pots under glass; but perhaps in the warmer sections we can offer them the heat and light to which they are accustomed, and they would provide interest and excitement at a season when a Daffodil is certainly not expected.

When a Daffodil not only performs in the autumn but bears *green* flowers, it is, indeed, a curiosity. The green-flowered Daf-fodil is *Narcissus viridiflorus*. Parkinson knew and figured it, naming it the "greene Autumn Daffodil," and saying that the flowers are the "same colour with the leaves and stalkes, which flower smelleth very sweete, somewhat like unto the rest of the Rush Daffodils; this," he goes on to say, "sheweth not his flower untill October, and the frosts quickly following after their flower-ing, cause them to perish." He describes it as rare and not easily grown, stating that "but few in these parts that have had it still enjoy it, in that it perished with all that had it."

It seems, indeed, to have disappeared from cultivation for a number of years, but A. H. Wolley-Dod, who accompanied George Maw on a hunt for the green Narcissus in 1883, gave an account [*] of Mr. Maw's finding it near Campamento, in Spain. He describes this interesting species as growing in local abundance on low coast hills between Gibraltar and Algeciras, extending a mile or two beyond the latter town, growing chiefly in damp hol-lows, though extending also to drier ground. He says it is extraordinarily difficult to see on account of its grass-green flowers and leaves amongst other grasses, and is more easily detected by its very strong scent than by sight.

In the *Botanical Magazine* (t. 1687), there is a portrait of this curious plant, showing it to be a strange spidery, almost evil-look-ing flower, with a very small neat cup and very long pointed reflexing perianth segments, dark green and borne in clusters of three. It has been said that many green flowers compensate with

[*] *Gardening Illustrated*, Oct. 28, 1933.

a powerful scent for the more obvious attractions they forgo,[5] and it must be so with the green Narcissus, for all are agreed that its fragrance is delicious. It is found not only in the south of Spain but in Morocco.

Another autumn-flowering Daffodil is *N. serotinus* L. "This minute plant," says Mr. Bowles, "is the most widely spread of the autumn-flowering species, being found in Southern Europe from Portugal to Greece, along the Mediterranean region of North Africa and in Palestine." It is described as a shapely little flower, flat and paper-white, the tiny neat cup boasting a touch of warm orange, and very fragrant in the way of a Paper-white Narcissus. A third in this uncommon company is *N. elegans* Spach. This occurs in Italy, Sicily, and North Africa. This, also, is a peculiar-looking individual. The cup is so small as to be almost non-existent, and the very long and twisted perianth segments stream out behind in a flyaway manner. The flowers are borne in clusters and are snowy white, and "give out a strong scent resembling that of Night-scented Stock, but with an additional odour which suggests tar or creosote." [6]

Yes, decidedly, growing these autumn Daffodils would be an exciting horticultural adventure. I see that Barr and Sons, London, offer *N. serotinus,* and the others will doubtless be found by the determined searcher.

[5] Jason Hill in *The Curious Gardener.*   [6] E. A. Bowles.

NOTHOSCORDUM *LILIACEAE*

False Onion

THIS is a small genus allied to the Onions. Its name, in fact, means "spurious Garlic," but there is nothing spurious about the odor of the leaves and stems when they are crushed. The flowers, however, of some of the species, are pleasantly fragrant.

There seem to be about ten species in the genus, and Nicholson says one is Chinese and the rest are found in tropical America and the Andes region. They are not very important to the gardener, and are of interest chiefly to the collector. In behavior and general appearance, they are much like Alliums. Occasionally they are grown in pots under glass, but the two kinds I have here, *N. bivalve* and *N. fragrans*, are perfectly hardy despite the statement to the contrary in "Hortus," that neither is hardy in the North. It is difficult to know just where "North" begins from a horticultural standpoint, but when a plant in my garden successfully withstands fifteen degrees below zero, I feel justified in calling it hardy in the North.

N. bivalve Britton (*N. striatum*)   *B.M.* t. 1524 (under Allium)

This inconspicuous little plant was sent me years ago by a Texas plant collector. It was tucked away in a corner of the rock garden among Anemones and *Corydalis bulbosa*, and there it has remained ever since. In the rich profusion of spring's offerings, it makes little impression and often flowers without being noticed; but when in the late summer it makes a second bid for attention by flowering again, we are very glad to see it.

In the early spring it sends up narrow leaves to a height of about eight inches, and between them a slender scape bearing a few-flowered umbel of pale straw-yellow flowers that have an agreeable fragrance. It has not increased very much, but it has lived a crowded life among pressing companions. It is said to be found from Virginia to Florida and the Southwest, so it appears to be a well distributed little plant.

273

N. fragrans Kunth   *B.R.* t. 898

A taller and much more vigorous species whose habitat, according to "Hortus," is in doubt; but it is said to be naturalized in Bermuda and the southern states. The Kew Hand-List attributes it to Mexico. It is, however, quite hardy, and I understand that it is capable of becoming an alarming nuisance once it is happily established in congenial surroundings.

I first saw it in the herb garden of Mrs. Mortimer Fox, near Peekskill, New York, and thought it rather handsome. It looks like a white Allium, the narrow, grasslike leaves forming good clumps, the flower scapes rising to a height of about eighteen inches or two feet. The flowers are borne in an umbel, each on a rather long pedicel, and are carried erectly, not drooping. They are white with lavender keels—a keel in the horticultural sense being exactly what it is in a nautical sense. They appear in early summer, and have a pleasing fragrance like that of Heliotrope, though not nearly so strong as in *Allium odorum*, which somewhat resembles it. It is a plant for the wild garden rather than more important sections of the grounds.

ORNITHOGALUM *LILIACEAE*

STAR OF BETHLEHEM

MANY persons who are well acquainted with the little Star of Bethlehem, are not aware of its family name or of how large and important this family is. The Ornithogalums are scattered over many parts of Europe, the Orient, with the greatest number in South Africa, and one, at least, in South America. They are a comely tribe, nearly all worth growing, but not all hardy enough to stand the rigors of our northern winters out of doors. The tender ones make charming window or greenhouse plants, however, and I think some experimenting with the reputedly sensitive kinds might show a greater cold resistance than we have credited them with. Last winter, a cold one, the lovely *O. arabicum,* a greenhouse kind, lived out in my cold New York garden, and blossomed freely in the spring.

The blossoms are borne on leafless scapes, sometimes in clusters, sometimes strung along the scape; they are six-petaled, usually starry, a few bell-shaped, commonly white, but a few are yellow. And some of the white-flowered kinds are among the rare flowers that stain their purity with green, and with the most charming results. Usually a greenish flower gives rise to the impression that something has gone frightfully wrong with its health, or that some tricky florist has been tampering with its diet. Not so the green-striped or greenish Ornithogalums—nothing could appear more pristine and fresh than they. The race generally is easy-going, thriving under any fair conditions, some of them holding their own and increasing freely in grass.

The name is an old one used by Dioscorides, and means "bird's milk," which in view of the prevalence of green in their coloration, is not very apt, or appetizing. The "Starre-flowers" were favorites of the early gardeners, and many grew in Parkinson's garden. Among their desirable qualities is their durability, the

Chinkerichees,[1] white or yellow, of South Africa lasting well in water, or when uncut for more than a month.

O. arabicum L.   *B.M.* t. 728

This beautiful and fragrant Star of Bethlehem grew in the gardens of Clusius and Parkinson, so the odor and charm of antiquity cling about it. It was called "the Arabian bulb" by the Turks when Clusius brought it from Constantinople to Vienna, and in Italy it was known as the Alexandrian Lily, or Jacintho del Paternoster. Parkinson seems to have flowered it out of doors in England, though he notes, "It is very impatient of our cold Winters." Last autumn a few bulbs left over from the potting up were planted in the rock garden here in sandy soil against a south-facing rock, and there in May they flowered as handsomely as did those in the windows indoors, though they had received only the light blanket of salt hay given to the rock garden generally. The question is, of course, will the bulbs repeat this performance in the coming spring?

Indoors or out, this Ornithogalum is a beauty, and I wonder if it could not be forced in quantity for use at Easter, something a little novel, very sweet, and extraordinarily long-lasting. Whether cut or uncut, the flower cluster lasts in good condition for nearly a month. The leaves are long and lax and apt to lie about, and from among them arises the flower-scape to a height of about two feet, carrying a wide cluster of large creamy blossoms, their creaminess enhanced by what appears to be a fat and shiny black pin-cushion (sometimes it is dark green) in the center, and each surrounded by yellow-headed "pins," the ovary and anthers. The fragrance is unusually delicious despite the fact that Parkinson describes it as "pretty sweete, but weake." The blossoms do not all open at once, but there are always enough to make a showy effect, and the same flowers open several days in succession, but they close in the afternoon before nightfall, when they appear like immense pearls clustered in some sumptuous ornament.

This Star of Bethlehem is widely distributed in the Mediterranean region. Mrs. Loudon says: "It is found in Barbary, Turkey and the Madeiras, besides numerous other places, but

[1] *O. lacteum* and *O. thrysoides.*

always growing in pure sand. It is quite hardy in British gardens if it be kept dry . . . if the soil is well drained and very sandy." [2] It is said to cover wide areas in Syria and Palestine.

O. nutans L.   B.M. t. 269
    Drooping Star of Bethlehem

A plant brought to us by a friend always, of course, possesses a special value. A few years ago, Mrs. North McLean of Shrub Oak, New York, brought me a bulb in full flower that I thought most curious and beautiful. It was very exciting, too, for it was the first really green flower that I had, at that time, ever seen. It turned out to be the plant that grew in Parkinson's garden as *Ornithogalum neapolitanum*, the Starre-flower of Naples. The leaves were four or five, narrow and rather flabby, and from among them arose the stout stalk nearly a foot high, strung with pendent flaring bells of large size. They were silver-green outside, and green and white inside, with the edges of both sides white, and with a silken sheen all over that gave them a most uncommon effect. Of course I planted it as she directed in a low spot at the back of the rock garden, where it did not receive the full sun all day; and it has bloomed for me twice with the coming of the end of April, and is engaged industriously now in raising up a family about it, which I watch with great interest. I was intrigued to find out more about this plant, and am pleased to note that it is a very old flower in gardens. All the ancient wise-acres knew about it. Casper Bauhin (1541–1613) reports it as sent him from Crete by one Honorius Belli. Clusius, Parkinson, and Jacquin all figured and described it, and it is proclaimed as a plant "which soon accommodates itself to any country; producing a numerous progeny both from roots and seeds, and by no means nice as to soil or situation; it is not long before it becomes a weed in the garden, from whence it is apt, like the *Hyacinthus racemosus*, to pass into the field or meadow." [3] It was not known as a wild flower, however, by either Parkinson or Gerard. Miller says it grows wild in abundance in the "Kingdom of Naples and is now become almost as common in England . . . and in many places where they have been thrown out of gardens they have

---

[2] *The Ladies' Flower-Garden of Ornamental Bulbous Plants.*
[3] *Botanical Magazine*, Vol. XIII, p. 269.

grown upon dung hills and in waste places as plentifully as weeds."

But how delightful that anything so exotic-looking and beautiful should grow as plentiful as a weed! And looking at the large, three-cornered pods that follow the blossoms and weigh down the stalk, one has hopes. Certainly it is not common in this country nowadays, for I have never seen it; but once it must have been fairly so, for Gray speaks of it as rarely escaped from gardens from Pennsylvania to the District of Columbia. If it is still to be found in these parts, I should like to hear of it.[4]

William Robinson says it is "very free in grass." The late Joseph Jacob speaks of it as everybody's plant, and says it is lovely to use with Tulips for cutting. And in Barr's catalogue, it is described as flowering in dense shade where few other plants will grow. Why do we not have more of this fine bulbous thing? When it is so easily raised from seed, there should be no difficulty in accumulating a stock. It would be exquisite rising from a bed of unfolding Fern fronds, a distinct and valuable addition to our shaded borders.

O. pyramidale (O. narbonense pyramidale)

I mention this species not because I know it, for ardent searchings have not thus far brought it to light, but because it is said to be a most desirable kind and hardier than *arabicum*. A graceful plant, and "there is no more difficulty with it than with the less beautiful squat-flowered *umbellatum*. The white flowers with their green stripe are borne in a long graceful spike, and are useful to form a clump in the herbaceous border and for cutting." [5] It grows wild in southwestern Europe, and Nicholson says it is naturalized in Britain. The conical clusters of small white green-striped starry flowers are six or eight inches long, and appear in summer. The leaves are few, and shorter than the flower scape. It is said to flourish almost anywhere. Another should-have!

According to the Rev. Hilderic Friend, the French gave the pretty name of Virgin's Spray to this plant.[6]

[4] Mrs. Earle in *Old Time Gardens* speaks of the bed of tall-growing Star of Bethlehem in her sister's garden as being very pretty, and the accompanying illustration shows it to be *O. nutans* growing most luxuriantly.

[5] *Hardy Bulbs for Amateurs*, by Joseph Jacob, 1924.

[6] *Flowers and Flower Lore.*

O. umbellatum L.   Red. *Lil.* t. 143
  Star of Bethlehem

So far as proper gardeners are concerned, this is surely the forgotten flower. However popular it may once have been—and if a
notable array of pet names is a sign of popularity, it must once
have been noticed and admired by many—*vox populi* now proclaims it a weed. Indeed, it is included in the list of troublesome
plants in W. C. Muenscher's *Weeds*,[7] troublesome locally from
New York to Ohio and Tennessee. In other countries, too, it
bears the accusatory name, and perhaps with good reason. Though
a native of southern Europe, it has become by its indomitable
colonizing proclivities a doughty citizen of half the world, following man's journeyings to far countries, and surviving strongly
under alien and, one would think, often uncongenial conditions.
Its spread has been assisted by the fact that where it has become
too plentiful, it is often thrown out of gardens with other so-called
rubbish. But no situation, apparently, comes amiss to this small
circuit rider; it simply settles down where it lands and makes
itself at home, lifting up its frail voice (too often unheard) in a
homily on making the best of things, and sending its numerous
progeny farther and farther afield the while. Of course gardeners
today expect a show for their money and trouble, and they do not
really like plants that take their hospitality for granted. The Star
of Bethlehem sins thus, and seems, moreover, to have no interest
in making a proper show of itself. It is little and low, and while
its corymb of white stars, each with a green line down the center,
is pretty enough, they remain open for a short time and then only
in the sunniest weather. The stars unfold lazily some time before
noon, and close long before their heavenly prototypes have
appeared in the sky; thus, Sleepy Dick, Eleven o'Clock Lady and
Six o'Clock Flower are among the names that it wears. The
French call it *Belle d'onze heures*. I have somewhere read that
the plains of Syria and Palestine are sheeted with it in the spring,
and this may account for its generally accepted name of Star of
Bethlehem.

At this late and somewhat disillusioned day, it may be absurd
to recall a time when I whole-heartedly believed in fairies, but

    [7] Macmillan, 1935.

so it was; and the Star of Bethlehem is forever associated in my mind with the little people. In the shady grass about our old spring house in Maryland, where in the shallow stream stood the shining pans of ropy yellow cream, in a region that we called the Fairy Hollow, this little plant grew thickly; and its ways seemed to me distinctly fairyish, especially its openings and closings—I could never catch it at them. At one time the rough grass would be gleaming with the flowers, and then, presto! they would all have assumed invisible cloaks and become one with the green herbage. Then there was the strange fact that both its leaves and its flowers were green and white!

Well, such memories keep many a flower in gardens that would otherwise be discarded. I could never throw out the Star of Bethlehem, quite, though I must admit to occasionally thinning its ranks; but give them a shady bank among ferns and Bloodroots and wild things to ramble over, or let them loose in a meadow— why not a meadow full of these white stars as well as of Buttercups? They are quite as pretty.

Once, long, long ago, its bulbs were eaten with relish by poor folk in pinching times both in Italy and in the countries of the Levant. It was doubtless brought to this country by the earliest settlers, for its name appears in a list of seventy-one kinds of seeds offered in a Boston newspaper of 1760. Like the hardy early settlers, it came to overcome hardship and make a home for itself —perhaps to escape persecution. A little kindness is its due.

OXALIS *OXALIDACEAE*

Wood Sorrel

Turning the pages of the great "Monographia" of the genus Oxalis, by Nikolaus Joseph Jacquin, published in Vienna in 1794, one marvels at the vast number of Wood Sorrels that grow in the temperate and tropical regions of the world, particularly in South Africa and the Americas, so few of which are in general cultivation. A few we are familiar with as pot or hanging basket plants, the so-called Bermuda Buttercup, the little pink *O. rosea*. A few intrude themselves upon us as the most maddening and ineradicable weeds. Chief among the latter is *O. corniculata,* which may be known by its purplish leaves and small yellow flowers. It appears to be a modest and harmless thing at first, but nothing could be further from the truth. It is a fast-working, sharp-shooting menace, insinuating and merciless, and once it has twined its way in among your choice mats of Androsace, Saxifraga, or whatever, only cruel mutilation of these mats will serve to extract it. It is as hardy as iron, a long-lived perennial, and increases by means of its creeping rootstock, and by shooting thrifty seeds in all directions. It is not certain where this little pest originated. In "Weeds," by W. C. Muenscher, it is said to have been introduced into Europe from America. Gray says it came from Europe *to* America. But it is not surprising that no country wishes to claim it; in any case, it seems now to be a citizen of the world.

There are some three hundred or more species of Wood Sorrel known. They grow from bulbs or tubers, and the majority have clover-like leaflets that droop or fold together at the approach of night, or in cloudy weather. The flowers are invariably five-petaled, the buds curiously twisted, and some of the species are very beautiful. Certain hardy kinds are of the first excellence as rock garden plants; a few others belong in the wild or woodland garden. A vast number are not hardy enough to live out in the

North. I am working my way among them in an effort to find which are suitable for garden use in the North, but have not got very far, as it is difficult to procure them, at least from American dealers. The results of my excursions follow:

O. Acetosella L.
   Common Wood Sorrel

A little plant of quaint and beguiling personality that droops its flowers at the approach of stormy weather, and folds its three pale green, heart-shaped leaflets as night draws on, or when the sun shines too strongly upon them. It grows naturally in deep woods on both sides of the water. Dr. Bailey ("Hortus") makes a distinction between the American and the European species, designating the former as *O. americana,* but not all botanists follow him. The leaves of the little Wood Sorrel all spring directly from the curiously beaded creeping rootstock. The delicate flowers, about an inch across, are pearly white, the petals notched and faintly veined with pink, or in a variety *rosea,* more definitely pink, the whole growing no more than three or four inches high. In the Old World, its pleasantly acid leaves were once much relished as a condiment, and it seems always and everywhere to have excited interest and affection. Few plants have been decorated with more names in the vernacular. In the Gaelic it was called *Feada coille,* Candle of the woods:

> Like the flaming light
> Of the wood-sorrel of the caverns.

In North America, it is found in cool woods from Nova Scotia and eastern Quebec to the far West, south to eastern New York (mountains of Ulster County), and in the mountains of North Carolina. It carpets the ground about old trees, flowering in May and June. But it is a difficult plant to settle in the garden—a real wilding not disposed to follow the strict ways of gardens. Its prevalence about Oaks and Hemlocks would argue a fancy for acid soil, and those who can give it real woodland conditions and the companionship of these forest trees, may stand a chance of succeeding with it. Here, where I must manufacture a second-hand habitat, it is not to be fooled and will not grow.

O. adenophylla Gill.   *B.M.* t. 8654

This beautiful Oxalis is very little known as yet in this country. It was first collected, I believe, in the south Chilean Andes by H. J. Elwes, and is much grown in rock gardens abroad. It is a plant of the first beauty and suitability for this purpose, thrusting up from a large scaly bulb a mass of rather large silvery green leaves, out of which spring in long succession, from early summer onward, exquisitely tender lilac-pink flowers with deeper-hued veining in their throats.

It is perfectly hardy, and asks only a snug pocket among the rocks in sun, or perhaps preferably half-shade in a pleasant loam, where it increases amiably from year to year, widening its tufts in the most gratifying manner, and becoming, as Mr. Farrer says, more and more reckless in the profusion of the fairy flowers. My first bulbs were a priceless gift from Dr. James Burlingham of Syracuse, and I later procured more from William Borsch of Maplewood, Oregon, purveyor of many rare and beautiful plants.

O. Bowiei (*O. purpurata Bowiei* Jacq.)

To find a South African Oxalis that would stand out over our winters, was indeed a boon. This beautiful species, which is usually consigned to pots under glass, has lived for several years in my garden in a warm corner. The bulbs were planted in October in the ordinary gritty soil of the rock garden, and almost at once sent up their beautiful lettuce-green somewhat fleshy leaves that are divided into three bluntly heart-shaped leaflets. These died down when winter gripped the garden, and I thought all was over for good; but late in the spring they again made their appearance, and in August the succession of flower stems began and lasted until after many hard frosts. The flowers are borne in open panicles of ten or twelve at the end of stalks some eight inches high, opening a few at a time. The color is a lively pure pink finely veined with deeper color. The buds are twisted and point downward, but, as they open, lift themselves until they are looking directly at the sun. The whole plant is minutely downy and is curiously sensitive to light. The flowers turn with the sun in an amusing manner, seldom appearing in the same position for long

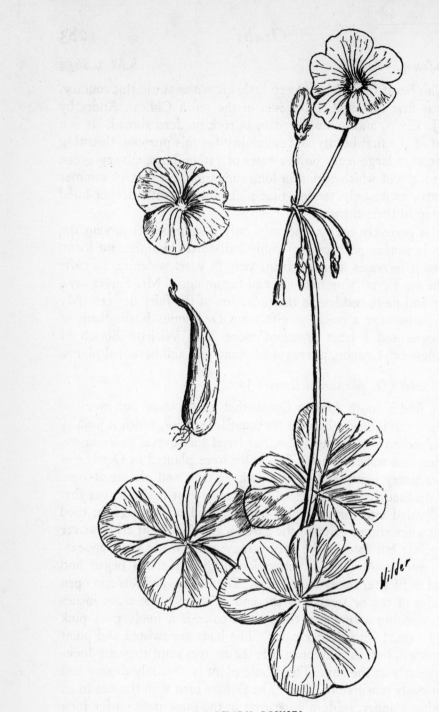

OXALIS BOWIEI

at a time; and as the light fails, the leaves droop to form a little tent. The flowers are tubular and open out flat only under a warm sun. In the rock garden, it makes a charming picture with tumbling masses of *Verbena venosa* behind it, and at its feet a little plantation of *Crocus pulchellus*. Where it is not hardy, the bulbs may be planted out in the spring, and wintered in pots of soil in a frost-proof place. This species, we read, was received from a Mr. Bowie by the Hon. and Rev. William Herbert, author of "Illustrations of the Amaryllidaceae," in 1823.

O. enneaphylla Cav.   *B.M.* t. 6256
    Nine-leaved Shamrock

This species is so beautiful that, according to Clarence Elliott, it makes *O. adenophylla* appear a "trifle overdressed in a slightly flimsy manner." As I have only just found that this plant that I have long looked for may be secured from William Borsch, Maplewood, Oregon, I must place the burden of description upon Mr. Elliott, who, as he says, made a dash out to the Falklands to collect it.

"It is a native of the Falkland Isles, Southern Patagonia, and Tierra del Fuego," writes Mr. Elliott in his splendid book, "Rock Garden Plants," [1] "and is, accordingly, imperturbably hardy. The root is a creeping, scaly, fleshy bulb, from the crown of which, in Spring, come leaves like blue-grey toby-frills, upon two- to three-inch stems, and among them, and carried just above, come the flowers in May and June. These are white waxy trumpets, an inch or more across, and with a delicious almond fragrance. Each year the scaly bulb-like root pushes out a fresh bulb, the old one becoming dormant, and so, in course of time, there will be a string of bulbs, like a string of beads, each as big as a hazel nut, only the latest, foremost one, active and growing, the back one alive and fleshy, but dormant. . . . To increase *O. enneaphylla*, the roots may be dug up every two or three years, just before they start into growth in Spring, and the connecting 'string' broken between the dormant bulbs. When broken apart in this way, and planted, the dormant bulbs will each produce its own new growing point, and make a vigorous flowering plant by the following year." Mr. Elliott recommends shade or partial shade for this choice plant, and a cozy pocket filled with the finest turfy loam,

[1] Published by Longmans, Green & Co.

mixed half and half with well rotted leafmold and a dash of silver sand. The bulbs should be planted not deeper than an inch under the surface.

O. lasiandra

This is a Mexican species tried here last year for the first time. The bulbs were planted in the spring, and began to flower little more than a month later, continuing throughout the summer and autumn. The leaves are like giant four-leaved clovers, each with a dark zone, and lovely in themselves, as are all Oxalis leaves. The flowers are borne in a loose, many-flowered corymb, each flower on a long pedicel, with the usual down-pointing buds opening to tubular flowers of a curious and effective coppery crimson color. I do not know yet if this species will live over the winter; probably not, though I gave it a sheltered situation in sandy soil. But the bulbs are inexpensive and certainly well worth treating as annuals in the interest of keeping bloom in the rock garden throughout the summer and fall. They are much used in Mexican gardens, and "against the creamy, sun-splashed wall of a patio," stand out in bold relief. Cecile Matschat [2] says it is equally at home as an edging plant, in the summer rock garden, and in hanging baskets or pots. My bulbs came from Gordon Ainsley, Campbell, California, and from him I also had O. Deppeii, which proved to be rather washy and not attractive.

O. oregana Nutt.
Oregon Wood Sorrel. Redwood Sorrel

The creeping rootstocks of this northwestern species were confided to a half-shaded situation at the back of the rock garden in the autumn of 1934. They survived the trying winter, and in the spring sent up large three-parted leaves, each with a paler blotch, and hairy on the undersides. That is very nearly all they did send up, for the pale flowers, an inch across, were so few and fleeting that it got to be a sort of garden game to catch them at all. Doubtless conditions were not to its mind, for it is said to produce carpets of pleasantly acid leaves and many flowers over a long period. It is native to Redwood forests and the Coast Range,

[2] *Mexican Plants in American Gardens.*

and, according to Ira Gabrielson, requires in cultivation quite heavy shade, a soil rich in leafmold, and plenty of moisture. Where made happy, he says, the creeping rootstock ranges widely and spreads a lovely carpet of leaves illumined by numerous white faces peering amongst them, often offering the only note of cheer in the gloomy forest light. The only thing I have proved is that it will stand our winters, and that it plays the same little games as others of its kind, the leaflets folding together when the weather is too hot or too cold, or when the light fails, as if shrinking from the hard facts of life.

O. violacea L. (*Ionoxalis violacea*)   *B.M.* t. 2215
    Violet Wood Sorrel   House, *Wild Flowers* Pl. 121

This charming little native I first saw flowering in Herbert Durand's garden, early in May, and received from him a few of the small brown scaly bulbs. It is a small tufted species with three parted leaves and a cluster of several soft-hued violet flowers, carried just above the leaves. Leaves and scape arise directly from the bulb. The clover-like leaves are very pretty in themselves, and Mr. Durand recommends this small woodlander as a companion for the yellow Star-Grass, *Hypoxis erecta*.

It is said to be common locally over a wide range of territory from eastern Massachusetts to Minnesota, and south to Florida and Texas, growing in rocky woods.

From Clarence Elliott I had the seed of *Oxalis rosea* that he brought from Chili. It was sown in the cold frame in the winter of 1933–34, and germinated in the spring, when it was dug up in little sods and planted between the stepping-stones of a path that takes its way through a plantation of Primroses, where it produced its pretty leaves and small pink flowers throughout the season. In Mr. Elliott's letter to me, he said: "Do not sow *Oxalis rosea* until frosts are over. Then sow it broadcast, thinly. It is invaluable for shade and dry places where little else will grow. You will be able to save your own seed for another year. Self-sown, it comes up in autumn here, and then is killed in winter." Sowing it in the frame was a mistake, but one that was not fatal as things turned out.

Other Wood Sorrels that it would be nice to try are the yellow-flowered *O. lobata* Sims, from Chili (*B.M.* t. 2386), *O. magel-*

lanica, from Magellan regions, a tiny species, "a delightful little plant for giving ground-cover over choice bulbs in the rock garden," and *O. tetraphylla,* a Mexican, said to have rosy-lilac blossoms. Where can they be had?

POLYGONATUM *LILIACEAE*

SOLOMON'S SEAL

FOUND in woods, thickets and on shaded banks in spring, the Solomon's Seals are among the most graceful of our native plants. They spring from an elongated, horizontal thickened rootstock, and their common name was anciently derived from the fact that every year when the plant has blossomed, fruited, and withered away, a round joint, suggestive of a seal, is added to the rootstock, so that it is presumably possible to tell the age of a plant from the number of its "seals." The stem describes a lovely curve, and is outlined along its upper half by oval pointed leaves that flutter back over the stem like the wings of a bird in flight. From the axils of the leaves dangle on short slender pedicels little tubular bells, creamy white tinged with green, followed by a pulpy blue-black berry.

One curious thing is noticeable concerning them which gives them an especially decorative quality when planted, as they always should be, in generous groups. All the stems curve in the same direction. Any one with an eye for line must be at once pleased by the beauty of this unison of green arches.

The Solomon's Seals may be grown in shaded borders, woodland or on north-sloping banks with fine effect, but it must be remembered that they quite die away after fruiting, so that it is well to plant ferns behind and about them to cover their defection.

P. *biflorum* Ell.
Hairy Solomon's Seal

This kind has a wide range. You may come upon it in any copse or woodsy place from New Brunswick and Ontario to Florida. It usually grows about eighteen inches tall, sometimes a little more, again less, according to the encouraging conditions with which it finds itself surrounded. One or two flowers hang from each slender pedicel.

P. giganteum Dietr. (*P. commutatum*)
Giant Solomon's Seal

Far handsomer than the above, indeed extraordinarily handsome, is the Giant Solomon's Seal, also a native but of much less extended range. It is very much taller, growing, indeed, it is said, upon occasion to a height of six feet, but my flourishing plantations have never attained to such dizzy loftiness. Between four and five feet, however, they do accomplish, and a fine colony with all the stems bending in the same direction is something to look at and admire on a spring day.

The dangling tubular bells when examined attentively are, though small, very lovely in themselves. They are curiously oblong, the perianth made up of six lobes creamy in color but exquisitely tinted with apple-green. There may be one little bell hung from each pedicel, or there may be as many as four or five. The whole plant is sleek, smooth, whereas *biflorum* is slightly hairy. This is a magnificent plant to use for filling the angle of a north wall, or to mass in wide shaded borders. It should be given the advantage of a rich humus-filled soil, not too dry, and it is very handsome for use along streams or pondsides, always keeping in mind the fact that it will die away after fruiting, and so planning something to follow it during the summer months.

There are Solomon's Seals in Europe, but since we may not have them, little need be said of them here. *P. multiflorum* is the commonest sort. This grows in many parts of Europe, and is familiarly known as Lady's Seal or David's Harp. In ancient times it was believed to seal or consolidate wounds or broken bones. This, of course, because of the old and fantastic doctrine of signatures, "the belief that plants bore outward signs of invisible virtues."

Gerard wrote lengthily of the virtues of this plant, and stated that "experience hath found out . . . that if any of what sexe or age whatsoever that chance to have any bones broken, in what parte of their bodies it be, their refuge is to stampe the rootes thereof, and give it to the patient in ale to drinke which soddeneth and gleweth together the bones in very short space and very strongly; yea, although the bones be but slenderly and unhandsomely wrapped up." A very handy plant to have about.

Reginald Farrer writes with admiration of a number of kinds, but of one in particular that sounds like a good thing for the rock garden. This is *P. roseum* (*B.M.* t. 5049), a little low one with rosy bells. Alas for the lack of it to add to the shaded side of the rock garden.

PUSCHKINIA *LILIACEAE*

STRIPED SQUILL

A SMALL genus of herbs with tunicated bulbs named for a Russian botanist, Count Pouschkin. Only one kind is in general cultivation. This is *P. scilloides*. Mr. Farrer names *P. hyacinthoides* "from the highest snows of Kurdistan," declaring it to be the smallest of the race and the palest blue. Such a one may well exist in that far locale, but I have never heard of its coming closer to hand.

P. scilloides Adams (*P. libanotica*)   *B.M.* t. 2244
Striped Squill

The Striped Squill is a pretty trinket of the early spring, a quaint and demure flower, "a little gray thing like the ghost of a Scilla come back to earth," but wearing a pale striped dimity gown rather than a bright blue stuff one. It comes from subalpine regions of Asia Minor, and was introduced only a little more than a hundred years ago. It flowers in April, early rather than late, the slender stem rising some five or six inches high between dark concave leaves, and hung with very pale blue bells, the color of skimmed milk, each segment with a deep blue line down the center.

Do what you will with this little flower, it cannot be made a showy garden ornament. Spread it in hundreds, or gather it in close colonies on some sunny ledge in the rock garden, and it remains its gentle, unobtrusive self. It is a flower meant for minute scrutiny, to hold in the hand or to bend above attentively, when its modest charms will be made plain to you: its delicate, almost transparent quality; the fluffy effect of the little bells assembled densely but carelessly on the slender stalk; the faint alluring fragrance, unexpected from a flower so small and inconspicuous.

The bulbs should be planted in September, three inches deep

and about three inches apart in sandy, nourishing, well drained soil. In the rock garden it likes a little sunny plain, and there increases very satisfactorily, or it may find a place at the edge of some cared-for border, or on the outskirts of a wild garden where it will readily meet the eye and be safe from the brutalities of the hoe.

In our climate, the shade from tall trees does not come amiss to it, and it likes shelter from rough winds. The bulbs need not be disturbed unless blossoming is falling off; but when this is the case, they may be dug up after the foliage has died down, the offsets detached from the mature bulbs, and all replanted in fresh soil. They are quite hardy as far north as Canada.

SCILLA *LILIACEAE*

Squill, Bluebell, Wild Hyacinth, Jacinth

Scilla is an extensive genus embracing about eighty species of hardy, half-hardy, and tender bulbous plants, native to Europe, temperate Asia in the more mountainous districts, and the mountains of tropical Africa. The name Scilla is an old Greek one used by Hippocrates, and means, according to Miller ("Gardener's Dictionary"), " 'I am molested'; because the bulb of this plant, by its acrimony, irritates the parts to which it is applied."

But there the irritation, if it in truth exists, ceases, for Scillas are a delight to the eye. They deal lavishly in tones of blue, and there are white and rose forms of some of the species as well. The flowers are either bell-shaped or starry, carried in a raceme, and the different kinds cover a long season with their blossoming, beginning very early in the spring and continuing through May, and beginning again in July or August and carrying on into September.

A soil composed of rich fibrous loam and sand is the most suitable for them, and they thrive in sun or shade. They require only to be planted and left in peace, "not fidgeted by a fork or harassed by a hoe," and when thus considered, will increase rapidly by offsets and self-sowing. They should be planted in early autumn while the bulb is at rest. The dwarf kinds are delightful for the rock garden, for scattering about shrubs, or for naturalizing in grassy places, while the taller kinds may be naturalized in light woodland, or freely used in the borders.

All Scillas are best after the first year of blossoming; their ranks close up and they make a fine show, increasing in beauty year after year. Can more be asked?

The dwarfer Scillas have much the appearance of Chionodoxas, but may be distinguished from Chionodoxas "chiefly by the stamens, which are threadlike filaments, whereas those of Chionodoxas are flattened and gathered into an erect cone."

In the early garden books and herbals, Scillas will be found under Hyacinthus. Linnaeus first gave them the separate identity of Scilla.

S. amoena L.   *B.M.* t. 341
   Star Hyacinth. Byzantine Squill

A species found in Austria, Germany, and the Levant, and introduced from the latter region to cultivation about 1590, so it is an old inhabitant of gardens. The bulb is roundish and of a purplish color, and from it arise in April or early May from five to seven keeled and channeled leaves, about five inches long and almost an inch broad, of a "lucid green," and commonly several purplish stalks that grow six or seven inches tall and bear five or six large starry violet-blue flowers, very like Borage blossoms.

Parkinson called this the "other starry Iacinth of Constantinople," and made special note of the prominent "whitish greene vmbone in the middle, beset with six blew chieus or threeds, tipt with blacke, so closely compassing the vmbone that the threeds seem so many prickes stucke into a clubbe." [1] It is a fairly hardy species, but should be planted out of the way of rough winds, as it is easily injured. Altogether, it is less effective than many other Scillas, and is not now often planted.

S. autumnalis L.   *B.M.* t. 919
   Autumnal Squill

Not a very conspicuous little plant, but it must be a pleasant find for the late summer and autumn wayfarer in Great Britain where it grows wild, though probably never very plentifully. "Flora Londinensis" states that it grows near Hampton Court and has been observed sparingly on Kew Green. Both Gerard and Parkinson mention it, and the latter describes its hue as a "bleake purple colour," and says, "I gathered diuers rootes for my garden, from the foote of a high banke by the Thames side, at the hither end of Chelsey, before you come at the Kings Bargehouse." And he notices a form with white flowers.

The Autumn Squill grows from a small roundish bulb sending up several slender stems in advance of the leaves, with a raceme of star-pointed flowers of a soft purplish rose color, with a greenish stripe on the back of each segment, in August or early Sep-

[1] *Paradisi in Sole*, p. 121.

tember. The leaves are several, narrow and much shorter than the flower scape, making their appearance when the blossoming is at its height, lasting over the winter, and dying off in spring. It grows naturally in pastures, and is said to be fairly plentiful in some parts of Cornwall and on the Isle of Wight. Nicholson states that it is also to be found in North Africa.

It is quite hardy, and a nice little plant for the rock garden, where its late flowering in sunny nooks is greatly appreciated.

S. bifolia L.   Lod. *Bot. Cab.* t. 1462, *B.M.* t. 746
Two-leaved Squill

The sleek red noses of this little Squill are always a welcome sight after the long winter. They push through the ground very early and flower hard on the heels of the earliest Crocuses and Winter Aconites—in this neighborhood about the middle of March, a full fortnight before their relative, the Siberian Squill.

It is said to be found in shady groves in various parts of Austria and Germany, and occasionally in Great Britain, especially on declivities above the Welsh coast and on the islands near by. Commonly the oval-oblong bulb produces but two leaves which are narrow, slightly keeled and concave; but occasionally a third leaf, smaller and like an afterthought, makes its appearance.

From between these arises the slightly flexuous stem, reddish, and but little taller than the leaves, not much more than three inches high as a rule, carrying a loose raceme of from four to eight starry flowers, the lower ones held off on little footstalks. These are scentless and, in the type, a soft slaty blue, not nearly so piercing a color as that of *Scilla sibirica*, but very soft and telling when grown in close masses about the feet of the little shrubs in the rock garden, or on a broader scale among shrubs of greater stature, or naturalized along the edges of lightly shaded paths. Not showy, these little flowers of the early spring, but of a very authentic charm for those with eyes to appreciate the small and exquisite.

It does not withstand storm and stress so valiantly as does the later-flowering *sibirica;* and so rather sheltered localities should be chosen for it because of the stormy time when it elects to bloom, and it should be permitted to increase its kind without fear of interference from the busy hoe. A quite sandy loam is the best for it, and it thrives in sun or partial shade.

This is a very variable species, and forms with pure white flowers are to be had, as well as various tones of pink and rose. The variety *carnea* is a pinkish ivory in tone, the scarcer *rubra* is a purer rose-salmon. A form from the Taurus Mountains, var. *taurica*, has crimson anthers that make its blue petals appear bluer; but this kind, though frequently offered, is not often received. If you find it, cherish it. It frequently produces three or four leaves, and the flowers are somewhat larger as well as more numerous than the ordinary kind. From trials, this seems to be the same thing that is sent out by some firms under the name of *Scilla sibirica taurica.*

S. chinensis Benth. (syn. *Barnardia scilloides*)   B.M. t. 3788
Chinese Autumn Squill   B.R. t. 1029

Autumn-flowering bulbs are not so many. There are, of course, Crocuses, Sternbergia, and Colchicums, none of them as much grown as they deserve to be, and the autumn-flowering Scillas are seen almost not at all. Only in the gardens of the very curious do they appear, and few if any catalogues on this side of the water list them. Yet they are pretty decorations for the late season, especially in the rock garden.

The one under consideration, *S. chinensis*, came to me from the well stocked garden of P. J. van Melle in Poughkeepsie. It is a small treasure, and I shall always be grateful to that generous gardener for letting me have a few bulbs. It is in full bloom toward the end of August or early in September, the erect strong little scape of about six inches in height closely set toward its upper portion with small, pinkish lilac blooms, appearing quite feathery with stamens, and lasting nearly a month in a presentable condition.

The leaves begin to shoot upward about the end of July, but make little progress, for the flower scape outstrips them. They are narrow and somewhat lax, falling away from the flower scapes as they mature, and lasting over the winter. An English catalogue says of it: "A little gem for small borders, rock garden and pots, producing in autumn dainty spikes of rose-coloured flowers."

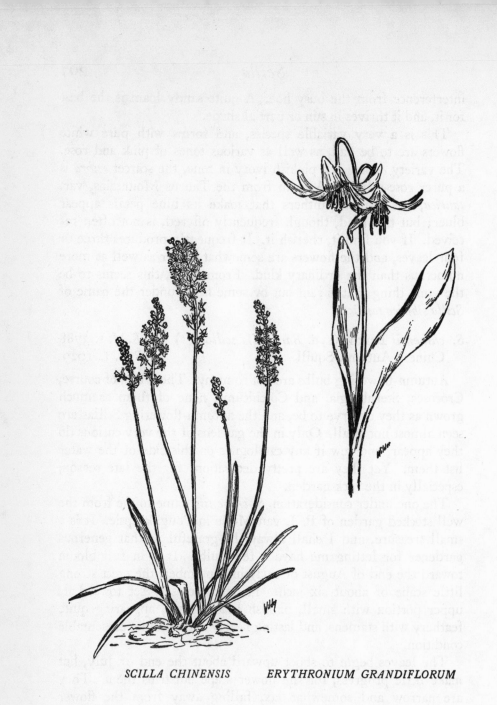

SCILLA CHINENSIS   *ERYTHRONIUM GRANDIFLORUM*

I have not tried it in a pot, but the rest is a true estimate of its value. Moreover, if you start with but one bulb, and are careful not to cut off the flower stalk after the blooms have faded, you will presently have a nice little family of Chinese Scillas presented to you with no trouble to yourself at all; but you must watch for these gratuitous babies, and not mistake them for young grass or garlics, and so root them out. In this garden they are growing on an east-facing slope of the rock garden in sandy soil.

Curiously in "Hortus," and in John Weathers' "The Bulb Book," they are spoken of as not hardy, and in the latter work, a frame or greenhouse is recommended for them. This is certainly not the case; they have weathered the last two exceptionally cold winters, 1933–35, without injury, both here and in Poughkeepsie.

In the rock garden at the New York Botanical Garden grows a bulbous plant labeled *Scilla japonica*. There is a *Scilla japonica* Baker, listed in the Kew Hand-List, but, examining my plants of *chinensis* and these *japonicas*, I see little or no difference between them. The plants at the Garden came into bloom about two weeks earlier, and the scape seemed more densely and evenly filled with fluffy blooms. These are, of course, not authentic botanical differences, but might well be caused by a variation in aspect and soil.

Mrs. Loudon, in "The Ladies' Flower Garden of Ornamental Bulbous Plants," speaks of *Barnardia japonicum* (*Scilla japonica*) as having been introduced from Japan in 1821. She says this is the *Ornithogalum japonicum* of Thunberg, having *purple* flowers, and attributes to it such tenderness of constitution as requires it to be grown in a pot.

S. hispanica Mill. (syn. *S. campanulata*)   *B.M.* t. 127
Spanish Bluebell or Wood Hyacinth

This is one of the big bears of the Scilla tribe. It grows from a foot to sixteen inches tall, and blooms in May. The flowers are bell-shaped, not star-shaped, and are open generously at the mouth. They grow on a substantial stalk, each with a little stalk of its own, forming a handsome spike. While somewhat resembling the English Bluebell, *Scilla nonscripta*, it is, as Parkinson notes, "greater in all parts, as well of leaves as flowers, many growing together at the toppe of the stalke, with many short greene leaves among them, hanging downe their heads with larger, greater, and wider open mouths, like unto bels of a darke blew colour, and no good sent." [2]

According to Nicholson, it was introduced from Spain and Portugal to cultivation in 1683; but, as Parkinson figured and described it in 1629, this must be a mistake. In any case, it was at once found to be a most accommodating and willing guest, and spread rapidly from garden to garden until few gardens of those early days but knew it; and its popularity has not since waned.

It is a plant for almost universal use. Beautiful planted in broad masses in light woodland, or naturalized in grassy places, lovely in half-shaded borders among ferns, particularly the white kinds, along woodland walks, or used freely in the borders. It is especially delightful used as an interplanting for the taller May-flowering Tulips, their bright hues with the softer tones of the Scillas lower down being most effective.

But they are not only *blue* bells. There is a great number of varieties on the market today, frosted white ones, pinks in all tones, beside the blues of varying depths and strength; and they are all fine robust plants, seemingly as hardy as iron, increasing readily, making it necessary from time to time, say every four or five years, to dig up the bulbs and redistribute them, giving to each a little more space. There will be a lot left over with which to start new plantations, or to furnish a favored neighbor with a "setting." Presently he, too, will be doing likewise, and so a pleasant chain has been started that will materially increase the beauty of the world. Given the same conditions of soil and exposure, the Spanish Bluebell will come into flower a little later than the English Bluebell.

Some of the many good varieties among the blues are: Amethyst; Blue King, dark lavender-blue; Blue Queen, a lighter tone; Excelsior, very tall and of a deep tone; La Belle, silvery lavender; Skyblue, late-flowering. Among the pinks, Frans Hals, Peach Blossom, and Rosalind are light and pure in tone. There are various deeper-toned pinks that verge on crimson and are not so effective. La Grandesse is a magnificent new pure white variety. The pinks and blues and whites planted in mixture produce a

[2] *Paradisus*, p. 123.

pretty chintzy pattern. The bulbs are rather large, and should be planted from four to six inches deep, according to size, in good sandy loam.

S. italica L.   Lod. *Bot. Cab.* t. 1015. *B.M.* t. 663
Italian Squill

Although this species was introduced to cultivation from southern Europe in 1605, and seems to have been well known in Parkinson's day, I do not find it listed now, and have never grown it. Of it Joseph Jacob ("Hardy Bulbs") says: "It is an interesting plant because it has been grown in British gardens ever since the very beginning of the seventeenth century, but for some reason or other, has never caught on. . . . It grows from nine to twelve inches in height, and when all the flowers are fully developed, they form a fat sugar-loaf shaped spike. They are a surprise packet, for when the flowers are first pushing up from the ground, they give one the idea that they are going to form a head very much after the style of a muscari or grape hyacinth."

The leaves are about six, much shorter than the scape, and bluntly channeled, almost recumbent, and encircling the flower scape. There is a good figure of it in Curtis' *Botanical Magazine*, where the flowers are described as fragrant, smelling like lilac, pale blue or gray. The anthers appear to be a very bright blue, in sharp contrast to the grayer blue of the starry flowers. The Kew Hand-List gives a white form.

English books pronounce it hardy, but that may not apply to our more severe climates. It is found growing naturally in the south of France, northern Italy, and also in southern Switzerland, "inhabiting rocky pastures in open situations on the mountains, ascending to considerable elevations above sea level." A light loam in a sunny position is recommended for it. The bulbs increase slowly by offsets, but I find a note in a back number of *Horticulture*, from Olympia, Washington, saying that they are easily raised from seed, planted in fall or spring, and take two or three years to reach flowering size.

It sounds like an alluring little plant for the rock garden, especially because of its Lilac scent. We have not too many fragrant rock plants.

S. nonscripta Hoffm. & Link. (syns. *S. festalis*, *S. nutans*)
Wild Hyacinth. Bluebell, Harebell, Jacinth

The modest Wild Hyacinth must go in constant fear of having its given name changed. I have known it as *S. nutans*, which means "nodding," *S. festalis*, which means "gay"—both names appropriate enough, it would seem; but the ways of botanists are inscrutable, and we now have *S. nonscripta*, and the poor gentle flower must be saying with the old lady in the nursery rhyme, "Lawk a mercy on me, this is none of I!" for *nonscripta* means "undescribed," [3] and surely the Wild Hyacinth has been described and redescribed by every writer on flowers, or gardening, for the last several centuries.

Turner, who in his "Names of Herbes," 1548, has it with all the Scillas, as have the early writers generally, under Hyacinthus, says: "The comune Hyacinthus is muche in Englande about Syon and Shene, and it is called in Englishe crowtoes, and in the North partes Crawtees. Some use the rootes for glew."

That is not all the confusion, but it is enough to relate here. It has a long list of common names, only one of which besides the above I will give, because it is so pretty and so descriptive. It is called in some parts of England Ring o' Bells, and the curving shepherd's-crook stalk with its dangling bells suggests just that.

But whatever name you find it under, it is a charming thing. Less assured, less erect, less robust than the Spanish Bluebell, it is yet something like it, and blooms at almost the same time in May. The bells may be blue in several tones, white, or pink, but they are narrower and more constricted than those of *S. hispanica*, and reflex at the tips. The leaves are numerous and pale green, and not as long as the stalk, which rises to a foot or more from the roundish bulb. And one must not forget to mention the fragile scent of these flowers which, where they are planted in masses, rides the spring breeze like a will-o'-the-wisp, now touching you, now lost, but very sweet when you get it, though Gerard describes it as strong and sweet, and "somewhat stuffing the head."

In "Wild Flowers," one of the books by that pleasant writer of

---

[3] Parkinson says, "Dodonaeus calleth it *Hyacinthus non scriptus*, because it was not written of by any Author before himselfe."

nearly a hundred years ago, Anne Pratt, we find this description of the place taken by the Bluebell or Wild Hyacinth in the English spring: "Scarcely a copse can be found throughout our land which is not then blue with its flowers, for it is to the woodland and the green lane, in Spring, what the buttercup is to the meadow. Growing near it we often find the beautiful pinkish-white blossoms of the wood-anemone, and before it fades away, the hedges are getting white, and becoming fragrant with the wreaths of the blooming May."

The utilitarian old herbalists had a practical use for the pretty Bluebell. Gerard says the root "is full of a slimy, glewish juyce which will serve to set feathers upon arrows instead of glew, or to paste bookes with: whereof is made the best starch next unto that of Wake-robin rootes." This starch, I read, was used to stiffen the grand linen ruffs once affected by great ladies.

But our use for them should be as Nature uses them in their homeland—to form misty pools of soft blue in woodland hollows among the browned fern fronds and the tender young green, or to stream down shaded hillsides in little rivulets, or to accompany us along shadowed walks with ferns and Bloodroot and the like. The "enameled blue" ones are far the prettiest and most effective, but there are for those who crave variety a Blush Queen (pink), and an *alba grandiflora*, a *rubra*, not very attractive, and doubtless others.

Plant the bulbs four or five inches down in the earth and a few inches apart in the autumn, by the hundred, if possible—the common kind are not expensive—and leave them alone. It may be many years before you will have to dig them up because of overcrowding. They seem able to stand a good deal of that without injury or visible discomfort. They are essentially for the wild garden, or informal treatment, and would look out of place where the Spanish Squill appears quite all right.

S. nonscripta is definitely a plant of western Europe, not found wild in Switzerland, Italy, eastern Europe or Scandinavia.

S. pratensis Waldst. & Kit.   *B.R. t. 63*
   Hungarian or Meadow Squill

Compared to the Scillas we have thus far been considering, the Meadow Squill is a newcomer. It was introduced from Dalmatia in 1827. A little colony has grown here for a number of years in a low place just beyond the shade of an apple tree where the soil is a little sandy and apt to be somewhat moist. There it receives the sum of its desires, to be moist while growing and dry while resting, for this low spot, which is damp in spring, becomes quite dry with the summer suns and thirsty apple-tree roots, and in the winter it is, of course, frozen.

Though it has been known to cultivation for more than a hundred years, this little bulbous plant has not got very far toward being a best seller. It is seldom seen; but many catalogues list it, and it is very pretty with a fluffy prettiness that is engaging. It grows about eight inches tall, with leaves somewhat flexuous, and almost, or quite, as long as the flower scape. The flowers are soft blue-purple, and are borne in a dense raceme. It flowers here the middle of May, the last of the Scillas to bloom. One of its chief charms is the very pleasing fragrance.

S. sibirica Andr.   Lod. *Bot. Cab.* t. 151. *B.M.* t. 1025
  Siberian Squill

This little Squill was introduced to cultivation from Siberia toward the end of the eighteenth century. Its burning blue color, its adaptability, its ready increase by means of seeds and offsets, made it an immediate favorite, and it has outstripped all others of its race in point of popularity. Few are the gardens in which the Siberian Squill does not greet the spring. It is, perhaps, the most popular of the smaller bulbous plants.

The bulb is small and ovoid, sending up several narrow leaves, and from one to six flower scapes about four inches tall, each carrying from one to three bright blue open bells in a loose raceme. They flower commonly before the Snowdrops are over and, planted close together, make the first really brilliant display of the year.

They take kindly to shaded situations, even the shade of evergreen trees, and will grow in grass, though the heavy, hungry turf of our country discourages their fecundity somewhat. They do as well in sunny places and, where they are not disturbed, seed freely, so that one's colonies increase in breadth year by year; and new colonies are started by means of winds and washing rains and birds in the most unexpected places. But we must look out for the slender spears of the seedlings lest we injure them and cheat ourselves of the precious increase.

Scilla sibirica is delightful scattered about the skirts of early-flowering shrubs, such as *Lonicera fragrantissima, Magnolia stellata,* the Shadblow, and the Forsythia. Sometimes narrow borders are edged with them, planted close together, when they look like a blue ribbon binding the border. A lightly rooting annual may be later sown over their heads—one of the dwarfer Sweet Alyssums, *Eschscholtzia caespitosa,* or, in partial shade, *Nemophila insignis* will carry on the blue-binding effect. Several sowings of this must be made at intervals of a few weeks to last the summer out.

The white variety, *alba,* is also prolific, and is especially lovely, as are all white flowers in woodland against a background of green. Another fine variety comes to me as *S. sibirica atrocaerulea.* It is taller, about six inches high, with large and more numerous bells of a rich blue color, somewhat less sharp than that of the ordinary *sibirica,* with bright blue anthers. The leaves are spoon-shaped. It is a very showy kind, but with me has proved less free of increase than the others of its race. I plant it in the rock garden in little close colonies, and there, encouraged by a sunny aspect, it flowers early and makes a conspicuous show. If a few spikes of any of these Siberian Squills are gathered in the hand, it will be perceived that they have a very pleasant, though not strong, fragrance. They come from Russia, Siberia, and Asia Minor.

S. verna Huds.

Sea Onion. Spring Star Hyacinth. Vernal Squill

In his delightful book, "Flowers," Sir Herbert Maxwell says that *Scilla verna* "abounds in short, wind-swept turf of our seaside 'heughs,' growing only four inches high, and not flowering before the end of May, whereas brought into the shelter of the garden, it flowers from the end of March and rises to a height of eight inches."

This has not been quite our experience with this little known (in America) British wild flower, but the difference in climatic conditions would account for this. It grows with me only about three inches high, the leaves appearing first, and flowers late in April or early in May, hurried on by our more ardent suns. The flowers are deep soft blue, arranged in a little hemispherical corymb, and are very fragrant, and so very welcome in my garden.

It is said to be common on the western and northern coasts of Great Britain, and to be frequent in the Orkney and Shetland islands, and on the east coast of Ireland. Anne Pratt in "The Flowering Plants of Great Britain," says, "Its clusters of star-like, sweetly scented flowers of brilliant blue and its numerous dark green smooth leaves, often attract the notice of those who wander on the shores of Cornwall, not only on the sea cliffs, but on heathy commons several miles inland. Its dry capsules, full of glossy black seeds, are conspicuous until very late in the year."

This little Squill is not often offered, but Barr and Sons of King Street, Covent Garden, London, can usually furnish it; and it makes a pleasant addition to the Scillas that are appropriate to grow in the rock garden.

Other Scillas that invite the curious searcher among plants, are the following:

S. maritima (*B.M.* t. 749), the White Squill or Sea Onion, is found on the shores of the Mediterranean, in sandy places in southern Spain, in Portugal, Morocco, Algeria, Corsica, southern France, Italy, Malta, Dalmatia, Greece, Syria, and Asia Minor; yet though so widely distributed, I do not find it in catalogues. "In Sicily, where it grows abundantly, it ascends to an elevation of 3,000 feet. Its range also includes the Canary Islands and the Cape of Good Hope. It is often grown under fig trees on the Italian Riviera, and is to be found in many botanical gardens, having first been recorded as cultivated in 1648, in the Oxford Botanic Garden." [4] It has a large, pear-shaped bulb which sends up a number of dark green leaves from which arises the succulent stem to a height of from one to three feet, terminating in a crowded spike of whitish flowers. The bulb has medicinal properties that are recognized today. Parkinson [5] gives a graphic description of the Sea Onion: "I relate it as I haue seene it, having shot forth his leaues in the ship by the way, as the Mariners that brought diuers rootes from out of the Straights, did sell them to mee and others for our use"; the rest is too long to give here.

[4] *A Modern Herbal,* by Mrs. M. Grieve. [5] *Paradisus,* p. 133.

S. puschkinioides, from Turkestan, early flowering, with pale blue flowers, I have not been able to come by.

S. peruviana, called the Cuban Lily, though it is not a native of that part of the world at all, but belongs to Mediterranean regions, is a handsome species often grown under glass in the North, which doubtless, south of Washington, would endure out of doors.

The only monograph of the genus Scilla I could find was in the first number of *Annals of Botany,* translated from the German of Messrs. Hoffmansegg and Link. They enumerate and describe twenty-seven species. I found this old book in the library of the New York Botanical Gardens, an amazing storehouse of horti-cultural literature made easily available to all students of the subject.

SISYRINCHIUM *IRIDACEAE*

GRASS FLOWERS

THERE are a vast number of these little Irids known, but few have been brought into cultivation, and perhaps few are worthy of this distinction, though several are of quite uncommon, if modest, beauty. Not all, at any rate, are hardy in cold climates. They belong wholly to the Western Hemisphere, north and south, though some of the Blue-eyed Grasses have wandered far afield and become naturalized in parts of Britain and probably elsewhere in Europe. They have short perennial rootstocks and tufted grasslike leaves that grow quickly into tidy little clumps. The flowers are round and have six divisions all alike borne on slender stems, often branching. They are easily raised from seed, easily cultivated, and self-sow in the garden if conditions are at all to their mind. The stature of the different kinds varies from a few inches to more than two feet.

S. angustifolium Mill. (*S. anceps*)   *B.M.* t. 464
  Blue-eyed Grass, Rush Lily

Every country-wise person, in whatever part of the land, is familiar with some sort of Blue-eyed Grass. In all grassy places, on hillsides, in fields, and by the roadside, its small blue eyes peer upward and attract our attention. They are not conspicuous plants, yet where they grow at all, they usually congregate in sufficient numbers to make a definite effect. On June 6, 1853, Thoreau wrote: "Blue-eyed grass now begins to give that slaty blue tint to meadows." It was one of Thoreau's favorites, for frequent mention is made of it in his diaries. On one occasion he wrote: "The Blue-eyed grass is one of the most beautiful of flowers. It might have been famous from Proserpine down. It will bear to be praised by poets."

The grasslike leaves are narrow and pointed, and a bright fresh green in hue; the slender flowering stem rises somewhat higher than the leaves, and displays its flowers in little umbeled clusters from May to July. The flowers vary from pale to deep blue in different specimens found, and even to wine-color, but there is always the yellow "eye" to lend a certain smartness to the small blooms, and the petals have a curious little barbed point. The flowers open only in sunshine, and they close before sunset. *S. angustifolia* is found from Newfoundland to British Columbia, south to Virginia, Pennsylvania, Michigan, Minnesota, and in the Rocky Mountains.

S. bellum S. Wats.

This little Blue-eyed Grass grows pretty much throughout California, and rather closely resembles its eastern relative. According to Lester Rowntree, "it stars the California spring meadows and responds to the sun in such crowded numbers that on bright days it turns many a grassy place from green to purple-blue." It is said, indeed, to constitute something of a nuisance to farmers in whose fields it elects to grow, as it makes stout little clumps strong enough to hold their own and make their way against the true grasses. I have a few clumps here, and they seemed hardy until the record winter of 1933–34, when they received a severe check, though not a fatal one. The clumps grow about a foot high, and there are six or seven round blue flowers to a stem. I can see little difference between it and the eastern species, though Californians claim it is prettier. It is called Nigger Babies in some localities.

It might be an amusing garden game for some one with time on his hands and a little unwanted space at command, to collect all the kinds of Blue-eyed Grasses that flourish in these United States. It would not be an easy undertaking, for few nurseries offer them, and few seedsmen carry the seed of any save the commonest. Certain western seedsmen offer the kinds local to their neighborhoods. If you are a walker along country ways, you may easily collect a number of different kinds. The differences between them will not be readily discerned by the casual wayfarer; but the curious searcher may care to engage in this minor horticultural sport, and his findings would be interesting and instructive. For the sake of such a one, I have compiled these data of the species and the localities in which they may be looked for (they are not at all complete, but go to show how many, and how widely distributed, are the members of this modest genus):

Northwest: *S. birameum* Piper, flowers dark blue, found in Vancouver and Washington; *S. Macounii* Bicknell, purple-blue, found in Comox and elsewhere on Vancouver Island; *S. idahoense* Bicknell, dark blue, found in wet meadows, Vancouver Island to Oregon and Idaho; *S. segetum* Bicknell, violet-blue, Washington and Oregon, west of the Cascade Mountains.

West: *S. radicatum* Bicknell, violet-blue, wet meadows, Wyoming, Idaho, Colorado, California; *S. halophilum* Greene, blue, alkaline meadows, Montana, Colorado, Nevada, Idaho; *S. heterocarpum* Bicknell, stem pale and often twisted, deep violet-blue, wet meadows and sandy ground, Wyoming; *S. alpestre* Bicknell, white or tinged purple, alpine meadows, Colorado; *S. septentrionale* Bicknell, pale rose to violet, wet meadows, Manitoba, North Dakota, Rocky Mountains; *S. campestre* Bicknell, pale blue or white, prairies of Wisconsin, Montana, New Mexico, North Dakota; *S. inalatum* A. Nelson, blue, dry open hillsides, Idaho; *S. montanum* Greene, dark purple, western Colorado, Gaspé Peninsula, Michigan, Minnesota.

East to Central West: *S. hastile* Bicknell, sandy shores, Belle Isle, Detroit River, Michigan; *S. albidum* Raf., white to violet, Ohio and West, Ontario to Wisconsin and southward, locally introduced in Connecticut; *S. mucronatum* Michx., violet, rarely white, meadows, fields, and open woods, western Massachusetts to Virginia and Michigan; *S. Farwelii* Bicknell, pale blue flowers on flexuous pedicels, southeast Michigan; *S. gramineum* Curtis, loose tufts, flowers blue, wet meadows and damp woods from New Hampshire to Minnesota and southward; *S. atlanticum* Bicknell, violet, damp soil, Maine to Florida, usually near the coast; *S. apiculatum* Bicknell, deep blue, lake shores, etc., Muskegon County, Michigan; *S. arenicola* Bicknell, not very abundant, sandy places along the coasts of Long Island and New Jersey.

S. bermudianum L.   *B.M.* t. 94
   Bermuda Star Grass

This Bermuda Star Grass is considerably more showy than any of its blue-eyed North American cousins. The flowers are of the usual round form, but they are larger and a richer blue, with a bright yellow eye, and sometimes as many as six erupt from a spathe. It is said to grow twenty inches high, and this may be its habit in Bermuda; here it is well under a foot high, nicely tufted, the stem flattened and winged, the leaves a quarter of an inch broad and rather thin in texture. It really makes a very good little rock plant where something sure and easy, and not too spectacular, is wanted. Its reputation for tenderness has not been borne out here, and the past three winters since it has lived in the garden, have been very trying. It begins to bloom here early in June, and continues well through the summer.

S. californicum Dryand. (*Hydastylus californicus*)   *B.M.* t. 983
  Golden-eyed Grass Flower

Although I have several times raised the Golden-eyed Grass from seed, and it germinates readily enough, I have not been able to keep it over a winter, either well protected out of doors or in a cold frame. It is undoubtedly not hardy as far north as New York, but doubtless would be reliable south of Philadelphia. Mr. Purdy says there are two forms, one that looks like a tiny Iris, making a compact little cluster by offsetting at the base. In this form the foliage is from three to six inches high, and in moist soil it will flower throughout the season. This dwarf form is found along the California coast, usually along the bluffs overlooking the ocean. The taller form is from the Sierra Nevadas at an elevation of from five to seven thousand feet, and in the mountains along the California-Oregon border. Presumably this mountain form would be hardier. I have not been able to secure seed of it. The Golden-eyed Grass Flower is much like the blue-eyed kind, but the flowers are larger and a bright yellow, and from three to seven are borne in a cluster at the top of an unbranched, broadly winged stem about a foot high. It sounds pretty and desirable, but it apparently is not for me.

S. filifolium Gaudich.   *B.M.* t. 6829
  Pale Maidens

There is no use saying there is nothing in a name. There assuredly is. Many a flower, as well as many a breakfast food, sells on its name. I was much intrigued by the pretty name of

Pale Maidens—it made a picture in my mind which, alas, has remained only a picture, for so far they have not materialized in my garden. Dr. Worth of Groton, New York, sent me some tiny seedlings which got lost during an overcrowded autumn planting spell, and Mr. Clarence Elliott, of Stevenage, England, sent me seeds which were put into the frames last fall; and what they will do is still on the knees of the gods. Mr. Elliott writes of it as "a rare and exquisite flower which I collected in the Falkland Islands," with rushlike leaves and hanging blossoms like white satin Snowdrops, with deep purple veins. Mr. Farrer writes of it as a rare treasure having a beauty that baffles words. It has fragrance as well. The rushlike leaves grow from four to six inches high, the stem carrying its burden of three to four charming bells being from six inches to a foot tall.

Mr. Elliott wrote me: "I see no reason why the two Sisyrinchiums, *S. filifolium* and *S. odoratissimum*, should not be hardy in New York State, as both came from really cold climates, especially *odoratissimum*. I found this right away down in the Straits of Magellan and in Tierra del Fuego. Anyway they will be worth trying, and I am sending you seeds of both."

At the last minute, seed of *odoratissimum* was found to be exhausted, so I am still awaiting it; but I have here before me a drawing of a charming slender plant with flowers shaped like a small Datura. "After the manner of its kind, the flowers issue in raceme formation out of the sepal, there being two, three, or four flowers according to the size of the plant (it makes no bones about flowering at an early age). Sometimes two inches across, these flowers are of a glistening creamy white in colour, gently penciled with finest purple. . . . The six petals of which the flower is composed reflex daintily after the manner of a Lilium; the whole flower exudes the delightful fragrance of *Daphne Cneorum*, or is it *Androsace hirtella*? I cannot just place its delightful aroma." [1] (Some compare it to that of Lily-of-the-Valley.) This species is said to be hardy out of doors in England, but its slender height of eighteen inches needs some support, or to be shielded from rough winds.

Both these Grass Flowers sound delightful and, as Mr. Elliott said, well worth trying. The faint heart never got anywhere in

[1] J. P. Shanahan, *Gardening Illustrated*.

gardening. Courage and curiosity are as important in the make-up of a gardener as patience and skill.

S. Douglasii A. Diet. (*S. grandiflorum* Dougl.)   *B.M.* t. 3509

With the lively little Grass Widow, we are back on firm and familiar ground. It is a native of our Northwest, found growing in damp meadows from British Columbia to Idaho, Utah and California, etc. Piper and Beattie [2] say that it is rare west of the Cascade Mountains, but common in the interior. It climbs the mountains to a considerable height. It has the largest flowers of any member of the race, and it is, perhaps, the most lovely. The flowers are bell-shaped, and hang like large rose-violet Snowdrops from slender pedicels among the narrow grassy leaves. They have a charming pellucid quality, and the sheen on the surface of the segments is like that on the inside of a sea shell. The stems grow about a foot tall, the leaves a little shorter, in scant stiff tufts. Sometimes it sends up the tips of its leaf-blades in the late autumn as an earnest of what is in store for us in the early spring. It usually flowers soon after the Snowdrops, and is a delightful plant for the rock garden, grown low down on the construction where the soil is not bone-dry, in little sociable congregations. The soil should be a rather cool and peaty one, and it will stand half-shade. The roots are planted in late summer or autumn, and left undisturbed as long as they are flowering well. They resent removal, and sometimes will sulk for a year after planting or transplanting.

There is a rare white form which, though its almost transparent texture makes it a thing of real beauty, is not as effective as the type. An Oregon correspondent writes me that there are forms to be found in many tones between the deepest rose-purple and the pure white, and that she has seen an occasional white kind spotted with purple. It is quite hardy and easy to grow, and, given moisture in spring, does not at all object to a summer baking, for that is what it is accustomed to.

Ira Gabrielson gives us a picture of it growing in its native habitat.[3] He says it is "one of the earliest, as well as the most showy, wild flowers in the vast country east of the Cascades. Here, depending on altitude and season, it spreads a shimmering

[2] *The Flora of the Northwest Coast.*   [3] *Western American Alpines.*

carpet of royal purple over acre after acre some time between February and June. Appearing with the clear yellow *Fritillaria pudica*, it makes an unforgettable color combination. The clumps of narrow grass-like foliage push up in all damp spots throughout the great plateau country, giving no hint of the surprising loveliness to follow when those amazing banners of royal purple silk are hung out to the breezes."

S. iridifolium H. B. & K. (*S. laxum*) *B.M.* t. 2319
                                    Lod. *Bot. Cabinet* t. 1679

Once started on a hunt for Sisyrinchiums, I wanted to try all I could find. And so a few years ago, I secured seed of the Iris-leaved Star Grass, which is said to be a common plant from Brazil to Chile. The seed germinated with the heartiest enthusiasm, and I had a fine lot of little plants to set out in the spring. (Seed was sown in a cold frame in the autumn.) The seedlings grew apace, and looked much like gray-leaved Bearded Iris plants. When autumn came, remembering their gentler home climate, I dug up a part of them and put them in a cold frame with the Californian Golden-eyed Grass, covering them warmly with salt hay. The others I left in the try-out bed. Curiously enough, these lived over the winter and flowered, while those in the cold frame died to a man, victims, apparently, of misplaced coddling; yet I do not think *iridifolium* could be considered a reliably hardy plant, and it is not pretty enough to excite one's protectiveness to any great degree. It began to flower here about the middle of June. From out the gray swordlike leaves issued a stiff stem to a height of about eighteen inches, bearing two or three short branches held close to its sides and two or three small leaves. The flowers, when they emerged in long succession from the spathes, were as round as buttons and pale yellow in color, veined with brown on the backs of the petals. Indeed the stout little stalk had a curious, buttoned-up appearance with all those round flowers outlining its upper half. There is a faint fragrance.

Other Grass Flowers that might engage the attention of the curious are *S. cuspidatum*, temperate South America; *S. graminifolium*, Chile; *S. junceum*, Peru, and *S. striatum*, Argentina, etc. From Margaret Armstrong's invaluable "Field Book of Western Wild Flowers," I take the names of two little yellow-flowered native species, *S. Elmeri,* yellow with purple lines, found in wet places in the Sierra Nevada, and *S. arizonicum,* with yellow flowers on branching stems. Seed is not offered so far as I can find, but may come to light some day.

The Grass Flowers are not dashing plants, they do not flaunt or glitter; but they have a quality and a quiet personality that make one like to number them among one's acquaintances.

SMILACINA *LILIACEAE*

Solomon's Plume, False Spikenard

S. racemosa Desf. (*Vagnera racemosa*)

The Solomon's Plume is an effective and easily grown perennial plant springing from a thickened fleshy rootstock, having many long fibrous roots, the scars of former stems showing ringlike along its length. The stems, often describing a zigzag course, arise to a height of from one to three feet, and are leafy all the way, ending in a "plume" of creamy white flowers from one to four inches long. They are faintly scented. The plume is followed in the late summer by branching clusters of red berries, speckled with purple. These are seized upon with avidity by birds with families to support.

This handsome plant grows in many parts of the United States and Canada, a common denizen of woodland places, transplanted easily and established in the shaded wild garden, or on the north side of a rock garden. When many are grown together, the effect is feathery and charming. It is often called Solomon's Seal, but the true Solomon's Seal is quite a different plant.

There are other native species of Smilacina, but this one will serve to illustrate the family.

STERNBERGIA *AMARYLLIDACEAE*

S. *lutea* Ker-Gawl.   *B.M.* t. 290
Winter Daffodil. Mt. Etna Lily   (under *Amaryllis lutea*)

ALTHOUGH it has been grown in European gardens since the sixteenth century, *Sternbergia lutea* is extremely rare in American gardens. In certain old Virginia gardens, it has long been cherished, and I believe it is grown somewhat in the Northwest; but otherwise it is almost unknown. Possibly this is because it has by certain writers been given a reputation for tenderness which is quite undeserved. It has grown in this cold garden for many years, even withstanding the record winter of 1933–34 without injury. Except for a very rare Crocus or two, there are no yellow-flowered bulbous plants blossoming in the autumn, so that the Sternbergia, aside from its own special attractiveness, is valuable for its glowing color at that season when we most appreciate it. The flowers are much like Crocuses in appearance, but of a thicker texture, and they never open out starrily as do so many Crocuses, but keep their vaselike form. Early authors called it the Winter or Autumn Daffodil, *Narcissus autumnalis major*,[1] or referred it to Colchicum, and Dutch florists exported it under this latter name at one time. It was also known as *Amaryllis lutea*. The genus was given its present generic name in honor of Count Caspar Sternberg, a noted German botanist (1761–1838). In the "Hortus Floridus" of Crispin de Pass (1615), wherein are so many beautiful drawings of bulbous and other plants popular in that far day, are depicted both a single and a double form of the Greater Autumne Narcissus. I can find no record elsewhere of a double Sternbergia, and it may have been a happy flight of the artist's imagination. He says it differs little from the single save in the number of petals, "which accord a greater grace to the flower."

The roundish bulbs of Sternbergias should be put into the ground as early as possible, preferably not later than the end of

[1] Parkinson's *Paradisus*, p. 77.

August, and set about four inches down and the same distance apart. Horticultural doctors do not agree as to the type of soil that best suits the plant, some declaring for a damp and others for a dry soil; but out of my own experience I think this is a case of the drys having it. My own bulbs are on a sunny slope of the rock garden in well drained rather stony soil, and they have done well and multiplied. Their native home lies on both sides of the Mediterranean to Syria and Persia, and this would indicate a liking for shelter and warmth.

To this end my bulbs are given a warm rock at their back, on the north side, which insures them the summer baking which seems to be required if they are to flower freely.

Not long after planting, dark, strap-shaped leaves, thick and durable, thrust up and grow finally to a length of eight inches. Out of the midst of these, about the middle of September, arise the golden Crocus-like flowers, one from each spathe, but several from each well grown bulb, about two inches long, and held up on stout, erect scapes three or four inches long. Both flowers and leaves are of substantial texture and withstand weather that would spoil the more fragile blooms of Crocus and Colchicum. In my climate the leaves last over the winter, appearing still richly green when we take off the blanket of salt hay in the early spring, and dying away before early summer. Patches of Sternbergias are lovely and welcome in the autumn garden either grown in the rock garden or along the edges of sunny shrubbery borders where the soil is well drained. If a companion for them is sought, nothing is more suitable than the earliest forms of *Crocus speciosus*, that are so very blue in tone. Colchicums blossom at the same time, but they are too pink to "go" well with these yellow flowers. *Colchicum autumnale album*, however, is suitable.

By some writers the Sternbergia is supposed to be the Lily of the Field mentioned in the Scriptures; and in support of this idea we read that "the fields of the Levant are overrun with the *Amaryllis lutea*, whose golden liliaceous flowers in autumn afford one of the most brilliant and gorgeous objects in nature."

There seem to be two forms of *S. lutea*, one with narrower leaves, thought by those so lucky as to possess it, to be superior. It is known as *S. l. angustifolia*. The late Sir William Lawrence, whose collection of bulbous plants at Burford was notable, wrote of the Sternbergias: "There are two species and a number of varieties of Sternbergia. In the one species, *S. lutea*, the flowers appear before or with the leaves; in the other, *S. siccula*, after the leaves are fully developed." And he describes several forms of *S. siccula*, including var. *Clusii*, which flowers in August, and *S. s. maroccana* from Tlemcen; also *S. s. graeca* (*cretica*), the smallest of the species. All these have hairbreadth differences of structure or aspect, and do not concern us in America who have difficulty enough in procuring the common kind at the present time. But with the hopeful weakening in certain directions of the quarantine against the importation of plants, we may also, one happy day, be concerned with these narrow distinctions.

There seems also to be a spring-flowering Sternbergia, *S. Fischeriana* (*B.M.* t. 744), or sometimes *S. lutea Fischeri*. This kind blooms in April, and the flowers are said to be large and of the characteristic bright warm yellow, and the leaves, which reach the height of a foot at full maturity, are somewhat glaucous. It comes from the mountain meadows of Asia Minor and the Caucasus to Persia. The bulbs should be consigned to the earth (if you are so lucky as to come upon any) in September, and a warm and sheltered locality given them.

Frequent lifting and replanting are not recommended for Sternbergias. Let them alone as long as they are flowering satisfactorily. If they show by not flowering that something is amiss, lift the bulbs after the foliage has died away, dry them off, separate the big ones from the small, enrich the ground with a little bonemeal, and reset the bulbs.

TRICYRTIS *LILIACEAE*

TOAD LILY

THE Toad Lilies are a small genus of perhaps half a dozen perennial plants with short creeping rhizomes. They are woodlanders and inhabit the mountains of the Far East—Japan, China, and the Himalayas. They are little known and grown, and when they are referred to at all, are generally recommended for culture under glass or in mild climates. They are curious rather than beautiful, but have a certain value because of their late flowering. Two species, at least, are quite hardy in the open as far north as Massachusetts, though they benefit from a light covering after the ground is frozen. They increase by means of underground rhizomes, which may be taken up in the spring or early autumn and divided.

T. hirta Hook. (syn. *T. japonica*) B.M. t. 5355
Toad Lily. Orchid Lily

The Japanese Toad Lily is an interesting rather than a beautiful plant. The stem, which is erect to a height of about three feet, and often branched, is covered with a sort of pale pile. The ovate, strongly veined leaves clasp the stem alternately and are somewhat hairy, but not spotted, as are those of some of the species. The blossoms, that may be as many as fifteen, are bell-shaped, of rather heavy texture, white or whitish, and sprayed on the interior thickly with livid spots. They appear in the axils of the leaves late in September and October, often meeting a sharp frost before they have run their course.

For this reason, they should be planted in rather sheltered positions, in warm borders or among small sheltering bushes at the back of a rock garden. A peaty soil, well drained and not too dry, is the best for them, and all the Toad Lilies prefer partial shade. Groups of them at the difficult shaded end of a border make a nice effect late in the season.

This species has proved quite hardy in my garden with only the usual light covering of salt hay or oak leaves. A variety *nigra* has dark stems and darker spots than the above, and flowers earlier. The Japanese Toad Lily was introduced in 1863, and is said to be widespread in the woods of Japan, but it has never achieved great popularity in western gardens. Its chief value lies in the late season of its flowering. When October comes, our critical faculties are somewhat dulled, and we are glad to see a fresh flower face instead of so many that are obviously on their last legs.

Other species of Tricyrtis are the following: *T. affinis* (Japan), smaller and daintier in all its parts, but with flowers similar to the above; the leaves purplish and marbled. *T. flava* (Japan) has flowers of a fairly good tone of yellow spotted with brown. *T. macropoda*, B.M. t. 6544 (Japan), hardy and much like *T. hirta*, but with the flowers disposed in a long corymb, the leaves four inches long; it flowers in summer. *T. pilosa* (*T. elegans*), B.M. t. 4955 (Himalayas), flowers in late spring and is taller than the others. The flowers are thick and creamy and covered with purple spots. I have not grown this, and do not know if it is hardy.

TULIPA *LILIACEAE*

My old friend, the late Rev. Joseph Jacob, one of England's famous gardening parsons, reported W. R. Dykes as once saying to him that, if he lived to the age of Methuselah, he might be able to say something definite about the species and wild forms of Tulips, but not till then. Mr. Dykes's searching scrutiny of the race was cut short by his tragic and untimely death, and though his wife subsequently published his notes, accompanied by her own accurate and beautiful drawings in color,[1] it may be taken for granted that even these exhaustive observations do not represent what would have been his final conclusions concerning this intriguing and perplexing group of bulbous plants. No one, to my knowledge, has taken up the study where Mr. Dykes left off, though much interest is evinced in the wild Tulips abroad.

American gardeners, too, are beginning to realize something of their fascination, and the attitude toward them has become much less oblique in the last ten years. Certain of them are frequently featured in flower shows, and they are grown in gardens far more often than formerly, and there is frequent mention of them in the horticultural press; but on the whole, the great hybrid Tulips, the Darwins, Cottages, Breeders and the like, still successfully hold the stage against the wild species.

As a matter of fact, there should be no rivalry among them, any more than there is between Pansies and wild Violets, between Grass Pinks and Carnations, or between Delphiniums and annual Larkspur. They are of the same race, and there is what might be termed a family likeness; but they are quite different in habit, requirements, and uses. What chiefly draws us to them is that they open up to us a whole world of venture and adventure, they entice us to trial and experiment, calling us from the beaten track to little winding paths into the unknown. Success with them is by no means a foregone conclusion, though quite possible, even

[1] *Notes on Tulip Species.*

322

probable, if we have luck or perseverance—perhaps they are the same thing—and when we meet with it, we find personalities among the wild Tulips and a vivid beauty of which we had no notion at all.

Twenty years ago when I first began hunting out the names of the wild Tulips in bulb catalogues, and risking a few, I had no idea what to do with them. My mistakes were many and costly, and I might well have been permanently discouraged; but there was that hankering for the unknown that all gardeners must confess to, and the twenty years have by and large taught me a little.

At first I grew only the fragrant *Tulipa silvestris*. This was followed by the gay and accommodating *T. Kaufmanniana;* then, growing bolder, I tried all the kinds that were from time to time available. Even now I cannot speak with the voice of authority, but only give my experience with a number of species in two gardens where the climatic and other conditions were quite different, for what it is worth; but, from first to last, growing them and getting to know them a little has been an unfailing source of surprise and delight.

During this period of experiment, I have not found any species that was not perfectly hardy over the coldest winters if planted in a perfectly drained and sunny position, but I learned that each must be treated as an individual with individual likes and dislikes. From Mr. Dykes, however, came the knowledge that all Tulips love sun and air, and that the soil in which they are grown should not only be well drained but contain some lime, and that bonemeal is an excellent fertilizer for them. Fresh manure is definitely not on their diet.

The rock garden, because of its sunny exposures and sharp drainage, turned out to be an excellent haven for most of them, particularly the dwarfer kinds; but I had to learn by sad experience that the bulbs resented bitterly being overshadowed by other foliage after they had flowered. I lost more than one colony of choice species by allowing some strong-growing plant to flop over it, thus retarding or preventing the ripening of the bulbs.

We plant the bulbs some time during November, late rather than early. In the *Journal of the R.H.S.*, September, 1925, Mr. Dykes suggests planting the bulbs of some species twelve inches below the surface of the ground, and he also advises setting them among the roots of shrubs which would suck the moisture from the ground and thus provide warmer and dryer conditions for their ripening. The wisdom of this latter course I soon discovered, for bulbs of *T. silvestris* planted among some bushes of Stanwell Perpetual Rose flowered freely every year, while those given more commodious accommodations multiplied their bulbs but minimized their blooms.

I have never, however, planted any Tulip bulb twelve inches down. We plant them from four to eight inches below the surface, according to size. Those with tall brittle stems are given some shelter, as a rock or low shrub to windward, for the stems are likely to be snapped off during rough winds. Also we now know that those bulbs that have a woolly lining to their jackets (*T. montanum* and others) require extra warmth and extra sharp drainage if they are to survive the damp of winter and the heavy rains of our summers. These we usually place upon a cushion of sand, and cover with the same material.

Many authorities insist upon the advisability of lifting and drying off the bulbs after the foliage has ripened. We have tried both ways many times, and can see little difference in the longevity of the bulbs, whether lifted and stored over the summer or left in the ground where they have been given sharply drained situations. Our heat-ridden summers seem to supply them with the ripening conditions they require. Whatever we do for them, it seems fairly certain that the Tulip species will never live on and on, spreading into wide colonies as do many Daffodils, Crocuses, and Scillas; but in nearly all cases, they will outstay the great hybrid Tulips that are planted in millions every year—a truth I have not before seen brought forward in their favor.

My bulbs of *T. silvestris* are the descendants of those first bulbs bought twenty years ago. Others that have lived in the garden for as much as ten years include *australis, persica, dasystemon, Clusiana, praestans, primulina,* and *Sprengeri.* Of others I have had a much shorter experience, but of none less than three or four years; but one does not come to unassailable conclusions after a few trials.

New conditions should immediately be tried when a situation

does not bring success. *T. Greigii,* for instance, one of the grand scarlets, failed time after time in the rock garden, producing horrid, sick-looking foliage and blasted buds; but when relegated in disgust to a corner of what had been a vegetable patch, it throve magnificently, fairly rioting in pale, purple-mottled foliage, crisp and handsome, and unfolding to our astonished gaze immense scarlet cups of absolute perfection, and in a short time has appreciably increased.

Before going on to specific cases, there is a last point to be noted in favor of including the wild Tulips in the garden's company. Certain of them begin to bloom before any of the hybrids have thought of getting under way, and others long outlast them; thus the Tulip season is prolonged by many weeks. And, to sum up, these essentials are to be borne in mind: late planting, not before November; deep planting, from four to eight inches, according to the size of the bulb; perfect drainage; sun and air and a rich soil in which some lime has been incorporated; no overshadowing by hearty herbaceous neighbors. These things heeded, a measure of success will certainly follow. A little prayer now and again, when you think of it, helps.

In an article on the species of Tulipa for the garden,[2] Sir A. D. Hall assigns the natural home of the genus to the "mountainous and steppe country that extends from Greece to the Altai Mountains; Kashmir and Palestine mark the boundaries in other directions, and one or two species, truly wild or colonists, extend along the Mediterranean and across to the Atlas. It is a region characterized by hot and almost rainless summers and intense winter cold, followed by a short spell of growing weather during which the Tulip reaches its flowering stage before it is dried up and rests as a bulb into the following season."

T. acuminata Vahl. (*T. cornuta; T. stenopetala*)

B.R. t. 127
Red. *Lil.* t. 445

This fantastic plant is not definitely a species but quite definitely a personality. It is generally regarded as a sport, but was once given a vague status as a species. It is said to have appeared

[2] *Journal of the Royal Horticultural Society,* June, 1935.

among gardeners about 1816 from the general direction of the Levant. It flowers here the 1st of May, hoisting on tall stems eccentric blossoms, red and yellow, with abnormally narrow and somewhat twisted petals. It has won in some quarters the name of Chinese Tulip, not, it is said, because it has any affinity with China, but because the very long and narrow segments suggest the finger nails of a mandarin. It is extremely effective for cutting, and belongs in the well drained sunny border.

T. australis Link & Schrad. (*T. Breyniana; T. Celsiana*)

B.M. t. 717, 9078

Red. *Lil.* t. 38

An engaging and very sweet-scented little Tulip allied to *T. silvestris*. It is shorter of stem than *silvestris*, however, and the flower is smaller with more pointed petals; and there is but one flower to a stem. Also it is a more reliable performer with me, flowering every year, but not increasing very rapidly. The color is bright yellow with the outer sides of the segments washed with reddish brown, the upper surface having a varnished look. In a sunny nook in the rock garden it grows less than eight inches high and blooms about the middle of May. It is a plant of subalpine pastures in France, Spain, Portugal, in the Valais in Switzerland, and in the Tyrol, the Apennines, and the Atlas Mountains. Sir A. D. Hall thinks it may be truly wild only in Sicily. He has seen it brought in bunches to the market in Bologna.

T. Batalinii Regel

A little Tulip for rock gardeners to dream about and to secure at the earliest possible moment. It hails from Asia Minor and is said to be only a color form of the brilliant *linifolia* and closely allied to *Maximowiczii*, but it has plenty of distinction of its own. It produces four or five stem leaves, and a stout little stem bearing a small generous cup with rather bluntly pointed segments of the softest cream-yellow hue, just verging toward shrimp. They are lightly fragrant. It crosses freely with its brilliant allies, and from these crosses, it is said, have been raised many beautiful forms in pinkish red, lemon, apricot and peach. I have not seen them offered in catalogues as yet.

T. biflora Pall.

B.M. t. 6518
Dykes t. 14

Perhaps the smallest of the Tulips, this is also the earliest to flower. It is too small to find a home in the wide world of the border, and belongs in the rock garden where, on a sunny little plain, it stages an amusing display at the end of March. From greenish red buds the flowers open pure white and starry, and there are usually three flowers to a slender stem, which may be no more than three inches tall. The leaves are narrow and strap-shaped and reddish on the backs and along the edges of the upper surface. In my garden, this small Caucasian species has not proved very long-lived.

T. Billietiana Jord.

B.M. t. 7253

This Tulip is not always given specific rank, but whether or not it deserves this distinction, it is an easy and friendly kind and a good stayer. It has grown in this garden for many years without lifting, and every year I look forward to its shallow yellow cups that appear on stems about a foot high when May is well under way. The rather blunt segments have a piping of red which gradually runs into the ground color as the flower matures. It may be grown in the rock garden or in narrow borders, but should not be contrasted with the larger May-flowering Tulips. It furnishes charming material for small vases. It is said to grow wild in the Swiss Alps.

T. chrysantha Boiss.

When we receive the bulbs of this Tulip, we know at once that we must give it a warm situation and a well drained soil with a cushion of sand to boot, for it has the telltale felt lining on the inside of the tunic. *Chrysantha* is a charming flower, blooming here during the first days of May. It grows under eight inches tall, and the single flower opens as flat as a star. It is pure yellow, flushed rosily on the backs of the segments. It is said that the higher it climbs in the mountains, the yellower it becomes, and the dwarfer in stature. It is found in "Northern Persia and Bokhara, in Afghanistan, Beluchistan, Cashmere, and the slopes of the Himalayas to Thibet, and from thence down into the plains of the Punjaub." Considering its sensitiveness to damp, it does very well in the garden.

T. Clusiana DC.   B.M. t. 1390
    Lady Tulip; Candy Tulip; Radish Tulip   Dykes t. 24

This gay and charming Tulip was named for the great botanist Clusius, who cultivated it in his garden in Flanders. It is allied to *stellata* and *chrysantha*, and is one of the few species quite often seen in gardens and at flower shows. It has been cultivated for more than three hundred years. Clusius reported that it was sent to Florence in 1606 with the statement that it had come from Persia. Parkinson knew it as the early Persian Tulip. Sir Daniel Hall says it is now apparently wild from Chital to Spain; but of the European localities it is noted that they are isolated and scattered, "however abundant the individuals may be in the spot where they do occur." It does not set seed, but wanders freely by stolons.

No prettier Tulip grows. The buds are long and slender and pointed, and up the backs of the snowy segments sweep carmine flames, so that the bud has exactly the appearance of a radish dressed for the table. When the flower is open, it discloses a warm reddish purple blotch. The stems grow something more than a foot tall as a rule, and usually carry three or four narrow leaves along their length. Given a warm sunny situation in rather sandy soil (especially in the rock garden), it proves a most reliable variety, blossoming year after year during the early days of May. It is charming for cutting, especially when cut in the bud stage. Reginald Farrer says it is frequently to be found in old olive orchards about Cannes. How charming it must appear beneath those hoary veterans of the Riviera! In my garden a colony of them rises up behind a mass of pale yellow Alyssum and deep purple Aubrietia with delightful effect.

T. dasystemon Regel (*T. tarda* Stapf.)   Dykes t. 16

Certainly one of the very prettiest of the wild Tulips, and one of the most amiable. In the rock garden or at the edge of a sunny border, it increases rapidly to form grand heart-warming colonies, even seeding itself where conditions are to its mind. It loves sunshine, and appears at its best when the sun's rays are falling upon its starry blossoms. These are greenish and inconspicuous in the bud, but open flat to a most generous width to show a bright yellow and white interior, some time about the middle of April. The strap-shaped foliage forms a rosette upon the ground from which arises the stocky little stem to a height of not more than three inches, carrying usually three blossoms. This small charmer comes from Turkestan.

T. Didieri Jord. B.M. t. 6639

This Tulip is commonly listed as bright red, but the form I once grew was yellowish and had the scent of Sweet Peas. It is a variable species and of neat form with nicely pointed petals and a tall stem. It belongs in the borders rather than in the rock garden, flowering in May. It is found in southern Europe, and one form which haunts the neighborhood of Saint-Jean-de-Maurienne has the name of *T. D. mauriana*. It is easy and long-lived in sunny borders.

T. Eichleri Regel B.M. t. 6191

The man who likes any color so long as it is red, will adore this Caucasian Tulip. It is magnificently red, though the outer segments are bloomy and paler, and there is in the interior a black blotch edged with yellow, and the flower is large and borne on a foot-high stem. The leaves are broad, and the stem carries three smaller leaves. Unlike most of the grand scarlets, it is an easy and reasonable plant, lasting well in the garden, and asking only sunshine and a well drained soil. It flowers about the same time as do the early Dutch Tulips, but does not belong with them. It should be given a situation at the end of some border where it will not be in competition with other forms. It makes a superb corner planting backed with the green of oncoming herbaceous plants.

T. Fosteriana Hoog Dykes t. 25
Book of the Tulip t. 9

In this most brilliant of all Tulips, the lover of red flowers will also find delight. It comes from central Asia, and is said to be the largest Tulip indigenous to that region. Its flowers are immense

—they may be ten inches in diameter—the petals broad and blunt and somewhat widely spaced when the flower is wide open. In the center of the varnished scarlet interior is a broad dark blotch edged with yellow. It grows a foot tall, and the leaves are exceptionally broad and distinctly veined.

I have in the garden, besides the type, the varieties Defiance and Red Emperor. I have to admit that the effect of their brilliance is a trifle overpowering, and the plants are too stocky to be graceful. Still, if you want a dazzling display, plant *Fosteriana* and its varieties. So far they have proved good doers here, but I cannot report upon them from long acquaintance. Certainly they want heat and light and a sharply drained soil.

T. Greigii Regel   B.M. t. 6177

This Tulip is first conspicuous for its pale foliage irregularly splashed and streaked with dark color. This foliage starts into growth early and is frequently injured by frost, so that it is well to keep a bit of the winter covering at hand to spread over it on cold nights. The flower is large and rather square at the base, the outer segments reflexing slightly to form what is termed a "waist." They are rather blunt, as are the inner segments. The color is a most shining orange-scarlet, and there is a purple blotch on the interior extending well up on the segments. Like nearly all the large scarlet Tulips, it is a trifle ungainly in appearance, its blossoms too large for its length of stem. It must be given a warm dry rich soil, and in this garden flowers in the early days of May.

T. Hageri Heldr.   B.M. t. 6242

With this Tulip we are back among the species suitable for the rock garden. It belongs to Greece and Asia Minor, "not extending westward of the Balkans." It is a little and rather quaint flower with a straight cup, opening from an oval greenish copper bud. The color of the expanded flower might be described as copper, tending toward olive, usually with an olive base. It grows only about five inches high; and while one would by no means go off one's head about its charms, it is nice for a sunny corner in the rock garden, and seems to be a fair stayer, though with me it has not increased. It is said to come from about Smyrna. It flowers here the first week in May, and there are usually three flowers to a stem.

T. *ingens* Hoog

Sir Daniel Hall says this Tulip is a bad doer, and has disappeared from most catalogues. It has made, however, three consecutive appearances in my garden, so I am inclined to feel very kindly toward it; and it is much more lovely and graceful than the majority of the large red-flowered Tulips, having a stem nearly eighteen inches tall and a flower whose rather narrow segments give it a casual and informal appearance, while the leaves are long and rather pale in color. The hue of the flower is a most rich and shining red on the interior, while the backs of the segments are a soft buff, and the black basal blotch lacks the usual disturbing yellow circle, a distinctly good point. It is here set on a high sunny plain in the rock garden against a small Spruce in very well drained soil. It flowers before the middle of May. *Ingens* is said to be a form of *T. lanata*, introduced from Turkestan rather recently, but *lanata* will have none of my garden, while *ingens* seems inclined to be at least tolerant. It seems to me a Tulip of real distinction.

T. *Kaufmanniana* Regel   B.M. t. 6887
Waterlily Tulip

Next to *biflora*, this is the earliest Tulip to bloom—in this garden, usually the very first of April; and surely it is the loveliest of the species. Its stems are short, its flowers large, but not for a single moment does the opprobrious adjective "squat" invade the mind of one looking at it, so entrancing are its flashing hues and lovely Lily-like form. It has many varieties, all desirable. The type has tapering cherry-colored buds that open to show a creamy interior merging to deep yellow at the center that is flecked at its apex with the cherry hue of the outer segments. These segments, which are rounded, reflex for about a third of their length, producing the Lily-like appearance, which gives the flower such grace and charm. And it is the most trustworthy of all the wild Tulips, settling down under ordinary garden conditions and flowering year after year as surely as spring comes round, and multiplying freely.

What more could be asked? But in addition, it gives us many exquisite varieties. One may buy them in mixture, or by individual names, and be sure of the greatest pleasure. The foliage of all is broad and of a hoary tone. I plant the *Kaufmannianas* low down in the rock garden in little groups, where they are inexpressibly gay during the early days of spring, or in plantations along sunny well drained borders, but never in competition with strong-growing perennials that would later overshadow them.

Some of the varieties that grow here are the following: *Aurea* is a golden yellow flower with a cherry exterior. Brilliant flowers late and is a rich cherry-red throughout; the foliage is dark in tone. Gaiety has silvery white flowers on such short stems that one hardly sees the cherry-colored stripe on the outsides of the segments after the flower has opened. Händel is a tall variety with cream and carmine blooms that have a circular band of rose-red in the center of the flower; the leaves are somewhat mottled. Primrose is one of the loveliest, a soft yellow flower deepening in tone toward the center.

Tulipa Kaufmanniana comes from Turkestan. Its early flowering exposes it to bad weather conditions, but it is seldom injured unless there are severe frosts. For a very gay show I like to scatter the bulbs of Chionodoxas about them. They bloom at the same time.

T. Kolpakowskyana Regel

B.M. t. 6710
Dykes t. 30

This is said to be a variable species. The form that grows here has usually two flowers to the five-inch stem. In the bud stage they hang their heads, but raise them as the flower opens. The flowers are soft yellow, tinged on the back with brownish red and a few streaks of green. The channeled leaves form a small rosette on the ground. There are no stem leaves. The plant flowers toward the end of April, and is a pretty ornament for a warm nook in the rock garden. It belongs to central Asia.

T. Kuschkensis

B.M. t. 9370

As might be suspected from its densely wool-lined tunic, this species is difficult to keep in the garden. It is one of the large red-flowered kinds, blood-red rather than scarlet, and has the usual oval blackish purple blotch edged with yellow at the center. This shows through the rather thin fabric of the flower. It blooms here early in May, and is said to come from Russian Turkestan.

T. *lanata* Regel

This species must be counted as one of my failures. It flowered once here, and then disappeared. I replaced it, and it duplicated the performance; but I am not devastated, for the big red Tulips, of which this is one of the biggest and reddest, are not among my favorites. One knows at once by its felt-lined tunic that *lanata* is going to be squeamish; and, even given the utmost consideration, it does not stay, at least not in this garden. Sir Daniel Hall says it is a native of Baldschuan, Bokhara, but it also occurs in Kashmir, where it is an introduction, and grows chiefly on the roofs of the temples and mosques. Clearly a low-brow rock garden would not suit it. The flowers are long in the bud and squarish at the base, very bright scarlet, slightly dusked over on the exterior.

T. *linifolia* Regel   B.M. t. 7998

In this small bit of brilliance, we have a perfect subject for the rock garden. It comes from northern Persia, and flowers here about April 24th. It has numerous narrow leaves slightly undulating in outline, and out of them arises on almost no stem at all, the glowing red flower, small and neat, with pointed, polished segments and a dark blotch at the heart. It flourishes here on a south-facing slope of the rock garden, and draws all eyes to it when it flowers.

T. *Maximowiczii* Regel

This is almost identical with the foregoing, and is sometimes considered a mere form of it. There is little to choose between them in their dwarfness, their glowing color, but in this garden it has a slightly taller stem, a larger black blotch, and flowers a fortnight later. Its range is said to extend from Armenia, the Caucasus, to northern Persia.

T. Micheliana

A Persian Tulip said to come from sandy, clayey steppes, with a large red flower having the usual yellow-bordered central black blotch. The leaves are somewhat mottled. It flowered here the 1st of May, but has died out and I shall not replace it.

T. Oculus-solis	*B.R.* tt. 204, 1143
Sun's-eye Tulip	Red. *Lil.* t. 219

Earlier to blossom than the red Tulips generally, this might find a special welcome. It comes into bloom soon after *Kaufmanniana,* but it tells the same old story of red and black and yellow —a deep cup, borne on a foot-tall stem, the exterior paler than the interior. It is said to come from the south of France, and the late Rev. Joseph Jacob says where it is happy it settles down to a long stay, seeding about freely. It has not done this in my garden.

T. Orphanidea Boiss.   B.M. t. 6310

A pretty little Greek Tulip much in the manner of *Hageri,* flowering with it, and thought by some authorities to be a hybrid between *Hageri* and *australis.* There are several forms, but the one I had a number of years ago and have now lost, had soft, orange-colored flowers, three on the short stem, greenish and pointed in the bud, and with bronze and green outer segments. The leaves were tinted purple, and formed a little rosette upon the ground.

T. persica

This little Tulip, which has persisted in my garden for more years than any other, seems to have no very stable standing as a separate species, but is deemed a cultivated form of *australis.* Sir Daniel Hall says there is no authority for the specific name *persica,* nor is any wild habitat known. For all that, it is a very distinct and valuable little flower, the latest of the species to bloom, save *Sprengeri,* in this garden about the 18th of May. It remains in bloom for a long time, too, and where it has increased to form little close colonies, is very valuable in the rock garden.

Its slightly undulating leaves form a rosette on the ground; the four- or five-inch stem also bears a few leaves and does not, with me, stand quite upright, so that the flower is always seen in a half-nodding position. The bud is narrow, greenish, and urn-shaped, and when the orange-yellow flower opens, the backs of the segments keep the green tint. If the sun is very warm, it opens wide, and its sweet fragrance is apparent to one bending above it.

T. polychroma (*T. Aucheriana, T. humilis*)   Dykes t. 12

Though suspect because of its felted bulbs, *T. polychroma* has lived wedged in a hot pocket in my rock garden for many years. Nicholson says it is allied to *Celsiana* and *stellata*, and was introduced from Persia in 1894. It grows about eight inches high, and bears on slender curving stems white flowers with yellow centers and a flush of soft mauve on the outer segments. It blooms here about April 10th.

T. praecox Tenore   *B.M.* t. 7920
Dykes t. 29

This is a species that does only fairly well in my garden. It comes from central and southern Europe, but when its great flower blooms on its fifteen-inch stem, it is a striking object. Mr. Farrer describes it as "of Southern Vineyards, the outsides of the flowers are blurred and dead and dull in the flat-sided triangular-looking bud, like the underside of a butterfly's wing, in no way preparing one for the satiny fury of pure scarlet that presently unfolds, staring out into the world with a menacing wide pupil of blackness." By many it is thought not to be a true species, but only a variant of *Oculus-solis*.

T. praestans Hoog   *B.M.* t. 7920

This is my favorite red Tulip, a narrow flower carried on a tall stem with wide silver-green oblong leaves clasping the stem. It flowers early, about April 25th, and planted on little heights in the rock garden is a sight to gladden any eyes. Its tone of scarlet is not deep but high and thin, a lovely flashing color, and the stem carries two or three flowers. The pale leaves are often pubescent and are marked by a raised midrib. The stem is slightly hairy.

Tubergen's variety is somewhat dwarfer, and seldom bears more than two flowers on a stem. Its tone is light vermilion, or as it is described, scarlet-orange. A third kind is Zwanenburg, described as looking like a Poinsettia. I grew it last year, but it was altogether too much of a good thing—too big, too red, too spectacular, for the rock garden. *Praestans* comes from Bokhara, and lasts very well in this garden.

T. primulina Baker   B.M. t. 6786

This pretty little Tulip has the peculiar habit of remaining closed until after midday, and remaining open long after sunset when most of its sisters have furled their buds. It flowers at the end of April, and from each bulb come two or three flowers. The buds are narrow and pointed, green tinted with brown; and even when the flower is open, though it is usually described as white, it is more greenish than any other hue. The inner segments are creamy with a soft yellow base, the outer segments are green on their outsides and streaked with green on their inner sides, so that the general effect of the flower is toward green. It is not very showy, but is nice and dwarf and has a very sweet scent. It was introduced to gardens from Algeria by the late Mr. Henry Elwes, and though from such a mild climate, it seems quite hardy here and lasts well in a sheltered situation where the soil is well drained.

T. pulchella Fenzl.   B.M. t. 6304

A very variable little species from high up in the Cilician Taurus, related to *T. violacea*. It is a delightful mite for the rock garden, growing no more than four inches tall. Early in April the oval pinkish buds peep up amidst the channeled foliage; some of them are almost stemless, others a little taller. It is prettier in the bud than when wide open, for it shows when fully expanded a gap between segments, which gives the flower a loose, unfinished appearance. The flowers may be rose, lilac, or light violet, sometimes with a clear blue or violet base, again with a yellow base. There is also *pulchella alba*, two kinds, one with a white and one with a blue base. All are engaging but have not proved reliable here after a year or two.

T. saxatilis Sieber.   B.M. t. 6374

Though I have planted it many times, this species has never seen fit to give me a single flower. After the manner of Tulips generally, if it is not going to bloom, it sends up a single leaf, not apparently wishing to leave one under any misapprehension as to its intentions.

Year after year my spirits sink with the appearance of that solitary ominous leaf, and it is some little comfort to read that several centuries ago Parkinson wrote of the "Tulip of Candie" (Crete) that he had "not yet heard that it has very often flowered in our Countrey." Mr. Dykes in modern times reported a similar stinginess of behavior, though he does say that one of the most effective pictures that ever appeared in his garden was produced by a hundred flowering specimens of the Cretan *T. saxatilis* backed by a mass of *T. Hageri*. To me, with my one poor leaf, this sounds almost like a vulgar profusion.

The color scheme of *T. saxatilis* is said to be spectacular, pure mauve segments with a deep yellow center and several flowers from each stem. It flowers late in May. Coming from the mountains of Crete where the summers are hot and dry, it undoubtedly requires a good summer baking, and to be given the hottest nook in the rock garden in stony loamy soil. And to facilitate the baking, one might take the bulbs up and store them over the summer in a dry place. All this I have tried, but to no end save that solitary broad leaf. I wish some one else better luck.

T. Sprengeri Baker   B.M. t. 2762

This is the latest Tulip to flower, coming after even the large hybrid kinds have had their day, and as such is valuable. It is a neat flower of medium size with pointed petals, buff on the exterior of the segments and of a curious low tone of red on the interior, not dark red, but somewhat muted. The stem is about ten inches high, and the numerous erect leaves are a rich olive-green. It does not make offsets very freely, but it is a good stayer in the garden, nevertheless; and it makes a quantity of seed which, if sown, will flower in the fourth year.

In some gardens, *Sprengeri* self-sows and, Mr. Dykes says,

sometimes establishes itself among Bearded Irises with astonishing results when the scarlet flowers suddenly appear amidst the purple Irises. It likes company and grows well among other plants. Its natural home is Armenia.

T. stellata Hooker　　　　　　　　　　　　　　Dykes t. 22

A dainty and captivating Tulip from the slopes of the Himalayas and thereabouts. It is a comparative newcomer in this garden, but one that is to be a guest always, I hope. It is much like *Clusiana*, but the flowers are smaller, the stems shorter. It made a brilliant show on the top of a mound in the rock garden, flowering about the 1st of May. The flowers have pointed segments, they are glistening white, and the backs of the segments are flushed with brightest cherry.

T. silvestris L.　　　　　　　　　　　　　　　*B.M.* t. 1202

Found growing plentifully in fields, meadows, and vineyards of central and southern Europe, this graceful sweet-scented Tulip is yet regarded as a doubtful native in these localities. Its wanderlust has carried it also to England, where it is sometimes believed to be a true native and called the Wild British Tulip, and Gray says it has escaped from gardens and run wild in eastern Pennsylvania. A gay little globe trotter this, and one that any wayfarer would be glad to meet on a bright spring day.

It is a charming species, usually with two or three flowers on a wandlike stem. The pointed, bronze-coated buds droop, but when the flowers open—and they open wide only under a warm sun, displaying the pure yellow interior—they bravely raise their heads. The backs of the segments are flushed wtih brown delicately veined with green, and the flowers have the fragrance of English Violets.

It is sometimes known as *T. florentina odorata*. The leaves are long and strap-shaped, sometimes a foot long, rather pale, and sometimes flecked with reddish color on the backs. The two or three pointed stem-leaves are also touched with brown as is the stem itself. From twelve to fifteen inches is the usual height.

Unfortunately this charming tramp does not always flower well. It increases rapidly, but too often makes forests of those ominous single leaves with blossoms only here and there. Undoubtedly, despite its specific name which leads one to plant it in shade, it wants the fullest sun and plenty of it, and a situation where it gets a baking during the summer. I have earlier in this section related my experience with it.

The form called Täbris, introduced from Persia, flowers more freely, but with me does not settle down in the garden as does the type, which has the happy knack of making itself at home abroad. I have also had *silvestris major*, and while this flowered to a bulb, it has not proved a good stayer, and, moreover, the flowers were so large that they missed entirely the special charm of the type—its captivating wild grace.

Give *silvestris* a hot situation, and let it grow, if possible, among the roots and shoots of some shrub, and plant with it the bulbs of the Heavenly Blue Grape Hyacinth. They bloom together and make the best of companions for picking and to strike the sight with pleasure.

T. turkestanica Regel   Dykes t. 10

This is one of the smallest of Tulips, only a trifle larger in all its parts than the minute *biflora*, but it makes more show, for it sometimes carries as many as six flowers on a stem. (Mr. Dykes says ten or twelve.) They are white with a small orange-colored base, very starry, and the backs of the segments are colored greenish brown. It flowers just after *biflora*, and if a choice is to be made, should be preferred. It is a nice little species for a choice nook in the rock garden.

T. violacea Boiss. & Buhse.   B.M. t. 7440

A dainty little Tulip from the Transcaspian region, this has been known in gardens only since about 1890. Its color is unusual, a warm mauve-red, varying to tints of carmine and pale rose with a central blotch of olive-green. The bud is a round oval, and the open flower is starry. The stem is very short, the leaves are narrow and lie upon the ground. *Violacea* blooms in the early days of April, and has two fine characteristics, a sweet scent and long-lastingness. It is said that flowers remain in good condition for ten days. But its wants must be considered. It requires a good summer baking, and it seems likely, though I have not yet tried it there, that the rock garden scree will be a good place for it.

T. Wilsoniana Hoog   Dykes t. 21

This is one of the most effective of the small Tulips and seems, despite its woolly bulbs, inclined to settle down and make itself at home on a dry hot slope of the rock garden. The small flowers are blood-red within and without, the segments pointed, and the stem no more than three inches high. The narrow leaves are stained with red on the backs as if the color had spread from the glowing flowers. It comes from Transcaspia, and flowers here at the end of April or very early in May.

This is only a small fraction of the many interesting Tulip species that are open to investigation by the curious and careful gardener. At present the bulbs of many kinds are expensive—chiefly, says Mr. Dykes, because most of them are very slow of increase by means of offsets. "There is, however, no difficulty in raising them from seed, provided that the climate is not too moist, though it is always five and often six or seven years before seedling bulbs are large enough to flower. However, once a bulb has begun to flower, it should go on flowering regularly year after year except when it is allowed to produce seed, and then it may miss a year." [3]

Happily a mere matter of years is nothing to a determined gardener. We are like a fisherman who sits hour upon hour contentedly awaiting a bite, and if the bite never comes, he has had a good time, anyway, and thought a lot of thoughts, and dreamed a lot of dreams. Success is not always the sole compensation for effort.

Garden Tulips

The big hybrid Tulip is the brightest feather in the cap of May, and so it has been since the sixteenth century. "It was as a garden flower," writes Sir Daniel Hall, "that the Tulip first entered Europe from Turkey. As is the case with so many cultivated plants, the actual origin is unknown, the evidence . . . points to a source in Persia or Iraq, but the species, one or many, out of which the infinitely variable group of garden Tulips has

[3] *Gardening Illustrated*, Dec. 8, 1923.

originated, cannot be traced. When it does appear in the records, it is already a 'made' flower, with many varieties and the peculiarities that we know to-day." ⁴ It was undoubtedly the accomplishment of eastern florists, this wonderfully varied flower, and it is strange to realize that before any of the wild Tulips were grown in European gardens, the hybrid Tulip was well known.

Though its past is veiled in the shadows of antiquity, it is said that the Tulip is a very "common motive in near-Eastern art, *e.g.*, on the faïence originating in Persia, Damascus, Anatolia or Rhodes." Its first appearance in horticultural literature, or perhaps one should say, herbalist literature, seems to have been in Matthiolus, "Historia plantarum," 1561, in which there is a figure of a Tulip.

There are various stories recounted as to its introduction to European gardens. One has it that Clusius received some bulbs and seeds in 1572 from A. G. Busbequius, Ambassador of the Emperor Ferdinand I to the Sultan. These he did not sow until 1575 "when they were old and shriveled and could scarcely grow."

Whether or not the first Tulips to be grown in European gardens made their bow in Vienna, cannot be accurately ascertained; but in any case the new and splendid flower made what we should call today an immediate hit. Soon all the world was growing seedlings; England, Germany, Austria, and the Low Countries. Chiefly the Low Countries, for the Dutch took the Tulip wholeheartedly to their well padded bosoms.

In Gerard's "Herbal" are several figures of Tulips which he calls Dalmation Caps, "a strange and forreine floure, one of the number of the bulbed floures, whereof there be sundry sorts, some greater, some lesser, with which all studious and painefull Herbarists desire to be better acquainted, because of their excellent diuersitie of most braue floures which it beareth." He goes on to tell of the diligent activity of "my louing friend M. Iames Garret, a curious searcher of Simples, and learned Apothecary of London," in raising Tulips from seed, both those of his own propagation and such as he received from his friends beyond the seas for the space of twenty years, "not being yet able to attaine to the end of his trauell, for that each new yeare bringeth forth new plants

⁴ *The Tulip*, by Sir Daniel Hall.

of sundry colours, not before seene; all which to describe particularly were to roll Sisiphus [5] stone, or number the sands."

Had the worthy Mr. Garret lived until today, he would still be rolling the Sisyphus stone, for Tulip seedlings are still as the sands of the sea in number, and far more various. In those early days three types were recognized: early, medium, and late. The flowers commonly had long pointed petals, but when the stout Dutch growers took them in hand, they preferred a flower of stockier build, and so the slender pointed petals gradually became rounder and broader, making the flower a shallow cup rather than a slender-waisted vase.

This is not the place to recount the story of that strange obsession, the Tulip Mania, which took possession of all classes of Hollanders during the years between 1634 and 1637, when single bulbs sold for many thousands of dollars. This was pure gambling and had little influence on the development of the Tulip as a garden flower, but while the gamblers gamboled, the sober growers went about their legitimate business of putting the versatile Tulip through new and undreamed paces.

The criterion of excellence where plants are concerned is seldom statical; the shifting winds of fashion blow upon them, and they change their figures and their garb according to its fortuitous dictates. So with the Tulip. Down the years it comes, a harlequin, a turncoat, a chameleon—butter in the hands of its lovers.

"Tulips bloom as they are told."

Today we have a number of groups of hybrid Tulips, each composed of more or less well defined types, though as time goes on, and crosses between the different types are consummated, group tends to approach group in certain individuals until they are hardly separable. These groups or classes of Tulips are variously named Earlies, Cottage or Hybrid, Darwins, Breeders, Parrot, Lily-flowered, Bizarre and Bijbloemen, Rembrandt, Triumph, and Mendel. An attempt is made here to indicate the character-

[5] Sisyphus, a fraudulent avaricious king of Corinth, whose task in the world of shades is to roll a huge stone to the top of a hill and fix it there. It so falls out that the stone no sooner reaches the hilltop, than it bounds down again.—Brewer.

istics of these various types, and a few outstanding varieties among the hundreds available are named in each group. The most important groups are the first four named.

The Hybrid Tulips are lovely used in colonies informally throughout borders and shrubberies, or with rank-and-file precision in formal beds, when they are often underplanted with such time-honored bedders as English Daisies, Wall-flowers, Forget-me-nots, Arabis, Violas, Pansies, and Primroses, their colors in harmony or contrast with the hue of the Tulips. When they are used in formal beds on terraces or lawns, it is best to plant new bulbs yearly; otherwise there will be irregularities of height and time of blossoming that will spoil the uniform effect aimed at.

In planting these formal beds, it is wise to dig out the soil of the whole bed to a depth of at least five inches, so that the bulbs will stand on a common bottom, so to speak. If holes are dug with a trowel, some bulbs will be deeper in the ground than others and take longer to come to blossoming, thus upsetting the epidemic perfection that such beds should present. The short-stemmed Earlies make fine bedders.

Shrubs and small trees in bloom with the early Tulips are the following: Japanese and Orchard Cherries, Flowering Almonds pink and white, *Prunus tomentosa, P. triloba,* Japanese Quince, *Spiraea Thunbergi, Magnolia stellata, Viburnum Carlesii,* White Kerria, the double-flowered Peaches, Wistaria (standard Wistarias are lovely with them), Forsythia, *Syringa oblata,* Dogwood pink and white. And besides the plants already enumerated, there are to combine with them *Anchusa myosotidiflora, Mertensia virginica, Pulmonaria angustifolia,* Bleeding-Heart, *Phlox subulata* in many colors, Grape Hyacinths, Daffodils, and Cowslips.

To bloom with the later-flowering Tulips, we have Lilacs in infinite variety, Crab Apples in pink or white, *Kerria japonica, Cercis canadensis,* Azaleas of many kinds, *Spiraea prunifolia, Rosa Hugonis, Viburnum tomentosum,* Halesia, *Kolkwitzia amabilis* (splendid with some of the off-toned Breeders), Dogwoods still lingering, besides such herbaceous plants as Bleeding-Hearts, Nepeta, Cerastium, Violas, *Phlox divaricata,* Flax, and Iberis, and such bulbous things as Camassias and the Spanish and English Bluebells. Late November is the best time to plant Tulips. The season of blossoming given is for the neighborhood of New York. It extends from early April to late May.

EARLY TULIPS

These flower in April, the first of the garden Tulips to bloom. As a rule, the stems are rather short and stout, the large flowers shallow rather than deep cups, the colors frank and pure, seldom evasive. They are ideal bedders, but they also look well planted informally about the borders. They are comely and trig and bright, and are not used as often or as freely as they should be. The Duc Van Thol forms flower first, a fortnight before the regular Earlies, while the group is extended to join the May-flowering varieties by such late bloomers as Couleur Cardinal. Many of the Earlies have a fine sweet scent. There are many double-flowered individuals in this group. These to me are most engaging and attractive, and they are delightful for cutting.

SINGLE EARLIES

Diadem, soft pink of a fine bland tone, fourteen inches; nice in the neighborhood of an apple tree with Grape Hyacinth. Alice Roosevelt, shrimp-pink and fragrant. Proserpine, large and globular and carmine-pink, delightfully fragrant. Ibis is rose-colored and very fine, fourteen inches. Rose Luisante, a fine rose-pink sort that looks well with a foreground of double Arabis, twelve inches.

De Wet, superb orange-colored flower, very luminous in effect, and very fragrant, seventeen inches. Fred Moore has many of its good qualities, and is less expensive, fourteen inches. Enchantress blends salmon-orange and yellow, and is a good outdoor Tulip, ten inches.

Of yellow-flowered Earlies there is Rising Sun, with especially large flowers. It has now lived in my garden for eight years without lifting, and is still presentable. Yellow Queen is paler than the last and somewhat taller. Cullinan is pale lemon with a rose-colored selvage. Mon Trésor and Goldfinch are fine for bedding.

The old Prince of Austria has such a delicious scent that one must put up with its scarlet yellow-based flowers. Vermilion Brilliant is a fine scarlet and an early bloomer. Couleur Cardinal is red of a dark tone and with a sort of violet bloom over it. It flowers late. Van der Neer more nearly approaches purple. White Earlies are White Swan, an oval flower on a tall stem; White Hawk, a rounded flower and a good bedder; Lady Boreel, the best of them all.

DOUBLE EARLIES

Mystery of India, a superb flower, the color a mingling of apricot, bronze, and pink. It is delightful arranged with branches of *Viburnum Carlesii* or with brown Pansies. Maréchal Niel is soft yellow washed with orange. Lady Godiva is pure yellow, fat, and as double as can be managed. Golden Giant bears out its name for size but is only semi-double—fragrant, however. Mr. Van der Hoef has a fine patina and a lovely fine tone of yellow, and if you are not too set upon an upright stem, the old Yellow Rose will delight both your eyes and your nose. Tea Rose, too, is exquisite in pale yellow suffused with rose.

Murillo has long been loved for her soft pink and white double flowers. Peach Blossom is gay and frivolous and very pink, and Triumphator is a fine deep pink bedder. Azalea is newer and very lovely, a pure bright pink flower flushed with deepest color, the outer petals flecked with green as are some of the Parrots.

Orange Nassau is grand among the warm-hued kinds and long-lasting. El Toreador is nearer scarlet, and Vuurbaak full scarlet. The old Schoonoord is still honored among white varieties, though perhaps the new Boule de Neige, large and like a white Peony, will be chosen in preference. Fortune is a tall variety on a strong stem, the flower a tender tone of rose-lilac with a satiny sheen. It is perfect with the early-flowering Lilac, *Syringa oblata*.

COTTAGE TULIPS

In some novel once read I remember that the heroine's "small white hand" was described as having the subtle fragrance of

Tulips. Not much stress is laid upon the Tulip as a fragrant flower, yet most of the Earlies and a great number of the Cottage varieties have a fruity or a Rose-like scent that adds much to their attractiveness. The Cottage Tulips, to my thinking, are the most beautiful of all. Their forms are exquisite, sometimes vaselike, or urn-shaped, again egg-shaped, the petals long and pointed, lovely in the bud, and dealing in fine, pure tones of pink and cherry and dazzling scarlet, a whole gamut of yellows from cream to the deepest tone, a few mauves and purples and gleaming white. The stems are long and slender, almost as tall as the Darwin, but commonly not so sturdy, so that the pose of the flower is less upright, more graceful. They begin to flower toward the end of April, and continue through May.

The Cottage Tulip is not new; it is, indeed, a survival. They are the descendants of old varieties that were long ago discarded at the behest of fashion, and lived on in old gardens, chiefly in Great Britain, patiently awaiting a knight errant. When the wheel turned, they were remembered, and a number of men rushed to the aid of beauty in distress. Chief among these rescuers were the Irishman, William Baylor Hartland, Peter Barr of Daffodil fame, and Walter T. Ware. These men fared to remote villages and hamlets and poked about in old gardens, "and so got together a varied and indeterminate group of flowers which were called Cottage Tulips." How grateful we should be to them!

Through the generosity of John Scheepers of New York, a vast number of Tulips have grown in my garden, the newest and many of the old kinds. To choose among them, as I go back over my notebooks of the past eight years, is a difficult matter. So many deserve recommendation for one reason or another that, where space is limited, one must almost pick at random. However, some of my prime favorites are the following:

Pink and cherry tones: Barbara Pratt, cherry with sunny lights; Dido, deep pure pink with topaz tones, long and lovely form; Inglescombe Pink, warm pink, an old and tried variety; Leda, enchanting and vivid pink, pale at the edges; Rosabella, large and opening wide, tinted like a shell, lovely for cutting.

Cream to yellow: Acushla, long and deep-throated, bright yellow with smart black anthers; Arethusa, exquisite, pale yellow and fragrant; Avis Kennicott, deep yellow, usually with a black base; Inglescombe Yellow, canary-colored, sometimes with a crimson edge; Magnolia, cream with cherry suffusion; Mongolia, egg-shaped flower of a soft deep yellow tone; Mrs. F. E. Dixon, soft yellow and superb form; Moonlight, lovely and fragrant; Mrs. John T. Scheepers, fine oval flower of clear pure color; Mrs. Moon, an old but fine variety of good color and long vaselike form; Walter T. Ware, the deepest yellow Cottage Tulip.

White: Albino, pure white and handsomely formed; Carrara, exquisite rounded form.

Rose and amber: These are quite indescribable in a few words, but all are of the first beauty and excellence; Ambrosia, Beauty of Bath, Eleanore Pratt, John Ruskin (sixteen inches), Marjorie Bowen, Hammar Hales, very long flower.

Red: Henry Correvon, brilliant self-red; Mayflower, immense flashing scarlet flower.

Lilac to purple: The Lizard, Union Jack, Ilias, Twilight.

Darwin Tulips

These are the tallest of all Tulips. The flowers are commonly cup-shaped, and have a squarish base, self-colored, and are borne on strong stems. Scentless. They flower in May. They are chiefly the accomplishment of Dutch growers. They garb themselves magnificently in pinks and scarlets and in mauves, purples, and dark red, almost to black, only occasionally in yellow. They are vigorous and strong-growing, and make splendid bedders.

Pink and cherry: Aphrodite, pale and exquisite; Clara Butt, old but excellent salmon-colored Tulip; Flamingo, pure pink; Kathleen Parlow, silvery pink, paling at the center; King George V, brilliant cherry; La Fiancée, pale pink; Mr. Farncombe Sanders, cherry; Princess Elizabeth, rose-pink; Princess Mary, deep rose-pink; Venus, the color of a June Rose.

Lavender, mauve, purple: Anton Mauve, deep violet; Blue Perfection, light violet; Duchess of Hohenberg, gray-lilac with faint pink tones; Insurpassable, bright pure lilac; King Mauve, mauve toning to rose; La Tristesse, cool tone of lavender; Lilac Wonder; Maya, lilac; Melicette, mauve with blue base; Ronald

Gunn, plum-purple; The Bishop, warm purple; Valentin, one of the finest of the lavender-flowered group.

Scarlet and red: Bourgogne, wine-red; City of Haarlem, dark red; Eclipse, rich red; Faust, wine-color; Giant, immense wine-colored flower; Jubilee, deepest red-violet; La Tulipe Noire, the darkest of all; Prince of Wales, superb cherry-red.

White: Helen Eakin; Mrs. Grullemans; White Giant.

Yellow: La Tosca; sulphur turning to cream.

BREEDERS

Flowering in May, the Breeder Tulips resemble the Darwins a good deal save that their flowers are more rounded, and have not the square base characteristic of most of the Darwins. Their stems are tall and strong, the colors most unusual, as they embrace many unflowerlike tones, bronze and fawn and brown among them.

Bronze and brown, etc.: Bronze Queen, Cardinal Manning; Copernicus; Dom Pedro; Garibaldi; Godet Parfait; Goldfinch; Indian Chief; Jessey; Louis XIV (fragrant); Mahony King; Mrs. Harold Brown.

Breeders of other colors are the following: Bacchus, violet; Dillenberg, salmon-orange; James A. McDonald, orange tones; Lucifer, orange with rose suffusions; Mrs. J. Ramsey Hunt, clear purple; Newton, plum-purple; Orange Glory, orange and terra cotta; Panorama, orange-scarlet; Roi Soleil, violet with blue tones; Velvet King, royal purple; William the Silent, the best of the purple Breeders.

LILY-FLOWERING TULIPS

These graceful flowers are the result of crosses between *Tulipa retroflexa* and certain pink Darwins. The long petals reflex like those of a Lily, and the flowers are carried on slender but sturdy stems. They are exquisite for cutting and flower in May with the Cottage, Breeder, and Darwin varieties.

Alaska is pure yellow; Captain Fryatt is a soft reddish violet; Elegans Alba is white with a carmine edge that does not spread as the flower matures; Marcellina is bright cherry-red with a white center; Retroflexer and its variety superba are pure yellow; Sirène is pure pink.

PARROT TULIPS

These are fantastic and often beautiful flowers, with the petals jaggedly cut and strangely marked. They are an old race of Tulips, probably sports that have occurred from time to time ever since the Tulip became a garden flower. It seems likely that what old van Oosten, certainly the most passionate and articulate Tulip lover of all time, described in his "Dutch Gardener," 1703, as of "uncommon shape and frightful to look upon, and for that reason called Monsters," may have been Parrot Tulips, though to our eyes today they are far from being frightful to look upon. Quite the contrary; and they are delightful for cutting but, being heavy-headed and not very stiff of stem, are less effective for garden decoration than other kinds.

Fantasy is the beautiful pink Parrot with enchanting apple-green markings; Gadelan is a blend of purples and soft rose; Sunshine is yellow, and Therese is brilliant rosy red. Gemma, which I have lost, is a white sort flushed with pink. Parrot Tulips bloom before the Cottage and Darwin kinds, just after the Earlies.

BIZARRE AND BIJBLOMEN TULIPS

These are the Tulips that rocked the little country of Holland on its foundations during the Tulip Mania period. Today this type is little grown, but in certain settings where a quaint formality is the note aimed at, they are very effective. The Bizarres have generally a yellow ground-color with flashes of scarlet or brown. The Bijblomens have a white ground flecked and striped with cherry or scarlet, and sometimes purple. Some good kinds are Black Boy, Hebe, Bonaparte, Cerise Primo, Cherbourg, Perle Schaep, Jupiter, Amphion, Le Duel, May Blossom, Louis XIV, Zebra, and King Arthur.

These and the Rembrandt Tulips, the so-called broken or rectified Darwins, flower at the same time as the other May Tulips.

The Rembrandts have flowers garbed in rich hues, amusingly striped or feathered with contrasting hues.

TRIUMPH TULIPS

These new and handsome varieties are useful to us in bridging the gap between the Earlies and the May-flowering varieties. Some fine varieties are the following: Cecilia, oval flower of fine yellow flushed with orange; Columbia, bright amaranth-red; Ensor, light orange; Johanna, light salmon-pink; Lohengrin, white suffused at the margins with pink; Snowdrift, white; Tucana, a blend of orange, carmine, and yellow.

UVULARIA *LILIACEAE*

BELLWORT

THE Bellworts are such pretty, albeit modest, flowers that it is surprising that they are not used more in shaded rock gardens, for they grow without special care and flower early in the spring. They are native plants, hardy, and comprising about four species. Their root is a thickened creeping rootstock, with alternate clasping leaves along the slender stem, and the flowers are creamy or yellow, and droop like fainting Lilies from the tip of the stem.

U. grandiflora Sm.   *B.M.* t. 1112
  Strawflower, Wood Daffodil

A lovely flower of warm yellow tone found in rich upland woods from Quebec to Ontario and far south and west, flowering here in April. My plants came from the Ozark Mountains, and are the finest I have seen, the flowers larger and of a richer tone of yellow than those secured from eastern localities. The leaves are long and oval and droop about the long, Lily-like flower with its graceful pointed segments. It is narrowly bell-shaped and nearly two inches long, and has a sort of swan's-neck pose that is very charming. Worthy to be grown in any collection of rock plants, or in choice places in the wild garden. After flowering, the whole plant dies away.

U. perfoliata L.   *B.M.* t. 955
  Mealy Bellwort. Mohawk Weed

This species is smaller in all its parts, has smooth foliage, somewhat glaucous, and paler flowers, less effective but still very pretty. It is widely distributed, North and South.

U. sessiliflora L.
  Wild Oats

This is a pale little plant, leaves and stems and flowers. The last have a faint greenish cast, but the same meek and attractive drooping pose as the others of its kind. It also has a wide distribution in dampish woods where the soil is somewhat sandy, and is easily established in the wild garden or shaded sections of the rock garden.

ZYGADENUS FREMONTII   CAMASSIA QUAMASH

ZYGADENUS *LILIACEAE*

ZYGADENUS is a genus of flowering herbs, with or without bulbs, not often seen in gardens. There are about twenty-five species, one of which is Siberian, one Japanese; the remainder are North American. They have long narrow leaves from the base of the stems, and flowers in irregular panicles on scapes from a foot to two feet high. They grow in sunny moist places, frequently associated with Camassias. "The Standard Cyclopedia of Horticulture" says, "Some or all of the species have poisonous seeds, bulbs, rhizomes, and foliage." One kind, the so-called Death Camass, known locally also as Poison Grass, Poison Sego, Soap-root and Alkali Grass, is frequently found inhabiting the same grounds as the true Camassias, and the bulbs are much alike, so that the Indians, to whom the latter are an important article of diet, must exercise the greatest care in gathering the bulbs. Even so, dire results are known to happen. The Death Camass is deadly to man and beast.

This plant, *Z. venenosus*, grows about two feet high, the leaves are long and narrow and many, and the scape carries an irregular head of creamy starry flowers, each with a yellow gland at the base. The Zygadenus are more suitable for use in wild gardens, or in damp waste places, than in the more formal sections of the garden, though a clump of *Z. Fremontii* in a low part of the rock garden, or at the edge of a rich border, is a point of interest.

Z. Fremontii Torr.

This species is the best for cultivation. The leaves are an inch wide and very numerous, falling away gracefully from the flower scape which arises in May to a height of about eighteen inches. The many starry flowers that compose the large irregular panicle are creamy white with a greenish cast, and each is carried on a long pedicel. Several scapes will come from a single bulb. It thrives in rich soil and is quite hardy. Found from southern Oregon through the Coast Ranges to San Diego, California.

ABBREVIATIONS OF PUBLICATIONS USED IN REFERENCE

B.M.—Botanical Magazine, London, 1787, still published monthly. Colored plates.

B.R.—Botanical Register, London, 1815–1847, 33 vols. Colored plates.

Gard. Illus.—Gardening Illustrated, London. Still published weekly.

Lod *Bot. Cab.*—Loddiges *Botanical Cabinet*, London, 1818–1824, 10 vols. Colored plates.

Maund's *B.G.*—Maund's *Botanic Garden*, London, 1825–1842, 9 vols. Colored plates.

Maw—*Monograph of the Genus Crocus*, by George Maw, London, 1886. Colored plates.

Nat. Hort. Mag.—National Horticultural Magazine, Washington, D.C. Published quarterly.

Pax. *Fl. Gard.*—J. Lindley and J. Paxton, *Flower Garden*, London, 1851, 3 vols. Colored plates.

Red. *Lil.—Redouté*, P. J., *Les Liliacées*, Paris, 1802–1816, 8 vols. Colored plates.

Sowerby's *Eng. Bot.*—J. Sowerby's *English Botany*, London, 1790–1814, 36 vols. Colored plates.

Sweet's *Brit. Fl. Gard.*—Sweet's *Brititsh Flower Garden*, London, 1823–1829, first series, 3 vols.; 1831–1838, second series, 4 vols. Colored plates.

INDEX

SYNONYMS IN ITALICS

Acaena, glauca, 14; inermis, 14.

Acidanthera bicolor, 27.

Acis, 218; *autumnalis,* 223; *hyemalis,* 223; *rosea,* 224; *tricophylla,* 224.

Adder's-tongue, 147.

"Addisonia," 101.

Alkali Grass, 354.

Allium (the race), 33–57; odorum, 13; stellatum, 13, 16, 33; Moly, 16; cyaneum, 16; *campanulatum,* 38; *azureum,* 39; unifolium, 42; *cyaneum dasystemon,* 44; *aureum,* 46–47; *pedemontanum,* 48; *lacteum,* 48; *Helleri,* 48; *cernuum obtusum,* 52; *reticulatum,* 54.

Almond, Flowering, 343.

Alpine Violet, 138.

Alyssum saxatile citrinum, 13.

"Amaryllidaceae," 253.

Amaryllis, Halleri, 227; *aureum,* 228; *lutea,* 317.

"American Botanist, The," 104, 148, 216.

"Among the Hills," 21.

Anagallis, 14.

Anchusa myosotidiflora, 106, 343.

Andrews, D. M., 9, 51, 103.

Androsace sarmentosa, 13, 136.

Anemone (the race), 58–66; blanda, 15; apennina, 15; nemorosa, 15; fulgens, 15.

Anemone, Wood, 62; double Wood, 63; American Wood, 63; Rue, 64; Japanese, 105, 133.

Anemonella thalictroides, 66.

Angel's Tears, 254–255.

"Annals of Botany," 306.

Antennaria dioica rosea, 13.

Anthericum, Liliago, 21–22; *Liliastrum,* 22.

Applegate, Elmer Ivan, 157.

Arabis procurrens, 13.

Armstrong, Margaret, 74, 78, 92, 178, 180, etc.

Arnold, Ralph, 166.

Arnott, S., 223.

Arum italicum, 67.

Asperula, odorata, 14; azurea setosa, 14.

Aubrietia, 14.

Backhouse, 248.

Bailey, Dr. L. H., 66, 231, 233.

Barnardia, scilloides, 297; *japonicum,* 299.

Barr, Peter, 244, 253, 255, 346.

Barr and Sons, 260, 263, 272.

Bauhin, Casper, 277.

Belamcanda chinensis, 20, 68–69.

Belle d'onze heures, 279.

Bellevalia romana, 241.

Bellis rotundifolia caerulescens, 14.

Bellwort, 351; Mealy, 351.

Berberis, verruculosa, 26, 67; *punctata,* 67.

Bermuda Buttercup, 281.

Bermuda Star Grass, 310.

Birches, 19.

Black Seranna, 167.

Blackstone, J., 173.

Bleeding-Heart, 343.

Bloodroot, 149.

Blue Dicks, 72.

Blue-eyed Grass, 308, etc.

Bluebell, English, 15, 20, 302; Spanish, 15, 20, 299.

"Book of the Iris, The," 213.

Borsch, William, 283.

"Botanical Cabinet," Loddiges, 226.

"Botanical Magazine, The," 47, 55, 69, 80, 202, 209, 231, 232, 234, 236, 241, 250, 271, 277, 301.

Bouncing Bet, 29, 68.

Bowles, E. A., 41, 63, 79, 105, 109, 111, 115, 118, 123, 124, 126, 136, 174, 186, 187, 189, 194, 206, 223, 252, 260, 270, etc.

Brevoortia Ida-Maia, 73.

"British Wild Flowers," 291.

Brodiaea (the race), 70–78; uniflora, 12, 27, 71; ixioides, 16; *parviflora,* 77.